The Education of Ernie Dumas

The Education of Ernie Dumas:

Chronicles of the Arkansas Political Mind

by Ernest Dumas

The Butler Center for Arkansas Studies

Central Arkansas Library System
100 Rock Street
Little Rock, Arkansas 72201
www.butlercenter.org
May 2019

ISBN 978-1-945624-20-9 (cloth)

Cover design: Tabitha Lahr and Mike Keckhaver
Book design: Mike Keckhaver
Copyeditor: Chris Dumas
Proofreader: Ali Welky

Cataloging-in-Publication data is on file at the Library of Congress
Names: Dumas, Ernest, 1937- author.
Title: The education of Ernie Dumas : chronicles of
the Arkansas political mind / Ernest Dumas.
Description: First edition. | Little Rock, Arkansas : Butler Center Books,
[2019] | Includes bibliographical references and index.
Identifiers: LCCN 2019010039 | ISBN 9781945624209
(hardcover : alk. paper)
Subjects: LCSH: Dumas, Ernest, 1937- | Journalists--Arkansas--Biography. |
Arkansas--Politics and government--1951-
Classification: LCC F415.3.D86 A3 2019 | DDC 976.7/04092 [B] --dc23
LC record available at https://lccn.loc.gov/2019010039

Butler Center Books, the publishing division of the Butler Center for
Arkansas Studies, was made possible by the generosity of
Dora Johnson Ragsdale and John G. Ragsdale Jr.

"Practical politics consists in ignoring facts."

"You can't use tact with a Congressman! A Congressman is a hog! You must take a stick and hit him on the snout!"

—Henry Adams, 1907

"God loves not him that does not love Arkansas."

—William Minor Quesenbury, 1878

Table of Contents

Preface and Acknowledgments

This book fulfills a contractual agreement between Bobby Roberts and me and, by his lights, my obligation to the commonweal of Arkansas. Dr. Roberts, see, is a historian and for years was director of the Central Arkansas Library System (CALS). For the purpose of gleaning more knowledge of Arkansas and Southern history and of spreading it to the needy public at large, the library established a publishing arm, Butler Center Books, an idea implemented with a grant from John G. Ragsdale Jr. Some years ago, Roberts began to wheedle me to write a memoir about more than a half century of writing about politics and government.

While no one should be even slightly enlightened by reading about my pedestrian life, he said, the stories about how and why things happened and the impulses that guided the men and women who were elected to office and made things happen or failed to make them happen would be important knowledge. Reporters who covered the events often saw and heard things that for professional, personal, or other seemingly obligatory reasons they did not share in print. If the stories were suitable for lunch or evening conversations, he thought, they ought to be accessible to the general public so that people could make their own judgments about historical values. The stray filaments that constituted the little stories I could tell should at least be available for historians in their endless search for ultimate truth.

For some years I put him off, because I was weary of deadlines and obligations, even when they came only once a week, which is my explanation for sheer indolence. Some day, in complete repose, I might do it, I said. Detecting my deteriorating faculties, Dr. Roberts warned that if I perished or became incapacitated without having written the book, I should do so with the certain knowledge that I had failed a moral obligation to my fellow man. In the fall of 2017, as I approached eighty years, David Stricklin, director of the CALS Butler Center for Arkansas Studies and still another historian with a mission, insisted that I sign a contract committing to write the book even if the contract contained no deadline, and he drew up such a contract. In want of peace and understanding, I did so and fell irresolutely to the task.

So, the acknowledgments should start with Roberts and Stricklin and former Butler Center Books manager Rod Lorenzen, who made me do it and actually offered gentle encouragement from time to time that they really did want the damned book done, and to Nate Coulter, who followed Roberts as the executive director of the library system and claimed to be as interested in the project as Roberts.

The acknowledgments should also include nearly all the politicians who appear in these pages, for, with a few exceptions that need not be mentioned, I found them always to be candid even when the events did not reflect very well on any assessment of their work. I am most grateful to Dale Bumpers and David Pryor, who had nearly twin careers in state and national government that covered forty-five years of this story. I spent at least a hundred hours in conversations with them about the matters covered in these pages, some twenty of them in oral histories that we recorded two decades ago on video and audio tapes and in transcripts.

The memories and writings of other reporters—I should mention particularly Gene Lyons, Rex Nelson, Steve Barnes, Anne Farris, and John Brummett, great storytellers themselves—were immensely helpful and provided some rich context. I must recognize the contributions of numerous old hands at the *Arkansas Gazette*, mostly now passed to glory, who shared reporting on elections and government with me for thirty years. I have stolen their stories anonymously and claimed them as my own and hope to earn their forgiveness.

The late and immortal George Fisher, the finest political cartoonist in history, deserves my gratitude, not simply for supplying the caricatures and cartoons that provide most of the illumination in this story, but for our friendship and our camaraderie for the last dozen years of the *Gazette,* when we talked daily about how to convey the essence of a political story in editorial graphics. The solutions were always his, but Fisher allowed me to think that I had helped sharpen the meaning of things. I must thank the proprietors of the *Arkansas Democrat-Gazette*, Rose Publishing Company, the University of Arkansas Press, the CALS Butler Center for Arkansas Studies, and Judi Woods, fierce guardian of the Fisher legacy, for permission to reprint a little of his work here to periodically revive flagging interest in my narrative.

Lest I be accused of plagiarism, I must acknowledge the source of both the form of this narrative and the title, Henry B. Adams, the nineteenth-century scion of two presidents and the author *The Education of Henry Adams*, which was first published in 1907 and recounted his disillusionment with American politics. I have scrubbed his name and substituted mine in the hope that confusion with the famous title might attract a few readers.

I am especially grateful to Ali Welky, Michael Keckhaver, and Glenn Whaley of the CALS Butler Center for Arkansas Studies. Without their devotion to the details of the narrative, including type and graphics, the whole effort would lack the appearance of professionalism.

With everything I do, I must share any credit but none of the blame with my wife, Elaine Kersey Dumas, who always encourages me when I need it and patiently reads everything I write to point out where my sentences make no sense. Finally, I must thank Chris Dumas, editor *par excellence*, for his thankless attention to style and the King's English and for accepting blame for any overabundance of commas, and also William Whitworth, the great editor-in-chief of *The Atlantic* and former colleague at the *Arkansas Gazette*, for reviewing the work and passing along ideas about how I might save myself some embarrassment.

I
Champagnolle

How I got into the business of writing for newspapers and about politicians and their labors is easy to explain. Ruth Jenkins, one of my high school teachers, told me to. Why I allowed it to happen when I hoped for a more estimable means of livelihood I am not even yet, sixty-five years hence, prepared to say, except to admit that I have always found it nearly impossible to resist even the mildest entreaties of any woman, including the one who would allow me for most of a century to look into the fair and open face of heaven. This is not to suggest that as a class women were ever very solicitous of my attention, for the truth is that I was never so beset. I merely mention that this is a part of my psychological profile that must be considered. As we move along with this story, the reader may have insights into how that came to be. Perhaps from deference, my keenly observant son, a scholar of Freud, has never offered any.

Nothing in my childhood environment and little in my experience should have guided me toward either journalism or politics, except, as I now imagine, the aforementioned patronesses who took an interest in a painfully bashful youngster. Champagnolle, a sparse community in the woods of eastern Union County where I was reared, did not have a rich literary tradition or even much book learning, but a few people along the dirt roads between the Ouachita River and the oil town of El Dorado had managed to go to high school and sometimes to get a diploma, although, to my knowledge, no one in the community had ever gone to college before my older brother, Wayne. My mother, Berta, who grew up farther south on a truck farm near the sawmill town of Strong, though sickly and possessing only one good eye, went to high school, passed the state teacher examination, and as a single girl taught in several tiny country schools. The last was Champagnolle School, which is where she met my father, a woodsman and hauler who lived across the creek about a mile from the school and who had gone to school there through its six grades. His two youngest brothers were her students. I do not have a clue about the quality of instruction at Champagnolle, except it would have been very good the year or so when my mother was the teacher.

After Berta married Clifton Dumas, Champagnolle's school closed and its handful of students were dispersed between the Old Union and Quinn districts. My brother and I were routed to Quinn when we started to school, and while there were only twenty-four of us in two brick buildings that once accommodated a pretty good enrollment, it was at least a better facility than Champagnolle's old wooden schoolhouse. Quinn had inside toilets, which were often accessible and sometimes functional. When Mary Hargett, who taught the first five or six grades at Quinn, would take to her bed, her husband, Johnny—the superintendent, custodian, bus driver, disciplinarian, and master for the two or three older boys whose parents wanted them to continue schooling—would climb out of the school bus before daylight and fetch my mother to ride the little bus with us to Quinn to teach Mary Hargett's grades. We were all in a single room, though Johnny Hargett sometimes took an older kid or two to another room for lessons, or discipline.

When I had reached the fourth grade, Quinn shuttered, too, and the state moved to consolidate school districts with enrollments smaller than 350, which was required by an initiated act that was proposed by the Arkansas Education Association and defeated narrowly by Arkansas voters in 1946 but adopted in 1948. My mother's professional career, even as a substitute teacher, ended with Quinn's closing. We had to ride the bus every day into the maturing boomtown of El Dorado and compete with all the rich, brainy brats who wore suede shoes and store-bought clothes.

If I inherited a recessive literary gene that Ruth Jenkins might have detected when I was in the twelfth grade at El Dorado, it would have been from my mother. She taught Wayne and me to read and write and had somehow collected a few books that furnished a library of one small bookcase in our house: *Tales of a Wayside Inn* by Henry Wadsworth Longfellow; *Modern Essays* (1921) selected by Christopher Morley; *The Poetical Works of William Cullen Bryant,* which gave me a leg up in high school when she had me memorize all eighty-one lines of Bryant's "Thanatopsis," the recitation of which would be a rite of passage to the eleventh grade; *The Century Handbook of Writing* (1918), still as good a grammar text as there is ("Do not complicate thought by persistent repetition of elements beginning with *that, which of, for,* or *but*, and NOT parallel in structure"); Shakespeare's *Merchant of Venice; Lord Byron's Shorter Poems*; and my favorite, the illustrated *Among the Giants* (1920) by Bertha M. Neher, a terrifying journey to the castles of banished giants who represented the six common human failings: carelessness, sloth, bad temper, foul language, selfishness, and untruth. Miss Neher wrote that "the mightiest and most hateful of all the giants was Untruth," a coward and dunce whose ability to transform himself into different pleasing visages seems now to have been foretelling of Donald Trump. The hero, Fenton, after confronting and dispensing with Giant Untruth, burned his castle to the ground and, after getting a little medical attention for his lacerations, erected another castle with this inscription over the portal:

Speak the truth!
Speak it boldly, never fear,
Speak it so that all may hear;
In the end it shall appear
Truth is best in age and youth.
Speak the truth!

Bad Temper and Untruth were the sorriest of the giants, and it was always liberating to reread Miss Neher's throbbing accounts of their demise at the hands of the noble Fenton.

From a traveling salesman who rolled up to our house in a cloud of dust, my mother ordered the full twenty-five-volume set of *Funk & Wagnalls Standard Encyclopedia*, which was shipped and paid for on the installment plan. I am quite sure ours was the only house between the city limits of El Dorado and Calion with an encyclopedia set.

Berta Dumas, I would figure out many years later, had some literary aspirations. Shy and suffering off and on from acute anxiety and depression, she sometimes wrote on tablets but never shared her work with us boys or, as far as I know, with my father. She often detected signs of resentment from other members of the extended Dumas family, including the many Armers and Perdues who together made up most of the white community around the junction of the Champagnolle and Armer roads. Her paranoia would extend to the little Baptist church at Old Union, where we were members and where my grandpa, Will Dumas, a carpenter, was a deacon. The *Arkansas Baptist Newsmagazine*, which was published at Little Rock, came to our house regularly. One month it printed an article that she had written and submitted, and on which the editor had put her byline. Although as far as I knew no one at the church ever mentioned the article, probably because no one was even aware of it, she discerned from glances and the sly manner of people at the church that there was deep resentment at what she had done, either because the flock disagreed with the doctrinal position that she took—infant immersion perhaps—or simply that she would be so presumptuous as to claim authorship of a published writing. Although my father and Grandpa Will said they had detected no such resentment, her brooding and occasional sobbing lasted many months. It seemed to have subsided after a year or so, and then she was emboldened to submit another article; it, too, was published. The silence and the averted looks at church this time proved to be too much. My mother insisted that we move our membership to a larger church nine miles away in El Dorado, where we could worship in more anonymity. She sent nothing else to the journal, as far as I know. Many years later, for a few months in 1964, I lived next door in North Little Rock's Lakewood subdivision to the revered editor of the *Arkansas Baptist*, Dr. Erwin C. McDonald, and I intended to work up the bravado to go next door and ask him about my mother's submissions and see if he might find them for me in the journal's archives. But we had to move suddenly when my housemate, the redoubtable writer Doug Smith, had too many beers one night, went to sleep with a cigarette in an overstuffed chair, and set the house afire. The owner told us to move, and I never got to ask Brother McDonald about my mother's articles.

Still, I can't say that my mother's literary aspirations, if she indeed had any beyond getting some spiritual matters off her chest, had the slightest effect on me. Words had no particular fascination to me as a child although, thanks mainly to my mother, I could spell, write passable sentences, and diagram them. But there might be something to the influence of newspapers in our household.

Rural Union County, which lies along the Louisiana border, was not a maelstrom of media activity before World War II, or after it either. El Dorado had two newspapers, the *Daily News* and the *Evening Times*, although truthfully they were a dual issue of the same paper, duplicate local stories appearing in both daily editions—in the morning paper with lightface headlines and in the afternoon *Times* with bolder head type. The same factual and grammatical errors and typographical miscues that annoyed afternoon readers bedeviled the next morning's subscribers as well. Printing both a morning and afternoon edition with the same staff and a few extra production men discouraged potential competition, although by the end of World War II fresh newspaper competition was rarely a threat anywhere and rapidly becoming extinct. The newspaper plant, part of Clyde E. Palmer's chain of papers that covered all of southwest Arkansas, also published a weekly paper for the town of Smackover, which allowed Palmer to soak up, for trifling production costs, the little advertising revenue that could be had in the small oil town and its satellite Norphlet. Out on Champagnolle Road, where we lived, and on Armer, Crain City, O'rear, East Main, and all the other little dirt roads that laced through the woods, hollows, and oil-fields east of the county seat, almost no one subscribed to the local papers and certainly not to the great statewide paper, the *Arkansas Gazette*.

But the Dumas family—that is, my part of it—always took the *Daily News*. Every morning except Sunday, the rural mail carrier, a friendly fellow with a beautiful purple birthmark on his forehead, thrust the paper from the window of his old black Plymouth into the mailbox that protruded onto the dirt road. There would have been no reason to expect Clifton and Berta Dumas to be the plutocrats who had a daily newspaper delivered to their home every day. My father, a logger and woodsman, had only a sixth-grade education, but that was all that was available to him. Although he read the newspaper thoroughly every day, he was not into the refinements of learning and books. My mother was a reader and a book lover, but I always assumed that it was my father who insisted on investing a few of the family's meager dollars in a newspaper subscription and sometimes another to the *Saturday Evening Post*. Clifton was a man of sublime temperament who I never heard raise his voice and who seems, in my memory's faint gaze, to have spent all his waking hours in toil, except for the time reading the newspaper or playing the violin and harmonica when his friend Walter Bird emerged from the woods at twilight with his own instruments to rehearse their short repertoire of fiddle tunes, which always included "The Eighth of January." I always thought my dad and old man Bird had composed the reel until Johnny Horton took it to the top of the hit parade in 1959, my last year of college. So poor was my education that it was not until I sat in Jimmy Driftwood's little rock house at Timbo, down the mountain from my wife's homeplace at Fox, and listened to Driftwood and George Fisher play and sing it, that I learned that Driftwood had set the words of "The Battle of New Orleans" to the tune in 1936 to get his pupils at Timbo School excited about American history.

Although the *Daily News* came to the house regularly and I must have riffled through it fairly often, I cannot say that I was a reverent newspaper reader beyond the stories on the sports pages about major league baseball and the exploits of the El Dorado Oilers of the Cotton States League. When Wayne learned to drive and got a permit, he and I occasionally went into town to see the Oilers play the Hot Springs Bathers or the Greenville (Mississippi) Buckshots. If we were lucky, we got to see the old fat righthander

Copeland "Iron Man" Goss pitch both ends of a Sunday doubleheader or centerfielder Pel Austin hit a couple of home runs. Pel retired from professional baseball when I was a senior and started coaching the high school basketball team. By then I was a reporter for the *Daily News* covering the games for the morning and afternoon papers and for my high school paper, the *Hi-Gusher*. Coach Austin would approach me after physical education class and talk about my stories in the *Daily News*, usually in a complimentary way but also with some graceful tips about how I might make his job easier. He said Joe Donnelly's mama—Joe was the big 6'3" center for the Wildcats—complained to him that Donald Barker, Lamar Drummond, and Sam Gladney, the team's big scorers, seemed to get all the attention in my game accounts in the *Daily News* and Joe was rarely mentioned outside the box score. Pel asked if I could find a way to mention Joe more, because he worked very hard and his mama seemed to think Coach had something to do with the coverage. It was my first experience with efforts to influence my reporting, and I succumbed. I would write: "Though he scored only four points and missed all five of his free throws, center Joe Donnelly ripped seven rebounds from the boards." Pel had problems with depression and took his own life.

The Oilers baseball team afforded me my first real contact with Arkansas politics. It was in the summer of 1954 and Wayne and I went to town to watch the Oilers play some team, perhaps the Greenville Buckshots or the Greenwood (Mississippi) Dodgers. Word leaked out that the Oilers were going to sell the slugger Harville Jakes if attendance did not pick up, and Wayne and I wanted to save Jakes. For the seventh-inning stretch, the owner or someone in management went to the screen back of home plate with a microphone and announced that they were happy to have their fine neighboring state senator, Jim Johnson, from across the river at Crossett, and his lovely wife, Virginia, at the game. Jim was running for the Democratic nomination for attorney general against Tom Gentry. Obviously, Jim shouldn't make a political speech between innings because fans were anxious to get back to the batting order, so he and Virginia belted out "On Mockingbird Hill." Their duet was not as good as Slim Whitman's version, but I thought they were pretty good. They had the words down pat.

> Got a three-cornered plow and an acre to till
> And a mule that I bought for a ten-dollar bill.
> There's a tumbledown shack and a rusty old mill.

But it's my home sweet home up on Mockingbird Hill.
Tra la la, tweedle dee dee dee,
It gives me a thrill
To wake up in the morning
To the mockingbird's trill.
Tra la la, tweedle dee dee dee,
There's peace and goodwill.
You're welcome as the flowers
On Mockingbird Hill.

Tom Gentry walloped Jim Johnson badly that summer in spite of Jim's adroit use of the U.S. Supreme Court's historic school-desegregation order, and then Gentry was beaten in the next election, in 1956, by El Dorado's own silver-haired racist, Bruce Bennett, while Jim was getting trounced by Orval E. Faubus in the governor's race.

Unsure of my memory, I asked Jim many years later if he and Virginia had sung "On Mockingbird Hill" at an El Dorado Oilers baseball game in 1954. "Damn, you have a helluva memory," Jim said. It might have been the same conversation in which he accused me of having destroyed his political career by reminding *Arkansas Gazette* readers every time he ran for justice of the Supreme Court that he had refused to shake hands with black voters in a 1968 race for the U.S. Senate against J. William Fulbright. He said my mention of the incident in columns or editorials made it seem that he considered himself too fancy to shake hands with a black man or woman when all he had meant in 1968, when he said that he was "not campaigning in the colored community," was that he knew he was not going to get black votes and it was pointless to go out of his way to inconvenience a black person by trying to shake his or her hand. Unfailingly gracious to me, Jim did not allow the old grievance to stop him from sending me a serviceable necktie most Christmases until 2010 when, suffering from incurable cancer, he killed himself.

If I was even vaguely aware of the momentous social movements manifested in the elections of 1954 and 1956 and that would occupy much of my reporting and commentary for sixty-five years, I do not recall it, although the causes must have confronted me every day even in the bucolic loneliness of Champagnolle Road. With rare exceptions, the very best that could be said of Southern white boys was that we were blithely ignorant of the inhumanity we saw around us every day, even when we did not directly

contribute to it. When the U.S. Supreme Court delivered its order to integrate the schools in *Brown v. Board of Education of Topeka, Kansas* in 1954,
the story would have been on the front page of the *El Dorado Daily News*
the next morning, but I do not recollect its seeming to have the slightest
importance to me or to anyone I knew.

It would not have occurred to me that the news might have any relevance
to the family that in some ways was more intertwined with mine than any
other, the Davises, an extended black family of men, women, and youngsters of uncertain consanguinity who lived in the woods about a mile north
of us. Dock Davis and my father worked side by side every weekday for
much of their lives, my father driving an International or GMC log truck
and often handling one end of a crosscut saw while Dock or sometimes
Marshall Wiley manned the other; Dock later used a gasoline-powered
chainsaw, and also controlled the mules and chains that pulled the logs
through the woods and onto my father's trailer. My father drove to El Dorado every Saturday to the home of one of the Anthony Wood Products clan,
collected the cash rewards for the week's deliveries to the Anthony skidways, and then shared them with Dock Davis. Mary, Martha, and Money
Davis, sisters of Dock I suppose, made the rounds by foot through the
white community every week, building fires and boiling water in outside
pots to wash folks' clothes and bed linens. Money's son Willie, a year or so
younger than me, would usually make the rounds with them and in the
summer we played. I was envious of Willie and the spawn of the Cato and
Marshall Wiley clans farther up Champagnolle Road, who were playing by
the roadside when I rode the school bus along the backroads to Quinn and
El Dorado. They did not have to go to school, there being none for their
kind out in the country to attend with any regularity. The offspring of the
Davis women seemed to die too often at an early age—medical care was
not an option that was available to them—or else, like Sam and Haywood
Davis, contracted some mental impairment that left them angry, brooding,
and, to white folk, fearsome.

I must admit that I can summon no firsthand memories of outward expressions of racism in the community besides references at the sawmills
where my father hauled his logs to the "nigger" hands at the mills. My
father and mother did not use the word, and I do not recall their ever discussing the race situation when I was a child. When I got into newspaper
reporting, my mother confided in me that segregation was morally wrong
and un-Christian but that I should never express such opinions in open

company because family members—I think she meant primarily an offensively pious elder brother of hers—and most other acquaintances would talk unkindly of me and try to poison my reputation.

But one incident does stand out. Part of the extended Dumas family of Perdues and Armers was an aged vagrant named Ed Armer, commonly called Cud'n Ed. He lived alone in a crumbling shack at the back of an abandoned field a quarter mile off the road, a house left to him by his father and probably his grandfather. Cud'n Ed was not known to have ever worked. He seemed to wear the same heavily layered and filthy clothes the year round, and when he came near you tried to inch around to stay upwind of him. How he survived was a mystery. My cousin Jerry Evers and I, squirrel hunting or something, once sneaked up to his shack and peered in a window to a room that was half filled with hundreds of empty blue Nabisco cracker boxes. Other than the Saltines that were probably stolen from stores in town, he must have lived on handouts around the community. He would appear at the edge of the woods near the shed where we kept feed for the chickens, hogs, and the milk cow, his limp gray hat nearly covering his rheumy eyes. He would stand there until my mother spotted him and took out some food, perhaps a few leftover biscuits and a tin of Vienna sausages or potted meat. Sometimes he worked up the courage to come to the door and ask for food or a dollar. He would hitchhike into El Dorado and go to Piggly Wiggly or Safeway, where the manager alerted employees to be on the lookout for him. Cud'n Ed had ridden to town with my father one Saturday and went to Safeway with him. The manager caught Ed sitting on the floor by the peanut-butter display with a nearly empty jar in his lap and his fingers and hairy face smeared with the contents. The manager told my father never to bring Ed there again. My father often took other routes into town if he thought Cud'n Ed might be on the road. He could not turn him down for a ride.

The final incident occurred when Ed bummed a ride with him on the log truck through Quinn Road to the Anthony sawmill on U.S. Highway 167. My father kept a long iron pipe on the floor of the cab that he used for leverage to loosen the chains and dump logs onto the skidway. Ed, I suppose, would try to cadge some crackers or some other foodstuff at the mill's ratty commissary, where my father and the black millhands kept credit. As they turned off the highway onto the narrow road that coursed through unpainted shacks where black millworkers and their families lived, a black man was strolling along the road. Cud'n Ed grabbed the pipe from the floor, reached out the passenger window, and took a swing at the man's head, bellowing "God-damned nigger." My father was able to swerve enough that Ed missed the man's head, and he told Ed he could never ride with him again, a commitment that he did not keep. My father was badly shaken by the incident.

Tenement rows like the one at the Anthony-Williams lumber mill were common around south Arkansas lumber and paper mills. The lumber mills, which paid negligible wages to millworkers, were one of the few kinds of factory jobs that were available to black men. Like my father, they all had credit at the commissary, which kept cigarettes, smoking tobacco, snuff, and chewing tobacco along with cartons and cans of foodstuffs and a few necessities like gloves, work socks, and knives. A fine little book called *Jelly Roll*, published in 1986, recorded the brutal existence that was life in a south Arkansas mill town. Brutal was not a word that Charles E. Thomas, the author, used to describe Jelly Roll, the name of the squalid community of shacks around the Calion Lumber Company on the south bank of the Ouachita River at Calion, a few miles down the road from our house. My father sometimes hauled logs there. The Thomas family owned the lumber company and what I call the housing, for lack of a more apt description; Charles Thomas was a professor of anthropology at Washington University at St. Louis when he decided to move back and run the old family business after his father's death. He set out to study and document the sociology of the Jelly Roll shantytown and the wretched (my word, not his) existence of the families there. *Jelly Roll* was not a searing piece of social criticism but an illuminating ethnography. You had to supply your own sorrow and moral judgment, but Thomas made it easy. Like the far more judgmental literature of Grif Stockley, Douglas Blackmon, Guy Lancaster, and others, Thomas's little book filled a gap in our knowledge of the dark corners of our Southern enclaves.

Jelly Roll and Champagnolle landing, a makeshift port on the Ouachita River near the Champagnolle Oil Field, were at the eastern end of our county road, and four miles away at the road's western terminus were the East Field, the flourishing city of El Dorado, and its belching refineries. On our short stretch of the dirt road, the bottomland oaks, tupelos, and birch trees along the springs and creeks were luxuriant with birds, squirrels, raccoons, rabbits, possums, and an occasional fox, and a boy with a can of worms could cut a birch limb and harvest enough panfish in an afternoon for a small supper. He could even swim safely in the wide bends of the cold waters, if he was careful about moccasins and the infrequent copperhead brooding in the tangle of birch roots.

Only three miles away in both directions, most dips in the road opened an entirely different vista—wide, dead valleys where hardly a trace of animal life or even vegetation could be seen. Thirty years earlier, in 1921, a speculator hit a gusher, the famous Busey Number 1, and the oil and gas rush was on. Within a few months, twenty-two trains a day loaded with oil were leaving El Dorado. Speculators and operators with trifling geological knowledge and little understanding of the faults and the dangers of drilling in the deep carbon sands—and even less concern about the terrible risk to the environment and public health—splashed oil, gas, saltwater, brine, and other poisonous minerals across the countryside, destroying forests and meadows and poisoning creeks, which fed into one another and finally into the Ouachita River four miles from my home.

My father told me of once seeing a portion of the river on fire, which was a common scene in the huge oil storage pits and nearby streams a few miles north of us in the devastated precincts of Standard-Umsted, Smackover, and Norphlet, where I sometimes went in the summer to play baseball with my cousins on the brown diamond under the smokestacks of the MacMillan Ring-Free Oil Refinery. The Ouachita meandered into northern Louisiana, where in the 1930s people threatened lawsuits to stop the upstream pollution in Arkansas that had despoiled their river and, after floods, poisoned their cotton farms and bottomland hardwoods.

We never fished or got into the Ouachita River, although my father claimed as a boy to have often swum across the river and back before the spring floods saturated the waters with salt, chloride, and mercury and slimed the banks with oil. To fish, he took my brother and me across the river into the swamps of Calhoun County, where still uncontaminated portions of the Champagnolle and Moro creeks would yield a string of largemouth bass and an occasionally edible carp.

It was an environmental disaster that would capture headlines worldwide today, but at the time and even in my youth it apparently caused little emotion but excitement—the lure of wealth and, even for poor African Americans, the chance for low-paying work. For a youngster, the ecological disaster was merely a curiosity. Walking home from school on an occasion when I missed the bus, I left a bridge crossing a creek and meandered a half mile downstream in search of some form of life, a small snake, a perch, even a minnow, but I found none. Ancient residues of oil lined the

banks and often the bottom of the shallow stream. Not a tree stood anywhere within fifty yards of the streambed, only an occasional long-fallen
tree trunk. I began to think about the physically and mentally disabled
relatives I knew who were born and lived within range of the refinery
emissions or contaminated groundwater. A distant cousin who was born
in sight of the oil scion H. L. Hunt's first well about two miles through the
woods from our home, which contaminated the creek that ran behind his
house and probably the family well, was mentally disabled, although my
father claimed that Whaley could recite some of the alphabet. I enjoyed the
discovery that H. L. Hunt's first well was a poor one and didn't bring the old
gambler and John Bircher much money.

It would be late in my newspaper career, reflecting on the casual observations of my youth, that I came to appreciate government's belated efforts—
even the weak initiatives of Arkansas regulatory agencies like the Oil and
Gas Commission and Pollution Control and Ecology Department—to roll
back a half century of heedless plunder and protect the human environment from future harm. Only a few years ago, I came across a scholarly
article by a scientist with the U.S. Geological Survey in the early stages
of the El Dorado oil boom criticizing the reckless exploration methods
he saw—not for the environmental and human harm caused by the gas
flaring and massive runoff from the holding pits, but because the methods
were so stupid and reckless that they left huge deposits of oil incapable of
production and wasted great oil wealth by spreading it across the lands
and streams. Some balm would be the realization late in life that, far from
a socialist plot to hamstring capitalist industry, environmental and safety
laws and regulations were a fulfillment of the promise of the government's
founding documents to protect people's life, health, and happiness.

But no more digressions from the story at hand—how I got into reporting on the affairs of government and politicians. My father told my brother
and me that if we could go to college we might study to be some kind of
engineer—almost anything but a lawyer. (He and a couple of other men,
who had driven trucks for a woman who owned an oil company, had hired
a lawyer to sue her when she never paid them, but the lawyer kept the
entire judgment as his fee payment and demanded more from them.) So
in the fall of 1954, my senior year, I enrolled in chemistry and advanced

math classes, and to balance them I took a journalism course under Ruth Jenkins, because my brother, who had taken the course, told me that writing stuff did not require any study. After the first issue of the high school newspaper came out, Mrs. Jenkins asked me if I would care to take a job after school at the *El Dorado Daily News*. Doing what? I asked. She said the paper needed a reporter, that I could do it, and that I ought to take the opportunity. So I skipped the bus after school that afternoon and walked down to the paper office and saw Robert T. Hays, the managing editor. He had me rewrite two or three news releases, examined my stories, and told me to report to the paper every day after school. I would go by the courthouse on the way from school to the office, collect the court news, write the obituaries delivered by the funeral homes, and cover the police and sheriff's offices in the evenings. Two splendid women reporters, Dewey Finley and Oleta Mitchell, the sharpest people in the whole operation, showed me how to do everything. I worked after school to about midnight and full days on Saturday and Sunday, covering all the high school and professional sports as well as the weekly news of drillings and discoveries in south Arkansas's oil and gas fields. The overtime, even at the minimum wage of seventy-five cents an hour, was so lucrative that I could buy an old Ford to get to school and home from work. That and weekend and summer work would support me through five years of college.

It helped that I could type faster than I could think, and it was the volume, more than the quality of my work, that enhanced my standing and value at the paper. I would later get a journalism degree from the oldest and most prestigious journalism school in the nation, but I picked up nothing there that I had not learned either from Dewey and Oleta, by reading the paper, or by the trial and error of actually writing for daily publication. One Sunday night in my first few months at the paper, I was left alone to take care of any news that might occur before the press rolled. A local eminence by the name of Lynwood "Schoolboy" Rowe called the paper and I answered. Schoolboy was a local legend, having singlehandedly led the high school athletic teams to state championships in about 1930 and then pitched the Detroit Tigers to national championships later in the decade. He was a major-league all-star for about five seasons and still holds the American League pitching record for consecutive victories, sixteen.

"Who am I speaking to?" he growled.

I told him my name. He said he did not want to see anything in the paper about his wreck in north Louisiana, mentioning the town. Did I understand? I asked him something about the wreck.

"I said I don't want to see anything in the paper. Can you understand that?"

Yes, sir, I said.

Unsure what I should do, I telephoned the police department in the Louisiana city and the desk sergeant read me the investigating officer's report. The accident was the previous day. Rowe had been charged with driving while intoxicated and someone was seriously injured. I wrote a short news story about it, attached a headline saying Schoolboy Rowe was charged in an accident in Louisiana, and took it to the composing room. It appeared on page two of the Monday morning paper. I worried about it that night and at school the next day, wondering if I had done the right thing. Schoolboy was the most admired person in town. His son, a gawky but likable kid, was a fellow student, having graduated the previous spring.

When I got to my desk after school, Bob Hays, wearing his customary scowl, limped over to my desk with the paper folded to the story about Schoolboy Rowe. (Bob had jumped off the East Hillsboro Street viaduct onto the Rock Island tracks near the paper but survived.)

"Ernie," he said, "who is responsible for this?" I said I was. He asked how it came about. I explained that Mr. Rowe had called about the wreck and that I had telephoned the police in Louisiana and gotten the details. I figured I was fired.

"Did Mr. Rowe tell you that he did not want to see this in the paper?"

"Yes, sir."

"But you just decided you knew better and you'd get the story and print it anyway?" he asked.

"Yes, sir, I guess so."

"Good job," he said, and walked away.

Boy, I thought, this is not a bad way to make a living.

One other event in my first months on the job was life-shaping. The night reporter spent a lot of time at the police station, the primary source of evening news, because the paper reported every wreck and most arrests that occurred before midnight. The patrolling officers brought in drunks from the slum around Washington Avenue and put them in the tank overnight. Sgt. J. G. Thomas and Patrolman L. J. Bryant, the evening cruise team, brought in an aging and frail black man so drunk that he could barely stand. The police were poking him with their nightsticks and laughing. They emptied his pockets and put the contents, including his billfold, on the shelf at the desk sergeant's window. The routine was that a person's belongings were kept in a big envelope until he was released from jail. Seeing his billfold lying on the counter, the old man instinctively reached for it. As his bony hand touched the billfold, L. J. Bryant brought his nightstick down on the man's hand with bone-crushing force. The old man crumpled to the floor with a loud wail. All the policemen laughed. Bryant jabbed his nightstick in the man's ribs and said, "Get up, nigger, get up. It'll be upside your head the next time." I wondered if I should write about the brutality. When I got back to the newspaper office I told the night editor, J. D. Beauchamp, about it. He laughed, too.

Such treatment, I began to observe, was routine for African Americans but never for whites who were brought to the station. I was sixteen. Racism entered my consciousness for the first time, and the reminders were unceasing after that, nowhere more than at the police station, but everywhere I went: the "colored" water fountains in squalid corners of the public buildings, a single "colored" restroom for both sexes, the absence of African Americans in all the public and commercial work forces—except for janitors and maids. For the first time, I began to reflect upon the obliviousness of my childhood, what I had seen but never cared about. It is an awakening moment that many white people have, especially in the South where multiracial contact is a daily experience, but probably also in all caste societies where status is predetermined by ethnic, religious, class, or tribal distinctions. It is a moment of self-examination, the conclusion of which is either gratitude for one's good luck in the accident of birth, or shame, or both.

Margaret Miller—along with her husband, Dale, who was known as "Slug" for his athletic exploits in college—ran her family business, Hollings -worth Feed Store, where we went from time to time to get feed for the hens, hogs, and milk cow along with vegetable seeds and tools. Governor Sid McMath had put Mrs. Miller on the board of trustees of Henderson State Teachers College at Arkadelphia, where she had met Slug. She asked one day in 1955 if I intended to go to college and where I would like to go. I didn't know. She said I should go to Henderson, because it was an easy drive from home—about eighty miles—and she was pretty sure she could get me a campus job. I said OK.

She arranged for me to work in the college's public relations office for

$37.50 a month. The public relations director/journalism teacher, Rudolph Gandy, had departed before school started, and the college president, Dr. Dean Depew McBrien, got Josephine Walton, a former English teacher who lived a few blocks from the college, to fill in at the public relations office for the year. I wrote most of the college's news releases that year and she lavishly praised everything I did. I loved her.

Since there was no longer a journalism teacher or journalism students, the weekly college paper, the *Oracle*, would have no editor and no staff when school started in the fall of 1956. Mrs. Walton, who was finishing her interim appointment as the PR officer, told the president and me that I would be the editor. One of my pals, Clarence Hall of Blytheville, later a fine novelist under the pen name B. C. Hall, had worked the previous summer at the *Courier News* in Blytheville. He agreed to share the responsibility with me, since we were likely to have no staff of writers to produce a paper every week. A freshman named Freddie Nuesch from Malvern volunteered to write sports. The *Oracle* office was situated across the hall from the president, who spent much of his time visiting with us, often reciting the clever limericks he found inscribed inside restroom stalls. Dr. McBrien thought they proved there was a lot of latent creative genius on campus.

We put out an insipid paper every week that year, but in the fall of 1957 we grew a little nervy. Governor Orval E. Faubus sent the National Guard to stop nine black children from entering Central High School at Little Rock, overriding the orders of U.S. courts. Dr. McBrien walked across the hall that week and told Clarence and me that the Henderson paper should not mention "that business up at Little Rock." He and the board of trustees, including Margaret Miller, had integrated the student body two years earlier, my freshman year, and it had received no coverage. But the integration of Central High School had inflamed the state and he did not want his college to get embroiled in the dispute. Any comment in the Henderson paper, he said, could get the college involved and focus attention on our integration and bring repercussions from the governor and the legislature. He reminded us that Henderson was a state institution, dependent upon the goodwill of the governor and the legislature. A few weeks later, Ben Donaldson, a bright student who occasionally penned a cartoon for us, drew one of the famous façade of Central High School with stacked bayonets in front. My recollection is that it bore no caption except perhaps something like "School Days." The president was furious and told us that we had violated his orders. We said, "Well, you just told us not to write anything about the integration stuff, and Little Rock and integration were not mentioned." He said he didn't want to see anything else, and he began to post himself by the *Oracle* box in the Student Union on Friday mornings, when the papers were delivered by the *Daily Siftings Herald* print shop.

In the spring of 1958, an article in the *Gazette*—or else an Associated Press article in the local paper—recounted some discussion of the school crisis at the Capitol, probably at a meeting of the Legislative Council, an interim committee of senior legislators, where there was talk of anti-school-integration bills that would be introduced at a special legislative session. We wrote a little editorial, the gist of which, in my vague recollection, was that the legislature evinced little real interest in education. All I remember is that, for some reason, we called the legislature "lethargic." We studiously avoided any direct mention of Faubus, Central High, or integration. It just talked about what was good for education. That Friday morning, a note was delivered to me in class that the president wanted to see me right away. Clarence got the same note. It seemed that the president had picked up the first copy of the paper when it was delivered to the Student Union, spotted the editorial, and had all the papers confiscated and destroyed. I told Clarence that I was too busy to see Dr. McBrien then and that I was going to go to El Dorado to go to work at the *Daily News*, as I did every weekend. He said he was going with me. Sunday night, after working all weekend, I was at home at Champagnolle with Clarence when J. Walton Coley, who had succeeded Mrs. Walton as the public relations director and "adviser" to the paper, reached me by phone and said the president was furious and talking about expelling us from school and ceasing publication of the paper.

Monday morning, we got fresh notices from the president's office to go see him. The three of us met in the doorway of the *Oracle* office. Dr. Mc-Brien said we had violated our implicit agreement with him and that if he had not stopped the paper's circulation Friday morning we would have jeopardized the college, the student body, and the faculty by putting the institution in the political crosshairs. He would be perfectly in his rights to expel us from school for insubordination, he said, and certainly we could not be trusted to produce the paper again. Mr. Coley heard the racket and joined the argument—on our side.

Finally, I went into our office and brought out an issue of the *Arkansas Traveler*, the four-day-a-week newspaper at the University of Arkansas at Fayetteville. It regularly carried Little Rock integration news on its front page, along with editorial attacks on the governor and funny pieces by a student named Charles Portis, a Korean War veteran and later the great novelist. I asked Dr. McBrien why the *Traveler* editors were not jeopardizing that institution's future the same way we were jeopardizing Henderson's when they were commenting on the crisis in nearly every issue and not in the insipid way we did. I tried to read to him a clever paragraph from Portis's piece. He grabbed the *Traveler* from my hand and said the University of Arkansas and its paper were irrelevant. His only interest was Henderson, not Fayetteville. Mr. Coley snatched the paper from the president—by this time, it was in shreds—and said "Ernie's right." He tried to read a headline or something to McBrien, who would have none of it. McBrien threw the paper scraps on the floor. I asked if the school would not land in the spotlight after all if the *Gazette* or *Democrat* at Little Rock wrote that, owing to the school crisis, Henderson had ceased publishing the college paper and expelled the editors. The president seemed stunned.

"You mean you would tell them?" he asked.

"No, sir," I said, but I speculated that the state papers would somehow find out, because the faculty, the student body, and townspeople would all know. You just can't keep those kinds of things a secret. Dr. McBrien said maybe we could work things out and continue publishing for the rest of the semester. "You can have the fucking paper," Clarence said, and walked out of the building.

Clarence and I drove to Columbia, Missouri, the next week and I enrolled at the University of Missouri School of Journalism for the fall semester. Clarence stayed around Henderson a year but did nothing more on the paper. He entered the graduate creative-writing program at the University of Iowa at Ames, which prepared him for college teaching and for writing quite a few high-quality gothic novels and many bodice rippers, written under pseudonyms like "Julia French."

II
Harry and Orval

On the day in November 1819 that William E. Woodruff printed the first *Arkansas Gazette* in a log house at Arkansas Post, the capital of the new Arkansas Territory, Napoleon brooded in his final exile on St. Helena's cursed rock; and on the humid June day in 1960 that I reported to work in the newspaper's stately neoclassical headquarters at Third and Louisiana streets in Little Rock, Ronald Reagan quit as boss of the Hollywood actors' union and converted to conservatism and the Republican Party. November 1819 should be a premier marker for Arkansawyers, for Arkansas's and the newspaper's destinies would be inextricably linked, more so probably than any other state and its media. The *Gazette* will be the fulcrum for these chronicles. The Emperor and The Gipper serve only to help the reader fix the time frame for the story in the firmament of history; we will have nothing further to do with either of them.

In the two years between my separation from Henderson State Teachers College and graduation in Missouri, the *Gazette* had achieved some national acclaim that added to its venerable tradition of courageous reporting, careful writing, and attention to the historical currents in what was commonly viewed by the rest of the country as a backwater state. In 1958, the paper received two Pulitzer Prizes, one for editorials written by Harry S. Ashmore, the newspaper's executive editor, about the school-integration crisis at Little Rock and another for community service for both its courageous editorial stand and its coverage of the events. It also received the Freedom House Award for protecting constitutional freedoms during that struggle. The newspaper was celebrated at the University of Missouri School of Journalism, and I began to go to the journalism library, which collected daily papers from around the country, to read the *Gazette*.

From this vantage point, I cannot say whether I had in mind going to work there after graduation, but my slumbering social conscience finally having been roused by what I had witnessed at the police precinct at El Dorado and by subsequent events like the dispute over our vapid little editorial in the college paper, I followed the blossoming civil rights movement with consuming interest. It manifested itself on the Missouri campus in a peculiar way, as a student protest against scholarships that the university was said to be giving to a few white boys from the racist South. Having inherited a little of my mother's self-consciousness, I worried that my classmates had found out that I was one of those Southern whiteys and wondered half seriously whether I should give back to the university the $600 I was getting each year from some kind of trust that memorialized Theodore Roosevelt. I never looked into Roosevelt's connections with journalism, but I flattered myself that my little scholarship might have had something to do with the former president's appearance in 1905 at the Little Rock city park near the *Gazette* building, where he manfully put down the state's Trumpian governor, Jeff Davis, who had introduced the great man by praising Arkansas's practice of lynching black men to maintain control over the race. Roosevelt responded that a better principle was the rule of law.

While the *Arkansas Gazette* almost overnight had become, nationally, the moral exemplar of what a great newspaper should be, back in my state it had once again become "that old red harlot," the honorific that Jeff Davis, the neo-Confederate governor, had hung on the paper fifty-five years earlier. Governor Faubus was hammering the newspaper and Harry Ashmore almost daily, and its circulation and advertising revenues had plummeted in the face of boycotts organized by the white citizens' council and conservative business interests.

In *An American Dilemma: The Negro Problem and Modern Democracy*, the 1944 treatise by the Swedish economist Gunnar Myrdal that triggered the court decisions that brought down *de jure* segregation in America, Myrdal wrote that the only hope of Negroes was an aroused press that would educate people about the terrible plight of the descendants of slaves in the South of Jim Crow. Only intense and inescapable national publicity, Myrdal concluded, could produce changes in the law and disinfect the unvisited recesses of the Southern social order. It would behoove the Southern press to undertake that job, but, outside the occasional African American newspaper, most Southern journals were either not inclined to challenge a social order that their owners and editors thought was intractable, or else, like James Jackson Kilpatrick, editor of the *Richmond News Leader*, they were fierce champions of white supremacy. Even reporting on racially tinged events was rarely done. A half dozen Southern editors, most notably Atlanta's Ralph McGill and Ashmore, who moved from his native South Carolina to Little Rock in 1947 to become an editorial writer and then executive editor of the *Gazette*, came to view segregation as the great shortcoming of the American experiment and as the inexorable issue of their time. But they wrote timidly about it, except to express confidence that the South's better angels would prevail when the inevitable day came—the inevitable day being an order by the U.S. Supreme Court that government-sponsored and -protected discrimination had to end. It would fall Ashmore's lot, and that of his newspaper, to assume the role that Myrdal envisioned.

Ashmore, like McGill, was hardly a firebrand. A South Carolinian with the educated aristocrat's preference for gradual and dignified evolution, Ashmore like many other Southerners had his conscience pricked on the battlefields of World War II. He was an infantry colonel in George Patton's Third Army and came home from Europe imbued with the idea that the greatest flaw in American democracy, particularly in the citadel of the confederacy where he was reared, had somehow to be fixed. A U.S. Marine hero in the Pacific, Colonel Sidney McMath, came home to Arkansas similarly impassioned. In Little Rock, Ashmore and McMath, by then the governor, became good friends, and in 1951 McMath had Ashmore address the Southern governors at a conference in Little Rock on their obligations to embrace or protect, as a matter of observing the rule of law, the civil rights that before long were certain to be coming through the courts.

Ashmore, McGill, and Hodding Carter of the Greenville (Mississippi) *Delta Democrat Times* were sometimes called on to debate the civil-rights issue in the North and East. The forums usually cast moderate Southerners, rather than hotspurs like Jack Kilpatrick, against the champions of full and immediate restoration of rights awarded by the Fourteenth Amendment. They asserted that, regardless of the rightness of the cause, the South needed to be given some forbearance when change was finally ordered. Ashmore became more and more embarrassed by his own appeals for forbearance and for gradual and piecemeal remedies, which he felt obliged to advance in these encounters with the NAACP and others—as if he were no more than a cat's-paw for the white supremacists and politicians like Strom Thurmond of South Carolina and Harry Byrd of Virginia.

As several school-segregation lawsuits advanced through the federal courts, the matter reached a critical juncture for Ashmore. The Fund for the Advancement of Education, a subsidiary of the Ford Foundation, decided in 1953 that it should use its resources to finally settle the question of whether Southern public schools provided the equal educational opportunities for black and white children that the Supreme Court in *Plessy v. Ferguson* in 1896 said would satisfy the Fourteenth Amendment's demand for equal protection of the laws and, if they didn't, exactly where and by how much they failed. It would pay for a massive research project in all the Southern states in hopes that the research could be done and published by the time the issue was ripe for a decision by the Supreme Court, probably in 1954. It asked Ashmore to head the project and to write the conclusions. The researchers would look at the funding for the separate school systems, teacher qualifications, the degree of enrollment of black children compared with white children, the length of school years, classroom sizes, and the quality of facilities. The report would provide the courts and the country with solid data, not mere theories and claims.

For a Southerner to take the mantle was almost certain to subject him to the reprobation of the political leadership and of a big majority of the citizenry of his community and state. Ashmore wanted to do it, but he asked the men who had hired him and who would bear any financial consequences, J. N. Heiskell, the *Gazette*'s editor, and Hugh B. Patterson Jr., the publisher, if the paper was willing to accept that risk. Patterson said he had to do it, not merely as a moral duty but as a matter of fiscal prudence.

"When that Supreme Court decision comes down," Patterson said, "every newspaper in the South is going to have to deal with the consequences, and we'll have the best-informed editor available—at Ford Foundation expense." Ashmore later said he had mentioned his new task to an old political acquaintance in Arkansas. "Son," Ashmore's friend told him, "it sounds to me like you have got yourself in the position of a man running for sonofabitch without opposition."

Hugh Patterson

As it happened, *The Negro and the Schools* by Harry S. Ashmore was released on May 16, 1954, one day before the Supreme Court handed down the momentous *Brown v. Board of Education* decision. Advance copies of the book had been sent weeks earlier to the Supreme Court and also to newspapers and other publications. They were preparing stories on the report's conclusions about the inequalities in black and white schools when the Supreme Court released the first *Brown* decision. While the book probably had little effect on the unanimous decision of the justices, Chief

Justice Earl Warren would later say that the text was studied thoroughly before the court rendered its *"Brown II"* decision in 1955, when it declared that schools had to be integrated "with all deliberate speed." If Arkansaw-yers had known that, Ashmore's and the *Gazette's* popularity doubtlessly would have suffered even more than they did.

The Negro and the Schools was not a polemic for integration and racial equality, but in columns of data and graphs about spending, enrollment, library holdings, population demographics, and migration in each of the states of Dixie, it laid out the incontrovertible facts, all woven into Ash-more's come-let-us-reason-together discourse on Southern history, its pe-culiar institutions, and his speculations about the difficulties that lay ahead in solving the problems that the courts were almost certain to say had to be solved. His short introduction concluded with a statement of Ashmore's typically hopeful philosophy about journalism, which he would soon have reasons to reconsider:

> In many important ways this volume puts to the test one of my cherished theories—that in addition to its usual functions of preparing a first draft of history, entertain-ing children of all ages, and promoting the sale of certain goods and services, journalism should serve as a two-way bridge between the world of ideas and the world of men. In any event, my experience as a journalist in a company of scholars has strengthened my conviction that no prob-lems are beyond resolution by reasonable men—not even the thorny ones that lie in the uncertain area between the polar attitudes of the American white, who does not yet accept the Negro as his equal, and the American Negro, who is no longer satisfied with anything less.

Four years later, after he and his newspaper found themselves in the cru-cible of the greatest civil-rights battle since the Civil War—when Faubus sent the militia to stop nine black children from attending Central High School and the paper condemned him for it—Ashmore wrote another book. *An Epitaph for Dixie* was more a screed than a paean to hope and reasoning humanity.

The editor's disillusionment was far-reaching for another reason. In the summer of 1954, weeks after the release of *The Negro and the Schools* and the first *Brown* decision, Ashmore had saved Orval Eugene Faubus's fledgling political career by writing an eloquent radio speech for him that defended his attendance at Commonwealth College, a radical self-help school near Mena, for a few months in 1935, at the depth of the Great Depression. Faubus would always concede that Ashmore's text was crucial to his winning the governor's office. It was perhaps also the greatest regret of Ashmore's life, for without it Faubus might never have been governor, and school integration at Little Rock and in the South might have taken an entirely different course. Governor Francis Cherry, although the true conservative in every sense that Faubus never was, would not have contravened the law in 1957 and used the limited might of the state to try to stop integration. Who knows, of course, what demagogue might have been elected governor in 1956 if Cherry and not Faubus had been elected in 1954? Might-have-beens perhaps should be reserved for gamblers and poets and never for historians, but I have always found it impossible not to extrapolate what the very personal nexus of the two men, Ashmore and Faubus—first vital confederates and then mortal enemies—meant to the future social and cultural development of the state and, importantly, to the newspaper that Ashmore led and to which I would devote my career. When Ashmore and Hugh Patterson persuaded J. N. Heiskell that the *Gazette* should oppose Faubus's efforts to prevent black children from attending white schools in Little Rock, the newspaper and Ashmore personally became lightning rods for Faubus and organizations like the white citizens' councils that were dedicated to the preservation of white supremacy. Within weeks of Ashmore's first editorial and Faubus's first attack on Ashmore and the paper in September 1957, the newspaper had lost seventeen percent of its daily subscribers and the afternoon *Arkansas Democrat* had surged into the lead in daily circulation. Partially owing to a boycott of *Gazette* advertisers promoted by the Capital Citizens' Council, the paper lost millions of dollars in advertising revenue. Seven years later, the *Gazette* would regain the lead, but the respite gave a new lease on life to the *Democrat*, the victim of a dwindling preference for afternoon newspapers everywhere and the declining utility of distributing them. Without it, the afternoon paper might soon have folded or else pleaded with Heiskell for a joint operating agreement, which became common for a few years in metropolitan markets.

In the Democratic runoff primary in 1954, Governor Cherry made Commonwealth College the central issue, only implying what he truly believed—that Faubus at least had once been a communist. He thought Faubus's Commonwealth sojourn proved it. Cherry ordinarily was not a hard-nosed politician. He had promised a frugal, circumspect, and honest administration and he had done little to curry favor with important interests or to reward friends. When the first glimmerings of his Commonwealth connection circulated, Faubus accused the governor of spreading the rumors and declared that he had never attended the school. Cherry and his advisers were torn about whether to jump on the Commonwealth story, which had seemed to stir little interest, and make it the central issue of the runoff campaign. When Cherry finally decided to go on television one evening for a full-bore attack on Faubus's honesty and, by implication, his patriotism, a young college student who was sort of his *aide de camp*, David H. Pryor of Camden, picked Cherry up at the Governor's Mansion to take him to the KARK studios a few blocks north on Spring Street for the big speech. Before he crawled into the Cadillac, Cherry veered off into the shrubbery and threw up. Cherry delivered the speech mechanically from his script. Pryor, who had keen instincts even then, thought that the speech went over badly and that it served only to create sympathy for the hillbilly Faubus. Cherry had proof of Faubus's lying about his Commonwealth attendance, a bound volume of the defunct college's newspaper, the *Fortnightly*, brought to the Governor's Mansion by the editor of the *Mena Star*. It carried proof of Faubus's enrollment and attendance at the school. Faubus then said that he went there only a few days and left disillusioned. But the school journal showed that Faubus, who grew up in a socialist household in Madison County, had been elected president of the student body, made the May Day speech at the college, and attended, as a delegate from the college, the All-Southern Conference for Civil and Trade Union Rights at Chattanooga, Tennessee, as well as another leftist gathering at nearby Monteagle, Tennessee. Near the end of his life Faubus would tell Roy Reed, his biographer, that he left the school after a Commonwealth lecturer, a communist refugee from Germany, declared that marriage was simply legalized prostitution. Faubus thought it was an insult to his dear mother.

Acting many years later on a tip from John F. Wells—who self-published a book called *Time Bomb*, contending that Faubus created the Central High crisis to further a plot formulated by Vladimir Lenin or Joseph Stalin, if not Karl Marx himself, to create racial strife in the United States—I went to the official papers of former governor Carl E. Bailey at the University of

Arkansas at Little Rock and discovered a typewritten letter by "Orval E. Faubus" to Governor Bailey in 1935 defending Commonwealth College, which a state legislative committee had been investigating for subversive activity. The letter urged Bailey to adopt a liberal stance and oppose the legislature's efforts to close the socialist school. Faubus's name was typed at the bottom but there was no signature.

Knowing that Johnny Wells, a *Gazette* reporter and editor in the early 1930s, had been an aide to Governor Bailey and a Cherry supporter, I was suspicious that he might have typed the letter and planted it in Bailey's papers to embarrass Faubus even years after his career had ended. I asked Faubus about it. He said he didn't recall writing the letter but that it was probably legitimate. Researching Faubus's Commonwealth connections when he was writing *Faubus: The Life and Times of an American Prodigal* in the 1980s, Roy Reed found a long article in the *Gazette* reporting on the legislature's Commonwealth hearings in which a student named "Arval Faubaus" had testified for the school and said he was not a communist. Faubus told Reed that if any of that had come out in 1954 he probably could not have survived the Commonwealth dustup and his political career would have ended. Even Ashmore's soaring sentences would not have saved him.

In the studio of the radio station, explaining his Commonwealth sojourn over a statewide hookup, Faubus read from Ashmore's hastily written text almost without looking up—he could still recite its beginning when he neared the end of his life: "When I went out from the green valley of my youth . . ." He said he looked up from the text midway in the speech, saw women moving closer to the microphone with tears running down their cheeks, and knew that he was going to win. Ashmore never expressed much pride in his authorship.

At the end of 1959, two years after writing the first editorial that condemned Faubus's defiance of federal court orders to integrate Central High School, Ashmore resigned as the *Gazette's* editor to join the Center for the Study of Democratic Institutions at Santa Barbara, California, and subsequently to become editor of the *Encyclopedia Britannica*. He may have felt that his departure was a service to the newspaper and its economic security by salving the hostility that the name Harry Ashmore brought it. He kept up with the paper and returned often over the years.

I began writing for the paper six months after Ashmore's departure. Some twenty years later, over drinks at our friend Fred Darragh's pool house on

Cantrell Road, Harry asked me how I was adjusting to being taken off the government beat after so many years and being made to write editorials. I said it was a hard adjustment to write opinions.

"Well," he said, "I think you'll find that writing editorials is like pissing in a blue-serge suit. It gives you a warm feeling, but no one pays any attention to what you did." He was right at least about that.

☐☐☐

My ego has never permitted me to accept the appearance that I owed my job at the *Arkansas Gazette*, and thus my career, to Jim Mooty, the speedy Arkansas Razorback, who could not have cared less about what happened to me. I graduated from high school a year before Mooty did, and he went on to become a first-team All-America halfback for the Razorbacks. The townspeople threw a parade for him around Christmastime in 1959 and the city declared "Jim Mooty Day." Home from the University of Missouri for the holidays, I was sent by the *Daily News* with a Speed Graphic camera to take pictures of the spectacle around the square in El Dorado and to write a story, which appeared in the morning paper in gaudy detail. The evening before I was to drive back to Missouri, I received a telephone call at home from A. R. Nelson, the managing editor of the *Gazette*, who said he was in town visiting his mother and had read my Jim Mooty story. Nelson, I would discover many years later, had been the daytime editor of the El Dorado papers in the 1940s. Nelson and a colleague named Copeland were each paid sixteen dollars a week to put out the morning and afternoon papers. As the day editor, Nelson was free in the evenings and covered the professional games of the El Dorado Oilers baseball team when they were in town and was paid two dollars a week by the Oilers to be the official scorekeeper for the league. The situation came to the attention of the publisher, Clyde E. Palmer, who called Nelson and Copeland in and said that he had learned that Nelson was getting an extra two dollars a week above his salary, which Palmer believed to be grossly unfair, especially to Copeland. He said Nelson should turn the two dollars over to the paper each week for redistribution among the other employees. Without a word, Nelson got up, put on his hat, and walked out the door, never to return. He went to work at the *Gazette*.

On this evening, Nelson said nothing about his old employer, but he thought I had written an exemplary piece on Mooty and wondered when I

was graduating at Missouri (the following May) and what I planned to do
then. I didn't have a clue. He offered me a job at the *Gazette* and I took it.
Nothing about the Jim Mooty story should have recommended me for a
job at the *Gazette*. Perhaps from residual vexation over his own treatment
at the *Daily News*, Nelson liked to hire El Dorado boys who worked at the
paper, and two of them, Rodney Dungan and Leroy Donald, respectively
one and two years my elders, said they had told Nelson he should hire me.
I have preferred that to the Jim Mooty explanation. When I received an
award from the University of Missouri at graduation that May, the university sent out a short news release about it. Nelson added a sentence that I
was going to work for the *Gazette* in June and put it at the bottom of the
front page in the first edition that circulated in El Dorado, but took it out
of the later editions that circulated in central Arkansas. He wanted people
at the *Daily News* to see it, as if anyone there cared.

When I settled in Little Rock in the summer of 1960, the city had fad-
ed from the national news, but race was not absent from the pages of the
Gazette or other newspapers in the state. The struggle over the pace of
integration in the Little Rock schools and then, gradually, elsewhere in the
state continued throughout the decade and beyond, and the civil rights
movement spread to Main Street lunch counters, swimming pools, department stores, workplaces, the dingy basement dining room of the State Capitol, and the police precincts where scores of African American protesters
were jailed and often brutalized. Rare was the day when the newspaper did
not carry an article about racial strife somewhere in Arkansas: if not Little
Rock or North Little Rock, then Pine Bluff, Fort Smith, Helena, Forrest
City, Gould, or Texarkana. National figures like the comedian Dick Grego-
ry arrived to get themselves arrested. William W. Hansen, a white kid who
led the Student Nonviolent Coordinating Committee in Little Rock for a
spell, got a few of his pummelings in Arkansas, especially after he married a
black woman. I watched him get bloodied by state troopers in the basement
of the Capitol in 1965, when he led a bunch of Philander Smith College
students there to get a plate lunch in the little cafeteria after the secretary
of state and governor had declared it a private club for whites. The troopers
also clubbed to the floor the *Pine Bluff Commercial*'s Capitol reporter, Bob
Lancaster, along with Hansen and the black students—men and women.
That night the governor went on television to falsely denounce Lancaster
as an integrationist provocateur who had abandoned his wife and child.
(The *Gazette* made me wear a suit and tie, which put a white man off lim-

its for police thrashings, unlike reporters like Lancaster whose employers didn't have a dress code.) U.S. District Judge J. Smith Henley promptly told the politicians that a government building could not be a private resort, so they just closed the cafeteria for a spell. It reopened quietly to legislators and capitol visitors of any color who didn't have the time or the thirst to get downhill to the Pitcher, now the White Water Tavern.

From the summer of 1960 until Faubus's transient retirement in 1967, he and Central High School never left the stage. In other political venues, race gave way to the old political shibboleths—government waste, lower taxes, prosperity, or roads—but every gubernatorial election turned inevitably on race. Faubus seemed at times to want to leave it in the past and talk only about the good things that he had done and still intended to do, as if he could hear the faint laments of old Sam Faubus, his daddy, about exploiting the prejudices of white Southerners—but then he always had to be sure that sufficient numbers of voters knew or suspected that each of his opponents was an integrationist or else not sufficiently segregationist.

It became my fascination to figure out the dynamics of political ambition. Every politician, from his or her first campaign stop to the last official action, confronts the dilemma of opportunism. How often, to what extent, and under what circumstances do you surrender your own moral beliefs and notions about good public policy to the pragmatism of politics? It sometimes comes down to why and how badly you want the job or to keep it. Rarer, it comes down to a person's confidence in voters, or else in his own ability to bring most of them around to his own persuasions. In my long experience, three Arkansas politicians—Winthrop Rockefeller, Dale Bumpers, and David Pryor—nearly always followed the unpopular course out of moral conviction, although Rockefeller did concoct an excuse, the Constitution's commerce clause, to oppose the Civil Rights Act of 1964. This confidence in the voters and himself—and perhaps his naïveté—sustained Bumpers, but not Rockefeller.

Orval Eugene Faubus, whose middle name memorialized the American socialist pioneer Eugene V. Debs, may be the best specimen of all time for such a study. Although he had few occasions even to glimpse African Americans in Madison County—a small colony of them south of Huntsville, an occasional itinerant railroad worker, or a visiting baseball team—Orval had adopted his daddy's view that they were kindred and mistreated slaves of capitalism. Orval was always in awe of his articulate and passionate old man, but even in his own later years he did not mind admitting that when he became interested in politics himself he hewed to the middle, not from any sense of conviction but because no one going under the label "socialist" was ever apt to have any success in politics in Arkansas. If a socialist was not on the ballot, his daddy often voted Republican, which was the closest thing to a liberal in that day, but Orval also sensed that an occasional Republican might have success in the Ozarks but never statewide.

As a candidate for governor in 1954, he ducked the integration issue by saying alternately that he would deal with it if and when it came and that Arkansawyers would nobly obey the law, whatever it was. When Jim Johnson made integration a burning issue in 1956, Faubus evaded it nimbly again by moving perceptibly to the right without resorting to the fire-breathing rhetoric of Johnson and his followers and by offering his own timid version of interposition. However, he had quietly done the opposite in his first year in office. As his hero, Sid McMath, had done a few years earlier, Faubus placed African Americans on the Democratic State Committee, collaborated with the National Association for the Advancement of Colored People to integrate the Employment Security Division, and even presented an Arkansas Traveler certificate to Daisy Bates, president of the Arkansas branch of the NAACP. As he would brag to Roy Reed and me one night in 1964, he had worked to equalize the pay of white and black state employees—there were a few in the lower echelons—and he had put a few on the boards of institutions serving African Americans. With his quiet assent, the first blacks were quietly enrolled in 1955 in several formerly white state colleges, including the one I attended, and he raised no objections when several public schools—notably at Fayetteville, Charleston, and Hoxie—integrated.

Reed's biography of Faubus documents the conniving and thuggery of the segregation hotspurs, all aimed at panicking the governor, as the day of the court-ordered integration at Central High School approached in September 1957. Many years later, Johnson would maintain that Faubus had sent word that he wanted threats of violence to support what he planned to do, to block integration as a means of protecting public order. Faubus would contend that the vacillating school superintendent, Virgil Blossom, who had designed the integration plan, wanted him to halt integration— but upon Faubus's own volition, not Blossom's. At what point Faubus's desperation and dithering gave way to resolve was never clear, although leaders of the Capital Citizens' Council, an affiliate of White America Incorporated, said he signaled to them at a night meeting, some days before the school opening, at Jimmy Karam's clothing store a few yards from the *Gazette* building that he was going to do something to stop the integration if he had their assurances that they would support him in the 1958 election. Arch W. Ford, the longtime state education commissioner, told me that Faubus summoned him and several other state government officials the Saturday before school opening to collect advice about what he should do. Ford and at least two others, Bill Berry of Stuttgart and Faubus's old friend J. Orville Cheney, counseled caution and obedience to the law. Two younger advisers, Claude Carpenter Jr. and Kay L. Matthews, thought sending the National Guard was the right course. Faubus was noncommittal, thanked them all, and asked Carpenter and Matthews to stay behind. Ford knew then what would happen.

Many observers believed it was a ranting speech to the Capital Citizens' Council by Marvin Griffin, the Georgia governor, that persuaded Faubus that the ground had shifted under him and that passive moderation was no longer a political option. Griffin and a few other Southern leaders said a Supreme Court order was not the law of the land and need not be followed. Griffin told the cheering crowd that he would never allow a black child to go to school with white kids in Georgia. A governor could just stop it. It was as simple as that, he said. Griffin and Roy Harris, the architect of massive resistance, spent the night at the Governor's Mansion and the next morning, over coffee, talked with Faubus about bird hunting. But Faubus never adopted the language of massive resistance. In all his remarks around the school opening and the National Guard deployment, at his conference with President Eisenhower, and for the rest of his life, Faubus would maintain that his purpose in sending the soldiers was to preserve order and public safety, not to stop desegregation. But his official order to the commander of the National Guard, which was entered in the court records, directed the troops to prevent black students from entering white schools and white students from entering black schools. Although he would attack the Supreme Court often in the years ahead, he would acknowledge, when he was pressed, that its orders were the law of the land and had to be obeyed. He was reputed by some to say, quite privately, that had he been a justice he would have joined the rest on the *Brown* decision. What was in his heart, no one could ever say.

So "1957," the popular historical reference, was altogether a political gambit, as Faubus would admit in moments of candid reflection, but his metamorphosis was no less fascinating as the passing years shed the momentary passions of 1957 and began to expose the judgment of history.

After the city's voters turned out segregationist school board members in a special election in 1959 and the reconstituted board reopened the high schools that Faubus had closed to avoid integration, the governor either lost enthusiasm for the fight or else divined that he had built enough political capital for the duration of whatever political career he wanted. Voters re-elected him in 1960, 1962, and 1964, but he did nothing overtly to thwart integration in Little Rock or anywhere else in the state, except to push a fruitless version of the pupil-placement laws that Southern states adopted to try to reduce the number of African American kids who might be allowed into integrated schools—and, at almost the last minute in 1960, to back a constitutional amendment that would have allowed schools to be closed in the face of court-ordered integration. Arkansas voters' massive rejection of the amendment, by a margin of three to one, ended all talk of official resistance to integration, certainly by Faubus and even by diehards like Jim Johnson.

Of course, especially in election cycles, Faubus continued to inveigh against the federal courts, the *Arkansas Gazette*, and, occasionally, the "silk-stocking crowd" in Little Rock that had pushed integration. Even then, his heart wasn't in it. He did it, at least I surmised, to remind the woolhat crowd of what he had done, in case time and circumstance had dimmed their memories, but he seemed to want to consign segregation and his crusade to stop it to the distant past, as if it were only then occurring to him that the light of history would not be kind to him. Members of his own family, including his father and especially a sister, were dismayed at what he had done in 1957. Sam Faubus quietly grieved about it and wrote letters to the *Gazette* favoring equality, without denouncing his son, and the paper published them over the pseudonym Jimmie Higgins, which was slang for a novice socialist. In 1963, Sam—who still published an occasional poem in *The Worker*, the paper of the Communist Party USA—told Patrick J. Owens, a *Gazette* reporter turned editorial writer at the *Pine Bluff Commercial*: "I think my son got embittered for some reason or other. I just don't know what it was." His sister Bonnie Lou Salcido never had much to do with him again, boycotting even his funeral. Perhaps as a gesture of reconciliation, when President John F. Kennedy came to Arkansas in October 1963 to dedicate the Greers Ferry Dam, Faubus brought his 76-year-old father and sat him by the president at a lunch after the dedication.

But campaigns still buoyed Faubus as much as ever. He was not an orator

but a passable speaker. He enjoyed the crowds around courthouse squares, where it was easy to gin up an impromptu rally, and he had the commoner's touch of seeming to listen earnestly to what folks had to tell him, staring alternately at his shoes and then into their eyes before patting them on the shoulder. Even after he had corralled all the fatcats, special interests, and malefactors of wealth into his corner, on the stump they continued to be the generic objects of his disdain. It was the rhetoric he had heard at Commonwealth College, shorn of polemical words like *capitalists*, *proletariat*, and *workers*. In the four or five years after "the crisis," probably out of bitterness over the criticism by the *Gazette* and his political enemies, Faubus adopted the language of bigotry, like "race mixers," that he had always eschewed—but that, too, subsided in 1964, the year of his last successful race, when he tried to align himself with President Lyndon Johnson's liberal Great Society. In his three forlorn comeback races, 1970, 1974, and

1986, he would clothe himself in the mantle of reformer who would bring young people and fresh ideas into the government. A 1974 cartoon by the *Gazette*'s George Fisher depicted Faubus with hippie-length hair and bell-bottom trousers, and another, which the *Gazette* did not publish, showed Faubus trying to get a pretty girl to join him on a nighttime hayride and reassuring her: "There's nothing to fear, honey. Your folks all know me." The voters never bought the conversion. His diminishing loyalists were always the never-say-die crowd. In 1988, he endorsed Jesse Jackson, the black civil rights leader, for president. "He speaks out for the underdogs of the nation," he said. It passed virtually unnoticed. The next year he attended a tribute dinner for Daisy Bates, his nemesis in the school crisis. He made a short speech there, praising her dedication to civil rights and claiming he never had any personal animosity toward her.

Two of Faubus's latter successful races, in 1962 and 1964, were Arkansas classics—watershed moments in Arkansas history—for they revealed a restlessness by voters about the status quo, a growing weariness over the racial vitriol, and an appetite, mainly among younger people, for a different course altogether.

III
Cox's Army

For a while, in the winter of 1961–62, Faubus toyed with the idea of retirement, or at least a respite from politics and the unrelenting anxieties of governing, which are particularly vexing when you have no one, not even a family member, with whom you care to share your misgivings, regrets, or apprehensions. He had had some health problems, traceable to stress, and it was clear that in 1962 he would have serious opponents for the first time since 1954. He dreaded one in particular, Sid McMath, the former governor who, along with Harry S. Truman, had been his earliest hero. Both Faubus and McMath had served as officers in some of the worst fighting in World War II, Faubus in the Battle of the Bulge and other European campaigns and McMath in the Pacific. After the war, both joined the "GI Revolt," a political reform movement that peaked in the first elections after the war, in 1946 and 1948. McMath was elected prosecuting attorney in Garland County in 1946, but the Madison County voters who had twice elected Faubus to the office of circuit clerk before the war rejected him for the office of county judge in 1946, in favor of a Republican who had not gone to war. Faubus

Sid McMath

acquired the local weekly, the *Madison County Record,* and his columns cheered McMath, the Marine hero from Hot Springs. When McMath was elected governor in 1948, he appointed the young man from Greasy Creek to the state Highway Commission, brought him into his office as executive secretary, and then made him the highway director. McMath would lament in 1962 that his big highway program had built the first paved road into Madison County and let Orval out.

McMath's mere entry into a race against him was a reproof of Faubus's desertion of the progressive movement, and a defeat at the hands of his old mentor would be especially bitter. McMath had counseled the White House and Justice Department in September 1957 about how to enforce the law without sending federal soldiers, which he thought would be too reminiscent of the Civil War. During the campaign, Faubus would accuse him of complicity in the "forced integration" of Central High and predicted that McMath would use force to integrate other Arkansas schools.

But McMath was not the only serious prospect. Congressman Dale Alford—who with the silent help of the governor had defeated Brooks Hays in a write-in campaign in 1958, after Hays had tried to broker a compromise between Faubus and President Eisenhower in 1957—had to run for *something*. Arkansas lost a seat in the House of Representatives after the 1960 census, and the legislature's reapportionment of the state into four districts threw Alford into a district with Representative Wilbur D. Mills. Alford knew he couldn't beat Mills; besides, Mills had persuaded House Democrats to accept Alford, who had opposed a Democratic nominee, and to include him in the seniority ranks. W. R. "Witt" Stephens, the president of Arkansas Louisiana Gas Company and the most powerful man in the state, worried that Alford might take on his man, Senator J. William Fulbright, who Stephens feared was vulnerable to a glib segregationist like Alford. Stephens sent his political agent, an insurance broker named Jack Gardner, to Alford with a message: It was pretty certain that Faubus would not run, and with Stephens's support Alford could walk into the governor's office. Alford jumped into the race. Privately, Stephens, like Faubus, had no use for the unctuous eye doctor and figured that Faubus, if he did run again, would take him out easily.

"Somebody said Dale Alford is like unto a wasp," Stephens confided. "He is bigger when he is first hatched than he'll ever be again." Jim Johnson tried to persuade Alford that Witt Stephens would never support him, but Alford decided the race was his best political option. Faubus did, indeed, announce that he would not run again, but after a spell he realized how miserable and useless he would feel out of office. His wife, Alta, sensed it and told him to run again. They ginned up a draft-Faubus movement, and he accepted the draft.

Marvin Melton, a big (literally) Jonesboro farmer and businessman who was president of the state Chamber of Commerce, got into the race and told McMath that if McMath got into a runoff with Faubus he would endorse McMath and together they would finally end the Faubus reign. Witt Stephens would take care of that, too. As Roy Reed recounted, Stephens knew that Melton had once helped start an insurance company by buying stock at a dollar a share and then had sold the stock for fifteen dollars a share. It sounded crooked. Those were the freewheeling days when anyone could start an insurance company in Arkansas with no real capital. Stephens tipped a newspaper reporter, who asked Melton about the stock. Melton decided to get out of the race. Five years later, Melton climbed into his single-engine Beechcraft to fly to Dallas and was never seen again.

The field of Faubus foes eventually included Kenneth C. Coffelt, a loud-mouthed trial lawyer who fancied himself to be the second coming of Huey P. Long; Vernon H. Whitten, a soft-spoken man who set out to fill the dignified-businessman slot in the field; and David A. Cox, a one-eyed rice farmer from the town of Weiner in Poinsett County, who rarely made the news but when he did inspired headlines like "Weiner Farmer Claims…"

Arkansawyers again got to see the most impressive politician in the state's history, though fleetingly. It had been ten years since McMath, two years out of the governor's office, almost upset the state's senior senator, John L. McClellan, in a farfetched comeback campaign after the "McMath highway scandal" in 1952 had cost him a third term. At an unusually fit sixty years old and soon to be promoted to brigadier general in the Marine Corps, McMath cut a fine figure on the stump with his trademark blue suit, red tie, and brimmed white hat. McMath nearly sprinted down sidewalks shaking hands, and he vaulted over balustrades in bank lobbies to meet secretaries, clerks, and bank executives. He was the best orator Arkansawyers had ever heard, unless they happened to have caught one of William Jennings Bryan's declamations in 1899 or 1910. But unlike other super-politicians like Bill Clinton, McMath couldn't remember people's names, calling women on his staff "Sweetheart" and the like. I traveled with him for three weeks—until Faubus's Selective Service director instructed Margaret Black, who ran the draft office in Union County, to put me at the top of the September draft and I left the campaign and the paper to head to Fort Polk, Louisiana, for infantry training. McMath always called me "Eddie," despite an aide's murmuring to him from time to time that it was Ernie. But personal campaigning and rallies were fading in importance, because television and radio gave most people about all the intimacy with politicians they coveted. McMath didn't have money for much of a media campaign. He made a short film in which he attacked Faubus's control of all the regulatory mechanisms of government, which were used to enrich his big supporters, like Witt Stephens, the gas executive and the majority owner of a dozen or so community banks. McMath pointed to a giant blowup of a menacing, cigar-chomping Stephens, who fifteen years earlier had been his own biggest supporter.

If your gold standard for a politician was high-mindedness, unflinching honesty, or mere individuality, then your candidate in the primary was David A. Cox. All the memorable utterances from that campaign and most others fell from the parched lips of the sunburned farmer, a rail-thin man who usually wore a starched white shirt and black trousers from which the long end of his belt drooped eight or nine inches, which suggested that sometime in the distant past he had shed many pounds but had never invested in a shorter belt. Cox had lost an eye, several fingers, and part of an ear as a youngster when he tried, as he explained it, to crawl through a barbed-wire fence with a loaded shotgun.

While no reporters were around, Cox showed up at the Capitol and paid his filing fee for the Democratic primary. Secretary of State Nancy Hall gave him a biographical form to fill out, which helped reporters identify who the candidates were, their ages, and something about their backgrounds. She said Cox told her he didn't want any publicity, so there was nothing on the form but his name and the town Weiner. The press couldn't find him and that is about all that appeared in the papers.

A couple of weeks later, Bill Shelton, the *Gazette* city editor, told me that a guy named Dave Cox had called and asked for the location of the office of Amis Guthridge, the head of the Capital Citizens' Council, the white-supremacy group that had fought school integration through the 1950s. Shelton asked him if he was the candidate for governor. He was. Cox told him he was going to go over to Guthridge's place and "clean that sonofabitch's plow."

The previous day I had covered a news conference at the Greyhound bus station on Broadway, where Guthridge and a couple of other Citizens' Council members put two African American women and their twenty-three children on a bus with tickets to get them to Hyannis Port, Massachusetts, where President Kennedy had a family compound. The Citizens' Councils in Arkansas and other Southern states that summer put poor black people on buses with a few dollars and shipped them to Hyannis Port—the famous Reverse Freedom Rides of that year. Guthridge made a grinning little speech in which he said he was sure the Kennedys would see to it that "these fine people" were given a good life up there.

I drove over to Guthridge's shabby little law office on West Markham

Street just as Cox spun into the gravel parking lot in his red Chevrolet Impala, on which he had strapped a sign saying "Dave Cox for Governor." He stormed into Guthridge's tiny office, where two black men were seated. Cox offered one of them a cigarette, which he declined.

"Hell," Cox said, "we might be riding on the same bus."

Guthridge came out of his cramped office and Cox accused him of "inhumanity, injustice and insulting the people of Arkansas." Guthridge took him inside his private office and tried to close the door. They argued for forty minutes. Cox demanded to know what the Capital Citizens' Council stood for, and Guthridge demanded Cox's position on integration. Cox launched into a long spiel that ended, "If God didn't create us all integrated, who did?" Guthridge had no answer. Cox wanted to know if Guthridge, as a lawyer, thought it was a just thing to do to put two poor women with their huge families on a bus for a New England town without telling them what was likely to be in store for them. Guthridge asked him what the people of Weiner would do if the government said they had to integrate.

"I guarantee you," Cox replied, "they would mix without incident if the courts said so."

As he barged out, Cox said to me, "I'm a humanitarian and I wouldn't give a blind man the wrong directions." Pointing at Guthridge, he said, "I think he would."

A week or so later, I drove up to Weiner on a Saturday for Cox's kickoff fish fry, which was to be in a small park beside the Union Pacific railroad tracks. He had a couple of tubs of fresh catfish sitting in the June sun, but the two men he had hired to fry them didn't show up—bought off by Orval Faubus, Cox guessed. The handful of hungry townspeople walked away. Amid bursts of cursing, Cox began to gather up a lot of liquor bottles to tote back across the rails to his car and asked for my help. He stumbled and fell while crossing the tracks and most of his whiskey drained between the crossties. We picked up the unbroken bottles and the fish and got them into his car. After he drove away, the town's mayor sauntered over and talked about Cox. Dave is an expert farmer, maybe the best around, the mayor said, but he would go off to Memphis and get drunk for days at a time and his house was just a mess. Shaking his head ruefully, the mayor said you could walk into Cox's living room and he'd be sitting on the floor working on a tractor engine right there, with oily parts all over the rug.

One of the first appearances of the candidates was at the convention of the Arkansas Press Association at Fort Smith. After their brief talks, the

five candidates who were present fielded a few questions from the newspaper folks, and a high school senior—there, no doubt, with an editor
parent—asked the candidates what advice they had for a person who was
graduating and going out into the world. Each of them got up and gave
some variation of the standard spiel: Arkansas is a state with rich opportunities, great colleges, good industries, and abundant natural resources; you
could build a wall around the state and it would be self-sufficient.

Cox, slouched deeply in a chair on the flank, was last. He strode to the
lectern, pulled up his britches, leaned into the microphone, and said: "I'd
tell 'em, *She's a low-wage state. Git out and git out fast!*" He went back and
flopped into his chair. It was a standard for honesty that I would never see
matched.

Shelton assigned three reporters to follow the three main candidates—
Faubus, McMath, and Alford—for the final three weeks of the campaign,
and each of us was supposed to drop off now and then and see what the
three also-rans were doing so that we might write profiles of them for the
Sunday paper before the primary. I caught Cox at one event and arranged
to travel with him the morning after the Mount Nebo Chicken Fry, an annual political event sponsored by the Arkansas Poultry Federation. I left
my car near the *Gazette* building that day and traveled to Mount Nebo
with a *Gazette* photographer. Cox caused some murmuring in the crowd at
that event by cursing several times and by declaiming, "I aim to live to see
the day when we've got a Negro president," although I believe he used the
cruder adjective. Before dawn the next morning, I met Cox at the nearby
Old South restaurant at Russellville for breakfast and the two of us took
off in his Impala. He had attached speakers on top of it. It was a fruitless
morning. We would park on the square at cities along the Arkansas River—Russellville, Clarksville, Booneville, Ozark—and he would get into an
argument with the first oldtimer he encountered, declare it a Faubus county, and move on. In Fort Smith, we stopped for a hamburger and a beer.
Like the rest of the day, lunch lapsed into a monologue about Faubus, the
racist culture of the state, and the special interests' control of the state government. The little people didn't have a chance, didn't know it, and didn't
care. And he kept downing beers.

In the late afternoon, spotting the bus station down the block, I told Cox
I had to get back to Little Rock and caught a bus. Arriving back in Little
Rock about midnight, I walked into the *Gazette* city room. The night editor
said they were wondering where the hell I was, and he showed me an As-

sociated Press story from Springdale. Cox had been arrested there earlier in the evening for being drunk in a public place. People complained that he was playing popular band music—Guy Lombardo, I believe—over his loudspeakers in a residential neighborhood and trying to make a speech. He spent the night in the Springdale jail in a cell with three snoring drunks. He couldn't make bond the next morning because he had only four dollars, which included a lucky two-dollar bill that he didn't want to give up. He tried to offer his glass eye as collateral, but the police wouldn't take it. They finally raised the small bond from policemen and inmate trusties and let him go. The municipal judge declared the bond forfeited when Cox didn't show up for his court appearance. Cox told a Springdale reporter that he was sick of Arkansas and was taking his campaign outside the state. He drove to Harrison, where Faubus had appeared on a Highway Department goodwill tour to show off his highway improvements.

"Give me a quart of whiskey and a crop-dusting plane and I'll do the same," Cox said. He declared that he had seen all he wanted to see of the mountains and hill people. "From now on, I'm going to stay in east Arkansas, and Crowley's Ridge will be the highest hill I'm going to get on." He headed for eastern Arkansas and home.

That was Friday. Saturday, Cox was arrested east of Crowley's Ridge in the county-seat town of Harrisburg, sixteen miles east of his home, for brandishing a gun in public and disturbing the peace. He had a pistol in the doorway of the town's bank. Cox offered a plausible excuse for his behavior and the municipal judge dismissed the charges.

For the *Gazette*'s profile before the election I asked Cox why he had run if he knew at the outset that he had no chance of winning.

"It's worth ten thousand dollars, or whatever I'm spending," he said, "just to be able to tell my granddaughters, when they read in the history books about what the governor did at Little Rock, that I did my best to get him out. I didn't just vote against him; I ran against him. It's just a shot in the dark, but you can't tell what will happen in Arkansas politics, if you can get your votes counted."

Faubus received 209,000 votes, a majority by only 6,000, but enough to avoid a runoff. A few machine counties might easily have delivered the winning margin. It was the next-to-last election under the poll-tax system, where a few people or just the county sheriff alone could hoard poll-tax receipts for scores of individuals and cast all the votes for a single candidate or a slate. McMath beat Alford for second place by 658 votes. McMath never ran for office again, but a survey of historians at the end of the century ranked him among the three most successful Arkansas governors of the twentieth century. Alford ran twice more, for governor in 1966 and for Congress in 1984, both times proving Witt Stephens's adage that, like a wasp, he was bigger when he was hatched than he would ever be again. Dave Cox finished last, which is where Faubus's pollster, Eugene Newsom, predicted he would be with an overly generous one percent. Cox's army of populists numbered exactly 2,149.

IV
The Prince and the Pauper

All across the South the civil rights movement was in full bloom in 1963 and 1964, but Arkansas and Faubus were shoved off the front pages and the network news by Alabama, Mississippi, Georgia, and Louisiana and by more authentic and tawdrier demagogues, like George C. Wallace, Ross Barnett, and Louisiana's Leander Perez. Orval Faubus seemed content to surrender the field to them, though he endorsed both Wallace and Barnett for governor. He was content to toss a few vulgar lines to the racist gallery from time to time, such as when he promised to run over any demonstrators who lay in the street in front of him. He denounced demonstrators, usually black students and occasionally white ones, and embraced the drivel that had once haunted him, that communists were behind much of the racial trouble and that the student sit-ins and other protesters were the progeny of Marxist teachers. But he did nothing to raise the hopes of segregationists that he would again use the government in any way to prevent integration anywhere in any form.

By the summer of 1963, the civil rights movement had reached a crescendo and even elected judges in Arkansas were beginning to recognize that the Fourteenth Amendment might mean what it said, although Bruce Bennett, the old Union County sojourner whom voters had restored to the attorney general's office, offered the opinion that the amendment ratified in 1865 was illegal.

Citing the First and Fourteenth Amendments, the Arkansas Supreme Court voided four laws written by Bennett and enacted by the legislature and Faubus in 1958 that sought to punish the NAACP and integration sympathizers. The U.S. Supreme Court in 1960 had unanimously struck down another of Bennett's laws from the same session (Act 10), which required every teacher in an Arkansas school or college to sign an affidavit every year listing organizations to which they had belonged or contributed. It was aimed at ridding the schools of teachers who were members of the NAACP or organizations like the Arkansas Council on Human Relations, which conservatives thought were subversive. My economics teacher at Henderson State Teachers College, Dr. Wladimir Naleszkiewicz, who was crippled in 1956 when Russian tanks and troops crushed the Hungarian uprising against the communists, lost his job in the 1959 school year because he would not sign such an affidavit. He had risked his life to flee such a regime. It was our little college paper's vague criticism of such legislative undertakings in the late spring of 1958 that got the paper banned and led to my severance from the school. In the spring and summer of 1963, Little Rock municipal judge Quinn Glover repeatedly dismissed charges brought against African Americans who engaged in lunch-counter sit-ins on Main Street, infuriating Bennett. The attorney general took over the race-baiting province, and Faubus seemed happy to let him.

In late August, Bayard Rustin, A. Philip Randolph, and an alliance of civil rights groups organized the March on Washington for Jobs and Freedom, which became the largest rally for human rights in the nation's history, at least before the Women's March in Washington the day after President Trump's inauguration in 2017. It was going to be a historic event, and I wanted to be there. I claimed a week's vacation, drove to Washington in my new Karmann Ghia, and ensconced myself in the throng around the Reflecting Pool. Mainly, I think I went to hear Mahalia Jackson, Marian Anderson, Joan Baez, and Bob Dylan sing, not to hear Dr. Martin Luther King speak, but I can't be sure. Daisy Bates, the heroine of the Little Rock crisis, spoke briefly at the outset when Myrlie Evers, whose husband, Medgar Evers, had been slain by a Klansman two months earlier, missed her flight to Washington. King's "I Have a Dream" speech was the most momentous since Lincoln's Gettysburg Address. It was so animating that I was still alert at three in the morning when a sheriff's deputy arrested me on a mountainside west of Crossville, Tennessee. I spent a couple of hours in the sheriff's dingy office in the Cross County Courthouse, where I had spent a few hours one night two years earlier, while on a junket to New York City to visit a friend who had gone to work for the New York Times. Both times, after my car and luggage were searched, I was fined for improper passing, although I had not seen a car for miles in either instance. The fine doubled this time, but it did not ruin the trip.

All the summer's events were dispiriting to the zealots. The Capital Citizens' Council, which had abandoned Faubus in 1962 to support Dale Alford, found itself with only a handful of committed soldiers and no clout even in school board races. The paragon of white supremacists was Theophilus Eugene "Bull" Connor, the commissioner of public safety at Birmingham, Alabama, and the boss of both the city's fire and police forces. Using fire hoses and police dogs, Connor led attacks on demonstrators, including children, during the Birmingham campaign of Rev. Martin Luther King's Southern Christian Leadership Conference. The television and newspaper images horrified much of the country and helped drive the passage of the Civil Rights Act of 1964, but to Amis Guthridge, Rev. Wesley Pruden, and the Citizens' Council remnants, Connor was a savior—even though he had just lost his job as fire and police commissioner four months earlier, when Birmingham voters changed the form of municipal government and also rejected his mayoral candidacy. No one could excite the rabble like Bull Connor.

Guthridge invited Connor to make a speech at a Citizens' Council meeting at Little Rock's Coachman's Inn. They hoped his appearance would raise enough money to pay the Coachman's two-hundred-dollar fee, replenish the group's depleted treasury, and refuel Arkansawyers' flagging concern about preserving the primacy of the white race.

In introducing Connor, Guthridge said he had asked Connor to intercede with Governor Wallace and get him to come to Little Rock to address a Citizens' Council rally, and he announced that Wallace had, indeed, agreed to do it. There was loud applause. Pruden begged the crowd to donate some money because the group was broke. But Guthridge reassured them it was not dead.

The *Gazette* had sent me to the Coachman's to cover the event. Guthridge alerted the crowd to my presence, which caused some restlessness, but he said, no, it was all right; I had to write what the paper told me to write, he said, and it would be better than no publicity. Bull Connor revealed that he had sent four men to Little Rock in 1957 to observe the integration at Central High School. He said his men had been spying on "Negro meetings" in Birmingham for years to be ready for the day when they started demonstrating and trying to integrate businesses, the schools, and public facilities.

"We were prepared," he said. "I went down and got me ten or twelve of the finest police dogs you ever saw and some high-pressure hoses. You can handle them with dogs and hoses, if you get them high-pressure hoses. Boy, I can knock them sixty feet with that thing."

If he didn't use the dogs and firehoses, Connor explained, he would have to shoot them.

"Ladies and gentlemen, that would have been wrong," he said, grinning. "That would have hurt people. Bull Connor doesn't want to hurt people."

He said he put hundreds of blacks in the Birmingham jail, and that it cost $400,000 to bail them out. If unions had not come up with $168,000, they would still be in jail, he said. "If I had anything to do with it, they'd be in jail for ten years."

Connor knew the crowd needed some heartening words. He promised that integration was going to be beaten all across the South, including Arkansas, but it was going to take four or five more years.

"I'll acknowledge that we are on the one-yard line and they got the ball," he said. "But, you know, yo daddy and mine—they was on the one-half-yard line and they had the bayonet in their backs, but they didn't give up." It was not clear what Connor was talking about, but it cheered the crowd.

Few if anyone there had heard that, back in Birmingham a few hours earlier, massive resistance had collapsed forever in Alabama, as it had in Little Rock in 1957. President Kennedy federalized the Alabama National Guard, which had been deployed to Birmingham by Governor George Wallace to block integration, and twenty-six black students walked into integrated classes in Birmingham under the protection of the guardsmen. The Birmingham police that Connor had commanded until four months earlier arrested twelve white men in a rowdy demonstration by segregationists at the West End High School. Several other Alabama schools integrated that day as well. Three months earlier, two black students had entered the University of Alabama at Tuscaloosa when Wallace stepped out of the doorway in the face of federalized troops sent by Kennedy.

George Wallace's great speech of deliverance for the Citizens' Council, which Bull Connor had arranged, was scheduled for December, but Wallace canceled it without explanation soon after President Kennedy's assassination on November 22. Little was heard from the Citizens' Council after Bull Connor's exhibition. No political candidate afterward wanted to have it even bruited about that he had the organization's support.

Kennedy's assassination at Dallas on November 22, seven weeks after Connor's histrionics, had a profound effect not only on the nation's sense of well-being and trust in its government and institutions but also on its politics. The immediate impact was the quick passage of Kennedy's legislation that, owing mainly to the resistance of conservative Southerners, including the Arkansas delegation, had stalled in Congress for almost three years— the first major civil-rights law since Reconstruction, tax reform, Medicare, and Medicaid. All were signed into law within a year of the assassination.

Kennedy's popularity had been soaring everywhere except in the South. In Arkansas, the grieving was peculiarly complicated. Kennedy had carried Arkansas in 1960 against Richard Nixon, although he had merely stepped across the state line at Texarkana to show that he had campaigned in the state, and the predominant Baptist church opposed him as a vicar of the pope. Arkansas should not have been fertile country for the charming Boston Brahmin, but Arkansas was still in the thrall of Franklin Roosevelt. I had driven to Texarkana for the *Gazette* to watch Kennedy straddle State Line Avenue and embrace Arkansas and then later over to West Memphis for Richard Nixon to do the same, so both could say they had campaigned in Arkansas. Faubus reluctantly supported the ticket as a gesture of loyalty, although he was critical of Kennedy as a high-collared Easterner and probably an integrationist. Faubus had appeared on the ballot in several states as the candidate of the National States Rights Party, but got only forty-five thousand of the sixty-nine million votes cast, fewer than were cast for the candidate of the Socialist Labor Party or the Prohibition Party (but a few more than the candidate of the Socialist Workers Party). So Kennedy's acceptance of the invitation to dedicate Greers Ferry Dam on the Little Red River proved to be vexing for the governor.

For two years, Faubus had criticized the civil rights bill that the Kennedy administration sent to Congress. Forcing people—businessmen particularly—to do things they don't want to do is not the right way to handle the situation, he said, though he didn't propose a better way to end discrimination in commerce or in public facilities. Faubus was to be the president's host for the big ceremony at the dam and in an appearance at the Arkansas Livestock Exposition in Little Rock.

It was a brilliant sunny day in early October and a strong breeze blew across the bluff above the river where the dedication took place. From my vantage point at the foot of the stage, the president looked unusually tanned, youthful, and exuberant among the pale delegation with which he shared the platform—the aging senators and congressmen and Faubus, who was only seven years the president's senior. A smiling Senator John L. McClellan was on the platform. McClellan was among the Southern senators who had harshly condemned the U.S. Supreme Court for its school-integration orders and he fought Kennedy's civil rights bill to its end, when Kennedy's successor signed it into law. The civil rights bill, like the Supreme Court's *Brown* decision, McClellan said, were intended to foment violence and racial discord in the South, where he said the races had been getting along fine. On that day, Faubus alone carried a dour expression, although he joined the general laughter when Kennedy joked about Wilbur Mills's power. Kennedy remarked that it was said in Washington that he would come to Arkansas and sing "Down by the Old Mills Stream" if

Wilbur wanted him to. The reason for Faubus's severity was soon clear. He was going to deftly take the young president to task for the civil rights bill before a joyous crowd eager to see the president—including Orval's own dad. He would sound the only sour note of the day.

Reading from his prepared speech, Faubus thanked the president for coming and for his concern for conservation, which the dam represented. It would transform the lives of people in the region, he said. Faubus would end on a happy note, too, but reading carefully from his text he said the Kennedy administration had spent too much time sponsoring "unworkable proposals" to correct social problems. Alluding to the civil rights bill trapped in the Senate Judiciary Committee, he said Kennedy would "deprive a citizen of the right to a trial by jury, interfere with a person's right to control his own business and even his own home, and take from the state without justification even more of the rights guaranteed by the Constitution."

"To abridge and destroy these basic rights," he continued, "will constitute civil wrongs, even though the efforts to abridge and destroy may masquerade under the name civil rights."

Kennedy sat impassively and when it came his turn thanked the governor and made not the vaguest allusion to his attack, instead lauding all six members of the state's delegation for their power and contributions to the nation's well-being. He talked about the government's mission to protect the environment and to channel the nation's natural resources to the good of the people. The delegation then flew to Little Rock for another public celebration.

Faubus, I would learn a few weeks later (after the president's assassination), had had some conflicting emotional pressures that day. His ailing father had come down from Madison County to see the president, whether at the son's invitation I never knew. I like to think it was Governor Faubus's idea. Faubus had to be the person responsible for seating his dad next to the president at lunch, in Faubus's seat. Sam and the president talked a few minutes before Kennedy jumped up to shake hands with a bevy of children.

The governor's sister Bonnie had written to Kennedy from California a few weeks before the dedication, apparently telling him that she and other family members did not agree with Orval on civil rights, that the president was stronger in the South than when he ran in 1960, and that she believed he would win by a landslide in 1964. Amazingly, the White House put the letter in the president's hands. Kennedy mentioned the letter to Sam Faubus in their brief conversation and told him he was grateful that his daughter had sent it. Sam told an Arkansas newsman in December that he had voted for Kennedy in 1960 and that Kennedy had been a great president. Bonnie had moved from Arkansas to California in about 1952 with her husband, who had been a Linotype operator for Faubus's weekly newspaper, the *Madison County Record*. She told the *Gazette* that they left because they could not make a living in Arkansas.

In death, President Kennedy was elevated to martyrdom, and his highly celebrated trip to Arkansas right before his assassination further sanctified him. People recalled the governor's attempt to embarrass the president at Greers Ferry and how Kennedy had handled the insulting lecture with grace.

The day of the assassination, a school principal told classes over the intercom that the president had been shot, and it was reported that the students broke into cheers. The common assumption was that they had heard their elders condemning Kennedy, whether for civil rights or for his Catholic theology. Statements and letters from Kennedy critics poured into the *Gazette* and other newspapers denying any blame for the president's murder.

⬚⬚⬚

Yet one more re-election lay ahead for the governor, and it would be the most satisfying campaign and election of his life. It may have proved liberating as well, because it allowed him in a perverse way to return to the green valley of his youth—as Harry Ashmore's surrogate phrase said in 1954—and to the populist zeal of his father.

Winthrop Rockefeller had arrived in Little Rock in 1953 looking for his own form of redemption and solace. The youngest scion of John D. Rockefeller Jr. and his liberal wife, Abigail, Winthrop was forty-one years old and aimless when he alighted from his maroon Cadillac at Little Rock's Sam Peck Hotel with his close African American friend Jimmy Hudson to see what kind of place Arkansas was. His parents had shipped Winthrop to an exclusive boarding school in Connecticut, and he had enrolled at Yale but was kicked out for misbehavior. He entered World War II as a private and emerged as a highly decorated lieutenant colonel. He received the bronze star and a purple heart for heroism during a kamikaze attack on his troopship in the invasion of Okinawa.

Back in New York and rudderless after the war, Winthrop was a precursor of Donald Trump, prowling nightclubs and catching the notice of the tabloids for his amours and drinking. He romanced a B-grade actress named Jievute "Bobo" Paulekiute Sears (her first husband was the Boston socialite John Sears) and they went to Florida for what was called "the wedding of the century," where a choir sang Negro spirituals. Bobo was the daughter of a coal miner who had emigrated from Lithuania. The couple split after a son, Winthrop Paul, was born, and the tabloids gorged on the divorce fight. There were suggestions in court that Winthrop had a vast pornography collection, suggestions circulated again in Rockefeller's Arkansas campaigns. Rumors went around that Bobo had caught him *in flagrante delicto* with a man, a story that was revived upon Bobo's death in 2008. In the divorce, she got custody of Win Paul and $5.5 million.

Scorned by his aristocratic family and humiliated by the scandalous publicity, Rockefeller drove to Arkansas, where his old soldier buddy Frank Newell, a Little Rock insurance man, said he might find a measure of solitude and happiness, a cocoon far from the glare and gossip of New York society. Newell drove him to the top of Petit Jean Mountain and its majestic overlooks. Rockefeller loved the place and bought a huge spread on a bluff with a panoramic vista of the meandering Arkansas River. In 1955 the legislature created the Arkansas Industrial Development Commission, and Faubus made Rockefeller the chairman. He threw himself into the job. Whether owing to Rockefeller or not, new industries poured into Arkansas, although most were low-wage companies like dry-goods factories. They were what Arkansas's poorly educated populace attracted.

Faubus was proud of the appointment and often bragged about what his AIDC and its chairman had done. The plutocrat from Hyde Park and the populist from Greasy Creek developed a casual but warm friendship. While Faubus was cultivating liberals in his first year in office, he was reported to have told a small gathering of them at Rockefeller's farm that the Supreme Court's *Brown* decision was right and that if he had been a member of the Court he would have joined the decision. As Jim Johnson prepared to run for governor in 1956, he coupled Faubus and Rockefeller as integrationist conspirators. *Arkansas Faith*, a crude journal published by Johnson and the white citizens' council, accused Faubus and Rockefeller of plotting to hire a black man as an investigator for the state Alcoholic Beverage Control Board—*and at a good salary*—and it said the two men, Faubus and Rockefeller, "would trade YOUR daughter for a mess of nigger votes."

When the legislature in 1957 passed four bills intended to ward off integration, Rockefeller warned the governor that the most insidious one, which created a state sovereignty commission with investigatory and subpoena powers to ferret out and prosecute integrationist activity, would create an Arkansas Gestapo. Faubus had agreed to the sovereignty commission in a deal with east Arkansas leaders—they would support his sales-tax increase for the schools in exchange for his support of a bill to create a Virginia-like sovereignty commission with powerful investigatory tools to stave off integration. Faubus suggested that the commission could investigate the NAACP and perhaps even outlaw it. When a legislative committee conducted a hearing on the sovereignty bill, a student leader from the University of Arkansas, David H. Pryor of Camden, drove to the Arkansas State Capitol to testify against it but was not recognized to speak. For eight months after the bill became law, Faubus would not appoint the commission members, but he did that autumn, after Johnson's collaborators filed a lawsuit in circuit court to mandamus him to make the appointments. The Arkansas Supreme Court eventually struck down most of the law's critical provisions as violations of the state and federal constitutions. Unlike Mississippi's and Virginia's, Arkansas's sovereignty commission met only twice and never did anything.

As school opening approached that fall, when Faubus was grappling with the competing forces over integration, Rockefeller implored the governor to stay out of the school business, because it would blow up and set back the state's industrialization. He told friends ruefully that he believed Faubus thought a greater danger lay on the other side—a takeover of the state by Amis Guthridge, Bruce Bennett, and Jim Johnson—if he didn't do something. Although he avoided a public breach with the governor in the three years that followed, Rockefeller made no secret of his displeasure with Faubus's defiance. Their friendship ceased. His prediction about a crippled industrialization drive proved accurate.

The Rockefeller clan had always been proper eastern Republicans, and in 1960 Winthrop began to try to energize the Arkansas party, which had been little more than a social club for sixty years, waiting eternally to harvest the patronage plums that followed the election of Republican presidents—postmasters, U.S. attorney, federal marshal, and the like. No Republican had been elected to a statewide office in Arkansas in the twentieth century, and few to local and legislative offices. By 1962, Rockefeller had wrested control of the Republican State Committee from the Old Guard, led by William L. Spicer of Fort Smith. Rockefeller approached me about joining his small staff in Little Rock's Tower Building as a public relations aide and speechwriter, with an oblique suggestion that it would be a foundation for his running for office before long. He wound up hiring John Ward from the *Arkansas Democrat*, a good newsman who would prove to be perhaps his best political asset. Rockefeller feinted at running for governor that year, but Sid McMath looked like a dynamic opponent for Faubus, one who would bring to the office sensibilities and a mission similar to his own.

In 1964, no such Democrat presented himself, owing obviously to the certain prospect that Rockefeller would run. Three Democrats, all unknowns, filed against Faubus and he dispatched them all effortlessly in the summer primary. The best was an unabashed and quixotic liberal named Joe Hubbard, who resigned as a Reserve Officers' Training Corps (ROTC) instructor at Arkansas Tech at Russellville to make the race, but he proved to be something of a phantasm. I arranged to travel with him for a few days, but when I showed up early one morning for the rendezvous at his tiny state headquarters on Russellville's Main Street, it was locked, and no one answered the doorbell at his home a few blocks away. His disappearances for a week at a time went unexplained.

Rockefeller announced in April that he was running, seven months after Faubus had attended and spoken at a testimonial dinner for him on the tenth anniversary of his arrival in Arkansas. Faubus soon afterward confirmed the obvious and said he would run for a sixth term but that it would absolutely be his last. Race was the tacit issue in the campaign, for Faubus's defiance of integration orders is what got him to an unprecedented fifth term—and it was also what impelled Rockefeller's deep impulse to remove Faubus and see if he could transform the social order of the state by good example and progressive policies. But whatever their private feelings, neither man wanted to run as an integrationist or a segregationist, or to accuse the other of being either. While the deep prejudices of people had not changed perceptibly since 1957, events had altered white people's tolerance of extremists, especially the noisemakers like Amis Guthridge, Wesley Pruden, and Bull Connor. From the torture and murder of young Emmett Till for allegedly flirting with a Mississippi white woman to Bull Connor's dogs and firehoses and the police clubbings of nonviolent demonstrators in Arkansas towns, the brutality of the warriors against integration made many whites at least defensive about their prejudices. It was reinforced in the summer of 1964, midway through the campaign, by the murders in Philadelphia, Mississippi, of three young voting-rights work-ers, two whites and an African American, whose bodies were discovered buried in an earthen dam after the state's leading politicians had claimed their disappearance was a hoax. People were less willing to be called segre-gationists, because even if they still intensely disliked the idea and practice of social equality, they had begun half-consciously to recognize the illegal-ity of segregation. At any rate, they wanted to refrain from the argument and hoped the issue might just subside.

Neither Faubus nor Rockefeller wanted to take on the issue directly. Fau-bus knew enough dog-whistles to keep the boys down at the forks of the creek aroused. He vowed to run over demonstrators who lay in the street in front of him, denounced a black associate at the Arkansas Council on Human Relations who tried to get seated in the Capitol cafeteria as a trou-blemaker (and the council itself as a communist-front group), and revealed that Rockefeller was a board member of the National Urban League, an establishment civil rights organization. But he also had met with leaders of the NAACP about increasing black employment in the government and sported the endorsement of Harold Flowers of Pine Bluff, a black lawyer who headed the Pine Bluff chapter of the NAACP and led the fledgling civil rights movement in the 1940s. Flowers called the governor a changed man. Faubus predicted that he would get the votes of most blacks. He con-demned the Civil Rights Act of 1964, which President Johnson signed in July, not because it advanced integration but because, he said, it took away individual rights. He did not elaborate that what it took away was a per-son's right to discriminate against others in hiring and services because of their race, religion, or national origin. Rockefeller objected to the critical public-accommodations section because he doubted its constitutionality, subsequently upheld unanimously by the Supreme Court, but Rockefeller urged people to accept and abide by the law, and Faubus did not.

Rather, Rockefeller chose to go after Faubus on more prosaic and safer grounds, like illegal gambling, prison corruption, voting fraud, and eco-nomic growth. Faubus had always taken the position that illegal gambling at Hot Springs was entirely a local matter, and there were endless rumors, never confirmed, that the casinos at Hot Springs ran regular payoffs to the Governor's Mansion.

That spring, two assistants to U.S. Attorney General Robert F. Kennedy spent an evening and the wee morning hours in Hot Springs casinos, ob-serving and participating in the wide-open gambling. The next day they announced that they were taking their evidence of a conspiracy to violate the state antigambling law to a federal grand jury. They never got a chance. Local interests, including the casinos, wanted to keep the matter in state hands, not the feds'. Coincidence or not, state Representative Roy H. Galyean, a somnolent Baptist preacher from Gravette, a town in the far northwest corner of the state, had a sudden seizure of piety and filed a resolution in the House calling for gambling in Hot Springs to be stopped. The House passed it, ninety-one to three. It was nonbinding, but Faubus sent the State Police on a peaceful raid of the casinos and ordered gambling to stop. "For the time being" was the message that the city got. (Gambling would resume after the election.) The Hot Springs Chamber of Commerce quickly circulated a petition for a constitutional amendment written by state Senator Q. Byrum Hurst that legalized and regulated up to ten casinos in Garland County. Faubus first feinted at endorsing it—his press secretary, Bob Troutt, privately promoted the gambling initiative—but finally had to join Rockefeller in opposing the amendment, which the voters defeated. To be sure of the religious vote, Faubus ordered another little slot-machine raid three weeks before the election.

Hurst and Senator Max Howell of Little Rock tried another sly gambit to make the Hot Springs clubs off limits for State Police raids. Inside the Joint Budget Committee, where the actual decision-making was secret, they inserted deep in the lengthy appropriation bill for the State Police a convoluted sentence that, when it was read a couple of times, seemed to mean that the Criminal Investigation Division couldn't supersede local law-enforcement authority over matters like wagering. Appropriation bills generally sailed through each house late in the session with no more than a one-sentence explanation from the chairman of the Joint Budget Committee—in the Senate, this was Robert Harvey of Swifton, a serious old farmer who saw himself as the public's steward of the treasury and who hated shenanigans. When budget bills were considered, senators and reporters mingled in and out of the chamber, and whoever was in the chamber shouted "ayes" for them. Harvey dropped by my desk and suggested I not leave the chamber and to watch for Senator Charles George of Cabot, a former basketball coach who studied the bills but rarely spoke. When the State Police bill came up, Harvey said it was the appropriation for the State Police and he would appreciate a good vote.

"Senator Harvey," George said from his seat on the front row, "could you look at Section 17 on page eight of the bill and tell me what that means?"

Harvey innocently turned to the page, squinted, and read the sentence without comment. George asked if it meant that the State Police could not conduct gambling raids. Harvey scratched his head and said, "Well, I guess you could read it that way. I don't know." Everyone grabbed their bill stacks and looked up the sentence. George moved that the sentence be deleted, and the Senate did so without a dissent.

The coincidence of national elections in 1964 presented both men with difficulties. Winthrop's liberal brother Nelson, the governor of New York, was running for the Republican nomination for president, eventually losing to Senator Barry Goldwater of Arizona, who was commonly viewed as representing the extremity of the party. Goldwater's ringing acknowledgment of his extremism in his acceptance speech—"Extremism in defense of liberty is no vice; moderation in the pursuit of justice is no virtue"— struck a chord. President Johnson passed and praised the Civil Rights Act, which Faubus said was the scourge of liberty. But Faubus, who had begun to praise Johnson's Great Society and its assault on poverty, wound up endorsing Johnson over Goldwater, whom he had also praised. Rockefeller endorsed his brother and then, after the nomination, Goldwater. Goldwater reciprocated and endorsed Rockefeller. President Johnson did not endorse Faubus.

For Faubus, running against Rockefeller—*a Rockefeller*—was an expedience that he had only dreamed about. It gave Faubus a chance to boast about his own humble beginnings and to mock Rockefeller's vast inheritance, as well as the rapacity of his forebear, granddaddy John D. Rockefeller. You could see the grin widen and hear the voice quaver every time Faubus launched into a trope about the legendary Rockefeller riches. He recalled his vagrant days, of sleeping under a newspaper on a Chicago bench and seeing John D. Rockefeller's long black limousine rolling down Michigan Avenue. He claimed that the robber barons Rockefeller and Jay Gould had him and other hobos tossed out of a Chicago park. (The *Gazette* rudely pointed out that Gould, the railroad baron, had died long before Faubus was born.) He remembered the cold mornings in his barren childhood home on Greasy Creek, when the wind whistled through the log slats and curdled the red-eye gravy on his plate before he could sop it up with his mama Addie's biscuits. He recalled riding behind the mules into Huntsville with his father and then riding home on the back of the wagon with a can of "Rockyfeller" coal oil squeezed tightly between his legs, a raw potato plugging the spout so that not a drop of the precious fuel spilled on the bumpy ride home around the mountain. It was that coal oil, purchased at the exorbitant rate of a dime for a half gallon, that helped furnish the great riches that Winthrop Rockefeller was now using to purchase the governor's office at Faubus's expense. Whether they were true or not, the stories gave some moral substance to Faubus's admonitions about the vast expense to Rockefeller of all the newspaper, radio, and television ads, slick home mailers, and the stylish campaign newspaper that arrived periodically in people's mailboxes.

Every prurient piece of gossip about Rockefeller that ever surfaced, Faubus worked into his campaign speeches somewhere, or else it found its way into some kind of campaign literature. The Reverend Corbett Mask of Benton, a hulking, unctuous Baptist who prayed over the state Senate to begin each session, circulated a letter supporting Faubus that accused Rockefeller of keeping a vast store of untaxed liquor at his Petit Jean estate and of serving liquor at parties and at cattle sales. In one joint appearance with Rockefeller before a crowd of ministers, Faubus said the governor of Arkansas should meet the standards of a Baptist deacon: "He should have had only one wife and not love whiskey." As long as he was governor, Faubus vowed, the Governor's Mansion "will not be the scene of drinking parties and the guest houses will not be the headquarters for beatniks from other states." Two years after leaving the governor's office, Faubus would lose the one-wife credential for deaconry. The reference to beatniks in guest houses apparently was an allusion to the Petit Jean residences, because the Governor's Mansion had no guest houses.

Two weeks before the election, Faubus came up with the *coup de grâce*. He accused the scion of robber barons of desecrating a cemetery, the final impudence of a true scoundrel. Faubus said Rockefeller, or his henchmen, had run over tombstones in a Lonoke cemetery to clear land for one of his farming operations. Rockefeller said it was a preposterous lie. Faubus repeated the charge. It seemed that workers clearing brush for Rockefeller at a grass farm or another farming operation accidentally struck a couple of headstones hidden in the high brush before they realized that it was an old burial plot and backed away. Rockefeller knew nothing about it. He overreacted and splurged on television ads countering the desecration charge, turning a silly political stunt into a major controversy.

Faubus's pollster, Gene Newsom, had Faubus with a slight lead ten days before the election. He got fifty-seven percent.

After the election and before his swearing-in in January, Faubus threw a small party at the Governor's Mansion for the reporters and cameramen who had covered the race for the newspapers, wire services, and radio and television stations. Faubus rarely socialized at the mansion and never with the media, although he had favorites like John Robert Starr of the Associated Press, Herbie Byrd of radio station KLRA, and George Douthit, the Capitol reporter for the *Arkansas Democrat*. But he relished the electoral victory over the billionaire and the businessmen and "silk-stocking crowd" in Little Rock (and the *Arkansas Gazette*) that supported him, and he needed to be sure that others recognized the significance of what he had done. However, he also wanted all the reporters to understand that it was a social event and was to be off the record.

It was on a brisk December evening. He and Alta, his wife, served punch and cookies. In the living room of the mansion, Faubus told campaign stories—he thought his cemetery gambit was the pivotal event of the race—and Harry Pearson, a reporter for the *Pine Bluff Commercial*, showed slides of pictures that he had taken during the campaign, of both Faubus and Rockefeller. After a couple of hours, Faubus signaled that it was time to break it up and everyone headed out. But as everyone passed onto the columned portico, Faubus held up Roy Reed and me for a moment—we had covered the race for the *Gazette*—and then suggested that we come back inside for a few minutes.

It was a remarkable hour or two. Reed and I would always wonder about the governor's motivations. Perhaps he pondered then that Roy might one day write his biography and that on this night he might engender some sympathy, although I doubt it. More likely, a part of him regretted the long breach with the newspaper whose editor had defended him at the pivotal moment in his political career, and that he yearned for some understanding, if only by a couple of reporters. Ernie Valachovic, the *Gazette*'s ace at the Capitol, did not drive a car and so had skipped the nighttime party. Perhaps it was something that Roy had written in his profile of the governor the Sunday before the election—he wrote that people still surged to Faubus on small-town squares "to touch the hem of his garment"—that kindled a need to explain himself, to get some recognition from a hostile quarter of the difficulties he had faced and the good he wanted to think that he had done in spite of them.

The *Gazette* editorials, he said, cast him as an archconservative when that was not his persona at all. His parents named him after the great socialist leader Eugene V. Debs—Eugene was Faubus's middle name—and he was proud of it. He said Debs, not Franklin Roosevelt, was the greatest American of the century, because it was Debs, not Roosevelt, who generated the great ideas that lifted so many people out of poverty and improved the lives of working people: Social Security and employer pensions, unemployment compensation, compensation for worker injuries, government-regulated job safety, and the forty-hour work week. Roosevelt just stole a few of Debs's ideas and implemented them. Debs ran for president three times and spent two long terms in prison for defying government strike-breaking actions and for violating sedition laws during World War I. President Woodrow Wilson wanted Debs to rot in prison, but Warren G. Harding freed him when his health deteriorated so that he could die in freedom.

Time and *Newsweek*, the news magazines, had irked Faubus by writing about the progressive "New South" governors. He said he had done more than any of them, because he governed a poorer state with greater barriers to progress. Roy or I would mention a contemporary governor who was supposed to be doing good things for education and implementing integration, or at least not fighting it—LeRoy Collins in Florida, Carl Sanders in Georgia, and Terry Sanford in North Carolina. Nah, Faubus said, his record was more liberal than any of them, and, besides, they governed far more prosperous states where it was easier to get things done.

He ticked off the things he had accomplished. He had reformed property assessments, or tried to, so that schools would get more money. He had raised the sales tax by half and dedicated the money to education. He had started a retirement system for state government employees. He had raised welfare benefits for the aged, blind, and disabled as often as he could. He had supported labor efforts. He had turned the snakepit that was the old state mental hospital into a modern mental-health hospital.

"Yes," Roy said, "but, governor, you're leaving out one thing." Faubus cut him off.

"I know what you're going to say—Central High School, 1957," Faubus said. (I'm paraphrasing what I remember.) "But you're ignoring the reality. You can have all the ideas you want about improving people's lives, but if you aren't in office, they're not good for anything. In politics, you have to trim your sails to the wind."

If he had not taken the stand he did and called out the National Guard, he said, Jim Johnson or Bruce Bennett would have been elected governor the next year. There was no doubt about it, he said. He would not have stood a chance of re-election in 1958 in the face of rising hysteria about integration.

"Now, Roy, you tell me. Who would you rather have been governor the last six years, Bruce Bennett or me?"

Roy laughed. "Well, if you put it that way, Governor, I guess you."

It was the only time I ever heard Faubus acknowledge that he had acted in 1957 solely for political gain and not upon conviction or upon his fear of violence at the school. He did later acknowledge to Reed, during their long conversations while Reed was prepar-

ing his biography of Faubus, that Johnson and Bennett would have been hard to beat in 1958 or afterward if he had not taken his stand.

Many years later, as Faubus was awaiting a ride at the Baptist Hospital after he had undergone a mild heart procedure, we talked again about the aftermath of the school crises of the 1950s and '60s. By then, he had turned himself, in his own mind, into a hero of the civil rights movement. He said it was the obligation of the federal government—the president essentially—to enforce the Constitution and the orders of the court, in the face of certain defiance all across the South. A governor couldn't do it. He had forced President Eisenhower to deploy federal power to assure people in every state that the law of the land had to be followed. If he had not forced Ike's hand, he said, the troubles would have persisted for many years. I could not tell for sure, but he seemed to believe it.

In 1988, he supported Rev. Jesse Jackson, the civil rights leader of the time, for president in the Democratic primaries. At least, he showed up at a rally in Little Rock and said so to a reporter.

V
Thermidor: 1966

Arkansas was not absent from the great cultural and political revolutions of the 1960s, but the convulsions over race, religious mores, and a miserable, unredemptive war in Vietnam were muted in an insular countryside where most people were too absorbed with the daily annoyances of existence to give much heed to big moral debates. A few college students would politely indulge a sort-of-radical speaker, like the prizefighter Cassius Clay or the raffish psychotherapist and sexologist Albert Ellis, but then drift back to the dorms and books or to a Dickson Street pub. But 1966 was a singular year when Arkansas, fed up with something (racial strife? corruption? economic stagnation?), moved perceptibly away from the past. People crowded into the Democratic primary that summer to boot out people connected in any way to the governing crowd and to nominate for governor an avenging populist, the noisiest white supremacist in the state. Three months later, in his stead they elected a rich, transplanted New York liberal committed to racial equality, higher taxes, superior schools, the arts, and abolition of the death penalty. It was not that the electorate was bipolar, but that people were having trouble figuring out what they believed and who might really represent their values. And they were disillusioned, finally, with Orval E. Faubus and the political order that he either nominally or dictatorially controlled.

The YD Revolt

It was first manifested in 1965 in the overthrow of Faubus acolytes in the Young Democratic Clubs of Arkansas, a cog in Faubus's political machine. Its president was John Browning, Faubus's administrative assistant, and the plan was to pass the baton at the state convention at Little Rock's Marion Hotel to Sheffield Nelson, a handsome blond fellow who had recently been president of the student body at Arkansas State Teachers College and who, by that time, was an assistant to Witt Stephens, president of Arkansas Louisiana Gas Company and the most powerful man in the state. Nelson would build a true rags-to-riches biography, his itinerant father having finally abandoned his wife and ragamuffin boy of fifteen in the rich Cache River bottomlands of Monroe County, which had borne the father none of the vestiges of agricultural wealth. Nelson managed to go to college and marry his high school sweetheart from Brinkley, who happened to be the daughter of state Representative Doris McCastlain, who happened to be a seatmate of Witt Stephens, who was finishing his second and last term in the legislature. Although the state Constitution prohibited it, Faubus would appoint Doris McCastlain state revenue commissioner the next year.

A band of young liberals (for lack of a better description) decided that with a little stealth they could take over the organization and use it to catapult Sam H. Boyce, the new prosecuting attorney at Newport, into the governor's office the next year. Boyce had the plump cheeks and beatific smile of a cherub, but he was a fighter. His nose seemed to betray too many solid punches. Boyce had done a little labor law and enjoyed union backing, such as it was in Arkansas. His band of insurgents was small but artful. It included the Hamilton boys, Joe and Henry—Joe managed to get elected to the legislature from conservative Boone County and, by wile and a raffish wit, to stay there for ten years—and James D. "Jim" McDougal, who would become internationally famous nearly thirty years later as the quarry of special prosecutor Kenneth W. Starr in the big Whitewater snipe hunt. McDougal would die ignominiously in a federal prison at Fort Worth in 1998 after being shunted into "the hole"—solitary confinement—for being sick and unable to urinate in a jar for one of the regular drug tests ordered by Starr.

Readers should index Jim McDougal in their memories, for his roguish part in the Young Democratic battle of 1964 foreshadowed similar roles in the great political battles ahead, the last as the antihero in the Whitewater saga that destroyed the political career of one man, Governor Jim Guy Tucker, and nearly another, Bill Clinton.

In 1956, at the age of fifteen, McDougal had hitchhiked sixty miles from the Bradford community in White County to Little Rock to shake hands with Adlai Stevenson, the cerebral Democratic nominee for president, which may have infused McDougal's lifetime zeal for politics, both its loftier and its clandestine planes. He could recite speeches of Lincoln, Franklin Roosevelt, and Winston Churchill with the appropriate flourishes, and it was he who plotted the churlish scheme that spoiled the first of Sheffield Nelson's many untimely and unsuccessful political ventures. The strategy was to create new Young Democrat chapters across the state, wherever Boyce had a law-school classmate or McDougal and the others had friends, and come to the convention with enough delegates to surprise the Faubus crowd. But the YD leaders got wind of it and did the same, with more resources, including state employees. The credentials committee for the convention, stacked with Faubus loyalists, was not going to recognize the Boyce delegations from a number of the new clubs.

Conventions are always a little late starting. On the morning of the YD convention, all the Boyce people were on hand early to carry out McDougal's strategy. Browning and the YD leaders had a hospitality suite upstairs in the Marion, where they gathered before going down to the ballroom for the opening session. When Browning, Nelson, and their cohorts left the suite and headed for the elevator, R. M. "Uncle Max" Allison, whom McDougal had given a dime-store walkie-talkie, alerted an accomplice in the Marion basement, who shut off power to the elevator, causing it to stall between floors. Allison, a slouching old man with a floppy brown fedora, was a familiar figure around the Marion. As a young man, Uncle Max had been afflicted with a permanent disability, which caused him to nod off in midsentence from a brain malfunction, and he spent his life in the service of politicians—most notably, U.S. Senator John Eldon Miller, Congressman Wilbur D. Mills, and David H. Pryor—and their causes. While Browning, Nelson, and others were trapped in the elevator and most delegates mingled around the ballroom and the entrance hall outside, Boyce people were in their seats and, at the scheduled moment for convening, Roy Lee Hight, a severely disabled young man who was the first vice president and the only Boyce supporter in the YD officialdom, arose and, in Browning's absence, called the convention to order. Someone nominated McDougal to be the temporary chairman of the convention and the Boyce crowd chorused "aye." McDougal, sitting down front with me and other reporters, vaulted onto the platform and called for a report from the credentials committee. Someone shouted that the convention should dispense with the committee's report and moved that all the delegates who had presented credentials be approved. That was seconded and the few dozen delegates who were seated shouted their approval. McDougal asked for nominations for president. Someone offered the name of Sam Boyce and moved that the convention elect him by acclamation. The motion was seconded and the seated delegates shouted "aye." It was all over in a couple of minutes. When the YD leaders were released from the elevator and rushed into the hall, Boyce was making his acceptance speech. They protested that the election was illegal and promised legal action, but the national YD organization recognized Boyce as the president. Boyce ran for governor the next year, but he split the progressive or moderate vote with former Congressman Brooks Hays and a couple of other decent but colorless candidates, which allowed Jim Johnson to lead the ticket and win the nomination.

The Horse Show Flap

The YD revolt was a chink in Faubus's armor, and things got no better in the new year. The governor's invincibility dissolved with one small scandal after another.

In January 1966, Faubus had the state auditor cut a warrant for $20,729.55 on the governor's emergency fund to the state Livestock and Poultry Commission, headed by his brother Doyle, to pay the delinquent bills of the Arkansas Horse Show Association, a private group of horse fanciers that had been headed by a big Faubus financier, T. J. Raney. The Raney family had set up a private high school for white kids in 1958, when Faubus closed Little Rock's high schools to avoid integrating them. The governor's gift of tax money to the group came to light when he filed a proclamation with the secretary of state, which was required when the governor spent money from his emergency fund, an account the legislature sets up every year for unanticipated crises. My *Gazette* colleague at the Capitol, Ernie Valachovic, ran across the proclamation while he was rummaging around the office of Secretary of State Kelly Bryant. A few legislators on the Legislative Joint Auditing Committee were emboldened to criticize the governor's giveaway of public funds to a group of rich friends to pay for their hobby of showing off their fancy horses at the state fairgrounds. Faubus had trouble justifying the check. He said the horse show's creditors thought it was a state agency and that he paid the debt to protect the state's image. It was not something a self-respecting populist would do.

The Midnight Pay Raises

Two months later came the Midnight Pay Raises. The governor's old Madison County pal and confidante, Mack Sturgis, had become weary of being the state purchasing agent in a cramped office on the Capitol's first floor, so Faubus told his appointees on the Highway Commission to make Sturgis the state highway director. Sturgis soon had a heart attack and decided to retire. But before retiring he got together with his next in command, the whimsically named Young William Whelchel, and, working at night on the agency's new computers, programmed pay raises for the upper echelon of the agency's staff and some 2,000 other employees. The "independent" Highway Commission knew nothing about the raises until Capitol reporters got wind of them. Many of the raises were illegal. The highway commissioners, all Faubus appointees, were furious and blamed the governor, since Sturgis was his man. The Mack Blackwell Amendment to the Constitution was supposed to make the highway agency independent of the governor and sheltered from politics. The commission fired Sturgis and rescinded the raises. Faubus admitted that he had told Sturgis to go ahead with the raises but said he was poorly informed about them and that, anyway, it was just an honest mistake. Another draft-Faubus movement had been percolating as the filing period for the 1966 election approached, but the Midnight Pay Raises silenced it.

Pensions for Pals

Kenneth S. Sulcer, a pink-cheeked man of forty, struck no one as a rising political star and certainly not a progressive or reformer. He had, after all, served seven somnolent terms in the state House of Representatives from the river town of Osceola in the ultimate machine county, Mississippi, which was run by A. A. "Shug" Banks and a few of the biggest plantation overseers in the state. While recounting the adventures of the legislature since Governor Francis Cherry's first term, the newspapers had rarely even mentioned Sulcer's name, although he had distinguished himself by sponsoring the bill creating the Arkansas Children's Colony for disabled children. Sulcer was painfully disabled himself—he ran real estate and furniture businesses—but, like Robert Dole, hid it deftly. But there he was at the Capitol announcing that he was running for governor in a field of prominent politicians and promising to bring rectitude and business savvy to the state government, where they were sorely in short supply. As an example of the backscratching he saw in the government, he mentioned a recently signed law creating the Quasi-Judicial Retirement System. As far as he could tell, it was passed to give tax-supported benefits to about seven of the governor's cronies.

None of us who covered the legislature recalled the bill, although hundreds of arcane and seemingly insignificant bills pass without debate every session and go unreported. The Quasi-Judicial Retirement Act had seven short sections, each describing a different set of qualifications that would make a person who had served on either the Public Service, Transportation, or Workmen's Compensation Commissions eligible for a state pension. The seven sections described the peculiar qualifications of seven men who had served for short periods (one only a few days) on one of the three commissions by appointment of a governor. Six were friends whom Faubus had appointed to one of three commissions for periods from a few days to several years. The other was William J. Smith, Faubus's legal counsel and legislative aide and senior partner at the state's largest law firm, Smith, Williams, Friday, Bowen, Eldridge and Clark. Smith, whom Governor Homer Adkins had appointed, had served on the Workmen's Compensation Commission for a short period in 1941. Smith renounced his pension after the story broke.

"Pensions for Pals," as an editorial writer called it, supercharged Sulcer's campaign for only a few days, but it permanently damaged Orval Faubus.

Prisons for Profit

Arkansas's two penitentiary units at Tucker and Cummins, north and southeast of Pine Bluff, were the state government's pride and joy in 1966, but by year's end they were the governor's shame. By using hardened criminals called "trusties" to take the place of paid guards, and by using inmate labor for farm and some small-trade production, Arkansas's prisons were the most efficient in America. Prison labor produced so much revenue for the state treasury every year that it sometimes exceeded the small appropriation of tax funds for the penitentiary. But it was a medieval and corrupt penal system that had sometimes brought infamy to the state. After the Civil War ended slavery, convict leasing introduced a way for Arkansas and other Southern states to make profitable use of the emancipated black man. Black men could be jailed on some minor or trumped-up charge— vagrancy was the most common one—and then leased out for planting and harvesting or to contractors for highway or levee labor. Doug Blackmon, a Stuttgart boy who worked for a time at the *Arkansas Democrat* and the *Daily Record* before reporting for the *Wall Street Journal*, wrote an absorbing book about the practice, although it dealt mainly not with Arkansas but with the horrific use of convicts in the mines of United States Steel Corporation and other companies in Alabama. Black men were arrested and turned over to the mining companies or others to work off their fines, sometimes for the rest of their lives. *Slavery by Another Name: The Re-Enslavement of Black Americans from the Civil War to World War II* won the Pulitzer Prize for history in 2009. Anyone even casually interested in the old debate over whether racism or genes played the key role in the stunted advance of African Americans in the one hundred years between Emancipation and the civil rights revolution ought to read it.

Arkansas may not have recorded the evils that Blackmon found in Alabama during the same period, but Governor George Donaghey was appalled by the abuses that he was sure were occurring in the prisons. Before leaving office in 1913 after his defeat by Joe T. Robinson, Donaghey, the father of the state's progressive tradition, pardoned 360 inmates, 37 percent of the inmate population, hoping that it would end the renting of prisoners for labor. Donaghey thought it forced men, often sentenced to prison for vagrancy or minor misdeeds, to work under inhumane conditions. He pardoned all the prisoners except just enough to cultivate the state prison farm. The legislature soon outlawed convict leasing.

Faubus often bragged about the efficient prisons and the use of trusties instead of free-world guards who had to be paid. It taught responsibility and also spared the taxpayers. A killer like Leslie Rutledge, an Independence County mountaineer who simultaneously shot down two brothers who were crossing his land, would be invited by the prison superintendent to bring his rifle when he reported to Cummins to serve his term for murder. Rutledge was made a long-line rider, supervising prisoners who were sent down for filching merchandise or writing hot checks, until Faubus, a few weeks after taking office in 1955, commuted his sentence and sent him home. His granddaughter of the same name was elected attorney general of Arkansas in 2014.

By his last term, even Faubus quietly recognized the endemic corruption of the system. The public could sense it if only by the frequency of prison escapes, which seemed to be announced in the newspapers every few days. It had to be for *something* that so many risked flight and its retributions. Former prisoners and sometimes relatives of inmates told of brutality and corruption and of bribes to get men paroled. The longtime superintendent, Lee Henslee, always assured Faubus that they were all lies, that prisoners were punished firmly but never cruelly, and that they were well fed and healthy. When Henslee retired in 1963 and Faubus put Dan D. Stephens, an avuncular lawyer at Clinton, in charge of the prisons, Faubus told Stephens to stop using the strap for punishment. Stephens was something of a reformer—he started an inmate band called the Dandees that sometimes played at events off the farm, and he built a prison medical clinic—but by 1965 he had reinstituted the strap, because he said discipline was breaking down. Sometimes, men on the rows would not meet their quota of okra or string beans and had to absorb a few lashes with the big leather strap. Faubus was concerned enough to ask a penology expert to evaluate the prisons for him. His report apparently was not favorable, but Faubus did not want to tarnish the penitentiary's image and never released it. He privately asked the State Police to investigate all the reports he was getting of cruelty and corruption at Cummins and Tucker. The night the troopers arrived at the small Tucker unit, the site of Death Row, the unit's barbarous director, Jim Bruton, fled and never returned. It was announced, without explanation, that he had resigned. Four years later, the Justice Department charged him with nineteen counts of violating the rights of inmates and of torture. Bruton and his trusties employed the infamous "Tucker Telephone," an old telephone magneto that sent electric shocks to a prisoner's genitals when the operator used the phone crank to "ring him up."

Although neither Faubus nor the State Police released its report on the depravity at the prison, word of it leaked out. Winthrop Rockefeller, running for governor again, this time against Jim Johnson, demanded that the report be made public. My wife and I had just bought our first home, and our tenant, in a tiny servant's quarter in the back yard, was Eugene Hale, a newly minted lawyer who was Faubus's office counsel and liaison with the prisons. Unknown to everyone but Faubus and the State Police, Hale had participated in the investigation with Duke Atkinson, Billy Skipper, and James Beach of the State Police, and he had helped prepare the report. On the Sunday afternoon before Rockefeller's inauguration, Hale gave the Little Rock media a lengthy statement of his own summarizing the horrors they had found. He had written it a week earlier and shared it with the *Pine Bluff Commercial*, a deal that he had made with a *Commercial* reporter for not writing about something else that the reporter had found. The *Commercial* published the account that Sunday morning. Hale described the prisons as "sadistic, sordid and barbaric" and said he had personally witnessed inmates being tortured. "It was unbelievable that such a degenerative situation existed in America, even if it is in a prison," he said. Hale moved out of our little cottage Monday morning and started to work in the office of the attorney general. He was fired in a few days.

The troopers' report confirmed everything Faubus had not wanted to hear. The system of giving "trusted" inmates, often the most brutal killers, control over others contributed to corruption and a culture of violence; the forced farm labor was often inhumane—fourteen hours a day in brutal heat with little nourishment and rest; beatings and deployment of the feared Tucker Telephone were frequent; bribery for favors or better treatment was widespread; liquor, cigarettes, and drugs were funneled into the prisons through a system of barter and bribes; new prisoners were raped by longtimers. The investigators criticized the food, which they said was sometimes nearly inedible. (They would have noted an exception on days when legislative committees paid visits to the prisons.) A slice of bread and a serving of rice was the typical meal. Inmates got meat once a month.

Faubus ordered his new prison superintendent, O. E. Bishop, to fire several wardens identified in the report and to relieve a few trusties at Tucker of their commands. Otherwise, he decided it was too late in his term to do anything and to just wait it out. Rockefeller would spend the entirety of his first term trying to bring civility and order to the penitentiary, which would become an international symbol of penal barbarity.

Arkansas Loan and Theft

Old Sam Faubus and Orval's mentors and classmates back at Commonwealth College might have been most piqued at the languid attitude of the government toward commercial abuses of consumers the longer Faubus stayed in office. An inherent danger of political longevity is that the government becomes a somnolent watchdog. Leland Duvall, a self-educated economic sage at the *Arkansas Gazette*, wrote about the frequency with which unscrupulous and fraudulent insurance and securities dealers preyed upon people. Someone could establish an insurance company in Arkansas and start selling policies with virtually no capital, and many operators did, often coming over from Texas, where regulators had cracked down. It was only during the succeeding administration of Rockefeller that the extent of the abuses became known. Rockefeller's insurance and securities commissioners canceled the licenses of hundreds of what Duvall had called "fly-by-night" insurance companies and securities brokers.

At the Capitol and in the boardrooms of scores of banks, there were murmurings in 1965 and 1966 about Arkansas Loan and Thrift Corporation, a rogue bank established by a Fort Smith used-car dealer with the not-so-secret help of Bruce Bennett, now reincarnated as the state's attorney general after his loss to Faubus in the 1960 governor's race. A number of powerful legislators—such as Representatives Paul Van Dalsem of Perryville and Chadd Durrett of El Dorado, and Senator Joe Lee Anderson of Helena—were supposed to be involved, and Faubus's regulators were either cozy with the founders of the bank or else obliged them by looking the other way. Bennett and the car dealer who would become AL&T's president, Ernest A. Bartlett Jr., started the company in December 1964. They had come into possession of the 1937 charter for a finance company called

United Loan and Investment Company that by 1964 was defunct. The old industrial-loan charter supplied AL&T's authority to start taking deposits and making loans like it was a bank or a savings and loan association. It promised to pay an interest rate of 5.75 percent, which was considerably more than banks or S&Ls paid, which caused a little consternation at those financial institutions. Bartlett advertised that your savings were safer in AL&T than if they were insured by the Federal Deposit Insurance Corporation, because they were backed by Savings Guaranty Corporation, which had a trademark seal that looked like the Great Seal of the United States. Actually, Savings Guaranty turned out not to own a penny of assets except a few shares of worthless AL&T stock. But many widows took their savings out of banks and placed them with AL&T, which had set up a string of offices from Van Buren to Helena.

Bruce Bennett

AL&T might have had a longer crack at poor investors had the voters not intervened. Among the veterans who lost in the 1966 Democratic primary was Bruce Bennett, to his and nearly everyone's shock. He was beaten by Joe Purcell, an unknown traffic judge at Benton with a campaign style so wooden that Doug Smith, my old house-burning roommate and at this time a *Gazette* political writer, lamented that voters had been known to fall asleep shaking his hand. Purcell's single political gambit was a big advertisement in the *Gazette* right before the primary, allegedly paid for by his friends and neighbors, who listed their names and telephone numbers and invited voters across the state to call them and ask about Joe's honesty and reliability. Two weeks after taking office, Purcell filed a lawsuit in Pulaski County Chancery Court to close AL&T, because it did not comply with state laws governing any kind of financial institution and was selling securities illegally. The suit was assigned to Judge Kennesaw Landis "Kay" Matthews, who had been Faubus's adviser in 1957 when he sent the National Guard to stop the integration of Central High School. Faubus had appointed Matthews to a vacant judgeship in 1965, and he was elected to another chancery seat in 1966. For a year, Matthews stymied any progress in the suit, sometimes rebuking lawyers for the state or for the Arkansas Bankers Association for disparaging the fine businessmen who ran AL&T. Finally, Governor Rockefeller's securities commissioner, Don Smith, contacted the federal Securities and Exchange Commission in Washington and urged the agency to investigate AL&T. It sent two staff lawyers to Van Buren in March 1968 and they soon asked U.S. District Judge John E. Miller at Fort Smith to put the company into receivership. He did.

I checked into a motel next door to the SEC lawyers and plowed through the boxes of company records to figure out how it had all happened. It was, to use two old metaphors, a simple scheme of backscratching and influence peddling. To skirt the state laws regulating financial and insurance institutions, Attorney General Bennett in his official capacity had issued five legal opinions in 1965 and 1966 advising state officials that they had no legal authority to regulate AL&T. The attorney general's office ordinarily put copies of its official opinions each day in a basket for reporters, but we had seen none of the opinions I found in the AL&T files. The opinions went to Representative Van Dalsem, the state Bank Department, the state Securities Commission, the savings and loan commissioner, and the state insurance

Joe Purcell

commissioner—with blind copies, naturally, to AL&T. Each regulator had asked about legal authority to regulate AL&T's activities. In response to queries from each of them, Bennett wrote: No, your laws do not apply to an institution like AL&T. Presumably, all of them knew that Bennett was a founder of AL&T, because it was general knowledge at the Capitol. Bartlett would testify at his criminal trial that, actually, William J. Smith, Faubus's legal adviser, had written Bennett's opinions. Smith denied it. A young assistant to Bennett who was fresh out of law school testified at Bartlett's criminal trial that he had sent letters to the State Securities Commission on the attorney general's stationery saying that he had examined the registration, prospectus, other documents, and the books of AL&T and that the company fully complied with all the requirements of securities law. Actually, he had examined nothing and only signed his name to letters that Bennett, his boss, handed him. Bennett gave him a few AL&T stock certificates for his trouble. As for Savings Guaranty Corporation, which insured people's deposits, the files showed that Van Dalsem, Faubus's House floor leader, had helped Bennett obtain an inactive insurance company from Representative J. H. Cottrell of Little Rock, the speaker of the House in 1965. Bennett sold it for $64,000 to AL&T, which changed the company's name to Savings Guaranty Corporation. When the examiner from the state Insurance Department came to check Savings Guaranty's assets to see if it had the minimum capital required by law, Bartlett wrote a check for $580,000 from AL&T and deposited it in Savings Guaranty's account. After the examiner certified that Savings Guaranty had the required capital, Bartlett transferred the money back to AL&T and left some AL&T stock certificates with the insurance arm as guaranty for the millions of depositors' dollars. For good measure, he gave the state insurance examiner a few shares of AL&T stock.

With rumors of impending legal troubles for AL&T and his involvement growing, Bennett made a final run for governor in the summer of 1968, finishing fourth in a six-person race for the Democratic nomination with only 15 percent of the vote. He was beaten by the perpetually frowning speaker of the House of Representatives named Crank, the mirthless wife of segregation hotspur Jim Johnson, and a buoyant liberal named Boswell. Dale Bumpers, a young lawyer at Charleston who was studying the candidates in preparation for a race himself in 1970, said Bennett was the most impressive-looking politician he had watched, but also the least congenial. Bennett shook hands with everyone he saw but never betrayed the slightest interest in them, even to ask their names. Bumpers made a mental note that he should always show people that they counted by asking their names and trying to establish some connection.

A federal grand jury in January 1969 indicted Bartlett, Bennett, and a pair of brothers from Booneville who were officers of the firm, Hoyt and Afton Borum, for fraud and conspiracy. The indictment said the company was an illegal operation and that the men had dissipated depositors' money by lending money to themselves, their companies, and friends with no expectation of repayment, and by giving themselves and their confederates large stock dividends although the company was broke. A jury convicted all but Bennett on numerous counts of securities, mail, and wire fraud;

conspiracy; and bribery. Bartlett and the Borum brothers went to prison. U.S. District Judge Oren Harris, an old friend of Bennett at El Dorado from the days when Harris was the congressman from south Arkansas, severed Bennett's case from the others and Bennett never went to trial. Back in 1955, when I was a reporter covering the Oil Belt Golf Tournament at the El Dorado Country Club for the *El Dorado Daily News*, I would spot Bennett and Harris, in their white suits and Panama hats, sipping cocktails near the eighteenth green. Bennett's doctor at El Dorado told Judge Harris that Bennett had cancer, and Harris gave his old friend continuances until the government gave up the prosecution. The U.S. attorney finally withdrew the charges in 1977, two years before Bennett's death.

After the government liquidated AL&T's assets, some two thousand people still lost most of their life savings. At a hearing in Fort Smith after Judge John Eldon Miller put the company into bankruptcy, a preacher asked the judge to give churches like his, which had put their building funds into AL&T, preference in distributing whatever money was recovered. He said they should recover all their money before any was distributed to ordinary people, because the churches' funds were "God's money." Miller, a former congressman and U.S. senator who was then eighty-one, told the preacher that God should have been smarter than to put his money into AL&T and that He would have to get in line with the widows.

A postscript to this sordid story: During Bartlett's trial, the government put on the stand Claude C. Carpenter Jr., a former Faubus aide who was named in the indictment as an unindicted co-conspirator. Carpenter, who had barely lost a race for lieutenant governor in 1966, was a law and business partner of Judge Kay Matthews, although he was not identified that way in the indictment or at the trial. He testified that Bennett and Bartlett had hired him to be counsel for AL&T in mid-January 1967. After his defeat in the 1966 primary, Bennett left the attorney general's office in mid-January 1967 and resumed his law practice at El Dorado. Carpenter said Bennett called and asked him to take his place as general counsel to AL&T—a job that Bennett had never acknowledged holding, because the conflict of writing official government opinions favoring a company that he partially owned and served as general counsel would have been obvious to a fifth-grader.

The day after the call, Bartlett showed up at Carpenter's office in the 1515 Building across from the State Capitol and gave him a check for $10,000 as a retainer. Later in the year, he got two more checks totaling $13,000, not because he had done any work for AL&T—he said he had done nothing—but because Bartlett was always showing up at his office unannounced and spending hours gabbing about the Arkansas Razorbacks and everything but AL&T. He said his law office's billings fell $7,000 that year because he was entertaining Bartlett, so he asked for a couple more checks.

Carpenter's morning of testimony introduced some unintended levity into the trial's tedium, about the bookkeeping legerdemain that was used in plucking the savings of some 2,300 depositors and putting it into the pockets of AL&T's officers, directors, and their families and friends. Usually, it was in the form of loans secured by worthless AL&T stock. Readers may find it as mind-boggling as the head-scratching members of the jury did.

The court-appointed receiver for AL&T had sued Carpenter and many others who were listed in the AL&T books as owing AL&T, usually for defaulting on their loans. Carpenter said he owed AL&T $89,000 because, in trying to settle a dispute between Bennett and Bartlett, he had signed a promissory note to AL&T that was supposed to simply satisfy the record. Bennett and Bartlett had helped establish a sister company of AL&T in Louisiana, called Louisiana Loan and Thrift, along with several disreputable politicians from the Bayou State, notably the flamboyant attorney general Jack P. F. Gremillion and Jim Garrison, the colorful New Orleans prosecutor who had tried to convict the patently innocent Clay Shaw of helping kill President Kennedy in 1963.

Incidentally, Louisiana Loan and Thrift ended the same way AL&T did, in bankruptcy and criminal court. Gremillion, like his friend Bennett, was charged with conspiracy and securities fraud in his dealings with LL&T. He was acquitted, but then convicted of perjury for lying about whether he had received consulting pay from LL&T. Gremillion served fifteen months in a federal prison at Fort Walton Beach, Florida, before Governor Edwin Edwards pardoned him. (Governor Edwards would subsequently do a little time himself.)

Carpenter said Bartlett was mad because Attorney General Bennett had sold his LL&T stock to a few Louisiana skunks so that he and the other AL&T officers would no longer have controlling interest in the company. Bartlett asked Carpenter to help him get Bennett out of AL&T entirely, so Carpenter arranged for a Borum relative to buy Bennett's shares for $89,000. It would be a few days before Troy Borum could come up with his $89,000, so Carpenter agreed to sign a promissory note for that sum to be put into the AL&T file until Troy Borum got his money together. Troy never got it together, and Carpenter was still on the hook. Carpenter admitted that he might have been snookered.

But he insisted that he never really did serious legal work for the $23,000 he was paid, or for the occasional pleasure trips he took with Bartlett at AL&T's expense. Bartlett once invited him to come over to Van Buren and see AL&T's new offices and sent an airplane to Little Rock to fetch him. They looked at the building and got on the plane to go back to Little Rock. Carpenter had consumed a little liquor and fell asleep. As the plane was gliding toward the runway at Little Rock he looked out the window and saw Pinnacle Mountain. No, the pilot told him, this is Albuquerque, not Little Rock. Since Carpenter's wife had long since been left waiting for him at Adams Field in Little Rock, they decided to fly on to Las Vegas and get in some gambling. On cross-examination, Bartlett's attorney, Sam Sexton, asked Carpenter if he was stoned on the flight.

"One is always reluctant to admit they were stoned, but I had had a couple of martinis," Carpenter said.

"A couple of martinis!" Sexton said. "Uh huh."

Carpenter and his wife also accompanied Bartlett and his wife to Destin, Florida, to celebrate the Bartletts' wedding anniversary at AL&T expense. Still, he said, he did so little actual work for AL&T that he always wondered why Bennett and Bartlett had made him the general counsel.

When I saw the date of their first encounter at Carpenter's office, the day on which Bartlett had handed him the first $10,000 check, I understood. It was January 24, 1967, the same day that a story appeared in the *Arkansas Gazette* about the lawsuit against AL&T that Attorney General Joe Purcell had lodged the day before in the court of Judge Matthews, Carpenter's law and business partner. I went over the timeline with William H. Bowen, a lawyer who had participated in the AL&T litigation for the intervening Arkansas Bankers Association and who had told me about how he had been treated in Matthews's court. Bowen said if my story about Bartlett's payments to Judge Matthews's partner appeared in the *Gazette*, he would file a complaint with the Supreme Court and seek to have the judge suspended.

I visited Judge Matthews in his office at the courthouse. I laid out Claude Carpenter's testimony and the remarkable coincidence that Carpenter was handed a big check from Arkansas Loan and Thrift the day after a suit against the company was filed in his court. Did his partner tell him about the check? Did he share the money? Should he have recused in the case at the outset? As I asked the questions, Matthews swiveled in his chair and stared out the window behind him. He said not a word. After a time, I said I was going to write a story about the coincidence and the course of the suit in his court. If he decided to comment he could call me at the *Gazette*. I wrote the article, and the editor or publisher sent it to the newspaper's lawyers at Rose, House, Meek, Barron, Nash and Williamson. The firm's senior partner, Archie House, recommended that the paper not publish the story, because it would destroy public confidence in the judiciary. The story never ran. For as long as he lived, Matthews, a dapper and jovial man, would leap to his feet whenever he saw me (usually in a restaurant), pump my hand, and tell his guests what a marvelous journalist I was. He apparently credited me with the decision not to print an article that would have jeopardized his judicial career.

Arkansas Monkey Trial I

None of these scandalous discoveries or the voters' disillusionment should leave the impression that the Enlightenment had settled upon Arkansas in 1966. The state's highest court ruled six to one that it was perfectly proper for the state to make it a criminal act for a teacher to talk about evolution in the classrooms, unless it was to denounce the godless theory.

Let me lay the groundwork. Forrest Rozzell, the executive secretary of the Arkansas Education Association, was the foremost guardian of public education in the quarter century after World War II. In every school crisis, whether it involved integration, school funding, consolidation, or intellectual freedom, his was the voice that was always heard at the moment when the rest fell mute. On September 24, 1957, the day after a mob encouraged by Faubus's defiance of court orders to desegregate Little Rock schools rampaged outside Central High School, Rozzell was to make a speech to the Greater Little Rock Federation of Women's Clubs on the status of education. Instead, the women got a lecture on the American heritage of rule by law. His deep voice quavering with rage, Rozzell told the ladies: "When there is a wild resort to jungle rule before the eyes of my daughter, a senior at Central High School, shall I dare not raise my voice again to insist that man must rely upon intelligence and cooperation rather than upon force and violence?" They heard him out and then turned to discussing their approaching style show.

In 1965, Rozzell decided that the state's antievolution law, adopted by the voters in 1928 in the wake of the Scopes trial in Tennessee, had to go, because it prevented any serious science instruction in the public schools. He found a biology teacher at Central High School, Susan Epperson, who had taught his daughter, to be the plaintiff in a suit against the state to strike down the law.

The suit was lodged in the court of Chancery Judge Murray O. Reed. Attorney General Bennett had to defend the law, and rather than let one of his deputies handle it, his usual practice, he was not going to pass up the opportunity for grandstanding with a stance that he knew would be wildly popular. Bennett would be on the ballot in a few weeks in his second run for governor, and what better lift could he get than to reprise William Jennings Bryan's performance at the Scopes trial in 1925? When the Arkansas evolution trial started, Bruce spotted my friendly countenance and winked. He felt better that an El Dorado boy would be recording his triumph in the state paper, although George Bentley, the *Gazette*'s courthouse reporter, actually wrote our story that day. The trial went badly for Bruce, an omen of things to come. To demolish Darwin's theory, he waved his King James Bible in front of the bench and tried to read one passage after another from Genesis. Each time, Judge Reed cut him off. The court, Reed said, needed no reminder of the biblical account of creation or of Darwin's theories. He was interested only in the constitutionality of the law. How, the judge wondered, did the evolution law comport with the religious-establishment and free-speech clauses of the First Amendment? That was not Bruce's field and he finally sat down. The Scopes trial at Dayton, Tennessee, had taken eight days; the Epperson trial took two hours and twenty minutes. Two months later, at the end of May, Reed rendered his decision. The 1928 act violated the free-speech rights of teachers and the establishment clause and was therefore invalid. Bennett appealed to the state Supreme Court in the fall of 1966.

The Arkansas court was the speediest appellate court in the land in handling its cases, but Monday after Monday, month after month, we anticipated its decision in the evolution case and it didn't come. It would be nearly two years, in November 1968, when the court finally ruled—a one-paragraph unsigned order upholding the old evolution law. One justice, Lyle Brown, the lone dissenter, signed his name. His law clerk, Pierce Wilson, subsequently confided how it came about. After the oral argument, the judges voted in conference four to three to reverse Judge Reed and uphold the antievolution law. Chief Justice Carleton Harris and justices John A. Fogleman, Conley Byrd, and Paul Ward voted to uphold the law, and Justices

George Rose Smith, J. Fred Jones, and Brown dissented. Fogleman wrote a lengthy majority opinion, and Brown a vigorous dissent. But Harris, the chief, who ordinarily resisted political influence, said evolution was such an explosive issue that the court needed to be united when it released its decision. The court's stature in the state was at stake, he said. Every few weeks, in conference, he tried to bridge the impasse and find a way for Smith, Jones, and Brown to join the

majority, but no one would budge. After a fresh term began in September 1968, he talked Smith and Jones into upholding the statute, but they said they would not join Fogleman's earnest and lengthy legal justification for the law. They would sign only if there were no legal pronouncements for which they would be accountable. Fogleman's opinion was scrapped. But Lyle Brown held out. He wanted his dissenting opinion published. In a final rancorous conference, Brown gave in, but flung his opinion across the conference table. He would not publish his opinion, but he vowed that he would be recorded as "no" for as long as he remained on the court.

The court delivered its decision the following Monday as a *per curiam* order. Unsigned by any justice, it said simply that the evolution law constituted "a valid exercise of the state's power to specify the curriculum in its public schools" and that Brown dissented. It carried no reference to the First Amendment. Rozzell had the decision appealed to the U.S. Supreme Court, which unanimously struck the statute down. "[T]he First Amendment does not permit the State to require that teaching and learning must be tailored to the principles or prohibitions of any religious sect or dogma,"

Justice Abe Fortas wrote. Banning a particular scientific theory because it seemed to conflict with Genesis's account of creation was a means of sponsoring religion, which was forbidden by the First Amendment.

Teachers and textbooks in Arkansas were finally free to talk about evolution theories, the foundation of modern medicine, anthropology, and genetics, but few ever did. Twelve years later, in 1981, the Arkansas legislature did what even its predecessors in the 1920s refused to do: pass a law mandating the teaching of Genesis's account of how God created the universe in six days, if the schools took up the matter of the universe's creation at all. Governor Frank White signed it and a federal court invalidated it. In most of old Dixie, the Enlightenment was still far behind the curve.

For the first time in fourteen years, Orval Faubus was not on the ballot in the 1966 primaries or in the general election, and there was no obvious political heir. So uncertain were the strength of the governor's coattails and the mood of the electorate that no one wanted to be widely perceived as the man who would carry on his legacy. Campaigns for nearly every office were exercises in tedium.

Justice Jim Johnson

Even Jim Johnson, whose race baiting and calumnies about his opponents had enlivened past campaigns, was almost a model of decorum. In his 1956 campaign, he had famously declared, "I am opposed to rape and murder and would speak out against them, and the greatest crime, even above these, is integration." But when he resigned from the Supreme Court to make the race in April 1966—he had defeated the scholarly justice Minor Millwee in 1958 for a seat on the court—he played down race. "There will be no schoolhouse door stands," he solemnly averred. He said he believed in "equal rights for all," although he acknowledged a preference for separation of the races. He ran this time as "Justice Jim" and nailed wooden planks, with "Justice Jim" stenciled on them, on fenceposts and trees along highways all over the state. Though weather beaten, they stood him in good stead for a couple of later elections. But he could not resist a few slurs about his opponents. His chief opponent in the Democratic primary was a colleague on the Supreme Court, Frank Holt, who resigned after Johnson did to join the race. Holt presented himself as a new kind of politician, a former prosecutor and judge who was unsullied by affiliation with the old factions. But the day before Holt announced that he was running, a reporter spotted him leaving the offices of Witt Stephens, the utility magnate and Faubus's chief financier. Johnson tagged him as the machine's candidate. Holt was the quiet, reserved younger brother of Jack Holt Sr., who had made three close but losing races for U.S. senator and governor in the 1940s and 1950s. Johnson referred to

Frank Holt

the genial Holt as "the pleasant vegetable." Holt's driver for much of that summer was a twenty-year-old Georgetown University student from Hot Springs named Bill Clinton.

In the general election, Johnson called Winthrop Rockefeller "the prissy sissy," "the Madison Avenue cowboy," and "the Santa Gertrudis steer," the latter a reference to the cattle on Rockefeller's Petit Jean Mountain ranch. (A steer is an ox that has been castrated.) The epithets were supposed to give credence to the rumor that Rockefeller was gay, which Johnson never uttered but which appeared in some unsigned literature. It infuriated Jeannette Rockefeller, his wife of ten years, when a *Gazette* reporter mentioned it to her.

"Who the hell am I supposed to be?" she asked.

Johnson and his campaign literature often called Rockefeller a rich New York playboy. After hearing that remark from Johnson at a political event, Rockefeller turned to a *Gazette* reporter standing beside him. "I wish they'd make up their mind whether I'm a queer or a playboy," he said. The anecdotal evidence leaned toward the latter. After all, he was kicked out of Yale in his third year after he was caught showering with a woman, and nearly twenty years later his first wife complained that Winthrop's womanizing had humiliated her in New York's café society.

Rumors circulated again that Rockefeller had a vast pornography archive on the mountain and that he also kept a cellar full of vintage wines, whiskey, and liqueurs from around the world. In 2008, I asked a panel of Rockefeller's old aides at a conference at Petit Jean if they knew whether any of that had been true. Marion Burton, his pilot and lawyer and later the governor's executive secretary, said that during that campaign Rockefeller got a tip that agents of the state Alcoholic Beverage Control Board were coming to the mountain on a specific day to investigate, perhaps to see if the reputed stash included untaxed liquor. Rockefeller's men loaded all the liquor in the back of a bob truck, covered it with canvas, and parked the truck on a downtown Little Rock street for a few days until the agents had inspected the Petit Jean premises.

Dr. Dale Alford, who got elected to Congress on Faubus's coattails in 1958, made a second race for governor and this time finished even below the man he had beaten that year, Brooks Hays. Hays, by then sixty-eight, waged a cheerful campaign but split the moderate vote with Holt, Sam Boyce, Kenneth Sulcer, and Raymond Rebsamen, a rich Little Rock businessman and philanthropist. Johnson beat Holt in the runoff.

Thousands of conservative Democrats, still segregationist at heart, nevertheless feared that Johnson—despite his calmer rhetoric—would stir up more racial troubles, and so they voted for the Republican. Rockefeller received 54.4 percent of the vote, a margin of only 49,121 votes. It was the first election after voters amended the state constitution to end the poll tax and set up a system of permanent voter registration. The amendment ended the voter intimidation widely associated with the poll tax, and African Americans voted in greater numbers across east Arkansas, almost uniformly for Rockefeller. Swept into office with him were the first Republican lieutenant governor since Reconstruction, Medal of Honor winner Maurice L. "Footsie" Britt, and the first Republican member of Congress since Reconstruction, John Paul Hammerschmidt, who beat the only liberal in the delegation, James W. Trimble.

Claude Carpenter and Bruce Bennett, who were widely associated with the racial troubles of the past decade, were beaten, as were several legislative giants, notably Representatives Paul Van Dalsem of Perryville and two former speakers and friends of Faubus, Glenn F. Walther and J. H. Cottrell of Little Rock. A tide of voters in Pulaski County, impelled by a "Throw the Rascals Out" campaign directed by women who had coalesced in the Central High School crisis, provided the margin in all five races. The cartoons of George Fisher in the *North Little Rock Times* (and reprinted in the *Arkansas Gazette*) inspired the movement. A court-ordered reapportionment had lumped Van Dalsem's tiny Perry County with Pulaski County in a thirteen-member House district. Speaking to a club of Little Rock

Paul Van Dalsem

businessmen he hoped would see him as an effective agent for them in the legislature, Van Dalsem joked that up in Perry County they didn't have any trouble with these uppity "university women," because the men kept them "barefoot and pregnant" and gave them a cow to milk. (This phrase became a national pop-cultural cliché.) Fisher's satirical illustrations, and the "Barefoot Women for Rule" organization, gave Herbert C. Rule III, a Yale-educated lawyer, a massive victory over Van Dalsem.

In south Arkansas, voters elected a young state representative from Camden, David H. Pryor, to Congress to replace Oren Harris, whom President Johnson had appointed to the U.S. District Court for the Western District. Pryor had been the leader of a tiny band of insurgents in the House of Representatives, championing fiscal reforms in county government and a new constitution. After college, he had started a crusading little newspaper at Camden, the *Ouachita Citizen*, to compete briefly with the daily newspaper that was part of the Hussman chain of monopoly papers across south Arkansas. Pryor defeated the son-in-law of the chain's owner in the Democratic runoff primary. While he was in law school at Fayetteville, Pryor was the *Gazette's* correspondent for northwest Arkansas—a fact that, if widely known, probably would have truncated his fabulous political career.

VI
Rockefeller

It is safe to say that not a dozen Arkansawyers knew what they were getting when they voted in the fall of 1966 to make Winthrop Rockefeller their governor, nor were many more of them sure of it when the experiment ended four years later and the heartbroken man, then only sixty years old, left the State Capitol to grieve the final miscarriage of his dreams. Twenty-five months later, he was dead. Rockefeller would remain—perhaps always will remain—the most liberal governor in Arkansas history and, by any definition of the word, among the most liberal in American history, although his wealth, family pedigree, and political party made it impossible for such a standing to gain popular credence. Jim Johnson, who in his most intemperate moments called Rockefeller a socialist, was a little closer to the mark than he suspected or intended, for the truth is that both men shared a political passion for what Johnson would call the common people—the difference being that Johnson loved them for what they were, prejudices, ignorance, and all, while Rockefeller loved them for what, with investment and guidance from a benevolent government and social institutions, they all might become, the prosperous and civic-minded citizens of an egalitarian society. The notion that the scion of the royal family of American capitalism was a secret agent bent on destroying business and privilege, which was the purpose of the socialist invective, was not going over with even the most delusional conspiracists, nor was it ever on Rockefeller's mind. He enjoyed wealth and loved giving it away.

As a politician, to the degree that he was a successful one, Rockefeller was the most enigmatic of the whole menagerie of characters who cast themselves upon the Arkansas democracy from 1819 forward. Shy in spite of a whole life in the glare of celebrity, inarticulate in spite of his intelligence, naïve in spite of the disillusioning familial, societal, and global conflicts in which he was involved, he nevertheless at the end threw himself into politics, an enterprise that required ego, ambition, self-confidence, and other traits that he seemed to possess negligibly if at all. What got into him? The expedient answer is that he had in abundance the one thing that is most essential in politics, money. His wealth obviously was the big enabler, but it also took something deeper, something subconscious.

The best explanation may be the popular one from the family biographies, like Ron Chernow's. When Rockefeller came to Arkansas, he was followed by descriptions of him as the black sheep of the great family, a drunken playboy who was perpetually rebuked by his displeased father and snubbed by his plutocratic siblings. As a chubby and clumsy boy in the family's nine-story mansion on West 54th Street in New York City or the Rockefeller estate at Pocantico Hills, up the Hudson River from Manhattan, he was often tormented by his older brothers, especially Nelson and Laurance, who taunted him as "Pudgy" and, when Winthrop developed a kidney ailment, got their kicks by reminding the lad that a cousin, also named Win-

Winthrop Rockefeller

throp, had died of a kidney disease. While his father was distant and perpetually reproving, his mother, Abigail, was protective and consoling.

"Abuse only makes him angry and much worse," she wrote of the boy, "while for love or kind treatment he will do anything."

All the other siblings accepted the familial archetype and were exemplars in preparatory school and the top universities, but not Winthrop, who stood out in prep schools in Connecticut and on the Columbia University campus for his achievements in cards, smoking, and pranks. Winthrop did an obligatory turn at Yale but admitted later that he mainly mastered the arts of smoking, drinking, and poker before he was expelled in his junior year over the co-ed shower incident. All the Rockefeller youngsters were given allowances in their school days away from home and were expected to maintain a precise ledger of how they spent the money and the value they got for it, but Winthrop's lack of diligence always disappointed his father. It would be so all his life. Even when the prodigal son transformed the Petit Jean mountaintop and made a name for himself in the state, the old man did not even deign to visit him in Arkansas to see what the boy had wrought. Winthrop made a documentary film and sent it to him.

To escape the constant censure of the family, especially his hectoring father, Winthrop left the East Coast and landed a job in the Texas oilfields as a roughneck for Humble Oil Company, by then a component of Standard Oil. He reveled in the hard work. Winthrop was taller and huskier than the other men and set out to prove that he could match their toughness and physicality, as well as their appetites for strong drink and language. He was not pushing a pencil or belaboring some arcane subject but actually getting things done with his own hands, achievements you could see. He liked the men better than he did the brainy nerds in prep school and college. But he didn't spurn privilege altogether. While he worked with the grunts on the rigs for seventy-five cents an hour, a pretty good wage for the time, he dined on the weekends at the country club with the company president. Just before the war came, he joined as a private and found the same rapport in the ranks of common men. He would leave the U.S. Army as a lieutenant colonel, highly decorated for bravery in the invasion of Okinawa. (Rockefeller is in the Infantry Officer Hall of Fame at Fort Benning, Georgia.)

Back in Gotham after the war, Winthrop returned to the recreational pursuits that so annoyed the family—partying, drinking, and romancing. The New York tabloids followed him like he was an early-day Donald Trump, although Winthrop, unlike Trump, never seemed to enjoy the publicity and certainly didn't engineer it. Although shy except after consuming a certain quotient of alcohol, he became a fixture in the tabloids' coverage of the Manhattan café society. Perhaps prefiguring his future fame in Arkansas, Winthrop won a dance contest in the famous Rainbow Room at Rockefeller Center by teaming with the Broadway singing star Mary Martin, who would later play the Little Rock nurse Nellie Forbush in the Rodgers and Hammerstein hit *South Pacific* in 1949. Apparently, he was ungainly only when he wasn't on the dance floor. You know the rest: Miss Lithuania, the Cinderella wedding, the humiliating divorce, and the escape with an old infantry confederate to a remote venue with lenient divorce laws. (Arkansas's quickie-divorce laws actually didn't figure into the divorce, which was consummated in Nevada.)

In Arkansas, Rockefeller soon found a contentment he had never known and, over time, a purpose in life—not just a purpose, but also a mission that went beyond distributing some of the vast inherited wealth to good causes, the *noblesse oblige* embraced by all of the Rockefeller family. Soon after he had redeveloped Petit Jean by moving tons of topsoil to the mountaintop for the farm and pasturelands, building an airstrip, and turning the estate into an agricultural showplace, he was approached by the state's new governor, Orval E. Faubus, about supervising the state's fledgling industrial program. The legislature had created the Arkansas Industrial Development Commission in 1955 and gave it an office in the Capitol, from which it was to recruit industry and jobs to the state. Faubus, who figured the cachet of the Rockefeller name would give the state a leg up against other Southern states, made Winthrop the chairman. Back in New York, he had headed a couple of fundraising drives and found that he actually enjoyed asking rich and important people to do things for philanthropic causes—*really* enjoyed it. He did the same at the AIDC, or from Petit Jean. He called executives who were known to be looking for expansion sites, and he made cold calls to CEOs and board chairmen at random industries just to make a pitch for their doing something in Arkansas. He had moved to Arkansas himself and found it rewarding—good climate, hard-working people, cheap energy, beautiful scenery. Often he would appeal to their charitable instincts. "Dammit, people need industry and jobs down here."

Industry and jobs did come. Many were cut-and-sew apparel operations or food-processing companies that paid barely more than minimum wage, but that was what the Arkansas population seemed capable of supporting. For counties and towns that had been losing population for thirty years, a shirt or shoe factory that hired thirty people, mostly at the minimum wage, was a nice dividend. If Arkansas did not have the least-educated and unhealthiest population in the country, it at least shared the bottom with Mississippi and West Virginia. Rockefeller became progressively obsessed with that equation. Real progress was not going to be made until those problems, especially education, were addressed and until opportunity was opened to African Americans. The family's philanthropy, through the Rockefeller Sanitary Commission, had ended the hookworm epidemic across the South and aided black colleges. Since visiting the Hampton Institute, a normal (teacher training) school for African American young men, when he was himself in prep school, Winthrop had pledged part of his allowance to the school every year. Within a year of settling on Petit Jean, Rockefeller gave the nearby city of Morrilton $1.2 million to build a new elementary school, built and staffed a medical clinic in the tiny adjoining county seat of Perryville, and gave hundreds of thousands of dollars to public and private colleges across the state.

After Faubus, against Rockefeller's advice, deployed soldiers to prevent integration at Central High School, Rockefeller persuaded himself that the economic and social transformation that had become a life mission could only be brought about by a political revolution. The old conservative order supported by the Democratic Party would have to be challenged by an invigorated Republican Party, which had been a walking corpse since 1895. He would have to lead the revolution, starting with his own party.

Having transfigured the party and then vanquished the Old Guard, at least nominally, Rockefeller took the oath of office the morning of January

10, 1967, and stood at the threshold of the "Era of Excellence" that he would promise a couple of hours later in his inaugural speech at the Robinson Auditorium. He had by then only half-formed ideas about how he expected to reach the sanctified era—vast investments in education at every level, in health services and in highways, reforms in the prison system, and higher taxes to pay for all of them—but he did little more than hint at them in his inaugural speech or, except for prisons, anytime during the long legislative session that followed—or, indeed, during his two-year term. He had found all his own ideas embraced and fortified in a study requested by Governor Faubus and the legislature in the fall of 1964 and published in a book called *Accelerating Economic Growth in Arkansas*. Faubus had appointed ten conservative businessmen and a country lawyer to the Arkansas Economic Expansion Study Commission, which was staffed by the University of Arkansas College of Business (that was long before Walmart and the Walton heirs acquired the college) and economists at the Industrial Research and Extension Center at Little Rock. The exhaustively researched 186-page report debunked the notion that industrial growth depended upon low taxes. Both logic and many studies, it said, suggested that state and local tax rates had little to do with either investment decisions or locations. If they did, Arkansas and other poor Southern states would already have been the richest and most industrialized in America, because their tax rates and per-capita tax loads were generally the lowest in the country. A few natural factors like geography could not be altered easily by government, but the climate and population growth in parts of the South were making the region more inviting to industry. The most important thing the state could do, the report said, was make a great investment in the state's poor and unproductive schools. State and local governments needed to invest far more in health-care systems and the transportation infrastructure. It suggested that cities and counties be given more taxing powers and that the state make greater and fairer use of personal and corporate income taxes, by which it apparently meant more graduated tax rates and brackets. Faubus immediately had the legislature in 1965 implement one of its recommendations, instituting a withholding system for personal income taxes. These eleven conservative commission members—big names in Arkansas business and each appointed by the governor or the legislature—shared, with business economists, Rockefeller's own bold ideas about taxation and investment in public services as he took office. What could go wrong?

A lot, his Arkansas advisers convinced him that January. The General Assembly comprised 132 Democrats and only three Republicans—not one of them in the Senate—and they were not going to be as hospitable as Rockefeller expected, either to his ideas or to the potential opposition that he and his two-party movement posed to most of them. Whatever were their own thoughts about his program, the men who assembled around Rockefeller—Dr. John Peterson, an economist; lawyers G. Thomas Eisele, Marion B. Burton, Bob K. Scott, and Robert Faulkner; and others, like newspaperman and publicist John Ward—thought he had to get over the shoals of distrust before asking lawmakers to adopt a program requiring much higher taxes, which most Arkansas voters were apt to hate. After he was gone, Rockefeller's advisers would describe the naïveté that he evinced, an almost childlike trust that people would either see the wisdom in what he wanted to do or else appreciate the sincerity and nobility of his effort. In two books that Ward wrote about Rockefeller's life, political career, and philanthropy, he described the boss's naïveté. Even when he grasped the political difficulties that his ideas faced, Rockefeller would be defiant, chiding his men for surrendering so easily to the negativists and defeatists, particularly on taxes.

"Dammit, we can do better than this," he would say. Right was worth fighting for. That battle would consume his second term, which he had promised from the outset would be his last. It would be his last chance to make his dream a reality.

Reality of a different sort arrived quickly in his first term. While the inaugural platitudes about introducing efficiency and integrity into state government earned good marks from nearly everyone, including Democratic legislators, Rockefeller introduced a few symbols of the change he intended on the first day. The flagbearing honor guard at his inauguration was integrated—a black soldier and a white soldier—and blacks had prominent roles in the inaugural ceremony, including a ringing dedicatory solo, "My Task" by Dorsey McCullough, a student at Philander Smith College. Several hundred African Americans were in the inaugural crowd. Rockefeller avoided any civil rights declarations but said he was going to bring African Americans into the government. Only 325 held jobs in the government that day, all in menial positions, but the number would rise to 1,800 by the time he left office in 1971, 170 of them in administrative positions. He promised better pay for teachers, prison reform, a merit system for state employees to end political patronage, state participation in the new federal Medicaid program to provide medical care for the poor, and a study of efficiency in government and of the need for constitutional revision.

Things went awry from the very start. On the first day of the new government, before Rockefeller was sworn in, Faubus sent to the Senate ninety-three appointments to state boards and commissions where terms were expiring and confirmation by the Senate was required. Ordinarily, outgoing governors left those appointments to their successors, even when they had been defeated by their successors, who, of course, had always before been from the same party. Rockefeller, operating from offices across the street in the National Old Line Building, sent a hasty note to the Senate asking it not to confirm the appointees until he had a chance to review them and to submit his own nominees. The Senate—thirty-five Democrats and no Republicans—retired into executive session, closed to the press, to discuss the situation and then confirmed all of Faubus's appointees. Rockefeller expressed his displeasure, and senators complained that he was using them as foils to build the Republican Party and to beat them in 1968. The third floor of the Capitol, particularly the south end where the senators dwelled, proved for four years to be a particularly inhospitable place for the governor.

A month into the legislative session, on February 10, the Senate went into one of its fairly regular private sessions where senators usually aired their grievances with the executive branch, such as a complaint by Senator Fred Stafford of Marked Tree that Rockefeller's new revenue commissioner, Bethel Larey, had fired a friend of the senator in the local revenue office. Stafford wanted the Senate not to confirm Rockefeller appointees to boards and commissions until he got satisfaction. When it emerged from the February 10 executive session, the Senate appointed former state Representative Glenn F. Walther of Little Rock, who had been defeated by another Democrat in the recent election, to the three-member Public Service Commission, which regulates utilities. An old statute allowed the Senate to make appointments to boards and commissions in the executive branch when governors did not make an appointment within thirty days of the end of a commissioner's term, but the Senate had never before exercised that option. Rockefeller simultaneously sent up his own nominee, Robert Downie, a Little Rock lawyer, but the Senate said it was a few minutes too late. A protracted legal battle followed. The Supreme Court, all Democrats, eventually ruled that, despite the timing, the appointment was Rockefeller's call and the job was Downie's. Allowing the legislature to perform an executive function violated the constitutional doctrine of separation of powers. The dispute only hardened the hostility between the chamber and the governor.

Unintentionally, I contributed to the animosity. Beginning with the Senate's first executive meeting on the first day of the session, it was the duty of reporters to find out what part of the public's business the senators were conducting behind closed doors. It was not hard at first. I would talk to Senator Robert Harvey of Swifton, an earnest conservative farmer who could not lie, or Senator William D. Moore, a former schoolteacher and union organizer in my hometown, who, if no one was within earshot, would confide what the topic of the secret meeting was: Senator Stafford, or Senator Guy H. "Mutt" Jones of Conway, or Senator Q. Byrum Hurst of Hot Springs had some grievance with the governor's office or the House of Representatives, usually an appointee to some board or commission from the aggrieved senator's district. When I approached him, the flustered senator then would have to explain his grievance to me, and I could put together a story for the paper.

Eventually, the Senate had an executive session to talk about the leaks from its private conversations and the possibility of a "bug" in the Senate chamber. The chairman of the Efficiency Committee, Senator Max Howell of Little Rock, reported to colleagues that Senate staffers had found what could have been the remnants of a monitoring contraption in a cushion on the press row to the side of the chamber. Senators also were warned about their obligation to be loyal to their colleagues and not to talk to reporters about what happened in the closed sessions. Everyone clammed up and didn't want to be seen talking to any reporter after a session. I noticed that the Associated Press had a telephone in the press room on the Capitol's first floor, and another on the reporter's desk off the well of the Senate, about four feet from my desk. The AP phones were connected. After we were chased out of the chamber at one session, I asked George Bartsch, the AP reporter, if he could just leave the receiver on his Senate phone open by putting an eraser under it so that the receiver did not depress the buttons that disconnected it. Could he then go to the pressroom two floors below, pick up his phone there, and perhaps hear enough of the discussion in the Senate to give us a clue about what was being discussed? A couple of days later, another executive session was called and we were ushered out of the chamber. Bartsch rushed up to me and said, "I did it." We went to the pressroom and, sure enough, we could hear the voices of senators who were near the well of the Senate. You could pick up enough of the conversation to figure out what the topic was and then glean enough facts from reluctant senators to fashion an article.

When the Senate resolved itself into its eighth executive session—the February 10 meeting in which it plotted to usurp Rockefeller's PSC appointment—Senator Dan T. Sprick of Little Rock told his colleagues as we were ushered out, "We might as well let the members of the press stay in here, because they're going to know everything that goes on anyway." When we reached the pressroom, Bartsch picked up his phone and scribbled down a raging speech that Sprick was making from his front-row desk a few feet from the AP's open phone line. Sprick insinuated that some senator was ratting on all his colleagues to reporters and that he hoped the senator, "whoever you are, carry your guilty feelings to your grave." From the muted discussions that followed, we gathered enough shards of comments to know that Rockefeller had failed to deliver his PSC appointment to the Senate by the thirtieth day and that they would need to act hastily to fill the job before he did. They appointed Walther.

A couple of days later, Sprick took the floor again, this time to condemn Bartsch, me, and the *Arkansas Democrat* reporter Bob Sallee as the mysterious "Senate bugs" who had set up a listening system to spy on the Senate, in collaboration with Winthrop Rockefeller. Sprick, who carried an elegant silver cigarette holder made fashionable by Holly Golightly in *Breakfast at Tiffany's*, walked to the press area and, pointing a finger in each of our faces, identified us by name as Rockefeller's co-conspirators. Poor Sallee, who knew about our listening arrangement but never participated in the coy newsgathering, for the expedient reason that his newspaper would not appear until the late afternoon of the following day, could only blush and shake his head. Sprick particularly hated my employer, the *Gazette* (he later sued the paper for slander), and me by association. Any question I ever asked him was met by a glare and silence. He told the Senate that he had followed us out of the chamber during the executive session on February 10 and down the stairs to the pressroom. The aging senator claimed to have clambered into an elevated flower bed outside the pressroom window, watched us on the AP's pressroom phone, and then run back inside the Capitol and followed us up the steps to the governor's office, which we entered. He said we alerted Rockefeller to the Senate's plan to fill the PSC vacancy in a few minutes. The senators all knew it was a yarn, because Sprick had stayed in the chamber during the executive session that day and actually introduced the resolution appointing Glenn Walther to the

PSC job, but they were happy to believe that Rockefeller was involved in some kind of treachery with reporters to foil their plan. It was a fine show on Sprick's part, and the AP carried Bartsch's straightforward account of it. My alarmed mother, reading in the *El Dorado Daily News* that her boy was the Senate bug, telephoned to see if I was going to jail for wiretapping the Senate.

For Rockefeller, the disillusionment was unending. He enjoyed a little success at lawmaking in the first legislative session. The legislature adopted his plan to consolidate fiscal agencies under one director and created a couple of "blue ribbon" study commissions—the usual resort when the state confronts intractable political issues. One commission studied conditions in the state penitentiary, and the other pondered the condition of the state's 1874 constitution and actually wrote a model constitution. The Constitutional Revision Study Commission recommended holding a convention to write a new constitution. The legislature put the question to voters at the 1968 general election and, to nearly everyone's surprise, it passed. An elected body of 100 delegates rewrote the state constitution, modeling it after the U.S. Constitution and stripping the old state charter of provisions that were written by post-Reconstruction and Great Depression–era politicians to curtail the powers of the government, particularly the governor. In 1970, Rockefeller would campaign for the new constitution as heartily as he would for his own re-election, but the same voters who defeated him by a margin of almost two to one also rejected the constitution that he thought would unshackle the government so that it could address the needs of the people. It magnified his grief and sense of failure.

Where he did not need the acquiescence of legislators, like toughening regulatory agencies that for years had taken a *laissez-faire* approach to their job of protecting consumers, Rockefeller had a modicum of success. He put John Norman Harkey, a Marine Corps Vietnam veteran and the prosecuting attorney at Batesville, who had been fined three years earlier for manhandling a policeman in a nightclub brawl at Hot Springs, in charge of the state Insurance Department and Don S. Smith, a Stamps boy who was teaching law at Emory University at Atlanta, in charge of the state Securities Division. Together, they revoked the charters of scores of crooked insurance companies and shut down dozens of broker dealers who watered stock and sold worthless securities. It was Smith who sicced the federal Securities and Exchange Commission on Arkansas Loan and Thrift Corporation, which cheated more than two thousand people out of their life savings.

More vexing for Rockefeller, who expected to introduce gravity as well as probity into the high reaches of government, was that his first term turned into an unending burlesque, owing mainly to two issues that had thrust themselves into his successful political campaign: gambling and prison corruption.

Although Rockefeller had relentlessly accused Faubus of allowing gambling—which was illegal except at racetracks—to flourish at Hot Springs and other places in their 1964 race, he was not a moralist on the issue. Faubus often accused Rockefeller of being a hypocrite because he owned a casino in Puerto Rico, a rumor apparently based on his brother Laurance Rockefeller's ownership of property in San Juan that included the Dorado Beach Hotel, which furnished gambling paraphernalia. Rockefeller swore he had no gambling interests, but Faubus was undeterred. When he took office in 1967, Rockefeller simply said that if people anywhere in the state found gambling in the community "obnoxious" he would shut it down. Early in the legislative session, Senator Q. Byrum Hurst, a lawyer friend of Owney Madden, the former New York mob boss, went to see the governor along with several other legislators, including Senators Sprick, Howell, and Oscar Alagood, all of Little Rock. Hurst had drawn up a bill to legalize casinos at private clubs in Hot Springs, tax their proceeds, and create a state commission to regulate them. The senators would later insist that Rockefeller had told them that if they could pass such a bill in both houses he would not veto it, although he might not sign it. In Arkansas, a bill becomes law without the governor's signature unless he vetoes it within five days of the bill's arrival in his office. The sponsors privately assured legislators from conservative rural sanctuaries that Rockefeller would not veto it and make an issue of their gambling votes, and they passed it in both houses. Legislators' constituents opposed gambling, but if Rockefeller signed it or let it become law, that would give them some political cover to vote for the bill. As soon as the House passed the bill, Hurst carried it to the governor's office to start the five days until it would become law. But the *Arkansas Gazette* editorial page went on a rampage. The *Gazette* roared against every form of gambling, including lotteries, until the newspaper's death in 1991. The editorials demanded that Rockefeller veto the bill, and on the final day he did. Legislators, especially in the Senate, claimed that the governor had betrayed them. If it were possible, relations with the legislative branch ebbed further.

And the melodrama continued. Jack Baker, a young reporter for the *Ga-*

zette, and Michael B. Smith, who reported for the *Pine Bluff Commercial*, were in a legislative committee room a few days later when they heard Representative J. Gayle Windsor of Little Rock mutter that he had been offered "ten bills"—commonly understood to mean ten $100 bills, or $1,000—to vote for the gambling bill. Both wrote stories about it without, at first, identifying Windsor as the legislator who was offered the bribe. Windsor wouldn't tell them who offered the bribe. The reporters implied that other legislators had been approached with a similar bargain. A felony had been reported on the front page of the morning paper, so the prosecuting attorney for Pulaski County, Richard B. Adkisson, summoned a grand jury and demanded that the two reporters identify the sources for their stories. Neither would say, and Circuit Judge William J. Kirby put them in jail until they spilled the names. I took Baker a couple of pairs of clean underwear, which he shared with Smith. Both were in a cell with James Dean Walker, the charismatic cop murderer whose religious conversion and exploits in and out of prison captivated people for a decade. Justice George Rose Smith of the Supreme Court soon ordered the release of the reporters. Windsor then volunteered that it was he whom the reporters had overheard and he went before the grand jury. So did Representative Bill G. Wells of Hermitage, although Wells said he had been offered the money as a campaign contribution, which he figured was a perfectly legal form of bribery. Wells was the Democratic nominee for lieutenant governor the next year. The grand jury and Adkisson concluded that no felony had been committed that the state could prove.

In the spring, Rockefeller appointed a thirty-three-year-old FBI agent from Texarkana, Lynn A. Davis, as director of the State Police. Legislators disputed the appointment because Davis had not been a legal voting resident of the state for the past ten years, as the law seemed to require of State Police directors. Eventually, the state Supreme Court held that Davis did not fulfill the residency requirement and the legislature refused to amend the law to make him eligible. But his short career during the legal battle provided more circus. Davis led troopers in the Criminal Investigation Division on a raid of clubs at Hot Springs and, with television cameras grinding, he and his men smashed the confiscated slot machines and put them on a bonfire. It marked the end of open gambling in the city until it reopened under Governor Mike Huckabee in 2005 under the guise of "games of skill."

But Davis wasn't through. One night he led troopers on a raid of back-room gambling businesses on the southern edge of Little Rock. They arrested twelve persons and charged them with gambling operations. The prosecuting attorney summoned Davis before another grand jury and asked him to say who tipped the police on the gambling. He refused and Judge Kirby had him locked up. This time, Rockefeller went to the jail and managed to pull Davis out of his cell to join him at a press conference, where the governor lamented, "No one can be pleased about this jailing, except gamblers and hardened criminals." The Supreme Court sprang Davis, but then shortly ruled that he was holding his job illegally. Davis would go on to practice law, write detective thrillers based on his experiences at the FBI and as chief of the Arkansas troopers, and serve as U.S. marshal for the Eastern District of Arkansas.

ㅁㅁㅁ

Rockefeller's striving to civilize the state penitentiary proved to be an even gaudier burlesque than the gambling crackdown, but on an international stage. Few in the legislature and probably few in Arkansas shared Rockefeller's notion that prisons needed to be humane zones where recalcitrants could be trained in the arts of chivalry and citizenship—"coddling" was the common word for it—but the shocking stories in Faubus's State Police report about the prisons had ended the reflexive defense of the Arkansas penitentiary as a model of efficiency. Rockefeller appointed John H. Haley, a liberal lawyer at the Rose, Meek, House, Barron, Nash and Williamson law firm at Little Rock, chairman of the five-member state Penitentiary Board. The other four members were holdover Faubus men who defended the institutions under their supervision.

While sharing Rockefeller's urgency to do something about the corruption and brutality, Haley was a little like John Norman Harkey, the brawling prosecutor who was Rockefeller's insurance commissioner. He liked bold risks. State Police investigators had reported suspicions and provided some evidence that paroles and cushy prison assignments were sold, and that for a little money inmates might get their records altered so that they earned extra good time and early releases. A young lawyer named Jim Guy Tucker, later a prosecutor himself, had just gone to work at the Rose firm. He headed Young Democrats for Rockefeller in the 1964 race against Faubus and did a couple of tours in Vietnam as a freelance reporter. Haley arranged fake commitment papers for a small-time criminal with the pseudonym "James Gus Turner," gave Tucker a few small bills, and had him hauled down to Cummins wearing some old clothes and a couple of days of stubble on his dimpled chin. Trusty inmates maintained the prison's records. The new prisoner was processed and his money was collected and held for him until his release. Tucker, a Harvard graduate, was assigned the next morning to the kitchen, where he helped an angry inmate chop up chickens. He was approached by the inmate who kept prisoner records and told that, if he was willing to forfeit the few bills he brought to the prison, his record might be altered so that his release would come a little early. Sure, Tucker said. Haley went to Rockefeller and told him proudly that he had planted Tucker inside Cummins to get evidence of the corruption. The governor exploded.

"Goddamn it," Rockefeller was reported to have said, "go down and get him out of there right now." All he needed, he said, was for some innocent kid to get his throat cut down there. Tucker's prison career lasted about forty-eight hours.

Barely a month into his governorship, Rockefeller had the chief at the Tucker unit, Pink Booher, fired; he then hired a thirty-nine-year-old criminology professor named Thomas O. Murton to run it. Murton had studied animal husbandry and mathematics and obtained a master's degree in criminology and penology at the University of California at Berkeley, where he did some research on the Alaska penal system. When Arkansas called, he was teaching criminology at Southern Illinois University at Carbondale.

Murton was slender, bespectacled, and soft-spoken, which belied a toughness and a deeply distrustful nature. Prison societies inevitably cultivate conspiratorial and paranoid dispositions, and Murton was particularly susceptible. When you met him, you knew this was not to be a job but a crusade, maybe one to change the world. He settled into a job where he was surrounded at all times by criminals, some of them armed, and few civilians. He knew who the real enemies were—the people in public positions who protected the venal and brutal correctional system. He didn't give much countenance to any of them, at times even to his boss, the governor. One day a month or so after Murton's arrival, I climbed on a bus with legislators who were going down to inspect the prison units at Cummins and Tucker for themselves and to gather evidence that the prisons were not nearly as corrupt and barbaric as the State Police investigators, Rockefeller, and now Murton maintained. At Cummins, Superintendent

Bishop met them in front of the prison administration building, where the grounds were neatly manicured. Inside, the halls were clean, and beds in the massive barracks were neatly made while the men could be glimpsed in the distance happily tending the crops, probably singing "Old Man River." The lawmakers were served superb meals while prisoners waved towels at their backs to stir up breezes to keep away the flies and the stifling heat. The whole place was Cap'n Bishop's pride and joy. Bishop had always been a likeable fellow. He had been the Union County sheriff when I visited him every day at the courthouse as a teenage reporter at the *El Dorado Daily News* in 1954.

When the bus arrived after lunch at the Tucker unit, Murton did not lead a welcoming party as Bishop had done at Cummins. The landscaping outside the administrative unit needed tending and watering. We finally climbed out of the bus and a guard let us inside out of the heat, or rather into the airless heat of the administrative unit. Murton could not be found at first but finally met the legislators in a stifling room with metal chairs and folding tables. There was nothing deferential about his manner. He wore blue jeans and a work shirt. Murton guessed that over at Cummins everything was spic and span and the barracks looked like they were ready for inspection. He was busy, he said, and had made no special preparation for them. You want to see what a prison is like?, he asked. This is it. He let the legislators tour Death Row, where inmates awaiting execution were held. Someone asked about the electric chair. Murton had dismantled Old Sparky and stored it in a closet. (Several months later, Murton asked the Board of Corrections to stop a $100 monthly retainer paid to a technician at radio station KLRA at Little Rock to be available to operate the death machine whenever the state needed to kill someone, but George Douthit, the Capitol reporter for the *Arkansas Democrat*, protested that the technician, who was his golfing partner, needed the money and would be hard to replace when the board needed an executioner. The board relented.) Murton made it clear that he had better things to do than entertain the legislators. They climbed back on the bus for Little Rock in a foul mood, entertaining yet another grievance against the governor.

Murton granted Rockefeller little more deference than he did the lawmakers, and the governor began to have private misgivings about hiring the crusader, as much as he admired his zeal and ideas. Murton publicly criticized Bishop's operations at the larger Cummins unit near Grady, referred to state legislators with sarcasm, told Arkansas reporters and the national media how rotten the prisons were before he came, and sometimes took an oblique slap at Rockefeller, his boss. When Bishop quit and Rockefeller sent word that Murton should be promoted to the Cummins unit and perhaps to be put in charge of both prison farms, the holdover Faubus appointees to the Board of Corrections resigned. The legislature, at Rockefeller's request, had amended the penitentiary's appropriation to include the position of commissioner of corrections. Murton said Rockefeller had promised him the job, but Rockefeller by then had decided Murton did not have the temperament for the job. Rockefeller learned one day that his prison superintendent was in Berkeley, California, talking to the media about the lousy Arkansas prisons and complaining about the lack of support from Rockefeller. "My patience has worn thin," Rockefeller said, when an Arkansas reporter asked him about Murton's California visit.

Since arriving at Cummins, Murton had made friends with many inmates and, indeed, had become a hero to much of the prison population, except the trusties he had stripped of power. One friend was Reuben Johnson, a fifty-nine-year-old Pine Bluff man who had been in prison for thirty-two years for murdering his brother and holding up a liquor store. Johnson told Murton—and then national reporters who descended on the prison at the end of January 1968—that he had witnessed prison guards and armed trusties killing many prisoners who fell behind in their payments to guards. They were buried on the grounds and sugar cane was planted on top of them. Murton had told Rockefeller's prison aide, Bob K. Scott, that he was sure there were murdered prisoners buried all over the Tucker and Cummins fields. Scott was dubious but told him, "Well, dig 'em up." Murton had men digging holes across the prison farm at Tucker during his tenure at that unit in 1967 but found no bodies.

On January 31, 1968, reporters from the *New York Times* and other media, having been tipped by Murton, showed up at Cummins when the digging started. Rockefeller was shocked to hear about it during the day. Reuben Johnson and Murton led everyone to a spot on the back side of Cummins where there were rows of depressions in the ground. With TV cameras grinding, inmates dug up three skeletons in rotted wooden boxes. Johnson announced that he was present when one of the men was shot and that he had helped bury him there. There were more depressions, but it started raining and the digging stopped for the day. Johnson and Murton said there were probably two hundred men buried in the pastures and cane fields at the prisons. The story went around the world.

The harshest reporting that day and for the next few weeks was done by Walter Rugaber, a lanky, drawling reporter for the *New York Times* at Atlanta whom Murton had cultivated. Rugaber was at Cummins the morning of the digging, ahead of the Little Rock media. He would later become editor and publisher of newspapers at Raleigh, North Carolina, and Roanoke, Virginia. When Rockefeller hesitated to release a State Police report on its investigation of the graves and the sordid tales of Reuben Johnson and other inmates, Rugaber wrote about his own study of the prisons. It appeared on the front page of the *Times* on March 28 under the headline "Arkansas Prisons: A Grisly Record."

"It is a picture," Rugaber began, "of prison officials yielding to the darkest strains of the human spirit, of inmates trapped in a nightmare of cruelty and fear."

On the day the graves were opened, Rockefeller was furious that Murton had called the press and begun the digging without his authorization or knowledge and without getting the required court order to open a grave. The head of the Criminal Investigation Division of the State Police, Major William C. Struebing, was on hand for the unearthing and said it was obvious that the graves were part of a paupers' cemetery that preceded the prison farm. Remnants of makeshift headstones lay around, and a shard of one nearby marker indicated that the person below had been buried in 1926. Rockefeller speculated that afternoon that the skeletons probably were inmates who had died of natural causes and whose bodies were not claimed. A few weeks later, the assistant state medical examiner, Dr. Rodney Carlton, said there was no evidence two of the men had been killed and that the third skeleton probably had been damaged when the grave collapsed. He said they had been buried twenty-five to thirty years and perhaps longer.

Rockefeller ordered Murton to open no more graves until the State Police had investigated and found evidence that crimes had been committed and also until it could be determined whether it had been a crime for Murton to open a grave without a court order. Murton was furious. He demanded that he be promoted to the new job of commissioner of corrections, but Rockefeller sent the corrections board a letter strongly recommending that Murton not get the job. Moreover, he said Murton had demonstrated that he was not qualified for any job in the prison system, because he had shown "callous disregard for the problems of his equals and his superiors."

The Board of Corrections—John Haley and four new Rockefeller appointees who replaced the four who had resigned—gathered at the Cummins unit on March 7. One of the new appointees was the Reverend William Lytle of Clarksville, a Presbyterian minister who had married the Murtons in New Mexico fourteen years earlier and whom Murton had urged the governor to appoint to the board. Murton brought the board a petition signed by more than a thousand prisoners supporting him. The board met privately with Murton for two hours and offered to let him stay on if he agreed to surrender any control of the farm operations, which he refused to do. It reconvened in open session and voted to fire him immediately.

It was a chaotic scene. Murton's wife, Margaret, and a sister of Murton visiting from New Mexico arrived, and Murton, half sobbing, told them that he had been fired. They hugged and cried. Ronnie Crabtree, an inmate friend of Murton who worked in the Cummins infirmary, walked down to the board room and the superintendent's adjoining office. Murton and the prisoner embraced and sobbed on the other's shoulder. Margaret Murton hugged Crabtree and said, "You're the best friend we've had in this state."

Murton told me about the petition from the inmates and said, "These men laid their lives on the line to help me and now their lives are in danger." Margaret Murton confronted Rev. Lytle and the other board members when they filed out of the meeting room. She sarcastically referred to each of them as "our *friend!*" and congratulated them on "my husband's lynching." She demanded to know how Lytle, who had married them, could have betrayed them. When Victor C. Urban, a Murton assistant whom the board named as his temporary replacement, appeared, she shouted, in words dripping with sarcasm, "Honey, so good to see you, and I want to tell you how much we *love* you." Four of Murton's employees, members of the same family, announced to reporters that they were quitting on the spot. When Marshall Rush of Pine Bluff, a Republican board member, emerged into the hall Mrs. Murton told him: "The only honest Arkansans I have met in this state are the inmates. I thank God for the experience of having known them."

Murton usually considered reporters his friends, or at least sympathizers, as I suppose we probably were. The Murtons moved in a few days to Oklahoma, where they settled for a time. About a week later, I received a telephone call from him. He had telephoned the *Gazette* to get the daily paper mailed to him in Oklahoma and apparently reached a clerk in the circulation department, who told him that the paper didn't take orders by phone without payment. He would need to send a check for a six-month subscription and include his address. Murton was outraged. He told me that he should have expected that "they" would get to the *Gazette,* too. I tried to explain that the woman probably did not even know who he was but was merely following the protocol for mail subscriptions. Why didn't he just... I had joined the cabal, too. Murton hung up abruptly and I never heard from him again.

But Rockefeller and the world did. That winter, Murton appeared before a U.S. Senate subcommittee in Washington investigating prison conditions and resurrected all his accusations about the horrors in the Arkansas penitentiary, which he said were emblematic of the "monster-producing factories" that were American prisons. He said his thirteen months in the Arkansas prisons proved that they were festering with "inmate abuse and official corruption, including death threats, shooting of prisoners, gratuitous beating with rubber hoses, blackjacks, brass knuckles, lashings, kickings, sexual perversion, and other forms of punishment."

"The Negro prisoners were segregated in even worse facilities than the whites," he said. "They ate only the scraps from the table after the whites finished eating."

Rockefeller called the chairman of the subcommittee, Senator Thomas J. Dodd of Connecticut, and asked to have the new corrections commissioner, Robert Sarver, appear before the subcommittee and tell the real story of conditions in the Arkansas prisons and the reforms that had been achieved. Sarver did. He said the strap and other torture devices had been eliminated, beatings had halted, prison control had been taken away from inmate trusties, and food and living conditions had been improved. Sarver did not get the national attention that Murton did.

Tom Murton never landed another job in a prison, but he wrote a best-selling book, *Accomplices to the Crime* (1969), about his Arkansas experiences. Hollywood turned Murton's story into the popular film *Brubaker,* starring Robert Redford. On the screen, the legendary actor bore little resemblance to the volatile and frenetic reformer. The movie, which left no doubt that the skeletons were murdered prisoners and that the penologist was a genuine hero, was nominated for an Academy Award for best screenplay. The Murtons moved to Alaska in 1970, but he couldn't find a job and the family lived awhile on food stamps. Murton soon divorced his wife, moved to Oklahoma, and started raising livestock. He rarely saw their four children again. He wrote another book about his thirteen months in Arkansas, *Crime and Punishment in Arkansas: Adventures in Wonderland* (1985), but it did not sell. He died of cancer in Oklahoma City in 1990.

The prisons beleaguered Rockefeller for the rest of his short political career and the state for another twenty years. A federal grand jury indicted Murton's predecessor at the Tucker prison, Jim Bruton, other penitentiary employees, and six inmate trusties for torture and generally violating the rights of inmates. A doughty prosecutor, Bobby Fussell, told the jury at the end of his summation that if they condoned Bruton's and his men's brutality by finding them not guilty, "may the Lord have mercy on you on judgment day." The jury acquitted six inmates who were following Bruton's orders and could not come to a conclusion on Bruton. To avoid a new trial, Bruton agreed to plead no contest to violating inmate rights and to spend a year in prison and pay a fine. In the privacy of Judge J. Smith Henley's chambers, where the infamous Tucker Telephone rested as an exhibit, Bruton's attorney, Reggie Eilbott of Pine Bluff, argued to the judge that the old telephone magneto, which was hooked up to a prisoner's genitals and cranked, was actually relatively harmless. It wouldn't hurt a flea, he said. Fussell admitted he couldn't be sure about the pain it inflicted and suggested they hook it up to Eilbott and test it. Eilbott reluctantly agreed. When Fussell cranked the old phone vigorously, the attorney bellowed and admitted that it might in fact hurt a flea. Judge Henley waived Bruton's prison sentence, because he said Bruton would be certain to be killed in prison. Judge Henley would put the prisons under federal court supervision for another thirteen years.

Governors were still elected for two-year terms, and Rockefeller in 1968 faced the prospect of a campaign in which he would have little to brag about, except a few regulatory reforms, and much that would be difficult to defend. He had hired and then fired a penologist who seemed to have produced little except chaos and a cascade of scandals that brought the state more international disrepute. He had tried to raise a few taxes—notably on cigarettes, tobacco products, and real-estate transfers—but the Democratic legislature happily stomped all the bills, along with others that sought an end to anticompetitive protections for industries like liquor. A singular achievement was the enactment at a special legislative session in March 1968 of Arkansas's first minimum-wage law, a rare accomplishment for a Republican anywhere, then or now. It created a minimum wage of $1.20 an hour by 1970. Rockefeller had famously uttered the remark, "What do I owe labor?" after some criticism by J. Bill Becker, president of the Arkansas State AFL-CIO, but tossed the wage bill into the special session as a challenge to Democrats, who generally but undeservedly enjoyed the support of unions. His message to legislators on opening day was that they must, finally, deal with the historic "exploitation" of Arkansas workers, an amazing plea from a Republican politician. Cornered, the House of Representatives passed the bill 88 to 4 and the Senate 24 to 9. Rockefeller still never got an endorsement from a union.

Events seemed to conspire against his re-election. A week after he signed the minimum-wage law, Dr. Martin Luther King was murdered at the Lorraine Motel at Memphis, where he had gone to show support for the city's striking sanitation workers. Rockefeller stopped plans by African American leaders for a protest march through Little Rock, which he thought might invite violence, and instead organized a memorial prayer service for the fallen civil rights leader on the Capitol steps, his wife Jeanette's idea. In front of a crowd of some three thousand, mostly African Americans, he and his wife joined hands with black leaders and led the throng singing "We Shall Overcome." No other state political leader in the country—most notably not in the South—did such a thing at that disquieting moment, when riots and angry protests beset cities from San Francisco to Washington. Photographs of the governor and first lady holding hands with black activists and singing the civil rights anthem was on the front pages of Arkansas papers, as was his call for the state and the country to finally address the problems of racism.

"Maybe this tragic incident and the loss of this great moderate leader—a man who believed in peaceful leadership—will awaken the eyes and minds and hearts and souls of the people throughout the nation," he said.

It was not Rockefeller's only act of courage in the still racially disturbed climate that year. Six weeks before the election, Rockefeller pardoned three African American men for the rape of a white girl in North Little Rock seven years earlier. No black man in Arkansas had ever been pardoned for such a charge involving a white woman. They were accused of raping a teenaged girl who was in a parked car in a wooded white neighborhood with her boyfriend. Rockefeller concluded that the men were innocent— the evidence was tainted and lie-detector tests showed that all three men were truthful when they said they had not raped the girl. Ordinary politicians would have at least waited until after the election to sign the pardons.

Martin Luther King was not a universal icon in 1968, certainly not in Arkansas, and some of the governor's advisers cautioned that it would be political suicide to engage segregationists so openly, especially with a re-election campaign only weeks away. Rockefeller brushed them aside. What was the point of being governor if not to show leadership in a time like this?

Then he promptly called another special session of the legislature, to try again to pass a few taxes, set up procedures for a constitutional convention, appropriate more money for the prisons, and—notably—pass a law to give cities the authority to allow restaurants and clubs to serve alcoholic beverages.

After Rockefeller's address to the joint session the first morning, when, as always, he labored through his prepared text and jumbled a few words here and there, I approached a number of legislators for reaction to his proposals. Senator Clarence E. Bell of Parkin, who had been Faubus's floor leader in the Senate, remarked, "I thought he had at least two and maybe three shots too many" before addressing the legislators. Senator Richard Earl Griffin of Crossett, who was standing nearby, chimed in that it was too bad the voters of Arkansas could not hear the governor's pitiful performance. I went downstairs to the governor's office to get his response. I ran into his press secretary, William G. Conley, in the doorway of the governor's suite. He said Rockefeller had left immediately after the speech; what did I need of him? I told him about Bell's remarks.

"Ernie," he said, "I was with him all morning and he had one small shot before he came here." My notebook was in my hip pocket, and after Conley walked away I scribbled his comment down. My article carrying the quotations from Bell and Conley appeared at the bottom of the *Gazette*'s front page the next morning. The headline carried Bell's charge that the governor had two or three drinks too many before his speech. Governor Jeff Davis, "the Wild Ass of the Ozarks," as he was known, had bragged about drinking at the turn of the century and ridiculed the Pecksniffian prohibitionists, but no other governor had ever admitted a preference for strong drink, and especially not in the mansion, the People's House. The incident encouraged the old rumors of Rockefeller's drinking and carousing, and there were allusions to it in his last two campaigns.

Rockefeller talked to a North Little Rock civic club at noon after my article appeared and a club member asked him how many drinks he had before he addressed the legislators. He grinned sheepishly and held up one finger. At a press conference a few days later he acknowledged that the drinking issue was a political liability, but he said it would have been hypocrisy to deny that he had a drink, and he said that alcohol did not impair his ability to serve the people.

Years later, after retiring as a public relations representative for the Aluminum Company of America, Conley returned to Little Rock and we met in an aisle in the Kroger store in Hillcrest. He said my deception in quoting him about the "one shot" without his consent shortened his life and that it was a wonder he was still alive. He observed that I did not have a pad and pencil in my hand when I talked to him in the governor's doorway that day and he had no reason to suspect that I would quote him.

Early the next morning after the governor's speech, Conley said, he had been awakened by G. Thomas Eisele, the governor's attorney and chief adviser, who told him to write a letter of resignation and be at the Governor's Mansion in an hour. Conley said he asked why he was being fired. Eisele asked him if he had seen the morning paper. Conley hadn't. Read Dumas's article on the legislators' reaction to Rockefeller's speech, Eisele instructed him. Conley said he stepped outside in his pajamas and retrieved the *Gazette* from the front steps. His heart sank when he saw his quote.

In the living room of the mansion, Rockefeller's top aides—Eisele, John Ward, and others—had gathered, and they roundly rebuked Conley for making the comment. They said he might have ended any chance of the governor being re-elected. Conley protested that I did not have a pencil and notepad in my hand and that he had not expected me to quote him.

"He's a newspaper reporter," Ward said. "That's what reporters do. They quote you." Ward had been a reporter for the *Arkansas Democrat* and would later be editor of the *Log Cabin Democrat* at Conway.

Conley and the other aides recriminated for an agonizing couple of hours in the mansion living room before someone came in and said Rockefeller was awake so they could go into his bedroom. Rockefeller was sitting on the edge of the bed in his pajamas. Eisele handed him Conley's resignation letter. Why is Conley quitting? Rockefeller asked. Eisele handed him the *Gazette*, folded to my story about "two or three shots too many." Scratching his head, Rockefeller scanned the article and started giggling.

"Hell, I'm not going to fire Conley for lying for me," Rockefeller said. "He knows I had three drinks if I had one. Now, get the hell out of here. I've got to get dressed."

The legislature blocked his mixed-drink bill, many not wanting to vote for his liquor bill and give him a pass on his drinking before the election. Rockefeller said that if the legislature was not going to authorize local-option elections to legalize mixed drinks, he might just start closing all the private clubs where drinking already occurred illegally.

"It's all right with me," he said, "but, goddamn it, I'll guarantee you one thing and that is I'll close every one of the clubs and I will arrest Mutt Jones's bootlegger and if he doesn't think I know who he is, he's wrong. I'll put him out of business." (Guy H. "Mutt" Jones was the state senator from Conway and Rockefeller's most virulent critic. He was convicted of income tax evasion in 1973 and expelled from the Senate.) Having survived the ensuing election, Rockefeller in January 1969 sent the mixed-drink bill to the legislature again; that time it became law.

Rockefeller's re-election seemed foredoomed to me, but I nearly always gave the electorate too little credit. He was lucky in his opponent, state Representative Marion H. Crank of Little River County, a savvy and

Guy "Mutt" Jones

knowledegable legislator whose deeply tanned face seemed always to carry the visage of a man in considerable pain or suffering from chronic dyspepsia. Crank might have been a liberal in a different time. He was a New Deal Democrat, having served in Roosevelt's Farmers Home Administration during the Great Depression. After World War II, he worked in China for the United Nations advising destitute farmers on irrigation and conservation and providing tools and seed. Back in Little River County, he taught school and opened a drygoods store in the town of Foreman. Witt Stephens, the political kingmaker, started a concrete business there, Arkansas Cement Corporation. When Crank, by then a state representative, helped pass Stephens's bill in 1957 to allow Arkansas Louisiana Gas Company to recover a good price from ratepayers for the gas the company produced from its own wells, Stephens rewarded him by making him a public relations consultant for the gas company and vice president for the cement company, which won a lot of contracts providing cement for roadbuilding.

Had Crank not won the Democratic primary, the election might have turned out differently for Rockefeller. Two of the candidates were articulate progressives somewhat in the mold of Dale Bumpers, who would beat Rockefeller two years later. Ted Boswell, a trial lawyer at Bryant who had won some big personal-injury cases, was a fiery stump speaker, and Frank Whitbeck, a Little Rock insurance executive, was one of the authors of the 1964 report on economic development that proved to be an inspiration for Rockefeller. The other serious candidates were Bruce Bennett, the silver-haired attorney general who was under investigation for his role in the Arkansas Loan and Thrift scandal, and Virginia Johnson, wife of Jim Johnson, Arkansas's most strident and persistent segregationist. Crank led the ticket in the Democratic preferential primary, but Mrs. Johnson and Boswell were in a virtual tie for the runoff spot. Crank's campaign manager, Jack Gardner, told me years later that he was told late on election night that Bennett had consented during the night to have a precinct or two in his (and my) home county of Union switch Mrs. Johnson's and Bennett's votes, which put her in the second spot by 409 votes over Boswell. Crank's team surmised that the newcomer Boswell would be hard to beat, but that Mrs. Johnson would have limited appeal. Crank beat Mrs. Johnson, Arkansas's first female candidate for governor, nearly two to one in the runoff. He would be the perfect foil for the governor, whose ads and commercials often led with "Cranking up the Old Machine."

Boswell's team had collected some good material on Crank to use in the runoff. Warren K. Bass, a Boswell friend, passed it along to Rockefeller shortly before the general election. In the legislature, Crank had put his wife and three children on the House payroll every session, and Rockefeller prepared to use it during the two weeks before the election. Ernest Valachovic, a *Gazette* Capitol reporter with me, picked up hints of it, perhaps from Crank himself, and wrote about it on the front page of the paper. Even Crank's eight-year-old daughter was paid twenty dollars a day as a clerk for the House. Then it was discovered from House records that Crank's running mate, Representative Bill G. Wells of Hermitage, who had won the nomination for lieutenant governor, also had his family on the House payroll as pages. Wells's four-year-old son earned $88 a week while the lawmaker's more accomplished spawn, who was six, earned $112 a week. Rockefeller called it "the Crank Family Plan."

To be fair, it was not uncommon for legislators to put their wives and even their children on the House or Senate payrolls, for at the time the annual salary that the Constitution allowed lawmakers was only $1,200 a year. As the speaker, Crank was pulling down an extra $150 a year. (For comparison, legislative salaries have been raised in the modern Republican era to $41,394 a year, plus per-diem pay and expenses.) Crank and Wells both made the point over and over, and contrasted their plight as poor Arkies with Rockefeller's great inherited family wealth. Crank said he could not send his children to fancy boarding schools like Rockefeller did his son, Winthrop Paul. Rockefeller won with 52 percent, a margin of 30,000 votes.

Marion Crank

□□□

Rockefeller had promised repeatedly to serve only two two-year terms, so now he had to deliver the program that would transform Arkansas into a modern and prosperous society—the Era of Excellence he had talked about in his inaugural address. Before the General Assembly convened in January after the election, he resolved to mend relations with the Democratic legislature as best he could. He invited legislators in groups to overnight visits to his mountaintop estate, with its panoramic vista of the meandering Arkansas River and the Ozarks. They would visit the Santa Gertrudis operations and sale barn, feast, relax, and talk a little about legislating for the people. That turned sour, too. The legislators took souvenirs from the guest cottages: toothbrushes, monogrammed towels and washcloths, hair dryers, pens, and table decorations. The Petit Jean staff valued the missing amenities at more than $3,000. Rockefeller was incensed privately, but that made it into the newspapers, too. Legislators were either embarrassed or incensed that they were made to look like petty thieves. The 1969 session started no better than the first one in 1967.

In his opening talk to the General Assembly, Rockefeller was generous in laying out his ambitious program, inviting legislators to work with him, offer suggestions, and make it more workable. He had talked during the last campaign about the need for greater investment in services like education that raised people's prospects for prosperity. His election was a mandate. The tax program he outlined would increase the general revenues of the state the following year by a full 50 percent. The money would go to the public schools, colleges and universities, parks, prisons, and law enforcement, and provide matching funds for physical and mental health services under the Medicaid program created by Congress four years earlier. While he pleaded for help and consultation, he also challenged the lawmakers. Teacher salaries in Arkansas, he said, bordered on immoral. Go back and tell your teachers, he said, that there is no need for better salaries, equipment, and supplies.

"Tell the next of kin of one who has perished on a stretch of unpatrolled highway. Tell the untrained and uneducated parents who struggle in poverty and who look helplessly at its ravages on the bodies and minds of their children. Tell the mother and father of an unmanageable mentally retarded youngster."

"So long as thousands of our people go to bed hungry or in pain, or in hopelessness every night, nobody in Arkansas, myself included, has the right to be callous or indifferent," he added. His taxes and broadened education and health programs would give people a leg up.

He had a stack of tax bills that he invited legislators to sponsor. But it fell largely to the Republicans—Senator Jim Caldwell of Rogers, a liberal Church of Christ minister (yes, seriously), and three northwest Arkansas Republicans in the House—to sponsor the bills.

Arkansawyers paid the lowest per-capita taxes in the country. Rockefeller proposed that the personal income tax be raised from a top rate of 5 percent to 12 percent on incomes above $40,000 a year—the highest state marginal rate in the country, although he pointed out that it would reduce people's federal tax burden, particularly for the wealthy, by increasing their deductions. His bill would cut taxes on people with very low incomes. The bills also would raise the sales and use tax from 3 to 4 percent; broaden the tax to apply to all kinds of services like architects, physicians, accountants, and repairs; raise excise taxes on cigarettes, cigars, tobacco products, beer, and hard liquor; increase the fees for liquor and beer retail permits; impose a tax on real estate transfers; and turn over to the state treasury abandoned assets left in financial institutions and insurance companies. The sales tax law would be amended to give poor families an annual rebate.

All the tax bills sat in committees without action, and Rockefeller asked to address the legislators again in joint session. He made another appeal for the legislators to address people's needs. Still, only a few bills made it to the floor for a vote in either house. The Senate allowed the big one, to raise personal income taxes to a top marginal rate of 12 percent, to come to a vote although it came out of the Revenue and Taxation Committee without a recommendation. Only Senator Morrell Gathright of Pine Bluff, a Democratic businessman, arose to speak on the bill, other than the sponsor's introductory remarks. Gathright said he was prepared to vote for a truly progressive tax structure, but that the tight brackets in the governor's bill punished low-to-middle-income families and he could not vote for it. The sponsor and Rockefeller's Senate liaison stood nearby in silence, although the sponsor, Caldwell, was Gathright's seatmate. When Gathright finished, I beckoned to him from my desk beside the podium and showed him in the *Legislative Digest* that the bill had been amended from its original form to eliminate or reduce income taxes for lower incomes. Gathright looked abashed and when the roll was about to be called, he went to the lectern and said he had been mistaken about the bill's impact and that he felt compelled to vote for it. The bill failed 3 to 31. Caldwell and Ben Allen of Little Rock joined him in voting for the bill. My gift to Rockefeller for the assorted troubles I had caused him was a single vote in favor of the income tax.

After the collapse of the governor's program, the House speaker, Hayes C. McClerkin of Texarkana, put together a $19 million revenue package—small increases in the excise taxes on beer, cigarettes, cigars, chewing tobacco, and snuff; a hike in the corporate income tax from 5 to 6 percent on profits of more than $25,000; and a tax on real estate transfers. Rockefeller signed a couple of them into law, let the others become law without his signature, and refused to sign scores of appropriation bills because he considered them inadequate to meet the state's needs. He let them become law without his signature. Signing the appropriations, he said, would make him a party to the state's failure to provide adequate resources for anemic programs like education.

He brooded throughout the year and decided he had to try again. Rockefeller was sure, John Ward would write later, that the people of Arkansas were appalled at the legislature's acceptance of the status quo. He would call the legislature into special session in 1970, well before the election, and give the legislators one more chance. If they failed again, he would break his promise and run for a third term, certain that most voters were behind him.

When the lawmakers assembled again, this time mutely, Rockefeller had tougher words about their failure to fund education, health care, and the prisons. He mocked them for defending the efficiency of the prisons and the profitability of the old prison farms.

"Belsen and Buchenwald were profitable institutions, too," he said. "They turned out beautiful lampshades."

This time, even the income tax bills never reached the floor for a vote. John I. Purtle, a maverick lawyer from Little Rock who had sponsored Governor Sid McMath's income tax bill in 1949 in his first legislative incarnation and was a future justice of the Arkansas Supreme Court, handled Rockefeller's 12-percent bill in the House. It died in committee.

While Little Rock had long since moderated its racial tension and people everywhere had achieved some level of pacification about the inevitability of school integration, Rockefeller did not get to enjoy a respite of peace in his crucial second term. Black militancy, led by Christian ministers, surged and, of course, virulent white backlash arose in the most inevitable quarters—farm towns in the central Delta, like Marianna and Forrest City, the latter named after the Confederate general who was the first leader of the Ku Klux Klan. Rockefeller met with the ministers who led boycotts of white merchants, expressed some vague support for their cause, and sent emissaries to the towns to bring the two sides together. When the Forrest City schools fired the Reverend J. F. Cooley, a teacher and black minister who was the leading spokesman for the protesters, the city seemed on the verge of violent conflict. A skinny and lame black lad at Memphis who had made a local name for himself as a troublemaker announced that he was going to prove that no poor black person in the Delta needed to fear the white bosses.

Using the *nom de plume* Sweet Willie Wine, Lance Watson planned a one-man march from the Mississippi River at West Memphis across the Delta along U.S. Highway 70 all the way to the Capitol steps at Little Rock. His March Against Fear in the heat of August 1969 brought warnings and fears of violence. Mayor Jerry Screeton of Hazen, who also had been a state senator, banker, and school board president, declared that Watson would not make it through his town. Rockefeller wanted Watson to cancel or postpone his march, but Watson was undeterred. The governor sent state troopers to patrol Watson's 130-mile trek to see that nothing happened to him. Screeton's townspeople wore black shirts the day that Watson reached Hazen, and nearby farmers barricaded the streets with their tractors and combines. Prairie County Sheriff Socrates E. "Crate" Grady met the spindly young man at the Hazen city limits with the greeting, "Do your feet hurt, Willie?" and escorted him through town.

"I came, I saw, I walked through Hazen," Watson pronounced afterward, for the sake of modesty avoiding haughty Caesar's Latin version, *Veni, vidi, vici.* Sweet Willie remained an activist in the Memphis brotherhood, in his graying years taking on the name Dr. Suhkara A. Yahweh.

⊔⊔⊔

Rockefeller's efforts to mediate the racial conflicts, to moderate attitudes on both sides, to gradually lower the barriers to employment and participation in the cultural life of the state, were far more than any Southern governor or any major Southern elected official did during that period, but many African Americans were still disappointed in him. You could not imagine that those efforts improved his voter appeal as he approached a decision about whether to break his vow to serve only two terms and continue the quest for the transformative victories that was the cause of his running for governor the first time six years earlier.

Nearly everyone but Rockefeller saw the futility of his ambition to serve another term. Eight Democrats, including the still unvanquished Faubus, filed to run against him. Still unsure of Rockefeller's weakness, Faubus supporters devised a plan to knock him off in the Republican primary so that Faubus would not have to face the expensive Rockefeller campaign in November. Only 29,000 people had voted in the Republican primary in 1968, when Rockefeller beat an unknown Republican 28,000 to 1,000.

On the last filing day in 1970, three men walked into the Capitol to file against Rockefeller in his primary: James "Uncle Mac" MacKrell, a popular radio evangelist and pastor who had waged a colorful campaign for governor in 1948; Lester Gibbs, a folksy old man who had filed for office a couple of times; and the Reverend Reginald Jeffery Hampton of Little

Rock, a black preacher. Faubus's men figured that Hampton would get tens of thousands of black votes and they would swamp Rockefeller in his own primary. The preacher, who was president of Shorter College in North Little Rock, said Rockefeller had been a great disappointment to black people.

At the Capitol, I asked Hampton about rumors that one of Faubus's big backers, Jess P. Odom of Little Rock, an insurance executive and developer, had paid his filing fee and would bankroll his campaign. Hampton replied that he had been assured that Odom would be "kind" to him financially, but he wouldn't say if Odom had paid his filing fee. I called Jess Odom, who said he intended to help Hampton financially but that his focus would be on electing Faubus again. He, too, wouldn't say if he had paid Hampton's filing fee.

The *New York Times*, to which I contributed Arkansas news for about twenty years, maintained an interest in the prodigal son Rockefeller's adventures in forlorn Arkansas. It published my piece about Hampton running against Rockefeller in the Republican primary and Jess Odom's role. Odom had not expected his financial support for Rockefeller's opponent to reach the *Times*, which was widely read in the nation's capital. He called me and asked if I had written the *Times*'s story. I said I had. He pleaded with me to call the *Times* and get them to run a retraction and to say that he had nothing to do with Hampton's challenge to Rockefeller.

Odom had applied to the U.S. Department of Housing and Urban Development for government support for the development of Maumelle, the new city that he planned to build on the Arkansas River northwest of Little Rock. The government's New Town initiative was an outgrowth of Lyndon Johnson's Model Cities program. The Urban Growth and New Community Development Act, signed by President Richard Nixon earlier in the year, allowed HUD to guarantee bonds, debentures, and other obligations by private developers like Odom who were establishing new towns outside dense and eroding urban centers. Odom stood to get up to $50 million in federal assistance in building the infrastructure for Maumelle. A HUD official had read the *Times* article and telephoned Odom to express his displeasure that he was part of a scheme to oust a Republican governor and help Faubus get back into office. Odom apparently told him that it wasn't so.

While he did not deny what either he or Hampton had told me, Odom said that if I didn't get the *Times* to retract the story I would jeopardize a development that would be big for central Arkansas. I told Odom he was free to tell the Nixon administration that he was misquoted but that I couldn't ask the *Times* to retract a story that was true. He thought I had doomed his dream. Odom would win the HUD grants after all, and Maumelle became one of the few successful new towns established before the program was scrapped in 1978. Maumelle has grown to be an upscale city of 20,000.

If Rockefeller's popularity was in sharp decline, Orval Faubus's was not on the upswing. An upstart named Dale Bumpers, who began the primary race last in a field of eight, easily defeated Faubus in the Democratic runoff and crushed Rockefeller and the segregationist candidate of the American Party in the general election while spending little money and avoiding even the mildest criticism of the governor.

After the legislature rejected his tax program and nearly every initiative that he proposed in 1969 and the special session of 1970, Rockefeller abandoned political caution altogether and appointed John W. Walker, a black civil rights lawyer with unusually sharp elbows, to the state Board of Education. Walker would be the first-ever African American on the board that supervised the public schools of the state. Walker had taken over the longstanding Little Rock school integration suit and was filing lawsuits to desegregate schools and public facilities all over the state. The Senate refused to confirm his appointment. As a courtesy, the Senate had always confirmed appointees to boards and commissions if the senator from the person's district approved. The five Pulaski County senators were silent on Walker's appointment, at least publicly. Rockefeller then appointed Dr. William H. Townsend, head of the more moderate integration group, the Council on Community Affairs, to the board, but the Senate rejected him, too. As he was leaving office, Rockefeller sent the Senate the name of Rev. Emery Washington, a black Episcopal priest at Forrest City, for the vacant board seat. Upon taking office, Bumpers asked the Senate to confirm Washington instead of filling the seat himself, and it obliged. Bumpers would confess that he had never found fault with anything Rockefeller had done as governor. He already had reason to be grateful to his predecessor.

When he ran for governor the first time in 1964, Rockefeller said he was opposed to the death penalty and would never carry out an execution if he were elected. One of his last official acts, on New Year's Eve, was to commute the death sentences of all fifteen men who were awaiting execution. He said their records and the severity of their crimes bore no relevance to his decision, and he knew that his was an unpopular stand in Arkansas. He was simply opposed to the penalty.

"My position on capital punishment has been clear since long before I became governor," he said. "I am unalterably opposed to it and will remain so as long as I live. What earthly mortal has the omnipotence to say who among us shall live and who shall die? I do not. Moreover, in that the law grants me authority to set aside the death penalty, I cannot and will not turn my back on lifelong Christian teachings and beliefs, merely to let history run out its course on a fallible and failing theory of punitive justice."

Dale Bumpers breathed a great sigh of relief that day. With Death Row emptied, he would never have to face the dilemma of signing a death warrant.

The election returns and Bumpers's landslide, which seemed to repudiate Rockefeller so utterly, brought him another defeat that he also took as a personal rebuke. Voters rejected a new state constitution, for which he had campaigned almost as hard as for his own re-election. For four years, Rockefeller had invested heavily of his own money in efforts to bring about a constitutional convention and then to ratify all the reforms that the convention's delegates formulated. He had been persuaded by the crusade of Virgil J. Butler of Batesville, across two spans in the legislature forty years apart, to rewrite the 1874 constitution. Butler, joined by David Pryor, a freshman representative and law student from Camden, started introducing bills calling for a constitutional convention in 1961. Butler believed that the constitutional restraints, which were placed on government at every level in 1874 to stymie the progressive reforms of Arkansas Republicans during Reconstruction (and again in 1933 when Butler was a naïve young representative), were at least partly responsible for Arkansas's backward condition, which melded with Rockefeller's own notions and with his newfound mission in life. Butler and Pryor could never pass their constitution bills, but when Rockefeller included Butler's bill in his administrative program in 1967 the legislature passed it. The legislation created a blue-ribbon commission to study the Constitution and recommend changes. When the commission reported a model draft and recommended holding a convention, the legislature at a special session approved Rockefeller's bill scheduling an election on whether to hold a convention and to elect the one hundred delegates. Rockefeller secretly paid for most of the campaign for a favorable vote (donors were not reported in those days), and the issue passed narrowly.

It soon became clear that the delegates faced a nearly hopeless task, neutralizing constitutional issues that bitterly divided the big and sometimes wealthy voting interests: the Constitution's rigid 10-percent ceiling on interest rates, the 1944 amendment that weakened unions by prohibiting labor contracts with union- or agency-shop clauses, and everything that had anything to with taxing and government spending. Still, the convention, in two long sessions in 1969 and 1970, produced a document full of reforms that excited Rockefeller. It strengthened the governor's power in such matters as vetoes, equalized the thresholds for passing tax increases, ordered a reorganization of the executive branch of state government, consolidated five constitutional offices, gave the officers four-year terms and lifted their pay ceilings while imposing term limits on them, required the nonpartisan election of judges and imposed ethical and organizational reforms on both district and appellate judges, reorganized county governments and created strong legislative bodies, and gave both counties and cities greater taxing and regulatory powers.

Rockefeller's campaign talks often included a line urging people to ratify the new constitution, and the Republican Party officially endorsed it. Bumpers endorsed the document, too, but not as often and as vociferously as Rockefeller did, and the Democratic Party at its state convention ducked the issue. Some would blame Bumpers for the defeat of the reforms, because his immense popularity might have carried the day if he had campaigned strenuously for the new charter. That was not likely. Opponents, led by the American Independent Party and a former Supreme Court justice, Ed F. McFaddin, characterized the document as a socialist plot to raise everyone's taxes and undermine their rights. Eighty-five thousand people who went to the polls did not vote on the issue at all, and 57 percent of those who did rejected it.

VII
"A Smile and a Shoeshine"

A survey of political scientists and historians in 1998 by Dr. Calvin R. Ledbetter Jr., professor of political science at the University of Arkansas at Little Rock and a practicing politician himself in his middle years, ranked Winthrop Rockefeller one of four "near great" Arkansas governors

Dale Bumpers

of the twentieth century but several ranks behind the single "great" governor, Dale Leon Bumpers. The academics were supposed to weigh the twenty-two men who were the Arkansas chief executive for more than a few weeks on several scales of accomplishment, and it was evident that they ranked Rockefeller high for striving and his successor higher for achieving what Rockefeller often strove for but failed to do. The nexus of the two men whose careers collided in the fall of 1970, so similar in values and motives but so opposite in abilities and style, is one of the compelling whimsies of history. Without the other man, Rockefeller's political career might be remembered as more calamitous than vital and Bumpers's career as, well, less than extraordinary. At the end of his own career of twenty-eight years, Bumpers acknowledged many debts to the man he had beaten so soundly, starting with Rockefeller's emptying Death Row of all the condemned killers that Bumpers would have had to execute or else grant clemency.

The Rockefeller and Bumpers elections raise the profoundest of political questions: whether momentous elections, such as those in 1966 and 1970, represent gravitational shifts in the body politic or the unusual suasion of charismatic politicians. Arkansas has experienced both. Orval Faubus admitted in his private moments that a shifting electorate in 1957 had turned him into a defiant segregationist for a while, in order to get re-elected. Then there was the iconic 1968 general election, when Arkansas voters on the same day re-elected an integrationist Republican governor and a conservative but internationalist Democratic U.S. senator while giving its electoral presidential votes to the race-baiting populist George C. Wallace. What were they thinking? In 1970, let there be no doubt that the election turned on the charm, eloquence, and simple messages of a man few had even heard of. Vice President Spiro T. Agnew, campaigning for Rockefeller at Fort Smith, said Bumpers was riding on nothing more than "a smile and a shoeshine," which was one of the old felon's (tax evasion, 1973) more shining moments, for it implied that he might have seen and appreciated Arthur Miller's great *Death of a Salesman,* although there was nothing more to a comparison of Bumpers and Willie Loman than a grin. Thirty years later, Bumpers would admit to me a little ruefully that he believed that a key to his election that year had, indeed, been a beaming snapshot of him taken by the former *Arkansas Gazette* photographer Willie Allen, which Bumpers plastered onto billboards, lapel pins, and newspaper ads.

If Rockefeller's motivation for enduring four brutal political campaigns and four tormented years in office was to raise up the state that had given him safe harbor from midlife's tempests, Bumpers was guided by a similar passion. It was to live up to his father's expectation that he would get into politics and do great things for the state and the country.

His father, who ran a hardware store at tiny Charleston and served a single term in the Arkansas House of Representatives, drove the thirteen-year-old Dale down to Booneville on July 9, 1938, to see President Franklin D. Roosevelt, who made a short speech there for U.S. Senator Hattie Caraway from the caboose of a train at the Rock Island Depot. Caraway was challenged by a young congressman from Malvern, John L. McClellan, who had opposed much of Roosevelt's agenda. The elder Bumpers wanted the boy to see the man who had saved the country. Dale and his older brother noticed that Roosevelt had to be helped to his feet and then leaned on his son James as he spoke, and they asked their father what was wrong with him. Rufus Bumpers shushed them, but on the way home he said: "Now, boys, let me tell you something. Franklin Roosevelt had polio when he was thirty-nine years old, and he can't walk. He has twelve pounds of steel braces on his legs. If Franklin Roosevelt can't even walk and has to carry twelve pounds of steel on his legs, you boys have good minds and good bodies and there is no reason why you can't be president."

"I've said a lot of times that for my father to say that was tantamount to being nominated," Bumpers said in 2002, after his longings to fulfill his father's dreams that his son might be president had vanished in the bygones of indecision and regret.

Rufus Bumpers, or R. W. as he was known, was a recurring figure in Dale Bumpers's speeches all his life. He was a big hearty man, unhandsome but owning a rich voice that made him the go-to guy to preside at funerals and civic and church events. He once ran for the office of state representative, and went to Little Rock for the legislative session in 1933, at the depth of the Great Depression. Being away from his business nearly ruined him so he never ran again, but he told his boys that it was the greatest thing they could do. Law, he said, was the best route to a political career, and both sons became lawyers. In Dale Bumpers's early stump speeches, his one standard line, to the point of boredom, was "My father taught me that politics is a noble profession." Politicians had a bad reputation, and he—and supposedly his father—thought the biggest reason was that politicians believed they always had to demonize their opponents to get elected. He never did. Privately, he would be ruthlessly judgmental about people, including his political allies, but never in public utterances. Good people usually did not have the thick skin to take the abuse of campaigns and office holding, so they too rarely offered themselves. Bumpers was not going to make the problem any graver.

When Bumpers was in law school at Northwestern University in Chicago in 1949, his father, mother, and an uncle of his girlfriend (and future wife) were killed when a drunk driver collided with their car on a hilltop in eastern Oklahoma, where they had just inspected the spinach crop on a farm his father had bought. Rufus Bumpers lived a week in agony. It further elevated him to sainthood.

With a law degree in hand, Bumpers returned to Charleston and ran his father's hardware store and did a little law practice on the side. In his first year, he grossed sixty-four dollars from the practice of law. His father's political blueprint did not seem to be working out for several years, until he won a jury trial of some local fame. Before long, he had more cases than he could handle. In fifteen years, he lost two jury trials. Jurors always hung on every word of his closing arguments, as the *New York Times* recorded one hundred U.S. senators as doing in Bumpers's last speech, on January 21, 1999, in defense of the impeached president, Bill Clinton—"a speech of rare eloquence," as the newspaper called it. Bumpers could recall when he discovered that he had that ability. A high school English teacher he adored, Miss Doll Means, had the class take turns reading verses from the epic poem *Beowulf*. When he had read a few verses, she asked the class, "Doesn't he have a beautiful voice and doesn't he read beautifully?" She added, "Wouldn't it be a tragedy if he didn't use that talent?" He called it a defining moment in his life.

Politics did not offer many opportunities in southern Franklin County. He finally decided to create one by running against the state representative, Mike Womack, who lived in Ozark, the much larger community north of the Arkansas River. He quickly realized the futility of wresting votes from the other guy's hometown. But the same brand of politics that would transfuse the career of Orval Faubus—race—presented itself to the young lawyer. Since he was the only lawyer in southern Franklin County he became the ex-officio counsel for the school board.

When the U.S. Supreme Court, on May 17, 1954, handed down *Brown v. Board of Education*, which outlawed racially separate schools, the superintendent, Woodrow "Woody" Haynes, asked Bumpers what they should do about it. Bumpers said they had to integrate the Charleston schools and that it was pointless to delay and be told by the courts to do it. Consolidating the separate schools was easy, because there was plenty of room in the white schools for the black kids. African American children through the eighth grade attended a one-room school two miles south of town, and the handful of high school students were bused thirty miles every day to the black high school in Fort Smith at Charleston's expense. Bumpers thought the superintendent and most of the school board wanted to do it, because it would save considerable money for a strapped little district. Bumpers naïvely thought at the time that schools everywhere in the South would integrate immediately, because it was now the law of the land. Charleston quietly and fully integrated its schools three months after *Brown*. It was the only school district in the South to do so. Bumpers said in 2002 that Woody Haynes should be recognized in the history books. There was some grumbling in town, but the town's young lawyer assured everyone that a lawful community had to follow the law, no matter how objectionable it might be to some people.

On the Sunday night before school opened, the superintendent and custodian came to his house to tell him that someone had painted "NIGGERS STAY HOME" in big green letters on the front of the school, which would greet children the next morning. Bumpers opened his hardware store and got several gallons of turpentine and several stiff-bristled brooms. The custodian scrubbed the walls clean during the night. Bumpers got up early the next morning and parked at the school to see the disappointment on the faces of the culprits—he was certain who they were—when they drove up to enjoy the commotion that their handiwork caused. One night soon afterward a black friend named Joe Ferguson, who worked at the brick plant outside Charleston and whose son was a high school student, told him that a truckload of white men were traveling around the black settlement south of town and shouting racial epithets and threats, which terrified his wife and small children and probably others in the little community. He didn't know whether they had guns. Bumpers knew it would be pointless to call the sheriff, so he drove out to the neighborhood, parked his 1954 Pontiac in Ferguson's front yard, and sat with the man in his porch swing. The hooligans drove by a couple of times but quieted when they saw Bumpers's car and went away.

Integration came off without a hitch in the fall of 1954, except that several high schools refused to play the Charleston football or basketball teams in their towns if Charleston fielded black players. Charleston did not suit out the black players, including a good running back, in those towns or else kept them at home. Bumpers late in life was remorseful about it, because he should have advised the school to insist on letting the black kids play and forcing the other team to forfeit if it refused to put its players on the same field or basketball court with black boys.

None of this made the papers then, nor did it for many years. Bumpers's seminal role in integration did not surface in the 1970 campaign, when it probably would have beaten him, although Faubus did glean from his political network in west Arkansas, as he told me that summer, that Bumpers was known in the area as "a flaming liberal" and an integrationist. But even the people of Charleston did not realize that theirs was the only school system in the South to fully integrate immediately after the *Brown* ruling and that it was Rufus Bumpers's mirthful boy who had instigated it. One of Bumpers's last acts as a U.S. senator was to get Charleston designated as a national commemorative site for having been the first town in the South to totally integrate its schools.

What was truly inexplicable was that by 1970 people seemed to have forgotten at least the particulars of Bumpers's role in the troubles that followed integration, which again did not make it much into the public prints—either the weeklies in the area or the daily papers at Fort Smith.

When Faubus defied the courts and blocked even the token integration at Little Rock in September 1957, a few Charleston townspeople grumbled, "Why did we have to do it here?"

When Faubus stopped integration at Central High School and then closed the high schools the next year, Bumpers would recall, the governor was much admired even in Charleston. Bumpers became fearful of trouble in Charleston and other communities from people angry about the federal government "forcing" integration. By that time, Bumpers had been elected to the school board. He was relieved when President Eisenhower sent a unit of the 101st Airborne to Little Rock to demonstrate that the law must be obeyed. Bumpers was trying a civil case on the third floor of the Logan County Courthouse at Paris when he heard the familiar rumble of machinery down Highway 22, vehicles from nearby Fort Chaffee that were heading to Little Rock to provide logistical support for the 101st Airborne.

"I want you to know that was the sweetest sound I ever heard," he recalled. "I felt so rejuvenated that the situation was going to be tranquilized." But of course it wasn't, not immediately. One member of the Charleston School Board moved that it rescind integration, reopen the schoolhouse for black children south of town, and bus the black high school kids back to Fort Smith. Bumpers told the other board members that they should not even entertain the motion. Two members wanted to resegregate and another just resigned. The chairman was indecisive but voted with Bumpers to stalemate the issue until the next school election, when the voters could settle the matter. Bumpers recruited a man to run for the vacant seat, and the segregationists fielded a candidate for the vacancy and also for Bumpers's seat. The town understood that if they voted for the Bumpers team the schools would remain integrated, and that if they lost, the town would return to separate school systems until they were forced to integrate. Bumpers won 308 to 173 and his friend by a similar margin. The chairman then voted with the pair to continue unified schools. That settled the question for good, except for some hard feelings.

Charleston's Methodists had another memory of Bumpers's integrationist impulses. The minister of the church asked Bumpers for money to repair the roof at the tiny African American Methodist church and Bumpers refused. He said they should forget the Civil War and invite the black Methodists to join the white congregation. The church had a board meeting to hear Bumpers's presentation and the board voted twenty to two to merge the congregations. Bumpers, who sang in the choir, said the little church was packed

Orval Faubus and Elizabeth Westmoreland

the next Sunday morning when the handful of African American families nervously trundled into the sanctuary.

Eight men filed for the Democratic nomination for governor in the summer of 1970, all but perhaps one—William S. Cheek of West Memphis, a racist with a ribald sense of humor—who were far better known than Bumpers. A Gene Newsom poll showed Bumpers with less than one percent name recognition in the state. It seemed certain that Faubus would lead the field and likely that Attorney General Joe Purcell would be second and in a runoff with the former governor. No one had ever had a bad word to say about Honest Joe. The others were House Speaker Hayes C. McClerkin of Texarkana; Bill G. Wells, the lieutenant governor candidate from 1968, blemished from having his toddlers on the House payroll; Robert C. Compton of El Dorado, a big trial lawyer who was past president of the Arkansas Bar Association; and Jim Malone of Lonoke, a catfish farmer with a reputation from former elections as a surrogate stump speaker for Faubus.

Orval Faubus had turned over a new leaf. He said he was running this time to create a better future for the young people and that he would have an entirely new team at the Capitol with fresh ideas. He had dropped his longtime mate, Alta Faubus, and taken up with a flashy young Wisconsin woman with a beehive hairdo named Elizabeth Westmoreland, who traveled the state with him in miniskirts. After Faubus bought television time one night to announce his decision to resume serving the people of the state, I called Alta at her home in Huntsville and asked if she had watched Orval's show and what her reaction was. She said he made a lot of promises to people, but she remembered that he also had promised to love, honor, and obey her. That promise apparently meant nothing, she said, and voters might take that into consideration. That little story ran alongside the article about his announcement. It was not a providential beginning for Faubus.

Two years earlier, Bumpers had been awakened one morning by his father-in-law, Babe Flanagan, who handed him $1,500 and told him to get dressed, go to Little Rock, and enter the race for governor. His old friend Woody Haynes suggested that he seek out Little Rock Mayor Martin Borchert for advice first, and he went to Borchert's office before going to the Capitol to file. Borchert told him he had little chance of winning and that he should wait two years; meantime, Borchert would arrange for him to speak to civic groups around the state and try out his wares. He did that, and Borchert, aside from family members, was his main supporter when he started in 1970. But Bumpers attended a state Jaycee convention and fortuitously met Deloss Walker, a Memphis advertising man and political consultant who had handled Bill Alexander's successful 1968 campaign for Congress in east Arkansas. Bumpers was Walker's notion of the ideal candidate. If he won the Democratic nomination, Bumpers was not going to attack any of the other candidates or Rockefeller, and he wanted to sell himself as someone who could bring people together, end the strife and division, and get things done. Bumpers thought the big field was an aid, not a hindrance, particularly for someone entirely new to politics. He had a simple message: He would invest heavily in public education, improve and expand the state's wretched parks, and improve public health, particularly for rural Arkansas.

If you can raise a little money, Walker said, we'll get your picture on a few billboards on key highways, get a little television time for you to sit on a stool and talk directly to people, and you go out and meet as many people in person as you can. That became the Bumpers campaign.

Twice, Bumpers talked his elder brother, Carroll, an Arizona industrial executive who had a Harvard law degree, into helping him get their sister Margaret, a Cleveland businesswoman, to contribute money to his campaign. She was resistant, calling it a foolish ego trip by the youngest sibling that she wanted no part of. Eventually, the sister and brother would twice contribute generous sums. Thirty-five thousand dollars from the siblings, along with ten thousand that he picked up for selling his herd of registered Hereford cattle, formed the bulk of Bumpers's financing for the preferential primary election. He was lucky, too. One day, a producer at the ABC station at Little Rock, KATV, called and said a show had been canceled suddenly. If Bumpers could get to the station quickly he could tape a prime-time thirty-minute show for only $150. He combed his hair, rushed to the station, sat on a stool with a yellow notepad on his knee, and talked flawlessly for thirty minutes.

He was flawless, too, in the retail politicking that was still a big part of campaigning. He asked everyone his or her name, asked about family members and perhaps a local connection, and always remembered to call them by their first names—Mildred, not Mrs. McGillicuddy—when he left them. None of the other seven candidates thought he had a chance and left him alone, except for an occasional funny dig by Bill Cheek, the other unknown.

Humor was a powerful tool in every speech he ever made, and would remain a force through his final oration at President Clinton's impeachment trial in the Senate. He had a joke or two or a funny anecdote for every occasion, although he sometimes lacked a filter that would steer him past inappropriate venues.

In the two-week runoff with Faubus, the desperate former governor called a press conference for the afternoon, when he said he was going to make a dramatic announcement. Bumpers asked a lawyer friend who was his campaign treasurer, Edward Lester, to go to the news conference and find out what the bombshell was. Bumpers was about to make a speech that evening at a big political rally at the Cotton Belt depot at Pine Bluff where Faubus also would speak. Lester told him that Faubus announced that he had been told that if he were elected his enemies would assassinate him within six months.

Bumpers spoke ahead of Faubus at a rally made up mostly of railroad workers and their families, big Faubus supporters, and he related the former governor's announcement earlier in the day. Bumpers told them that he knew that they all cared deeply about Orval Faubus. He said they owed it to Orval to save his life. They had it in their capacity to do that.

"If I'm elected, he will have nothing to fear," Bumpers said, smiling broadly. "You can save Orval's life by voting for me. You owe it to him." The crowd laughed. Faubus never mentioned the assassination threat in his talk and got polite applause.

Faubus led in the first primary but with a disappointing 36 percent. Bumpers trailed with 20 percent, but he was certain of winning in two weeks. He did, with almost 60 percent of an even higher turnout.

An Associated Press article by Robert Shaw a few days after Bumpers's surprising victory in the first election caused a momentary scare. Shaw went to Charleston to find out who this upstart was. Joe Hyatt, who was in

"I wear the chains I forged in life," said the Ghost of Faubus's Past.

Bumpers's Methodist Sunday School class, praised him as a teacher. People packed Bumpers's classes on Sunday morning, because they were always provocative, the AP reported. For example, Bumpers would toss out the idea that the biblical story of God's parting the Red Sea for the Israelites might be an allegory and that God might not have physically parted the vast waters. It would stir a lively debate in the class.

Bumpers read Shaw's story with horror. "I knew how the people on the *Titanic* felt," he said. Faubus jumped on the story and chided Bumpers for not believing in a literal interpretation of the Word of God. He ran a big ad in the *Jonesboro Sun* with the bold headline "What about the Bible, Mr. Bumpers?" If he does not believe that God parted the Red Sea, Faubus demanded, what else about the Good Book does Bumpers not believe? A reporter called Bumpers's headquarters to get a reaction. Bumpers tele-phoned the Right Reverend Paul V. Galloway, the retired Methodist bishop of Arkansas.

"Dale, I've been waiting for your call," Galloway said. He called the re-porter and offered a defense for Bumpers's apostasy.

It was the first time that Bumpers suffered a personal attack, which was rare for a political candidate on the verge of a major victory. Faubus re-alized that it was too late to create an unwholesome narrative about the man. Other than the Red Sea story, Faubus merely repeated that Bumpers was known in his town as a flaming lib-eral. If he knew about Bumpers's seminal role in integration, he didn't exploit it in the runoff. It is probable that he did not, because none of the rest of us did either. Late in the first primary campaign, Fau-bus had remarked at a rally that one of his opponents was known in his com-munity as a big Rockefeller supporter in the past, and he implied that Rockefel-ler had put the man and maybe others into the race to defeat him in the Dem-ocratic primary. I asked Faubus after the speech if he was talking about Bumpers. He smiled but said the man he alluded to had no support around the state, and he was not going to elevate him by giving him the attention.

Dale Bumpers

Having nothing else to attack, Faubus devoted himself to making nega-tives of Bumpers's good looks, charm, and eloquence. He said the newspa-pers—mainly the *Gazette*—wanted Bumpers to win their election because it would set up a fall campaign between two men who were so similar in everything, including, he implied, wealth.

"The *Arkansas Gazette* wants to set up the same sort of gently contested race you would find for the king and queen of a charity ball at some coun-try club," Faubus said at rallies. "Bumpers versus Rockefeller—battling it out, tux to tux, cocktail to cocktail, boyish grin to boyish grin. No hard feelings. It's nothing serious."

Bumpers mocked him, but gently. With a grin, he bragged about all the big country clubs they had at Charleston. People would assume, correctly, that the town of 1,400 had no country club, although someone had developed a cow-pasture golf course on a creek nine miles east of Charleston at the crossroads community of Ratcliff, right across the road from the Full Gospel Bible Church and the Ratcliff Baptist Church.

Before we leave Orval Faubus again, one other encounter deserves mention. After the 1970 race for governor, and still another in 1974, life turned brutal for Orval and Liz, his second wife, in his hometown of Huntsville. Both of them had repeated run-ins with the local constabulary and townspeople, and in 1978, some $200,000 in debt, they fled to Houston, Texas. There, sometime in 1979 or 1980, Faubus placed a telephone call to Senator Dale Bumpers in Washington. They had a cordial conversation and then Faubus asked a favor. He was trying to get a grant from the U.S. Department of Labor for a job-training program that he wanted to institute in the Houston area. His request seemed to have hit a snag in the Labor bureaucracy. Could Bumpers check into it and give the project a push, something senators and congressman, notably Arkansas's, had been known to do? Bumpers asked who Faubus's contact was at the Labor Department—who was in charge of signing off on the project?

"Ernest Green," Faubus replied. Green had been the leader of the Little Rock Nine, the first African American graduate of Central High School, one of the nine whom National Guardsmen had turned away in September 1957 on Faubus's orders.

Bumpers was astonished. He told Faubus it was unlikely that Ernie Green would ever award him a grant.

"Why not?" Faubus asked. He said he had never meant any harm to Green and that his actions in 1957 were not intended to hurt Green, nor were they based upon any ill will toward the young man. Bumpers imagined that Green would have different emotions about it.

I do not remember if Bumpers made even an obligatory call to Green, but Faubus never got the grant. He and Liz fought, she ran him off, and he returned to Arkansas and accepted a job running the state's little veterans affairs office for Governor Frank White in 1981. She obtained a divorce, spurned Faubus's pleas for reconciliation, and was murdered in her home in March 1983.

A poll right after the runoff election showed Bumpers that he would defeat Rockefeller two to one. Unless he made a grievous error, he would win easily, no matter how much the governor spent. (Charles Allbright, an old colleague at the *Gazette* who wrote speeches and statements for the governor, told me later that Rockefeller spent some $10 million, counting all the staff work on the campaign. Contributions flowed into the Bumpers campaign unsolicited, but he spent less than $250,000.) Not making a grievous error meant playing everything safely. Rockefeller challenged him to a series of debates, which trailing candidates always do. Bumpers, as leading candidates nearly always do, avoided the debate by dithering until it was too late, which he would later lament was a cheap thing to do. Rockefeller, and all of us in the media, challenged Bumpers about what he would do about taxes. He talked about pouring money into education, public health, and parks. Would he raise taxes, like Rockefeller had tried repeatedly to do and was promising again to do? Bumpers wouldn't say. Neither would he make a no-tax pledge. He said he needed to dig into the state's finances and see what could be done with existing taxes. He also would admit later that he simply did not want to spend the fall debating taxes, which would surely winnow his huge lead.

For all of his confidence and aplomb, Bumpers approached his inauguration with trepidation. He knew he was a neophyte at governing and that persuading legislators, all with different egos and ambitions, might take a different set of skills than winning over a mass of voters. Every new governor confronts those unknowns. But Bumpers faced one uniquely. He worried, even before taking office, about misconduct in the government that would be under his aegis, not just in his office or in positions under his direct control but in the vast apparatus of government, more than 25,000 employees. He would be responsible for all of them—they would be the Bumpers administration. He had monitored all the misdeeds that came to light in the last part of the Faubus reign—Arkansas Loan and Thrift, Pensions for Pals, the Midnight Pay Raises, the Horse Show Scandal—and even in the Rockefeller administration, which had to stymie an influence-peddling scheme by a handful of the governor's men and endure a little corruption by a Republican underling in the revenue agency. Rockefeller told Bumpers after the election that his biggest problem would be finding highly competent and honest people to run the programs, particularly at the low salaries the state paid. For Bumpers, unlike any other elected official in my knowledge, the fear of ethical misconduct became an almost morbid obsession.

Only a few weeks in office, he developed suspicions that a young man on his staff was trying to use the influence of the governor's office to affect liquor permits at the state Alcoholic Beverage Control Board. Bumpers got his resignation. Later, he demanded the resignation of the director of the agency, based on reports that the man was carting off liquor from stores that he was regulating without paying for it, as if collecting tribute from the people who owed their livelihoods to him was an emolument of the job.

A couple of months into his administration, the State Police reported to him that an African American woman in Dallas County had told a state trooper that a member of the state Pardons and Paroles Board had come to her home and asked for a payment of perhaps a thousand dollars to get her son paroled from the penitentiary. He explained that he would have to "split it with the man," apparently meaning the governor. She didn't have a thousand dollars. The man had been appointed to the Paroles Board by Rockefeller and was in the middle of his term. Bumpers sent Major W. A. Tudor of the State Police to Fordyce, who hid in the woman's home with a recording device after she arranged for the board member to return. Tudor got the man on tape asking for the bribe. Bumpers had a member of his staff call the man and tell him to come to the Capitol to see the governor. Bumpers had him sit down and write a letter of resignation before leaving his office. He had Tudor turn the evidence over to the prosecuting attorney in the district, who refused to prosecute the man.

At the end of his career, Bumpers recalled that the incident made him sick. He imagined that if the bribe attempt had first surfaced in the media it would have reflected on him and it would have been hard to persuade everybody that he wasn't crooked. He began to imagine his three children reading or hearing from classmates about corruption in their daddy's administration. He thought about it every day and every night. He started giving short lectures to everyone he appointed to boards and commissions and administrative jobs. He told them it was easy to do a little expense padding here and there, or to influence a liquor permit or a bank or insurance charter, but he expected them to be honest in everything they did and he would stand behind them whenever any criticism surfaced. They would be on their own if they committed even the slightest ethical or legal misdeed.

Betty, his wife, told him one evening early in his term that she had been shopping at a men's clothing store in downtown Little Rock when the manager approached her and said someone had bought a suit for the governor and that he should come down to be fitted. She told him that if her husband came down to be fitted for a suit he would pay for it himself. It only magnified Bumpers's worries.

Martin Borchert, the former Little Rock mayor who was his first major supporter, joined his staff first as a legislative liaison and then as a permanent executive assistant. Bumpers learned from his prison superintendent that Borchert's building supply company had submitted a bid on some small supply project at the penitentiary. Bumpers told Borchert that he had to withdraw the bid and never do anything like that again, because it gave the appearance of misconduct. Borchert protested that his products were just as good as anyone else's and that if his company's bid was not the lowest he would never use his influence to get the contract. But he obeyed.

Gifts, just small mementos, began to arrive at the Governor's Mansion or at his office. He dictated a form letter to go to everyone explaining that he could not accept gifts of any magnitude from anyone but appreciated the thought. The gifts were returned. One day in the spring of 1971 he received a small package with a Rolex watch, the big price tag still attached. It was from Henry M. "Mike" Berg, a Camden jeweler whom Faubus had appointed to the State Police Commission. Berg's six-year term was expiring and he wanted to be reappointed. Bumpers returned the Rolex with the form letter and didn't reappoint Berg. A short time later Tudor (who had not yet been made to resign) told the governor that a new inmate who was being processed at the Cummins prison claimed that Berg had hired him to assassinate Bumpers, the payment to be made when the deed was done. But the man got arrested and convicted for a smaller crime before he could get around to killing Bumpers. He obviously hoped to get his commitment shortened by telling about the murder for hire. Tudor wanted to know what Bumpers wanted done with the story. Bumpers told him to send a trooper to the jeweler and tell him that if any harm ever came to Bumpers or any member of his family they were coming after him.

"I'll do it myself," Tudor said. Berg, a hermitic germophobe who wore white gloves every time I saw him, would figure from time to time in speculation about the unsolved mystery of the disappearance in 1957 of Maud Crawford, a prominent Camden lawyer whose firm was involved in the investigation of alleged Mafia control of some labor unions. No evidence linking Berg to the crime ever surfaced.

Hilary Jones of Jasper, one of Bumpers's original supporters, brought a delegation, including a couple of legislators, to the Capitol to visit with him on behalf of a roadbuilder who was a friend of Jones. The man had done a small road job for the state Highway Department, and the agency had fined him $13,000 for liquidated damages because he had not finished the job in the time agreed upon in the contract. They wanted the governor to tell the highway director, Ward Goodman, not to assess the fine against the man's company because bad weather had slowed the work. Bumpers told them that if he called Goodman and asked him not to collect the fine Goodman might oblige, but that he would have to do the same for others who were assessed liquidated damages for failing to fulfill the terms of their contracts. He thought people had not voted for him to bestow favors on anyone. Jones stood up and said: "That's the reason I voted for you. Let's go, boys."

While we were cruising down to his Grant County farm one morning in 1977, Witt Stephens, the financier and former gas-utility president, explained his lifelong enmity toward Bumpers. As a lawyer at Charleston, Bumpers had sued Stephens Production Company several times for violating royalty contracts or damaging the owners' lands. Stephens said he was willing to forgive Bumpers for all of that after Bumpers defeated Faubus in the 1970 primaries, and he sent the candidate a check for either five or ten thousand dollars—my memory about which fails me—for the fall campaign against Rockefeller. Stephens said Bumpers returned the check, and Stephens took the message to be that Bumpers thought he was too good to take money from an old pol like Stephens. Then he went to the Capitol to visit with Bumpers about an issue that he thought was vital to the state's largest gas-distribution company. It needed a rate increase so that it could explore for gas in the developing Anadarko Basin in the Texas and Oklahoma panhandles, western Kansas, and Colorado. He asked Bumpers to invite the new chairman of the Public Service Commission, Pat Moran, over to the governor's office so the three could discuss the importance of his companies' competing for gas in the rich basin and the need for more revenue. Bumpers refused to call Moran or to exercise even the slightest influence. Stephens thought it was spite against him.

Bumpers recalled the incident later and said that he had tried to explain to Stephens that *ex parte* communications like that were improper and that Stephens was supposed to submit his case for a rate increase to the commission and make the arguments there. He would not attempt to influence the commissioners either way, and he suggested to Stephens that it would be improper for him or anyone at his company to have any dealings with

Witt Stephens

the three commissioners outside the formal rate proceedings. Then he lectured Stephens that the old way of doing business—getting the governor's office to intercede in regulatory matters—was over, which infuriated the utility executive.

A few weeks later, when I was in the office of Robert C. Downie, one of the commissioners, he pardoned himself to go to the bathroom and knocked a letter off the corner of his desk as he left, a little ostentatiously. I picked it up and used his copying machine to make a duplicate. It was a personal letter from Stephens telling the commissioners that it was vital that he get a rate increase to explore the Anadarko Basin. I wrote an article about it for the *Gazette*. Arkansas Louisiana Gas Company applied for a rate increase and got a small one that Stephens always considered inadequate. He blamed it on Bumpers's spite.

The enmity between the Stephens brothers and Bumpers never healed. In 1986, Witt arranged for Bumpers to join his group for lunch in the Stephens building one day, perhaps to reach some rapprochement with the man who had now served two terms in the U.S. Senate and was about to win another, or perhaps just to set some old matters straight. James O. Powell, editor of the editorial page of the *Gazette*, was there and described the scene. Witt seemed to have some notes in his lap and brought up the old gas-field disputes, when Bumpers was a young country lawyer tending to the grievances of neighbors who had royalty interests in the gas production in the fields of Franklin County. They argued and finally Bumpers said something like, "Why, you senile old bastard, that just didn't happen." Someone from the Stephens company went back and told brother Jack that Bumpers had called his elder brother a "senile old bastard." Jack was furious and swore that he would beat Bumpers in the next election, even if he had to do it alone. A few days later, Meredith Oakley, the political reporter for the *Arkansas Democrat*, wrote a story that Jack Stephens, by then a Republican, was weighing a race against Bumpers in the approaching election. Bumpers was worried, because while Stephens was an intensely private person who avoided even the most trivial public appearance, he had the money to run a powerful media campaign. Bumpers was in a dentist's chair a few weeks afterward and the dentist told him not to worry, because Stephens was an official resident of Florida and was ineligible to vote or run for office in Arkansas. In his stead, Asa Hutchinson, later a congressman and governor, would make the gamble that year and lose.

$$\square\square\square$$

None of the agitations in the governor's office brought Bumpers as much panic as a wild charge by one of his opponents in the 1972 governor's race that Bumpers had taken a bribe from a Buffalo, New York, company that owned part of the Southland Greyhound Corporation dog-racing track at West Memphis. Mack Harbour, a wavy-haired hospital administrator at Paragould, charged that Bumpers had flown to Buffalo sometime during the governor's race in 1970 and picked up a sack at the airport. He implied that it contained a payoff from Emprise Corporation of Buffalo, an owner of the track that was suspected of having Mafia ties. The payoff was for the governor not doing something about Emprise, although what he should or could have done was not clear.

Bumpers pronounced the charge absolutely false. He recalled having flown with his wife and daughter from his sister's home in Cleveland in September 1970 to Boston, where his daughter had undergone spinal surgery, but he said the commercial flight did not go to Buffalo. That was about the end of it, but Bumpers could not get over it. Betty, his wife, told him repeatedly to stop worrying about it, because no one paid any attention to the absurd charge. Bumpers was sure that thousands of people would believe it and that school classmates of his children would bring it up. He couldn't sleep. His secretary checked airline schedules for the previous September to see if the plane might have touched down at Buffalo without their remembering it. It hadn't. Ten years later, Harbour was fired as the hospital administrator, convicted of theft of property, and sentenced to seven years in prison.

Soon after the Harbour incident, Bumpers went to Kansas City, Missouri, to make a speech at the Truman Day dinner and spent some time with the former president. Truman had made the hardest decision any president ever had to make, to drop atomic bombs on Hiroshima and Nagasaki and end World War II. Bumpers was personally grateful, because when the bombs fell his Marine unit was leaving southern California for the invasion of Japan. He told Truman about all his anxieties about possible misdeeds in his government and about whether his decisions would turn out to be bad ones. He said he went to bed in turmoil every night.

"Now, son, let me tell you something," he recalled Truman telling him. "People elected you to do what you think is right. So, when you're lying out there at the Mansion looking at the ceiling, I can save you a lot of sleep. Just think about that fact. They're busy with their lives. They don't have time to deal with the nitty-gritty that you deal with every day. They want you to do what you think is right. So, when you're in trouble, get the best advice you can get on both sides of the issue. Pick the one that makes more sense to you and go with it. That's all the people expect of you."

He felt immense relief. But not compared to the relief he felt when he resigned in December 1974, a couple of weeks before the end of his term, so that he could be sworn in as a U.S. senator. The next morning he awoke and all the anxieties and fears had vanished. They would return every time he contemplated running for president, in 1976, in 1980, in 1984, and in 1988. Charges like Mack Harbour's would be everyday events if he ran for president and particularly if he were elected. He would marvel at Bill Clinton's imperturbability during years of investigations growing out of a small and silly land transaction that he and his wife had made in 1978 when he was the Arkansas attorney general. Late in life, Bumpers was quite sure that he would not have lived through a term as president. Clinton had loved every day that he was governor and every day that he was president. Bumpers said he was miserable every day that he was governor and he suspected that he would have been far more miserable as president.

If all those problems represented a sort of insecurity that is rare in politicians, Bumpers never evinced any of it in his public performance as governor. From the day he first announced in 1970 until his career ended, he was the quintessence of self-confidence. In speeches and in negotiations or wheedling with legislators, he was certain that he was right, and he nearly always got his way.

For a man with no experience dealing with a legislative body beyond the little Charleston school board, which comprised his neighbors and friends, Bumpers demonstrated an uncanny instinct for aligning lawmakers with his objectives. In one of the first battles, he formed a permanent bond with the legislators that served him the rest of his tenure. The Arkansas Municipal League and the Association of Arkansas Counties, which lobbied the legislature and the governor every two years for a larger slice of the state tax pie, came up with a scheme to take a permanent layer of the state's constantly expanding general revenues. Seven percent of the general revenues of the state would be taken off the top each year, before any distributions for the state's fiscal agencies, the public schools, or any of the agencies and institutions of government. Four percent would go to the cities and three percent to the counties. Together, county and city officials formed a powerful phalanx that every legislator found too formidable to defy. They got returning legislators and candidates in 1970 to commit to vote for the turnback bill. City and county services were underfunded, and raising taxes locally was too treacherous. Besides, cities and counties were allowed little home rule under the state Constitution. The legislature had to give cities and counties specific taxing powers, and it had given them few beyond those specified in the Constitution, which mainly were property taxes. Moreover, city and county officials had not sought greater taxing powers. It was easier for legislators and the governor to fade the heat for raising taxes.

Bumpers declared that the automatic turnback to local governments was no way to run a government. He said local officials who would spend the money, and who were elected just as he and legislators were, should show the leadership and take responsibility for funding a city's or county's needs. He asked legislators to vote against the turnback bill, but they said that while they agreed it was a reckless policy that endangered funding for schools, colleges, and health services, they had made solid commitments. It would be suicide to renege on their pledges when county judges and city officials were so potent in their districts.

"All right," Bumpers said, "I'll have political leaders in all seventy-five counties mad at me, but I will veto the bill if you will at least back me up by not overriding my veto." They did. Neither house took an override vote.

To give local officials more taxing power, which they were not begging for, Bumpers offered expanded home rule. The key bill allowed local governments to levy a small personal income tax or a payroll tax that would collect some revenues from commuting employees outside the city or county. The legislature approved the tax bill, but over the next forty-five years not a single city or county sought to take advantage of the taxing power. The legislature in 1981 gave cities and counties the local option of levying sales taxes, which landed more heavily on low-income people, and most counties and major cities took advantage of it.

On some occasions, in particularly tense political conflicts, Bumpers would evince a mischievous uncertainty—a seeming unwillingness to take a hard stand, or perhaps a hope that the issue might be resolved somehow without him. He would be criticized as indecisive, but in the end there would always seem to have been an uncanny calculation to his indecision.

The powerful delegation in the Senate and House from Pine Bluff introduced a bill to dedicate all the state's highway revenue to the building of a superhighway between Pine Bluff and Little Rock until the highway was built. Legislators felt obliged to the Pine Bluff men to vote for it and to force the Highway Department to temporarily abandon its timetable for statewide roadwork, including projects in their districts, until the Pine Bluff highway was finished. Many of them went to the governor or his legislative aides for quiet assurances that the governor would veto the bill if they passed it. He told them that if it was such a bad bill they should vote against it; after all, he had to run in Jefferson County, too. The bill passed and he let it lie on his desk until the final day, when he vetoed it, to the great relief of 90 percent of the legislators.

The same strategy prevailed when Senator Guy H. "Mutt" Jones of Conway introduced and passed a bill splitting the Fifth Judicial District into two court districts in order to protect the judges and political machine in Faulkner and Conway Counties from Alex Streett, an aggressive young prosecuting attorney in Pope County, the largest county in the district, who was going after election fraud and misconduct in the Faulkner and Conway County Courthouses. Bumpers told legislators they should vote their own consciences rather than being intimidated by the political powers and he wouldn't say, publicly or privately, where he stood. He vetoed that bill, too, and made the veto stick, even though a gubernatorial veto in Arkansas, unlike most other states, can be overridden by a simple majority of lawmakers.

Poor Lee County, nearly 60 percent of whose population was black and lived in poverty, posed the hardest dilemma. A federal grant from VISTA (Volunteers in Service to America)—the domestic counterpart to President John F. Kennedy's Peace Corps program—had set up a medical clinic at Marianna, where poor and black people had had virtually no access to health care. It was staffed by a young doctor and managed by a young black man named Olly Neal. Medical practitioners in the area, business people, the hospital, and apparently most white residents hated the place and wanted it closed. It was bruited about in the white community that the clinic was a hotbed of radicalism and that Neal was planning a massive insurrection, like the one whites thought was in the offing in the nearby community of Elaine in 1919, when white vigilantes, aided by a militia sent by Governor Charles Brough, slew hundreds of black people in their homes, cotton fields, and marshes, and at the railroad station where blacks gathered to greet the troops. Indeed, the clinic had become a source of emergent black pride and its defense a rallying stage for activism. Neal seemed to be behind a growing boycott of the white-owned businesses. There was sporadic violence.

When Bumpers took office, it was time for the VISTA program to be renewed, and a state's governor had to sign off on the renewal of such programs. He was under intense pressure from the whole region to deflect the VISTA grant. Lee County was one of only two counties in the state—the other was adjoining Phillips—that Bumpers had not carried in the recent election. Rockefeller had gotten the black votes and Bumpers the whites. The governor pondered and vacillated. He wouldn't tell anyone what he would do. He sent three or four friends to the county for a few days to assess the situation. They came back and told him that there was no doubt the Lee County Cooperative Clinic served a vital need but that the community was near an explosion. Still, he delayed. I asked my friend Irene Samuel, who was on his staff and who had been one of the heroines in the Little Rock school crisis, what she thought the governor was going to do. She shrugged. She had pestered him to tell her on the promise she would keep it a secret.

"Irene," he said, "did you go to work for me because you thought I would do the right thing?" She said yes. He walked away. She took the gesture to mean he would renew the clinic's lease on life but she could not be sure.

In 2002, Bumpers told me that he had talked one day to the preeminent leader in the community, Lon Mann, who owned a cotton plantation and gin, headed the chamber of commerce and the school board, and also was a critic of Olly Neal, the clinic, and the boycott. He said Mann had confided that the clinic indeed served a vital purpose but that he could never say that and could not publicly support Bumpers if he renewed the VISTA grant. Bumpers renewed the grant. He sent nine state troopers to the community for several days to keep the peace. Neal got a law degree and was later appointed and elected to the state Court of Appeals, where he served for twelve years.

□□□

What Bumpers did in four years—the volume and sweep of legislation and executive initiatives—has never been matched by any governor. The institutions and services he put in place form the government we have to-day. After his election, Bumpers asked his old friend Ben Allen, a state senator and a lawyer who had found himself sometimes opposite Bumpers in the courtroom, what he should do now that he would soon have the job. He had talked about no programs other than spending more on education and specifically teachers, improving the parks system, and doing something about the poor quality of medical care in rural areas.

"Champ, for starters, just take Rockefeller's program and pass it," Allen said. Much of the Rockefeller program that had gone down to defeat encompassed proposals made in 1962 by a group of reformers called Democrats for Arkansas, headed by political scientist Calvin Ledbetter Jr. and Dr. David Luck, a liberal doctor at Arkadelphia. Bumpers had already talked to Governor Rockefeller about reorganizing the executive branch along the lines of a study that Rockefeller had hired the national accounting firm of Peat, Marwick, Mitchell & Company to do. Rockefeller couldn't get the bill introduced.

"Be my guest," Rockefeller said. Bumpers made a few changes in the Rockefeller bill, got a couple of Old Guard legislators to sponsor it for him, and passed it in the first few weeks of his term.

Lining up some sixty-five state agencies under thirteen department heads streamlined accountability, but it was largely window dressing, except for one department. All the so-called welfare agencies, including the mental hospitals, children's welfare programs, rehabilitation institutions, and programs for the disabled and aging, were put under a single director, Dr. Roger A. Bost, a wiry little man with a reedy voice and big ideas who had been the Bumpers family pediatrician and a school board chairman at Fort Smith. Bost learned all about the federal Medicaid law enacted in 1965 and federal mental health services. Arkansas was last among the fifty states in delivering medical care for the poor under the Medicaid law. It spent $10 million a year, almost all of it on nursing home care for the aged, and left untapped $25 million in federal aid for other social and medical services. In four years, the $10 million grew to $100 million in federal and state spending on medical care for the indigent. Legislators on the Joint Budget Committee protested that the federal government someday might cut back its spending and leave the state holding the bag, but Bumpers and Bost belabored them into approving the budgets. The state made thousands of children and medically indigent people eligible for subsidized health coverage. Centers for severely disabled children were built at Warren, Jonesboro, and Arkadelphia to meet the huge demand on the state's single children's colony at Conway. The state de-emphasized institutional care for the mentally ill and moved to community mental health centers, subsidized with federal funds. Arkansas became the first state to provide statewide nutritional services for the aged. With Medicaid funding, the state's struggling children's hospital at Little Rock, which had an average patient population of twenty-five, was transformed into a world-class rehabilitation center for children.

Bost would later organize area health education centers around the state, where physician graduates would do their residencies and perhaps locate their practices outside the metropolitan areas. Bumpers passed a bill expanding physician training at the University of Arkansas for Medical Sciences to turn out more doctors, and another to retire the student loans of new physicians who would practice for a few years in a small town, and passed a bill, strenuously opposed by the state association of physicians, to give hospital and pharmaceutical privileges to osteopaths. Bumpers saw that osteopaths were often the family physicians in small towns across the border in Oklahoma and thought the law might help fill the need for primary-care doctors in rural Arkansas. (The state in 2018 started two osteopathic schools to train primary-care doctors.) The state began rebuilding the University of Arkansas for Medical Sciences with surpluses produced by Bumpers's tax program.

Arch W. Ford had been the state commissioner of education since 1953. In the closing days of the 1970 campaign, Bumpers asked for my thoughts about various department heads, including Ford, which I was reluctant to give except some general observations about the character of the men. He thought Ford was something of a seat warmer because, after all, he had been the commissioner during all the crisis years over school integration. He figured he would replace Ford right away. I noted that Ford's son, Joe, was a member of the state Senate. Bumpers did not fire Ford, which he would later say was one of the wisest decisions he made. He invited Ford up to his office for consultation in the opening days and Ford was full of ideas about what ought to be done. Arkansas was one of the few states that did not supply free textbooks to high school students. Arkansas voters had amended the Constitution in 1968 to allow the state to fund kindergartens, but the legislature had refused to appropriate money for them. He thought the state should require schools to educate disabled children or provide private education for them. The state had two postsecondary technical schools, at Morrilton and Pine Bluff, and two community colleges, at Helena and Fort Smith, and Ford thought they should be accessible to kids all over the state.

In four years, all of those things were done. All required enabling legislation and appropriations. Kindergarten was the hardest. Bumpers visited the Joint Budget Committee three mornings in a row to plead for the passage of the first $500,000 appropriation. It passed the House of Representatives but not the Senate, where, time after time, the appropriation failed by a single vote. Legislators protested that the state could not afford the cost of schooling five-year-olds, and others, like Melvin Chambers, the senator from Magnolia, thought kindergartens were a communist plot to undermine America by tearing tots away from their moms at a vulnerable age. The Senate finally approved the first $1 million appropriation in 1973 and the Magnolia senator voted for it. Arkansas teacher salaries ranked fiftieth among the states. The state provided average raises of $500 a year for the next four years.

A constitutional amendment adopted in 1964 had allowed the creation of community college districts after a vote by people in the districts, but only two had been created, because paying for them was a community obligation. Voters could approve a property tax to support the schools. Over the strenuous objections of the state's four-year colleges and universities, Bumpers persuaded the legislature to change the enabling law for the colleges to give them state operating funds for the first time. A rush by legislators to authorize community college elections followed. It ended, at least at that session, when Senator Nick Wilson of Pocahontas, at that time a virulent opponent of the little schools, introduced a bill to create a community college at the southern tip of his district in the remote mountaintop hamlet of Fox, which was situated halfway between Mozart and Turkey Creek, a few miles from the newly commissioned Ozark Folk Center. The bill said the college would be named "Folk U." Wilson, whose puckish humor often got him into political trouble, had met my wife, who is from Fox. Wilson told me to tell her that evening that if the legislature passed the bill and the governor signed it, which he hoped they wouldn't do, he would try to get her hired as the chancellor. I wrote a short article for the *Gazette* about the bill and the proposed name of the college and the paper printed it, which Wilson seemed not to have expected of the priggish newspapers of that time. His friend, who was editor of Wilson's prim hometown weekly, the *Pocahontas Star Herald*, did not pass that news about their senator on to local readers. But the bill achieved Wilson's purpose, which was to stop the surge for two-year colleges, at least momentarily. The two community colleges and four technical schools increased to twenty-one in a decade and served every part of the state. Wilson, by then converted to a champion of the schools, sponsored and passed legislation in 1991 to convert most of the colleges and vocational schools to technical colleges, supported by a corporate income tax.

Arkansas Agricultural, Mechanical, and Normal College, the troubled black institution at Pine Bluff, was made a part of the University of Arkansas system, and its state funding was equalized with the white schools. Arkansas Agricultural and Mechanical College at Monticello also was made a part of the University of Arkansas system. A search of Arkansas's laws going back a century listed all the laws that required segregation in some way, including the labeling of blood by race, and a single statute repealed all of them. Bumpers vetoed bills passed by the legislature to allow the segregationist private academies that were springing up in east Arkansas to enroll their teachers in the state-subsidized teacher-retirement system, a step that would have encouraged communities to abandon the public schools and create taxpayer-supported private academies for the white kids.

Bumpers was the first governor who could be called an environmentalist. During the campaign, he called Arkansas's parks a disgrace for a state with so much natural beauty and so many historically significant places that needed preserving. The state spent more money on the parks in his four years than in all previous years combined. The state created a passel of new parks: Village Creek, Moro Bay, Woolly Hollow, Pinnacle Mountain, the Ozark Folk Center, Crater of Diamonds, Historic Washington, Toltec Mounds, and Logoly. The Nature Conservancy bought the land for Logoly (Columbia County) in 1974, Bumpers's last year, to preserve it until the state Parks and Tourism Department could get funding for it, which they did in 1975.

Middle South Utilities was planning to build a string of nuclear- and coal-powered generating plants to replace aging plants with oil and gas boilers. Bumpers and Don S. Smith, a member of the Public Service Commission, developed a bill requiring utilities to get approval from the commission to build the plants after proving both the need for and the environmental suitability of the plants. The commission would reduce the size of the big coal-fired plants in Jefferson and Independence Counties because the volume of greenhouse gases they would emit would be too great. In 2010, the Arkansas Supreme Court held that the Public Service Commission and American Electric Power had violated that statute by not proving both the need for and environmental compatibility of a big coal-powered plant in Howard County before giving it a permit to build the plant. (The plant went on line anyway, in 2012.)

Bumpers had his Planning Department identify rare scenic areas and species that were endangered and needed preserving, and then tried to get an appropriation of a million dollars to purchase and preserve the areas, which opponents referred to as wildernesses. Senator Virgil T. Fletcher of Benton said that down in Saline County they didn't need to set aside a wilderness because they could create one anytime they wanted to without any stupid law. It was one of fewer than a dozen bills Bumpers could not pass in 1971 and 1973.

Another was to designate five mountain streams (Buffalo River, Mulberry River, Eleven Point River, Kings River, and Big Piney Creek) as wild and scenic rivers, where damming and development would be limited. The roguish Nick Wilson of Pocahontas, a freshman who was ordinarily an ally, got the bill amended in the Senate to include the Arkansas River, which would have meant dynamiting all the dams in the Arkansas River Navigation System. That killed the bill. Wilson admitted to Bumpers at lunch forty years later that he actually had favored the scenic rivers bill, but chose to kill it because he felt obliged to his constituents, most of whom wanted to develop the Eleven Point River in his district for tourism rather than keep it in its pristine state. Bumpers also could not pass a bill that prohibited the sale of beverages in nonreturnable containers, the kind that typically wound up as roadside trash. His successor, David Pryor, would succeed with a similar bill in 1975 but, owing to a rebellion by fast-food merchants, had to call a hasty session that summer to repeal the law before it was to take effect. Bumpers also offered a bill, which ultimately was defeated, to create a merit system for state employees so that professional workers would no longer depend upon political allegiance for their jobs. The Parks and Tourism Department and the state parks themselves had been big platforms for political patronage, but Bumpers professionalized the staff. The chief parks professional, Richard Davies, retired forty-five years later.

Bumpers wanted to liberalize workers' compensation benefits and to grant the state the authority to begin a turnpike system, like Oklahoma's, to build major highways without waiting for motor-vehicle tax receipts to trickle in. Both bills died in the legislature.

The governor's fear of and absorption with misconduct in the government translated into the first real public ethics law in Arkansas, although it passed the nervous Senate without a vote to spare. The law prohibited officials and employees anywhere in the state government, including legislators, from using their offices for personal gain or to get privileges for themselves, their business partners, or their relatives, or to receive supplements to their salaries from any quarter. It required all public officials to file public reports annually showing any firm in which they had an interest exceeding $1,000 and their positions in corporations from which they had received more than $1,500 the previous year. Attorneys in the legislature had to list the state agencies before which they had brought cases. The penalties for violating the law were jail, fines, and forfeiture of their offices. Another act required candidates for legislative and state office for the first time to list their campaign expenditures. An effort to limit campaign spending failed.

A few issues fell into the governor's lap—and out. Congress referred to the states the Equal Rights Amendment for women in 1972, and Bumpers endorsed it and pushed for its ratification by the legislature. Bumpers and women's groups had enough senators committed to it to assure its passage there but, at the pivotal moment before the vote, Senator Mutt Jones of Conway offered an amendment qualifying the proposed law to say that women could not serve in the armed forces, and the Senate adopted it. It rendered any action by the legislature pointless, since the proposed law would be different from that ratified by the other states.

Although some version of many of the bills that Bumpers pushed through the legislature had been proposed and defeated in the past, they merely attracted the opposition of muscular special interests, not the general public. Taxes were another matter. While most people could be persuaded that the state needed to spend more money on a lot of services, particularly roads and highways, they tended not to like any particular form of taxation. Without higher taxes, little that Bumpers wanted to do could be achieved. While he had equivocated about taxes throughout the campaign, infuriating Rockefeller, he admitted privately that he would have to seek higher taxes. The massive Rockefeller tax program, which would have raised the state's general revenues by half or more, offered him cover. Anything less than Rockefeller had proposed would be viewed as a relief. The program that Bumpers laid out, after getting his reorganization bill passed, was only about a fourth of Rockefeller's plan in terms of the revenues it would raise for the state. In volume, that was easily achievable: a mere hike in sales-and-use taxes. Clarence E. Bell of Parkin, a powerful senator who could carry much of the conservative Delta, was happy to sponsor a sales tax increase of any amount. The sales tax could be passed by a simple majority in both houses, while most other taxes—any that existed in 1934—required a three-fourths majority under a perverse law put into the Constitution that year, at the depth of the Great Depression. But Bumpers said it was an unfair tax that placed a huge burden on low-income people and very little on the wealthy. He would impose no taxes rather than raise the sales tax. He prepared a bill raising the income tax, but not nearly as high (12 percent on the highest income brackets) as both Rockefeller and Sid McMath had proposed before him. Income tax rates and brackets had never been raised since the tax was imposed in 1927. His bill raised the tax rate on the top income bracket from 5 to 9 percent. Legislators and his advisers told him that reaching 75 percent on such a bill was impossible. His plan was to raise a few other minor taxes as well. He would expand the sales tax to cover a few services and the purchases by utilities, railroads, pipelines, and bus and truck companies, which had been exempt from the tax.

The income tax, he said, would be no burden to people who were well to do, and people would recover part of the taxes by claiming the deduction on their federal tax returns. But it would prove harder than he imagined. He and his aides lined up commitments from three-fourths of the members of both houses, but he would learn that oral commitments were not enough. Legislators would check the calendar on the day the bill would come up and leave the chambers, hide in the restrooms or the phone booth, or simply disappear for an hour when the troublesome bill came up for a vote. Needing twenty-seven votes in the Senate and seventy-five in the House, it failed 25 to 8 and 23 to 6 on successive days in the Senate while the governor's aides were scouring the halls for missing senators. Although Bumpers declared that he was staying with the bill "until the last dog dies," he was finally persuaded to amend it. He took off the top bracket and its 9 percent rate, leaving a top marginal rate of 7 percent. Then it passed 29 to 6. In the House, with a top rate of 7 percent, it was even harder than in the Senate. There it failed repeatedly for days, 73 to 24, 73 to 19, 72 to 22, and 72 to 18. Bumpers said he would keep insisting on roll calls until every representative lived up to his commitment to vote for the bill. It passed 77 to 17. Not one legislator in either house who voted for the bill was defeated in the next election.

But the legislature was going to have to make up for the loss of revenue from shaving off the 9 percent bracket. Bumpers announced that he was going to make it up by raising the excise tax on cigarettes from 12.5 cents to 17.5 cents a package. I followed him down the stairs after the announcement. Why did he choose the cigarette tax? I asked. He said it was the only sizable tax source that could be raised by a simple majority. No, I said, cigarettes were already taxed in 1934, so it would take a three-fourths vote. He looked at Ben Allen, his leader in the Senate, who grinned sheepishly and shrugged. He said he thought cigarettes needed only a simple majority.

Both houses approved the smokers' tax increase anyway, although it again took three votes in three days in the Senate. On the last vote, the roll call ended at 26 to 6, one vote short of passage. Lieutenant Governor Bob Riley, who was presiding, kept asking, "Anyone else wishing to vote? Anyone else wishing to vote?" As Riley was about to bang the gavel and tell the clerk to cast up the vote, the rear portals to the Senate swung open and Bumpers's liaison, Martin Borchert, stood there clutching Senator George E. "Butch" Locke of Hamburg, who was holding up his unzipped pants. Borchert had yanked him out of a stall in the men's room a few feet away.

"Locke votes aye," Locke said wearily, and the doors closed.

The new taxes were supposed to raise $27 million the first year, but they produced twice that. Commodity prices soared that year and the next couple of years, and industrial growth and new jobs hit records. The surpluses every year developed the state parks, rebuilt the state medical school, and addressed long unmet capital needs at all the colleges and universities. Two years later, in Bumpers's second term, they raised motor-fuel taxes and earmarked all the revenues from the increase for rural roads.

The 1971 session was the most productive assembly in the state's history. It lasted eighty calendar days, the longest since 1912, when voters amended the Constitution to cut off the lawmakers' six-dollars-a-day *per diem* after the sixtieth day of every session, a reform that encouraged them to stop dawdling and get the work done. In 1912, six dollars a day and expenses were a powerful incentive to hang out in the capital rather than go back home, drink your own whiskey, sleep with your own wife, and find lucrative toil. The legislature passed and the governor signed 829 laws, 171 more than during the long 1969 session, but far more remarkable was the record number of highly controversial and truly consequential acts, and the fact that all of this was done under the aegis of a man wholly inexperienced in governing, one who seemed to settle into the office on his first day with an almost whimsical paucity of ideas about what he wanted to do and could do. What were the lessons to be learned here?

The same elections that brought Bumpers into office also altered the composition of the legislature, bringing a new cadre of largely progressive men (women were still exceedingly rare) into both legislative houses. They championed almost every cause that the young governor raised, but he also wanted the Old Guard—senators like Max Howell of Little Rock, Knox Nelson of Pine Bluff, Clarence E. Bell of Parkin, and Olen Hendrix of Prescott, and representatives like William F. Foster of England, Wayne Hampton of Stuttgart, and Jim Shaver of Wynne—to be part of his team and to sponsor hard bills. Bargaining and persuasion seemed to be instinctive abilities.

A freshman legislator marveled at his skill. After Bumpers had pulled in a clutch of senators to make the case for some difficult bill, one of the senior lawmakers, perhaps Max Howell, who had already been there nearly a quarter century, would explain matters to the neophyte governor: "Governor, we all want you to succeed but a lot of us who have been around here a long time just can't go along with you on this." Bumpers would reply deferentially, "Max, I understand perfectly. I just want you to vote your conscience on this and everything else. There will be lots of other chances for us to work together. You do what you need to do on this." Then Howell would vote for the bill.

Sometimes Bumpers went around them. He wanted to give full privileges to osteopaths in the hopes it would produce family physicians for rural parts of the state. Max Howell agreed to sponsor the bill for him. The bill lay in Howell's Judiciary Committee awhile and then lay doggo at the bottom of the Senate's calendar of business for much of the session. Howell's law firm—Howell, Price and Worsham—often represented many groups whose businesses and professions were regulated by the state, including (with Eugene Warren) the Arkansas Medical Society, which strenuously opposed giving osteopaths hospital and prescription-writing privileges. When George Bean, the state's lone practicing osteopath, went to Bumpers to point out that Howell's bill never moved up on the Senate calendar (I confess to telling him that while he was treating my sore back), the governor asked Senator Hendrix, who represented a southwestern Arkansas area with almost no medical services, to file a new bill to do the job. Bumpers went to the Public Health Committee's hearing and said he personally wanted the bill to become law. It did, with Max Howell's (apparently) reluctant vote. He would vote for nearly every bill in Bumpers's program.

Bumpers followed a similar strategy in getting the legislature finally to repeal the liquor industry's old fair-trade law, which had prevented competitive pricing by requiring every retail store to price every bottle of booze at least 15 percent above the wholesale price.

Senator Robert Harvey, a farmer and Vanderbilt law graduate, said at the end of the session that Bumpers's secret was hard work. Harvey had been in the legislature since Ben T. Laney was governor in 1947, and he had never seen a governor work so hard. You just couldn't vote against someone who worked so hard and seemed so earnest, Harvey said. Bumpers would show up at committee meetings to talk about his bills or budgets or why some tax exemption should be defeated. He had a legislative staff of five men who gathered early every morning at the Governor's Mansion or the Capitol office to go over the status of every bill he thought was important, to talk about amendments and why certain legislators were opposed and how they might be persuaded. He collared legislators in the hallways or in committee rooms, and his liaisons herded a steady stream of them to his office for the personal treatment. If they had political problems back home, say with a tax increase or with a powerful interest, he would promise to go to their bailiwicks and campaign for them.

The dilemma of Bill Walmsley, a freshman senator from Batesville, was illustrative. Poultry was the biggest industry in his district and the biggest figure was J. K. Southerland, who ran a poultry operation with 800 employees and was president of the area's biggest bank. At every legislative session, one or more industries wanted a small tax break, usually an exemption from sales-and-use taxes for equipment or some commodity used in the manufacturing process—something to improve the bottom line a little. Lawmakers found them irresistible. One exemption was as justifiable as any other, so if you voted for one you had no argument for opposing another. Bumpers was raising taxes, so it made no sense to be giving up revenue on the other side. A bill exempted some components in poultry processing from sales taxes and Bumpers wanted it stopped. The bill passed the House of Representatives and on the day it came to a vote in the Senate, Walmsley was attending the funeral of a friend at Batesville. The bill failed by one vote and its supporters served notice of getting another vote the next day, when Walmsley was expected to deliver the decisive vote. Bumpers called him and said he expected him to vote against the bill.

"Governor, you're asking me to commit *hari-kari*," Walmsley said. He would incur the opposition of the biggest businesses in his district and hundreds of their workers, and it would almost certainly beat him at the next election. The bill would be of negligible help for the industry, no help to the employees, and also of only a little consequence to the state treasury, but Bumpers thought the principle was too important. He suggested that Walmsley tell people that the governor had put it to him personally and threatened to give no consideration to him and the district for either patronage or capital improvements if he voted for the bill.

Walmsley finally consented and the next day at the end of the roll call he cast the deciding vote that killed the bill. Within a half hour, pages were bringing him notes to call J. K. Southerland, Lynn Lanier, and other poultry executives. He returned their calls, collected their censure, and took the notes down to the governor's office. Bumpers had his executive secretary, Archie Schaffer III, call the men and invite them to a meeting Saturday morning in the board room of Southerland's bank at Batesville. Bumpers met them there along with Walmsley and Paul Henry, the state representative. Bumpers thanked the men for bringing so many jobs and so much prosperity to the community and sort of apologized for his principled stand to avoid cutting their taxes while asking the rest of the population to bear a greater tax burden. He went around the room pointing out how each of the men was serving on or seeking appointment to important state boards like Livestock and Poultry or Banking and left a hint that they might not be appointed or reappointed. He said he had put great pressure on their young senator to jeopardize his own political career in order to go with the governor and against important leaders in the community. Now he hoped they would give the young man their allegiance, because he was doing his best to do what was right for all the people of the state. The meeting broke up with handshakes and merriment all around. Walmsley couldn't believe it. He did not get an opponent in the next election.

It was not Walmsley's last political lesson. Somewhere in his second legislative session, he noticed that the Senate elders, several of whom rarely helped the governor's program, still got favors from the governor's office—even a new state park (Village Creek and Woolly Hollow) in the case of Senators Clarence E. Bell and Mutt Jones, or the appointment of their supporters to state boards and commissions. He took his peeve to the governor. He had stood with Bumpers through thick and thin, voting for and often sponsoring politically difficult bills, but the rewards seemed sometimes to go to men who always looked after their own narrow interests. He said he felt a little unappreciated.

"Well, Bill," Bumpers said, "have you sponsored anything that you didn't think was in the best interest of the state or your people up there?"

"No sir."

"Well, have you voted for anything that you thought wasn't right or good for your people?"

"No sir."

"Well, Bill, I don't see how I owe you a damned thing."

"No sir," Walmsley replied, "I guess you don't."

He walked out of the Capitol into the sunlight, he told me years later, and never in his life had he felt so proud of himself.

VIII
The Natural

In February 1957, David Hampton Pryor of Camden and his dormitory mate at the University of Arkansas at Fayetteville, Kenneth Cole "Kenny" Danforth of El Dorado, drove down to the Capitol at Little Rock to testify against a race-baiting bill that was sailing through the legislature. Segregationist rabble-rousers like state Senator Jim Johnson had a passel of bills to deter school integration by letting schools use public funds to fight integration in court, punish groups like the National Association for the Advancement of Colored People, and intimidate teachers and others who might espouse civil rights. The truly scary bill, the one Pryor and Danforth intended to testify against, created a "state sovereignty commission" that would have extralegal powers to investigate and punish people who expressed any sympathy for equal rights for African Americans. Pryor and Danforth had grown up in deeply segregated towns thirty miles apart and went to schools reserved for white children, but, perhaps by mutual persuasion, they had shed the bigotries of their upbringing. Both had begun to practice the trade of their choice, journalism—Danforth as editor of the student newspaper, the *Traveler*, and Pryor as an irregular columnist and editorial writer. Pryor deplored the rising hysteria that was evident in the 1956 elections and the preparations for the legislative session of 1957. The occasional compliments from professors and students buoyed him, and he was thinking that this might be a pretty good career.

When the roommates reached the Capitol for the big hearing on the sovereignty commission, they were met at the foot of the Capitol steps by Storm Whaley, the normally gladdening redhead who was an administrator and public relations hand for the university and who was stationed at the university's nearby medical campus.

You must not do this, said Whaley, who apparently had been alerted by the president's office at Fayetteville that the students were going to Little Rock to testify. Pryor was president of the student body and had told people what he was going to do. He would seem to be speaking for the student body or the student government. Whaley said their opposition to the sovereignty commission, which was part of Governor Faubus's program, in such a big forum could jeopardize the university, which depended upon the governor and the legislature for financial support. The newspapers were likely to report what they said. It was the same argument I would hear that fall when B. C. Hall and I were editing the little weekly paper at Henderson State Teachers College.

Whether by pre-arrangement or not, Pryor and Danforth could not get recognized to speak at the hearing in the chamber of the House of Representatives. The chairman said there were too many speakers, like the Malvern Baptist preacher Dr. Hoyt Chastain, who brought down the house by shouting that he supported segregation because the communists opposed it, and Pryor's old neighbor at Camden, former governor Ben T. Laney, who said the people of Arkansas would never stand for integration. Danforth and Pryor checked into the Marion Hotel overnight and spent the evening listening to legislators harangue about the segregation legislation in the Marion's all-night coffee shop and its basement grill, the Gar Hole, where hideous needlenose fish swam menacingly in a giant glass tank behind the bar. The whole experience was life-changing, especially for Pryor, engendering a passion for politics and governing. "An eye-opening and inspired education in practical politics," he would call it a half century later in his memoir. Danforth would carry on as a journalist at the *Arkansas Gazette*, *Time* magazine, and *National Geographic*. Pryor would go into politics.

Only one member of the 100-member House of Representatives voted against the sovereignty bill, Representative Ray S. Smith Jr. of Hot Springs, who would become one of his best friends in Pryor's later years in the legislature and the governor's office. Ray Smith furnished a profile in courage that Pryor took to heart. Pryor marveled that Smith did not even get an opponent at the next election and, although he followed the same course on other tough issues, served another twenty-five years. A dozen men in the Senate fought the bill—notably Max Howell of Little Rock, Mutt Jones of Conway, Sam Levine of Pine Bluff, and Robert Hays Williams of Russellville. Jones pronounced it "the most vicious legislation a democratic body ever enacted upon its people." In the racial cauldron that followed Faubus's effort that fall to thwart school integration by using the National Guard, all but Sam Levine fell mute.

As for Faubus, he seemed to be a reluctant advocate of creating a state gestapo to enforce segregation, but he had made a quiet deal with the east Arkansas political powers. Hugh Patterson, the publisher of the *Gazette*, and Forrest Rozzell, the head of the Arkansas Education Association, had persuaded Faubus to seek a one-cent increase in the sales tax for the public schools. It stood little chance of passage but east Arkansas interests, like R. B. McCullough, a Forrest City lawyer, struck a deal with Faubus that they would help pass his sales tax if he committed to pushing the segregation package, including the sovereignty commission, and signing all the bills into law. The sales tax passed and McCullough would become the attorney for the short-lived sovereignty commission. Faubus stalled on appointing the citizen members of the commission for months, until Jim Johnson arranged to sue him. Faubus observed that the commission could outlaw the NAACP, which might make the law unconstitutional, but nevertheless he thought it had adequate safeguards. As soon as he appointed the public members, a lawsuit challenged the act, and two years later the Arkansas Supreme Court ruled that its key provisions were unconstitutional. The commission never met again and, unlike the Mississippi and Virginia sovereignty commissions, the agency never undertook a single investigation or, apparently, spied on a single person, although the State Police would take on that role for Faubus.

For Pryor, the sovereignty skirmish at the Capitol stoked a latent penchant for a political life. If anyone ever had politics in his DNA, it was David Pryor. His mother, Susie Pryor, was nineteen years old when the 19th amendment was ratified, giving women the right to vote. When she was twenty-one, she became the first woman in Arkansas to run for public office, losing a race for county clerk of Ouachita County to a World War I veteran who had lost a leg in the war. But then she became one of the first women in the state to be elected to a school board. His father, Edgar Pryor, a car dealer, was twice elected county sheriff. Politics was the dinner-table talk. Ben Laney, the former governor and Dixiecrat leader, was a neighbor. John L. McClellan practiced law in the town, and the Pryors supported him when he ran successfully for the U.S. Senate in 1942 and every race after that until 1972, when Pryor ran against him. The district's congressman, Oren Harris, was a family friend and would later make the young Pryor a congressional page. At age twenty, Pryor worked in the re-election campaign of Governor Francis Cherry and suffered that bitter defeat with him.

A fascination with the machinations and tactics of running for office and also with the mysteries of actually getting things done in a democratic government was not the young man's only aptitude for a political career. His disposition was perfect for it. Everyone in the first grade was his friend. He was elected president of the class and, as he would tell it, he immediately began calculating how he could get elected president of the second grade. He expected to be the head of the class, and the class always expected him to be. He made top grades and was co-captain of the Camden Panthers

football team his senior year. As the tailback in the old single-wing formation that Camden used, Pryor passed, ran, and kicked for the Panthers,
which meant that he was at the center of the action on nearly every play.
He averaged 4.3 yards a carry and made first-team all-district. He enrolled
at Henderson State Teachers College at Arkadelphia, where he immediately made friends with nearly everyone. No one was too low or too prestigious to escape his merry greetings. Whenever he encountered the college's
somber president, Dr. Dean Depew McBrien, in the halls, Pryor would
exclaim, "Hey, Dean, how are you?" on his assumption that "Dean" was
McBrien's title, not his first name. The president had a member of his staff
find Pryor after class one day and tell him that the president considered it
impertinent for a student to shout at him by his first name and that if he
was going to speak to the president at all he should address the president
as "Doctor McBrien." My own trifling impertinence five years later in publishing a vapid editorial on the Arkansas legislature against Dr. McBrien's
instructions merited a threat of expulsion from the college, although he
never acted on the threat. Both Pryor and I left, although his salutation
offenses apparently were not the cause of his leaving.

Pryor transferred to the University of Arkansas at Fayetteville and grav-
itated into its more vibrant culture of campus and civilian politics. He had
decided that politics and public service were what he was cut out to do, and
he was going to major in political science, government, and history. At the
end of his first year at the university, in the summer of 1954, he received a
call out of the blue at the dormitory from Governor Cherry asking him to
drive him in his re-election campaign. Chauffeuring gave Pryor the rare
chance to observe politics at close hand at its very highest level and learn
from the man he thought, at the time, to be its canniest practitioner. The
white-haired judge, dour and dignified, had shocked people two years earlier by overtaking Governor Sid McMath and three other major officeholders with a series of "talkathons," in which he would sit before a radio microphone for up to twenty-four and a half hours (in his first one) answering
questions called in by listeners and appealing for money to carry on his
crusade for rectitude in government. He promised an end to politics and
backscratching in the operations of government and an administration of
immaculate probity and efficiency.

Cherry governed pretty much as he had promised, but his opponents
in 1954 tried to manufacture a few scandals: They blamed him for a rate
increase for Arkansas Power and Light approved by the state Public Service

Commission, accused him of secretly giving Hot Springs gambling operators the green light to resume the casino gambling that had supposedly
been chased into the shadows by McMath, and caused him to waffle on his
unpopular plan to assess all property in the state at 100 percent of its value.
But Cherry's conservatism had taken a sanctimonious tone, which Pryor
divined soon enough did not serve him well. Cherry referred to "dead-
beats" who undeservedly got welfare checks. He proposed that people be
required to give the state liens on their real estate in exchange for getting
old-age and disability checks, but the legislature did not pass his bill. He
was still able to remove 2,300 people from the rolls in four months. Orval
Faubus, then still his daddy Sam's boy, said Cherry wanted to make a poor
widow give up the $200 she had saved to pay for her burial. Cherry's con-
servatism was genuine even if it was naïve. He came to be viewed as heedless of the strivings of common people. Sixty-five years later, a Republican
governor would be a hero for lopping a hundred thousand poor people
from health-insurance rolls.

Still, Pryor adored Cherry, who was as uncommonly kind to him as he
was dour and unyielding to many others, especially legislators, state officials, and others whose goodwill and favor the governor needed from
time to time. He had refused to build a statewide political organization,
calling it the bane of government and public service. The young driver,
who was still not old enough to vote, got to see how real politics worked,
and it was not a lesson from a civics textbook. At a rally at Perryville north
of Little Rock, state Representative Paul Van Dalsem, a bulldog of a man
and a bully, asked Cherry to come to his house after the speaking. There,
Van Dalsem told him that he wanted his friend Carl Adams, the county
judge of little Perry County, to be appointed state welfare commissioner.
He wanted a point-blank commitment from the governor, which Cherry wouldn't give. Wandering around the house, Pryor spotted two of the
governor's opponents, Faubus and Senator Mutt Jones, sitting on beds in
other rooms. Faubus apparently supplied the right answer that night. The
following March, he made Adams his welfare commissioner.

Long after that campaign, Pryor would discern another valuable lesson
from chauffeuring. A big weakness of the governor was that he actually
had a distaste for retail politics—talking to ordinary people, listening to
them, and asking them for their vote. When the governor and his driver
arrived in a town for one of the rallies that were the staple of campaigning
in pre-television days, Cherry had Pryor park the car a few blocks away

and go to the rally while Cherry sat in the car listening to Harry Caray and the St. Louis Cardinals or perhaps Guy Lombardo and his orchestra. Pryor would sprint back and fetch Cherry when it was time for him to speak. Faubus would mingle in the crowd trying to see everyone and, while gripping the person's hand and staring at the ground, pretend to absorb and ponder everything the person told him. But it was still stunning when the governor did not receive a clear majority in the preferential primary.

Cherry and everyone else in the campaign fell into a funk, because the conventional wisdom was that an incumbent would not win a runoff. In desperation, Cherry decided to go all out on the Commonwealth College story and the implication that Orval Faubus was not a decorated combat soldier with the heart of a common man but a subversive. The televised Army-McCarthy hearings in Washington, which looked into communist infiltration of the armed forces, had just ended and the nation was transfixed by Senator Joseph McCarthy's bullying and lying and finally by Army lawyer Joseph Welch's famous squelch when McCarthy attacked the loyalty of a young lawyer in Welch's firm: "Let us not assassinate this lad further, Senator. You've done enough. Have you no sense of decency, sir, at long last? Have you left no sense of decency?" Edward R. Murrow had delivered his own screed against McCarthy in the television documentary *See It Now*: "We will not walk in fear, one of another. We will not be driven by fear into an age of unreason." McCarthy's great popularity had collapsed. Arkansas's own senior senator from Camden, John McClellan, had led a walkout of Democratic senators from the Republican-run subcommittee to protest McCarthy's tactics, and J. William Fulbright, an early critic, was a sponsor of the resolution late that year that censured McCarthy and effectively ended his career.

Francis Cherry was no Joe McCarthy—his opposite, in fact, in terms of rectitude and decency—but he enabled Faubus to collect sympathy for having his patriotism assaulted. Harry Ashmore, who penned Faubus's defense of his Commonwealth sojourn, was Faubus's Murrow. Cherry, who had piled up a 64 percent landslide against Governor McMath two years earlier, lost to Faubus by a narrow margin. Pryor never saw anyone else so demolished by defeat. The governor sobbed in the car as Pryor drove back to the mansion from his headquarters on election night, his sorrow perhaps magnified by regret over what he thought he had to do to win. Pryor promised him that night that he would one day even the score. For the youngster, the heady experience of a close relationship with a great leader ended in particularly bitter disillusionment, not so much with Cherry but with voters and with politics. He returned to Fayetteville determined to follow another course and get a degree in business.

Not for long. How to get into position to change the laws and improve people's prospects for happiness—those were provocative fields of study and pining. How to sell things and make money at it was a tedious subject and depressing to contemplate as a career. Even his body had rebelled at his turn of mind. That fall, Pryor went back to Camden for a few days, where he developed a mysterious infection that nearly cost him his vision and then his life. He recuperated from a string of surgeries and relapses and returned to college a year later, in the fall of 1955, and for two years focused his passion on politics rather than scholarship. In the back of his mind was his youthful boast to the fatherly Cherry on the night of the defeat that he would one day avenge the terrible injustice at the hands of Orval Faubus. For two years, he followed Faubus's modest work at the Capitol, the degrading 1956 primary campaign in which the governor tried to steer a moderate course while promising segregation just avidly enough to stymie the hotspur Jim Johnson, and the 1957 legislative session, where massive resistance carried the day and he had his first hands-on experience, in the sovereignty commission debate, with the thrall of pervasive fear and hatred.

In the summer of 1956, Congressman Harris arranged a job for Pryor on the graveyard shift in the U.S. House of Representatives' mail office. Pryor got to sit in the Senate and House galleries, hang around the U.S. Capitol, and see and hear all the great figures of the day—Everett Dirksen, Sam Rayburn, Lyndon Johnson, Walter George, John F. Kennedy, Russell Long, Hubert Humphrey. He was reading *Profiles in Courage* on a bench in the Capitol when Kennedy tapped him on the knee and asked what he thought of the book. They were heady experiences for a youngster. He was about to return to Camden to get ready for the fall term at Fayetteville when Paul Chambers, the Democratic national committeeman from Arkansas, who had once run a car agency at Camden, asked him to serve as the sergeant at arms for the Arkansas delegation to the Democratic National Convention in Chicago, the convention that sacrificed the brilliant Adlai Stevenson, for the second time, to Dwight Eisenhower. When they showed up at the historic Palmer House the day before the convention to get into their room, they learned that their reservation had been canceled by Senator McClellan and that the hotel was full. Chambers had audaciously run for the U.S. Senate in 1954 against McClellan and Sid McMath and had finished a distant third. Chambers was outraged at the room cancellation, so the hotel finally provided them cots among racks of men's suits in the sample room of a clothing salesman at the end of a dark basement corridor. When the convention ended, Chambers ducked out early and left Pryor with the Palmer House bill for their week's stay. Pryor's mom wired the money. There were lessons to learn every day. But the experience was worth Susie's money. Stevenson, Lyndon Johnson, and Governor Averill Harriman came to the Arkansas delegation's caucuses to make their pitches. From the floor, Pryor heard all the historic speeches—Frank Clement's thundering keynote diatribe ("How long, O America, how long?"), Kennedy's eloquent nomination of Stevenson, Eleanor Roosevelt's plea for the urbane statesman, and Jack Kennedy's memorable concession speech after he lost the vice-presidential nomination to Estes Kefauver.

Journalism was the most appealing prospect when Pryor graduated from the university in 1957, and on the way back to Camden he dropped by the *Arkansas Gazette* and offered his services to A. R. Nelson, the managing editor. Nelson did not need another reporter. Pryor tried the *Pine Bluff Commercial* and the *Fordyce News Advocate,* to no avail, and then called Nelson and offered to write for the *Gazette* free for three months to prove himself. Nelson still wasn't interested. Back home, he talked to people about starting a weekly newspaper in competition with the *Camden News*, a daily paper in Clyde Palmer's (and later Walter Hussman's) chain of dailies and weeklies that covered most of southwest Arkansas. It was a foolhardy notion even in that day of newspapers' prime. But Pryor acquired an interest in an old print shop and he, his mother, and his new bride, Barbara Lunsford, began to print the *Ouachita Citizen*. Susie Pryor wrote society news while Barbara reported, wrote obituaries, sold advertising, and wrote a regular column called "Something Good" about people in the community performing good deeds. Pryor covered government and civic news; wrote blistering editorials about Faubus, state government, and the shortcomings of local officials; collected debts; and tried to stay current on notes at the bank. The *Gazette*'s editorial section on Sundays often republished excerpts from Pryor's editorials, along with those from other newspapers that dared to offer a slant on the affairs of government.

Governor Faubus took notice. Campaigning for re-election on the square at Camden in the summer of 1958, Faubus went to the microphone holding three journals that had ridiculed him after the school crisis, one of them Pryor's little paper, which had endorsed Faubus's principal opponent, Chris Finkbeiner, a big cheery man who made wieners at his meatpacking plant at Little Rock and piloted his Beechcraft Bonanza to political events all over the state. (Finkbeiner was killed six years later when his plane crashed after takeoff at Fayetteville.)

"*Life*," Faubus said, waving a copy, "is a magazine for people who can't read. *Time* is for people who can't see. And the *Ouachita Citizen* is for people who can't think!" In other venues, Faubus would flaunt a copy of the *Gazette* instead of Pryor's little Camden paper. Pryor watched as the crowd, including lifelong acquaintances, cheered. Pryor thought he caught the baleful glares of a few neighbors standing nearby. He ducked away and went home. Faubus beat Finkbeiner and Lee Ward in a landslide and carried Ouachita County easily, as did two other objects of Pryor's editorial scorn, Attorney General Bruce Bennett of neighboring El Dorado and Jim Johnson, who beat an eminent justice of the Arkansas Supreme Court, Minor W. Millwee. Fourteen years later, in another political campaign, Johnson would refer to Pryor and his supporters as "a mess of trash." On the rare occasion that the *Camden News,* which was run by Clyde Palmer's son-in-law, Walter E. Hussman, editorialized on matters of state, it found no fault with anything Faubus or the other men in power said or did. But the daily paper's economic clout with advertisers, not its timidity or its support of demagogic politicians, kept Pryor's brash little weekly from gaining a foothold in the market. The *Citizen* was fast delivering the whole family into penury, and in 1960 Pryor sold it.

Facing bleak prospects for any success in the newspaper business, Pryor figured that it was as good a time as any to start the political career that he had decided was his destiny. He went to Bill Andrews, the state representative from Ouachita County and a family friend, and asked if he intended to continue to line up behind Faubus in the legislature and to keep kowtowing to the courthouse gang. If he did, then Pryor was going to oppose him in the Democratic primary in 1960. Andrews told Pryor that he had no practical choice but to stick with the establishment and to work with Faubus, or else he would be completely ineffective. Pryor ran against him, campaigning door to door with his wife and often his newborn son in a stroller. The Faubus organization, figuring African Americans would vote for Pryor, induced the band director at the black high school in south Camden to run for the seat along with Andrews, expecting that he would split the small anti-Faubus vote with Pryor and perhaps get into the runoff rather than Pryor and save the seat for Andrews.

Pryor still carried every box in the county. He absorbed political lessons every day. He traded in his old Chevrolet for a flashy little Opel, which was made in Germany, although General Motors owned the company. He drove to the little Camden suburb of Chidester, parked in front of the town's gas-

David Pryor

oline station, handed each of the old men sitting in chairs under the overhang a thimble—the gimmick he and Barbara had hit upon—and took a seat with the old whittlers and began to talk about the heat. One of them looked up, saw his car, and asked, "What kind of car is that?"

"It's an Opel," Pryor said and recounted its great features: superior gas mileage, easy steering, and quick pickup. He said it was made in Germany.

The old man shifted his stare back to his whittling. "They killed my boy," he muttered.

Pryor drove back to the GM dealer and traded the Opel for his old Chevy.

His father, who died of leukemia when Pryor was eighteen, taught him the "politics of neutralization." Don't make enemies of your opponent's friends and supporters. Disagree with your opponent but don't vilify him; you both just happen to be seeking the same office. If people say they have already committed to vote for your opponent, tell them that they are morally obliged to do so but that you would like to have their votes the next time. Be gracious in either defeat or victory and always gallantly praise the man or woman who beat you or lost to you. That would be critical to his future electoral success, but Pryor would live to see the day, with the election of Donald Trump in 2016, that the opposite strategy would become the norm.

Joining the Arkansas legislature in 1961 with a reputation as a Faubus adversary and maybe an integrationist did not augur a career of legislative accomplishment. A foe of the popular governor would have been taxed to pass a resolution praising the father of the country on the occasion of his birthday or to designate clay pottery as the official Arkansas art form.

Pryor fell into the company of a band of likeminded dissidents, whom the *Gazette* began to call the Young Turks: Representatives Hardy W. Croxton of Rogers, Virgil Butler of Batesville, Jim Brandon of Little Rock, Joe Hamilton of Harrison, and Ray S. Smith Jr. of Hot Springs. None except Smith could pass a bill of any note, although Butler had served a spell in the legislature during the Great Depression. They rallied behind the aging Butler's crusade for a new constitution and widening the democracy through election reform. The 1964 amendment ending the poll tax and creating a system of free and permanent voter registration was a byproduct of their work and Winthrop Rockefeller's. Butler believed that the restrictive provisions put into the Constitution by the Redeemers in 1874 to thwart the Reconstruction governors, and another round of restrictions during the Great Depression, were the main reason that Arkansas was so far behind the rest of the country in education and living standards. Pryor would devote his later years as governor, fruitlessly, to reforming the Constitution.

His first crusade was to trim the omnipotent power of county judges, whose unfettered control of the administration of counties, sometimes in alliance with the sheriff, was a playbook for corruption. The county judge picked who supplied the labor, gravel, culverts, and equipment for road improvements, who sold the county the supplies for all the departments, and how much the county paid them. He could reward friends and punish foes and sometimes gain monetarily from the friendships. Pryor introduced a bill at the first legislative session to require county judges to get bids on any purchase or project amounting to more than $300 and award the business to the lowest competent bidder. County judges, naturally, opposed the bill, and it could not get out of committee. He introduced it at every session. Faubus wandered over to him one evening in the Skyway hall on top of the old Hotel Lafayette and said he agreed that Pryor's bill was badly needed. If Pryor could pass it, the governor said, he would happily sign it into law.

In a few days, Representative Harry B. Colay of Magnolia, an aging family friend, introduced Pryor's bill with a few insignificant changes. It sailed through both houses and Faubus signed Colay's bill into law. The old man was credited with reforming county government. Colay sought Pryor out privately to apologize for upstaging him. Faubus and House leaders made him do it, he said. Colay's best friend wanted to be on the board of trustees of Southern State College (now Southern Arkansas University) at Magnolia, and Faubus's price for making the appointment was that Colay had to take over Pryor's bill and put his own name on it. The strategy was to make apostates like Pryor and Brandon look ineffective to voters back home. They must have nothing to show for having been elected and served.

The 26-year-old freshman's virility in a chamber of mostly staid old men was compromised by his circumstances. Pryor had enrolled full time in law school at Fayetteville and commuted frantically between Camden, Little Rock, and Fayetteville and the demands of family, law classes, and the legislature. At Fayetteville, he became the *Arkansas Gazette's* correspondent, providing the newspaper with the occasional tidbits of news of the sort that community stringers from around the state provided the two statewide papers, with small remuneration. Stringers rarely were identified in bylines or else Pryor's association with the "integrationist" paper would have increased Pryor's alienation in a government that generally considered the *Gazette* a hostile force.

One day in the summer of 1963, a student group at the university invited Dr. Albert Ellis, a famous New York psychotherapist, to give a talk on the campus. Ellis had written the book *Sex and the Single Man* in 1962 and joined the ranks of men and women—Alfred Kinsey, Masters and Johnson (William and Virginia), and Dr. Ruth (Westheimer)—who were breaking taboos by talking publicly and permissively about sex and kindling the Sexual Revolution. The university first tried to block the talk, which only attracted attention and increased the fervor of anticipation. Pryor covered the event for the *Gazette*.

Ellis did not disappoint. One remark stood out, at least for me. Leroy Donald was absent from the state desk that evening and I went over, took Pryor's notes on the telephone, and wrote the story for the *Gazette's* front page. Ellis's provocative remark was that any man who had not had sex by the age of thirty was apt to be in for a life of mental instability. In 1963, it was a shocking statement. He seemed to be encouraging promiscuity. Pryor recognized it and, at the end of our conversation, he wanted to make sure that I was not going to put his byline on the story. The bearer of bad news often is the person shot. At the top of the article I typed only "Gazette State News Service." To quell the storm over Ellis's apostasy, the president of the university in the days afterward made it clear that Dr. Ellis's atrocious remarks did not represent the views of the university. Governor Faubus condemned Dr. Ellis and said the university should not have let him on the campus. Legislators fumed and suggested that the state should take reprisals against the school. Although I only followed the newspaper's byline policy in not placing his byline on the story, I would always maintain with Pryor that I had saved his political career by not giving him a byline on the sensational sex story.

Actually, Orval Faubus should be credited with saving, or at least advancing, Pryor's career, and it was intentional. It was one of the many discordant impulses that littered Faubus's life. Pryor was settling into a profitable legal practice at Camden with his friend Harry Barnes in July 1965 when Fred Coleman, a railroad lobbyist from Arkansas, telephoned him from Washington with a heads-up that Oren Harris was about to retire and be appointed to a new federal judgeship. Coleman, a close friend of Harris, who was himself young Pryor's first patron, thought Pryor could get a jump on everyone else in running for Harris's south Arkansas seat in the special election that would soon follow. But President Lyndon B. Johnson announced Harris's appointment the next day. State Auditor Jimmie "Red" Jones bought a house in Pine Bluff so that he would be living in the district at the special congressional election. Jones, an amiable man who had not a single critic in the state and whose familiar name had appeared on every poll-tax receipt and on every state ballot for the previous ten years, would be certain to lead the ticket and probably to win in a special primary and election. Dean Murphy of Hope, a brash-talking truck-stop operator who had given Harris the scare of his career in the 1964 election, announced that he would run again. Richard S. Arnold of Texarkana, a legal scholar with an impeccable family pedigree (President Clinton almost appointed him to the U.S. Supreme Court in 1994), soon announced for the seat. Charles L. "Chuck" Honey of Prescott, a lawyer who would later have a career in the state House of Representatives, entered the race, as did a prominent Pine Bluff lawyer named John Harris Jones. Pryor had no money, no organization outside Ouachita County, and little name recognition. Barely two weeks after the president's nomination, the Senate confirmed Harris for the judgeship. Since his congressional seat would be vacant for seventeen months, Governor Faubus was expected to schedule a special primary and election for a couple of months away so that the district would have representation. It would leave no time for the novice to build a campaign that would give him a realistic chance.

Faubus announced instead that special primaries and a special election would be too costly for the state and that there was no urgency in giving the district representation in Washington. The House had just passed the Voting Rights Act, which curtailed voting restrictions on African Americans across most of the South (Harris had voted against it, like every other member of the state's delegation), and nothing else important seemed to be on the agenda in Washington. Faubus called a special election to coincide with the general election in November 1966, fourteen months away, and special party primaries a few weeks earlier. For Pryor, a full year's preparation seemed to be a fortuitous stroke of luck, delivered to him by his biggest enemy.

His good fortune was not accidental, he would learn later. It was another affirmation of his lifelong gift—to make friends of everyone he met. At the law school at Fayetteville, he had developed a close friendship with Farrell Faubus, the governor's troubled son, who had enrolled at the same time. They shared classes, exchanged notes when one or the other—usually Pryor—missed classes, drank a little beer together, and occasionally played a round of golf at a public course in Fayetteville. Pryor liked him, thought he was brilliant in spite of his clumsiness, and worried about his mental health. Other law students avoided Farrell, either because of misgivings about his controversial father or owing to his own social ineptness. He was overweight and was blundering in the most trivial social circumstance. His father always seemed embarrassed by his son, who sought out a friend wherever he could find one, including people like Pryor who were not fans of his father.

In August 1965, after the Senate confirmed Oren Harris for the judgeship, Farrell went to his father and urged him not to call an early special election for the congressional seat, because it would be the only chance that his friend David Pryor might have to build a credible campaign. He told his father that Pryor was about the only classmate who befriended him and was about the most decent man he knew. He asked his father to delay the election for his friend and also for him.

(For a moment, excuse my skipping ahead eight years, to 1974, when Faubus tried a second comeback, this time against David Pryor. I followed him around the state for a couple of weeks, along with Farrell and Farrell's miniskirted girlfriend, Trinket Bean, who traveled together behind Orval in a station wagon on some days and tried to distribute cards to people Orval missed as he went from store to store shaking hands. Faubus never cast a glance at either his son or the girl, as if he had no idea who they were, and obviously hoped I would not write about them. In the evenings, Farrell would pound on the door of my motel room with a bottle of whiskey and with Trinket in tow. He wanted to discuss campaign strategy with an earnestness that was heartbreaking, and I had to run them out to get some sleep. I accorded Orval some grace and mentioned the couple only once, deep in an article. Farrell's old friend Pryor was Faubus's victorious opponent that summer. Two years later, after fights with his father and stepmother at Huntsville and a family commitment to the State Hospital at Little Rock, a final attempt at suicide succeeded at the home of Farrell's aunt in Seattle. He emptied several bottles of drugs into his stomach.) As his own tortured old age neared its end, Orval Faubus sought out old enemies, from Daisy Bates to journalist Paul Greenberg, in search of grace or forgiveness. One was David Pryor. Faubus said that he regretted their political disagreements and that he had always liked Pryor. He thanked Pryor, then a U.S. senator approaching retirement, for befriending his son and said that he was proud both to have pleased his son on that distant occasion and to have played a part in Pryor's successful career. When Faubus scheduled the special primaries and election a year away, Jimmie "Red" Jones decided not to run for Congress after all. An early special election, if Faubus had called it, would have allowed Jones to test his strength in a regional election without abandoning an office that he could safely hold for the rest of his life. When Faubus delayed the election a year, Jones chose certainty over an uncertain future in Washington and ran for auditor again, unopposed. The congressional primaries in the summer of 1966 (all the candidates appeared twice on the same ballot: to finish the last six weeks of Harris's term after the general election, and then to serve the following two years) came down to a contest between Richard Arnold's engulfing media campaign and David and Barbara Pryor's relentless boy-and-girl-next-door personal greetings. Pryor's beaming young wife, a vision of incarnate April in colorful print dresses, was nearly always at his side.

With the little money he had for media buys, Pryor simply paid local radio stations to announce that he would be in towns to make a talk at a certain time and place, but he was often met with no crowd. He and Barbara arrived at an intersection at the tiny town of Sparkman just north of his legislative district to find only two persons, one of whom promptly climbed onto a bus and left. Pryor made his talk to one old man, who happened to be a mechanic who had once asked Pryor, his state representative, to use his clout to get the Fordyce Telephone Company or Southwestern Bell Telephone Company to run a line out to his house in the woods between Camden and Sparkman. Pryor started to give his talk anyway while the old man kept muttering a single refrain: "Never got me no telephone, never got me no telephone . . ." Then he followed Pryor down the street as he went from store to store to meet clerks and customers, chanting to everyone, "Got a big crowd, didn't he? Never got me no telephone . . ." Pryor would remember the man all his life as the personification of the democratic experiment. The man had wanted telephone service like all the townspeople had, and Representative Pryor couldn't deliver.

Pryor led the balloting for both the short and full terms with about 35 percent of the votes and Arnold entered the runoffs with about 21 percent. Then the campaign got nasty. Flyers announcing that "Black Power Supports David Pryor" mushroomed across the district. The flyers claimed, falsely, that the radical SNCC (Student Nonviolent Coordinating Committee) and Stokely Carmichael, one of the original Mississippi Freedom Riders and the founder of the Black Panther Party, had endorsed Pryor. SNCC was demonstrating at lunch counters in Little Rock and swimming pools at Pine Bluff and other cities, and had recently tried to enter the cafeteria in the basement of the State Capitol, which Faubus and Secretary of State Kelly Bryant had converted to a private club that granted membership only to whites. The flyers, which were signed "The Arkansas Committee of Concern," carried the famous quote from Carmichael, ". . .we will bring whites to their knees every time they mess with us." Pryor thought he had to buy television and radio time to denounce the flyers but decided that it would only widen their impact. He would always say that he never believed that Arnold was behind the flyers. But Arnold was behind the attacks that Pryor was controlled by "out-of-state union bosses," including Jimmy Hoffa, the Teamsters Union head and suspected mob impresario who had been convicted of jury tampering.

"Union bosses" was the nomenclature commonly applied in those days to union organizers and officers, even in objective news accounts, and it followed Pryor everywhere for ten years. He had won the endorsement of the wood and paper workers' unions, which was good for a few votes around the unionized wood and paper mills, and also the pipefitters and oil-workers unions. He went to the gates of all the unionized and nonunion mills in the district to shake hands and talk to workers at shift changes.

The 1966 congressional race would be one of the last big Arkansas elections where intense personal campaigning could be said to have made the difference. Glad-handing was not Richard Arnold's style. A scholar and honor graduate of Yale University who sometimes wrote papers in Latin, he was comfortable in the lecture hall or arguing constitutional law in the courtroom, but he became laconic and even diffident in casual repar-

Wilbur Mills

tee with the men and women upon whom you had to force yourself when you went around introducing yourself and asking for votes. He seemed to have trouble asking a person to vote for him, although he knew Pryor was right and that you had to do it. Arnold had married the daughter of Walter E. Hussman Sr., the publisher and principal owner of all the daily newspapers in the district except Pine Bluff. Hussman himself had married the daughter of Clyde E. Palmer, who built the chain of newspapers, radio stations, and television stations that blanketed south Arkansas, and inherited the empire upon Palmer's death in 1957. (Palmer's grandson, Walter E. Hussman Jr., now runs the media organization, which includes the *Arkansas Democrat-Gazette*.) The Palmer papers were the principal organ of Arnold's campaign. Long stories under the byline "Palmer Arkansas News Bureau" appeared regularly in all the newspapers, carrying Arnold's attacks on Pryor's record as a state legislator and his subservience to union bosses. Right before the runoff election, Arnold delivered a long prime-time attack on Pryor on the TV stations covering south Arkansas.

"If you want the Teamsters Union to have a congressman from the Fourth District, if you want another rubberstamp for Walter Reuther and Jimmy Hoffa in Washington, D.C.," Arnold said, "then vote for David Pryor on August 9." He said Pryor would be unduly influenced by the liberal newspapers at Pine Bluff and Little Rock (the *Pine Bluff Commercial* and *Arkansas Gazette*), which had editorialized favorably for Pryor.

Pryor thought the show was devastating, but he had no money to respond before the election on Tuesday. Bertie Murphy of El Dorado, whose husband was chairman of Murphy Oil Corporation, showed up at Camden and gave him $1,000 to respond on television. The rest of the Murphy family supported Arnold. Pryor's short speech referred to Richard Arnold repeatedly as his good friend, who he said knew better than the attacks. He denied Arnold's charge that he had received campaign money from Hoffa and Reuther. Campaign funding disclosures were not required in those days.

Pryor received nearly 65 percent of the votes in the runoff and beat Lynn Lowe of Texarkana, the Republican nominee, in the general election. As a U.S. senator in 1980, he joined Senator Dale Bumpers in nominating Arnold for the U.S. Eighth Circuit Court of Appeals. Arnold was appointed by President Jimmy Carter, and President Clinton would have appointed him to the Supreme Court had he not been diagnosed with cancer in the 1990s.

Making friends big and small was good politics, but holding the favor of divine providence was even better. The best friend to have in Washington in 1967 was Wilbur Daigh Mills, the chairman of the House Ways and Means Committee, who had been in Congress for thirty years and had practiced a camaraderie that recognized no distinctions between liberals and conservatives or between Republicans and Democrats. Every bill Mills shoved from his tax-writing committee, like the Medicare and Medicaid Act of 1965, had to have major Republican as well as Democratic support. Mills was chairman of the Committee on Committees, which recommended committee assignments to the speaker. Because Pryor was elected at both a special and a general election, he took office ahead of the other freshmen and got a bump in seniority. Mills wanted to give the youngster a leg up and wondered what committee assignment he would like to have. Appropriations, Pryor replied. Every member of Congress wanted to be on the Appropriations Committee, because everyone on Capitol Hill or in the executive branch and every lobbyist beseeched the friendship of the men who clutched the nation's purse strings.

No, no, Mills said, that is impossible. Eighty new representatives were about to be sworn in, but the election had created no vacancies on the Democratic side of Appropriations. Besides, many representatives with seniority were on the Appropriations waiting list.

On January 10, when all the members were to be sworn in, Mills's friend Representative John E. Fogarty of Rhode Island stood up in his office in the Longworth building to walk across Independence Avenue to take the oath of office for his fourteenth term and fell dead of a heart attack. Mills telephoned Speaker John W. McCormack of Massachusetts and told him to put freshman Pryor in Fogarty's slot on Appropriations. Three days after Fogarty's funeral, Pryor took his seat on Appropriations.

Fogarty had spent his twenty years on the Appropriations Committee fighting for better health and medical research, especially for the elderly and the mentally and physically disabled. Pryor tried his best to channel the old union bricklayer. He took up the cause of men and women in nursing homes, which were haphazardly regulated. He modified his name and worked part time as an orderly in nursing homes in the District of Columbia and northern Virginia, kept notes, and then exposed the mistreatment and unsanitary disregard of patients that he had found in nursing homes that housed the poorest people. Pryor's crusade brought him some national attention but a cold rebuff from the House leadership, which never cared for greenhorns who upstaged their seniors. In the end, his efforts brought stiffer federal and state standards and regulations of nursing homes, but Representative Claude Pepper of Florida, in his second congressional career, this time as a House member, would years later achieve Pryor's goal of creating a Select Committee on Aging to pursue solutions for the problems of the aging.

The year 1967 was not a propitious time for an aspiring politician from the South, especially a man of conscience, to be starting a congressional career. The civil rights revolution was in full swing and the country had plunged deeply into war in Southeast Asia. No member of Congress could duck the issues, no matter his or her constituency, especially when the same man, President Lyndon Johnson, was pursuing victory both in Asia and against segregation in his beloved South, albeit knowing that he was dooming the Democratic Party in Dixie for a half century or more. After passage of the Civil Rights Act of 1964 and the Voting Rights Act of 1965, both Democratic initiatives, rural districts across the Deep South began to turn to the Republican Party. Arkansas was not in play because, alone among the Southern states, the GOP was personified by a liberal and a passionate advocate of social justice, Winthrop Rockefeller. Johnson hammered the Senate and the House of Representatives into coming together to pass a law outlawing racial discrimination in housing, the Fair Housing Act of 1968. Only a few Southern congressmen who represented liberal urban districts, like Claude Pepper in Florida and Hale Boggs in New Orleans, could vote for the bill. Like the other five members of the Arkansas delegation, Pryor quietly cast a no. But he would make up for it.

By the arrival of the Democratic National Convention at Chicago in 1968, Democrats were sundered by the war in Vietnam, which had ignited protests in Washington and on college campuses, and by Southern resistance to civil rights. Rev. Martin Luther King and Senator Robert F.

Kennedy, both civil rights activists and foes of the war, had been slain in the months before the convention. Leading Democratic politicians in Arkansas stayed away from the convention, and Pryor was counseled to stay away from the fray and visit his constituents. But he had great memories of the 1956 convention in the same city, where he was the ceremonial sergeant at arms for the Arkansas delegation. He went to Chicago in 1968 as a delegate, and the party put him on the Credentials Committee, where the crucial battle over seating white or black delegates from Mississippi played out. While the national Democratic Party had been trying to diversify delegations to represent women and African Americans, Mississippi sent an all-white delegation of segregationists. Blacks were 35 percent of the Mississippi population, although few of them were able to vote in 1966, a year after passage of the Voting Rights Act. Mississippi still had not ratified the Thirteenth Amendment, which abolished slavery in America, and wouldn't until 1995, one hundred thirty years after Arkansas ratified it. Even then, Mississippi wouldn't send word of the ratification to the national archivist in Washington so that it would be official. The archivist finally got the state to make it official in 2013.

African Americans had organized the Mississippi Freedom Democratic Party in 1968 and gone to Chicago seeking recognition as the state's delegation. The white Mississippians refused to compromise by accepting a few black delegates, insisting on all whites or nothing. Breaking with other Southern members of the Credentials Committee, Pryor voted with the majority to seat the Freedom Party delegates. Mississippi's four congressmen and two senators did not speak to Pryor, several of them for many years. A few in his own delegation were shocked at his vote. He encountered hostility back home. At a big east Arkansas political fish fry at the Carlisle high school stadium, a man spotted Pryor from the bleachers, ran onto the field cursing him for his Mississippi vote, jumped on his back, and started pounding his head. Bobby Glover, the young mayor of Carlisle, who had been a local athletic hero, wrestled the man off Pryor and sent him on his way. When Pryor became governor six years later, Glover, by then a state representative, was one of his staunchest allies, but Pryor would always consider Glover's greatest favor to have been keeping the hotheaded racist from stomping him in front of a crowd of two thousand voters.

Vietnam proved even more troublesome. As a freshman on the Appropriations Committee in January 1967, Pryor had to assume an immediate role in funding the war. It had been two and a half years since the bogus attack on American ships in the Gulf of Tonkin sent Senator J. William Fulbright of Arkansas to the floor of the Senate to manage the resolution that would serve as the government's mandate to take whatever combat role in the revolution the administration thought would win it. Despite repeated escalations, the war went badly in every evaluation except the administration's public accounts. Public support was beginning to crumble, Fulbright himself regretted his role, and campus demonstrations were spreading. President Johnson summoned General William Westmoreland, the head of the Military Assistance Command in Vietnam, to come home and help him market the conflict, the first time in American history that a president had brought a wartime field commander home from the front to sell a war to Congress and the country. Johnson asked the chairman of the Appropriations Committee to bring a delegation to the White House to meet with Westmoreland before his televised address to Congress. The square-jawed general was the personification of the heroic warrior. There—his first visit to the White House—Pryor sat with leading members of Congress, the president, and Secretary of Defense Robert S. McNamara, listening to the great general outline the strategy for winning the war for the South Vietnamese and American people and bringing the boys home victorious. He waited for probing questions, if not rebuttals, from the wise old men of Congress. Pryor asked a couple himself but felt uninformed and irresolute. They all left submissive. In his soaring speech to Congress, Westmoreland drew cheers when he declared that his command would "prevail in Vietnam over the Communist aggressor." The tone was a little stronger than an earlier talk to the Associated Press's editors' luncheon in which he said, "I do not see any end of the war in sight."

Soon afterward, the president asked Pryor to accompany him on a political trip to Texas, where he hoped to shore up what he perceived to be flagging support in his native state. Though he projected confidence in the war effort, he seemed in private to be moody and disconsolate. Flying back that night on Air Force One over south Arkansas, Pryor looked down and saw the lights of what he thought was probably Camden. Johnson, sitting beside him, had grown quiet and was frowning.

"Mr. President," Pryor said, "it looks like we might be flying directly over Camden, Arkansas. That's my hometown. If you look straight down at the ground, you might see Jim's Cafe on Washington Street."

Johnson leaned across him to the window, peered into the darkness for a few seconds, lunged back, and closed his eyes.

"God-amighty," the president muttered, "I wish I was at Jim's Cafe right now."

More than a year later, when Pryor went to Chicago for the fateful Democratic National Convention, the war seemed to be going no better in spite of the soaring enemy body counts that the command put out regularly. Johnson and Vice President Hubert Humphrey cultivated the young Southerner. The seating of the Mississippi delegates having been settled, the real battle was over the war and the competing allegiance to Humphrey and the antiwar candidates, principally Senator Eugene McCarthy of Minnesota. Humphrey and Johnson wanted Pryor to speak for the moderate war plank they wanted in the platform. Pryor tried to call Senator Fulbright in his office in Washington to seek advice, but Fulbright was on the floor. Pryor agreed to do it and delivered a short speech to the convention supporting the plank, which he thought was a compromise version, to the dismay of many of his friends in the House of Representatives and at home, and to his own regret. Representative Thomas P. "Tip" O'Neill of Massachusetts, the future speaker, had made a powerful speech on the House floor against the war, arguing that America was intervening in a civil war in which Americans had no interest and for an altogether unrighteous cause. It had a profound impact on Pryor, but still he felt compelled to go along with the president and especially with Hubert Humphrey. His wife, Barbara, had told Pryor almost from the beginning that it was an unworthy cause that Americans would regret.

Not long after the Democratic Convention, in late 1968, Pryor climbed onto an American Airlines flight at Little Rock to return to Washington, and as he was making his way down the aisle in the coach class a young uniformed soldier stopped him. He recognized Pryor and said he was from his south Arkansas district, naming the town, Pryor would remember. Pryor asked him where he was headed. The soldier was shipping out to Vietnam.

"Man, we're lucky to have people like you doing this," Pryor told him. He thanked the soldier for his service and went to his seat in the rear of the cabin.

A Friday morning a few months later, he got on an American Airlines flight in Washington to go back to Arkansas. As he was walking through the cabin he spotted the same young man in uniform, stopped, and introduced himself.

"Hi, I'm David Pryor," he said.

"I know," the soldier said.

"I thought you were going to Vietnam," Pryor said.

"Well, I'm back," the soldier replied. He pulled a blanket off his lap, revealing two stumps for legs.

Pryor had trouble breathing. He couldn't speak for a few seconds. The young man spoke for him.

"I would not have minded," he said. "I wouldn't mind losing my legs had I ever known what I was there for."

Pryor thanked him again for his sacrifice and stumbled back to his seat. He sat numbly for the flight to Little Rock. When he returned to Washington the next week, he wrote a newsletter to his constituents. He said he would not support the war any longer, through appropriations or anything else.

IX
The Senate Contagion

John Little McClellan and David Hampton Pryor, who engaged in one
of the iconic Arkansas political battles of the twentieth century, had little in common except geographical and familial connections, matching
upbringings in the small-town culture of south Arkansas's piney plain, a
shared personal modesty that was rare among politicians, and all-consuming ambitions to be United States senators. That is to say that they contrast-
ed almost exclusively in their personal styles, the instincts that animated
their ambitions, and the aspirations of their respective generations. When
they clashed in the U.S. Senate race in 1972, McClellan was seventy-six
and a true senator of the old South, and Pryor was exactly half his age,
thirty-eight, and on the leeward side of Jim Crow and the civil rights revolution.

It was McClellan's last election and perhaps the most satisfying of his
twelve campaigns, because he was beaten yet managed not to lose. Mc-
Clellan suffered only two defeats in fifty-six years—the first one in a race
for mayor of Malvern in 1921 and the last in his first race for the Senate in
1938—while Pryor suffered a single defeat, at the hands of John McClellan,
in thirty-six years of running for and holding public office.

The everyday countenance of the two men that voters saw was a shocking
contrast. Pryor always seemed cheerful and sociable—"the happy warrior,"
to use the William Wordsworth sobriquet that was usually attached to politicians like Hubert Humphrey and Joseph Biden. Years later in the Senate,
Pryor was easily the best-liked member, because he was jovial with all his
colleagues and every employee in the Capitol and the Senate office building where he spent most of his days. He kept up with everyone's children,
including the parking policeman's. McClellan, on the other hand, always
seemed dour and distrustful, presenting to the public a visage that seemed
to have been aged by waves of grief and disappointment. Factually, it was.

Al Capp, whose rich comic strip *Li'l Abner* we all followed in the Sunday
papers in the 1940s and '50s, lampooned the culture of the midcentury
South (the physical Dogpatch of *Li'l Abner* came to the Arkansas Ozarks
in the 1960s) with such characters as Senator Jack S. Phogbound, whose
scowling bluster and barely disguised bigotry Capp intended to represent
Dixie's race-baiting demagogues of the era. Actually, Phogbound's original
model probably was Huey P. Long, "The Kingfish," who was assassinated in

1935. McClellan had become a familiar face on early television sets in the 1950s for his grimacing lectures, with young Robert F. Kennedy at his side, in the televised Senate committee hearings on labor racketeering and Joe McCarthy's communist purges. The televised hearings were Americans' first graphic encounter with their national government at work.

Depending on the episode and where you lived, Senator Jack S. (pronounced "Jackass") Phogbound might have been seen as Joe McCarthy, J. Strom Thurmond of South Carolina, Richard Russell of Georgia, or John McClellan. But McClellan was no demagogue. While he sided with the demagogues on every civil rights cause in the Senate, including the Southern Manifesto, he avoided the race-baiting flourishes of Thurmond and the rest. Sherry Laymon, McClellan's admiring biographer, said he simply recognized the political necessity of abiding by the overwhelming sentiment of white people, who were 90 percent of the Arkansas electorate, but carefully avoided the race baiting. It also must be considered that African Americans were already voting in Arkansas primaries and elections after World War II, albeit not in huge numbers, but they did not vote in large numbers in Mississippi and much of the rest of Dixie until after the passage of the Voting Rights Act in 1965. Unlike Eastland and Thurmond, John McClellan had to think about black voters, who could be pivotal in a close election.

Another Capp character, Joe Bftsplk, a miserable little man dressed in black who walked under a perpetual black storm cloud, was a more apt caricature of McClellan. Frost and icicles covered Bftsplk's nose even in midsummer. Joe was a well-meaning and generous man, but misfortune befell anyone who was unlucky enough to be around him. Naturally, he was a lonely and sad man.

Misfortune followed John McClellan from the moment of his birth in the farm community of Ain, halfway between Grapevine and Cross Roads in Grant County. His mother got sick at his birth and died within a few days. Grandparents who were sharecroppers largely raised him, but his father, who remarried and had other kids, was still a big figure in his life—a harsh taskmaster who insisted that the boy toil hard in the fields and then, at the age of ten, start reading law with him. His father became a lawyer and then John, too, at the age of seventeen, when he passed the Arkansas bar. No other requirement for a law license existed then.

He also married a Sheridan girl at the age of seventeen, who bore him a son, Max McClellan, in 1916. John joined the Army Corps, and when he came back on an unexpected furlough he confronted what was only described as an unhappy situation. His wife, Eula, almost at this same time bore him a second child, Doris. They quickly divorced—she sued on grounds of desertion and he didn't contest it—and she died of blood poisoning after calling the children to her bedside and telling them never to have anything to do with the McClellans.

John moved across the Saline River to Malvern and started practicing law. He ran for mayor and lost, a result that he would blame on a cabal of businessmen who tried to extract a promise to fire the town's water commissioner if he got elected, which he agreed only to study and pray about. The other guy promised to do it and, after the election, did. But McClellan soon married Lucille Nell Smith, the daughter of a furniture dealer, and served as the town's city attorney. Lucille bore him a son, John Jr., in 1926, the same year that he was elected prosecuting attorney by besting two men who accused him of being a divorcee. It was the brief heyday of the Ku Klux Klan in central Arkansas, where being a divorcee, a black, a Jew, a Catholic, or an imbiber of hard drink was a disqualification for public service. McClellan got a reputation as a trench fighter whom you didn't want to reckon with. After a stint as the prosecutor, when he earned the reputation as a well-prepared and tough litigator in front of juries, he ran against the district's congressman, David D. Glover, a fellow congregant at the First Baptist Church. McClellan had spoken for Glover in previous campaigns, and the congressman said he was thinking about retiring before long and encouraged McClellan to run for his seat when he did retire. It sounded like a good plan. When Ed Freeman, a Pine Bluff newspaper publisher, urged McClellan to run against Governor J. Marion Futrell, McClellan told him he was instead thinking about a career in Congress. Freeman's paper speculated that McClellan would run against Glover. Glover considered it a betrayal and announced that he was running again. McClellan, now himself aggrieved, thought he was being threatened by the old lawyer's six sons and filed against him. On the stump—town-square speechifying was the common campaign event of the times—McClellan would deftly taunt the old man, who was sixty-six, and discombobulate him. At one rally, Glover got so overwrought that he accidentally threw a glass of water from the stage into a woman's lap. From the platform, McClellan apologized to the woman for having agitated Glover so much, but he lamented that it was an all-too-common event in Washington.

After beating Glover handily, McClellan took his wife and five children to Washington in January 1935. Lucille had borne two more children, Mary Alice and Jimmy. Mrs. McClellan headed back to Arkansas with the children for the first summer congressional recess, ahead of McClellan. When they got to Memphis she became sick and was hospitalized with spinal meningitis. McClellan arranged for an Army airplane to fly him to Memphis, but she was in a coma when he arrived and died in a few hours. The children were quarantined. He left them with a caretaker and went

John McClellan

back to Washington, where he suffered bouts of depression. The next year he met Norma Cheatham, a widow with one child. She worked at the federal General Accounting Office. They were married in 1936 and the five McClellan children moved to Washington with them.

His political career after that was typically Southern: As a conservative, he was obliged to publicly condemn Franklin Roosevelt's big spending on national recovery while spending every federal dollar he could get for flood control, drainage, roads, and other public works projects in south Arkansas. In 1938, he ran against Senator Hattie Caraway, the first woman elected to the U.S. Senate (in 1932) and an ardent New Dealer, and was beaten—thanks, he believed, to his betrayal by Homer Adkins, the Internal Revenue Service director for Arkansas and the future governor, and to the votes of all the WPA workers who thought they owed their meager livelihoods to Hattie and FDR. McClellan ran again for the Senate in 1942 against Jack Holt, the popular Arkansas attorney general, and two sitting congressmen and beat them all. He was re-elected in 1948 and 1954, the second time against former Governor Sid McMath, and in 1960 and 1966 without serious opposition.

Through it all, he developed a not-entirely-original theory about politics: loyalty had to be the abiding standard. He kept a mental ledger, if not a physical one, of real and imagined betrayals and of debts. None was ever forgotten. Bob Riley, who was blinded in his right eye in World War II when he led an assault on a Japanese machine-gun emplacement on Guam and had his own political career—the state legislature, lieutenant governor,

a loss to Pryor in the 1974 governor's race—remembered running into Mc-
Clellan in the 1960s. Riley wore his trademark black eyepatch to mask his
wartime wounds. He extended his hand and introduced himself.

"I know who you are," McClellan replied, declining the handshake. He
said Riley had helped Hattie Caraway in 1938. Riley was fourteen in 1938.

Nick Wilson had a more poignant account. In 1973, he joined McClellan
and others for a tour of Blanchard Springs Caverns, where the National
Forest Service was developing the spectacular cave for tourism. Standing
outside, Wilson, a freshman state senator from up the road at Pocahontas,
told McClellan that he would like to talk to him about getting the Farmers
Home Administration to turn loose a grant for sewer-treatment lines in the
little town of Imboden. McClellan told him to call his office in Washington
the next morning at eight o'clock and ask to be put through directly to him.

Before Wilson could call the next morning, the manager of the Little
Rock FHA office called and asked him to arrange for the mayor of Imboden to meet him in the town in a couple of hours to get a check for the
sewer system. Before they hung up, the manager told Wilson, with unctuous politeness, "Senator, in the future could you just call me directly when
you need something rather than bother Senator McClellan?"

The next year, an aide to McClellan called and said the senator was expecting Wilson's support in the Senate race against Pryor and Ted Boswell.
Wilson said he had to support his old friend Boswell. When Boswell lost in
the first primary, the aide called again to ensure Wilson's support against
Pryor. Wilson said no, now he had to support his friend David. Five years
later, Wilson journeyed to Washington with Attorney General Bill Clinton
and Representatives Julian D. Streett of Camden, Ray S. Smith Jr. of Hot
Springs, and Joseph K. Mahony of El Dorado to beseech McClellan's help
in getting the U.S. Treasury Department to lift its cap on the amount of
housing revenue bonds a state could issue and for which investors could
claim interest earnings on their tax returns. Truthfully, the new Arkansas
attorney general just wanted to use the occasion to hobnob with the state's
congressional delegation. After dismissing U.S. Attorney General Griffin
Bell, who had come to introduce his new deputy to the senator, McClellan
welcomed the five Arkies into his office and sat them down around his
desk. After curtly rebuking an aide who was returning to work that day
after a siege of heart trouble for carrying a pack of cigarettes in his shirt
pocket—those joints are why you are having heart trouble and skipping
work, he told the aide—McClellan asked Clinton and the three state rep-

resentatives at length about various relatives and business associates, and told a story or two to each of them. But he never spoke to Wilson or even acknowledged his presence by as much as a glance. His gaze shifted among Wilson's four colleagues without a hint that Wilson was even in the room. To John McClellan, Wilson did not exist.

◻◻◻

But we were exploring the Joe Bftsplk dynamic in the life of John McClellan. A month after McClellan was sworn in as the new U.S. senator from Arkansas in 1943, a bellhop delivered a telegram telling him that his eldest son, Max, had died of spinal meningitis in Casablanca, Morocco, during the Army's invasion of North Africa. Max was buried there until the war's end. The Army exhumed Max's body and brought it back in 1949 to Sheridan, where he was born, for burial next to his mother. While McClellan, his wife, and three other children gathered there for Max's burial, they learned that his second son, John Jr., known as Johnny, had been in a car wreck at Fayetteville, where he was enrolled in law school, and was hospitalized with a broken arm and nose. After the burial, they climbed onto a plane and flew to Fayetteville to visit Johnny, only to learn at the airport that he had died an hour earlier. Jimmy McClellan, the youngest boy, enrolled in the law school and when he got his law degree joined a firm at Little Rock with C. Hamilton Moses, the industrialist, and Senator McClellan's son-in-law, Harry "Buddy" McDermott, who had married McClellan's daughter Mary Alice. McClellan talked about retiring and practicing law with his son at Ham Moses's firm, where he would be the "rainmaker." While Jimmy McClellan was taking a test for his pilot's license in 1958, he crashed his twin-engine plane and died. Only Senator McClellan's daughters, Doris and Mary Alice, survived him.

◻◻◻

In February 1972, when McClellan announced that he wanted a sixth term in the Senate, he confronted another slight of nearly familial gravity. Young David Pryor, the neighboring boy whose father had saved McClellan's political career in 1942, determined to end it by running against the old man. Pryor was not motivated by animus. Despite their largely generational differences on issues like segregation and war, he did not regard

McClellan as a political enemy, and the senator thought of him as an acolyte and perhaps his successor. It was simply that McClellan stood in the way of the young man's own ambition. The Senate had been Pryor's goal since he was in high school and did a summertime stint as an intern at the national Capitol, where he had planted a dime behind a granite column in the basement as a lucky charm that would bring him back one shining day to climax what he hoped would be a lifelong political career.

Pryor was starting his sixth year in the House of Representatives and feeling inconsequential. Aside from a low-ranking seat on the Appropriations Committee, which enabled him to get a little pork for south Arkansas, he was a virtual cipher in the 435-member House. What he could do as a member of the House Appropriations Committee paled alongside the casual handiwork of John McClellan, who by 1972 was chair of the Senate Appropriations Committee. Only the previous June, President Richard Nixon had gone to Tulsa to dedicate the 450 miles of the Arkansas River Navigation System and its eighteen locks and dams, at that time the largest public-works project ever undertaken and completed by the Army Corps of Engineers. It was now called the McClellan-Kerr Navigation System, after the two neighboring senators (Kerr, from Oklahoma, was chairman of the Appropriations Committee) who for twenty years had pushed enabling legislation and appropriations for Arkansas River work through the Senate. It all had started with the passage of the Rivers and Harbors Act in 1946, when McClellan was a mere freshman on the Senate Appropriations Committee.

It would take Pryor decades and survival in a dozen political races before he would be able to swing any weight in the deliberations in the House over any field of national policy. Two other young Arkansas congressmen— John Paul Hammerschmidt in the Third District comprising the Ozarks and William V. Alexander in the First District along the Mississippi River Delta—were rising stars in the Arkansas firmament and presumed to be contemplating the retirement of McClellan and the slightly younger junior senator, J. William Fulbright. But could McClellan be beaten? He was nearly defeated in 1952 by McMath, his last serious opponent. In McClellan's previous race, in 1966, an old fuddy-duddy named Foster Johnson, who spent no money and virtually no effort beyond walking around downtown Little Rock wearing clanging body-length sandwich boards proclaiming his name, got 91,000 votes. Pryor figured McClellan had the entire business and political establishment locked up, but he calculated that the old man's popular support was weak. McClellan also had accumulated some hostility, especially with labor, African Americans, and the little clot of liberals in Pulaski and Washington counties. McClellan's celebrated investigation of labor racketeering, including the steamfitters and pipefitters union in south Arkansas run by Earl and Ermon Griffin, would provide some enthusiasm for a Pryor campaign. There would be some union political aid, although it would not match the business and bank funding that McClellan could expect.

If he waited another six years, when McClellan promised to retire, Pryor likely would face every ambitious young politician in the state, including the sitting governor, Dale Bumpers. Eight days after McClellan announced that he was running again, Pryor announced. So did Ted Boswell, a youthful but silver-haired trial lawyer, and the unquenchable Foster Johnson, whose indestructible knees and sandwich boards bore him through three U.S. Senate elections in six years.

For McClellan, Pryor's decision to try to take his seat away from him was both another grievance and a cause for lamentation. Back in October 1967, when Pryor had been in Congress only eleven months, Camden threw a John McClellan Appreciation Day. Both men were on the program and, while they were freshening up, McClellan told the young man that he was the kind of person who ought to succeed him one day. Had McClellan planted the seed then for what he would consider a sort of betrayal in 1972? He also had to remember a similar remark by the aging Congressman D. D. Glover to young John McClellan in 1934, which caused the young prosecutor to mention the possibility of a future congressional race to a Pine Bluff newspaper publisher, who then published speculation about a McClellan challenge to Glover, which angered Glover and in the end produced the race that McClellan had not exactly planned but that had hastened the trajectory of his career.

More bothersome was another memory, from 1942, when David Pryor's father raised the money to keep McClellan in the race for the Senate, the pivotal moment in his long career. Raising money had always been an anguishing matter for McClellan. He didn't want to get into the closing stage of a campaign without the money to see it through.

When Senator Joe T. Robinson died soon after being sworn in for a new term in 1937 and the new governor, Carl E. Bailey, crowned himself as the Democratic nominee in a special Senate election, rebellious Democrats sought a candidate to run against him as an independent. McClellan was their first choice but, after briefly testing his financial support around the state, he went back to Washington chastened and a little grumpy. At the last minute, Congressman John E. Miller, who was little known outside his northeast Arkansas district, flew to Little Rock, got the independent nomination at a rump convention at the Marion Hotel, and then beat Governor Bailey in a landslide. The Senate seat would have been McClellan's for the taking. So two years later he was not going to play so hard to get. He took on Senator Hattie Caraway—Senator Huey P. Long, who was gunned down in the Louisiana Capitol at Baton Rouge, was no longer there to salvage her re-election—but, as he feared, McClellan ran out of money at the end and she beat him by a bare 11,000 votes.

Trying again in 1942 for Senator Robinson's old seat after President Roosevelt cleared the way by appointing Senator Miller to the federal bench for life, McClellan found himself running against the firebrand attorney general, Jack Holt, and two congressmen, David D. Terry of Little Rock and Clyde T. Ellis of Bentonville, the father of rural electrification. On a Saturday morning a few weeks before the Democratic primary, Sheriff Edgar Pryor walked from the courthouse to McClellan's nearby law office and found him typing a letter announcing that he was stopping his campaign and conceding the election. Mad and depressed, McClellan had exhausted his campaign funds and had nothing left for a final binge of advertising. Edgar Pryor called three business friends and the president of Citizens Bank and they went to the downtown bank and signed notes totaling $10,000. The $10,000 propelled McClellan into a near tie with Holt in the preferential primary and a runoff victory over Holt. Now, the son of the benefactor to whom he owed his long career was claiming his seat. How could providence be so cruel?

Long after his defeat that year, Pryor would wonder if he should have approached McClellan long before the filing period and told him of his interest in running, because McClellan might have chosen to step down on his own, owing to his age and dispiriting health, and avoid the hard campaign and the prospect of a humiliating defeat at the end of an illustrious career. Pryor said he had thought briefly about it but figured McClellan would be infuriated and therefore start even earlier to rebuild his network and a war chest.

Doubtlessly, McClellan had hired a polltaker and knew that he had a struggle. Delivering millions of dollars for public works like the Arkansas River navigation project—"McClellan-Kerr," the signs along the Arkansas locks and dams called it—had earned him the eternal loyalty of the movers and shakers, but all of it meant little to the multitudes. By 1972, most people wanted to forget the civil rights battles of the 1950s and '60s, in which he had raised his sepulchral voice for the preservation of Jim Crow. Youthful and handsome and with an ebullient wife and good-looking boys who seemingly were always at his side, Pryor had a good image all over the state and an especially worshipful following in south Arkansas, McClellan's old grounds. Average folks down there didn't count the old man as one of their own but rather as an ancient Washington figure. Pryor didn't use the civil rights issue against McClellan, because it would still have been a big loser, and he was privately abashed that he had felt compelled to vote against the single civil-rights legislation of his House tenure, the Fair Housing Act of 1968, as McClellan also had done in the Senate. Many in his district were still sore at Pryor for voting to seat the black delegation over Mississippi's white segregationists at the 1968 Democratic National Convention. There was no point in reminding them of that apostasy of the white race. Pryor's big goal was to diminish the importance of McClellan's vast seniority. He talked about using the Senate power not just for bricks and mortar but to build a good life for people through better health care, education, and help for the aged. And he was now against the increasingly unpopular Vietnam War. McClellan voted for all the war appropriations and said he was standing behind the fighting men.

How could McClellan make himself relevant to the modernists—the younger generation and all the women who were freshly energized about their secondary status in the workplace, the marketplace, the halls of government, the law, every facet of life?

The ERA.

The Equal Rights Amendment to the U.S. Constitution, which would abolish the legal distinctions between men and women, had been around since 1921, when it was first introduced in the U.S. House of Representatives a year after the ratification of the Nineteenth Amendment, which gave women the right to vote. Opposed by working-class women who feared it would take away special workplace protections for women, the ERA got nowhere. It was reintroduced in 1971 by U.S. Representative Martha Griffiths of California and approved that fall by the House. In the Senate, where power shifted to Southern states, it was viewed as a leftist scheme.

McClellan's biographer suggested that McClellan didn't merely cave in that winter to pressures from women, including his own daughter, to support the ERA but that he engineered it while seeming to be resistant. A band of women, including a few leaders of the Women's Emergency Committee, who had led the movement to reopen public high schools at Little Rock that had been closed by Governor Faubus, went to Washington to lobby for referring the ERA to the states. When they visited McClellan, he was noncommittal but mentioned his fears about how the amendment could harm women. He promised to think about it.

That summer, in the midst of his renomination campaign, I drifted into McClellan's big campaign headquarters in downtown Little Rock. Behind an elevated desk in the center of the activity sat Margaret Kolb, a Baptist church leader who had run the telephone tree for the Women's Emergency Committee and had been kept under surveillance by the State Police.

"What are you doing here?" I asked. She said she was doing everything she could to re-elect John McClellan. I expressed amazement she would be working for the conservative senator when two candidates who really suited her politics, Pryor and Boswell, were in the race. She said she had gone to see McClellan in Washington along with her good friend at the liberal Pulaski Heights Baptist Church, Mary Alice McDermott, McClellan's youngest daughter. Kolb was making the case for the ERA to McClellan when he interrupted her.

"If I support the ERA—and if I sponsor it—will you support me in the campaign?" he asked. She swallowed and said yes. "No," he said, "I mean *really* support me. Not just vote for me. Will you work openly and publicly for me and urge your friends to do it?" She said she would.

McClellan signed the amendment as a co-sponsor and pushed it through the Judiciary Committee over the opposition of the chairman, Senator James O. Eastland of Mississippi, and other Southern senators, including Estes Kefauver of Tennessee and Richard Russell of Georgia, who contended that the ERA would nullify rape, dower, and workplace laws and rules that protected women. Senator Fulbright joined McClellan as a sponsor. The ERA finally passed, 63 to 19, largely with Republican votes, but never reached the threshold of thirty-eight ratifying states. How much McClellan's role cooled the ardor for progressive women's natural champions, Pryor and Boswell, could not be measured, but Pryor had counted on that solid bloc. McClellan also lined up a few African Americans, including I. S. McClinton at Little Rock, to proclaim their support for him, even while former Justice Jim Johnson was calling Pryor's supporters "a mess of trash."

Crowds at the small daily campaign events had been shrinking for years—

meeting a politician personally was no longer much of a thrill if you could see them up close on television—but McClellan seemed to take the small crowds personally. I traveled with him—more often behind him—for five weeks. When his plane landed at the little municipal airport at Harrison, the band of supporters who were supposed to meet him at the airport and ferry him to the square was absent. The hangar and control center were deserted. Paul Berry, an aide, went in to make some calls to find out where they were. McClellan sat on the hot plane, disconsolate. He motioned for me to sit with him. He started asking me about where I had grown up and what my daddy did. He asked about my education—where I went to college, what I studied, what degrees I got. He finally fell into silence and after a spell murmured, "I never went to college."

All his life, he said, he had regretted not going to college. He thought his life would have been richer, his abilities and achievements greater. He had merely read law with his father when he was a youngster and learned enough to get a license to practice law. In Congress, he was surrounded by men with good educations who had a superior knowledge of the world. He always felt inadequate and that he was just striving to prove to others that he was somehow up to the job.

"Well, senator," I said, "I find it hard to believe that any member of the Senate, or anyone else, ever doubted your abilities." He stared out the window in search of Berry and a supporter or two and muttered, "Thank you."

His melancholy proved to be well founded. The primary returns gave him a bare lead over Pryor, 220,000 to 206,000. Boswell got 60,000 votes and Foster Johnson another 9,000. The conventional wisdom, supported by nearly every election in modern times, was that an incumbent officeholder would be beaten in a runoff, unless he was awfully close to the threshold of 50 percent plus one, or else the losers were of disparate philosophies from the surviving challenger and closer to the incumbent. Pryor and Boswell were political twins and Boswell endorsed Pryor in the runoff. The Pryor headquarters that Tuesday night was bedlam, McClellan's a wake. The expectation was that Pryor voters would be buoyed for the runoff, McClellan's dispirited and likely to stay at home.

Wednesday morning, as he had many times before, Wilton R. "Witt" Stephens, the kingmaker of Arkansas politics, arose and decided to put his foot on the scales for McClellan, although the senator had never been an ally and had once been a staunch foe. Witt Stephens had always pulled strings for Homer Adkins, who McClellan thought betrayed him in the

1942 Senate race. In the 1952 Senate race, Stephens's friend Sid McMath tried to unseat the senator, and McClellan got wind of a Stephens vow to spend $10,000 to defeat him.

Stephens, who by 1972 was both CEO of Arkansas Louisiana Gas Company and partner in the largest investment firm off Wall Street, was easily the most powerful man in Arkansas and had been since the death in 1941 of Harvey Couch, the industrialist who ran a railroad and the major electric utilities in three states of the Middle South and kept a tight tether on nearly every consequential politician in Arkansas for twenty-five years. Arkansas Power and Light Company (today Entergy Arkansas) and its bosses—first Couch and then C. Hamilton Moses—had backed McClellan after he first won his Senate seat, most notably when he was challenged by McMath. Moses formed a law firm at Little Rock with one of McClellan's sons and his son-in-law and gave Senator McClellan a private office there.

As a youngster, Witt Stephens had figured out that politics was not merely a sport but that it mattered for the greater public good and also for his own felicity. He made his first small fortune by putting his faith in President Franklin D. Roosevelt, who he hoped would not only provide food and makeshift jobs for the masses suffering from the Depression and a biblical flood and drought, but also rescue a calamitous state government. Arkansas was the only state that defaulted on its debt after the great financial collapse. Arkansas's debt was fabulously large for such a small and poor state—$165 million in road bonds and tens of millions more in school and levee bonds.

At the age of twenty-five, Witt got a job in 1932 working for his father's friend at a Little Rock brokerage that traded municipal bonds—toil that must have been as propitious then as selling beach houses during the hurricane season. When Roosevelt took office the next spring, Stephens bet that he would get around to redeeming the bonds and restoring the state's credit. He bought all of the worthless bonds that he could for nickels on the dollar and marketed many of them to his father's friends in banking around south Arkansas. When the Reconstruction Finance Corporation redeemed them, Stephens's faith was rewarded. Those who shared the rewards were friends for life and Stephens never forgot them, or their children. His brokerage boomed during the recovery and the war, and then he got into the natural-gas business. When Roosevelt and Harry Truman set out in 1945 to break up the utility trusts, Stephens went to Washington to beseech a Securities and Exchange Commission administrative judge to let him buy the Fort Smith Gas Company for $1.2 million. He needed $160,000 in equity capital to go along with the securities and loans that he was pledging. An SEC attorney kept badgering the hayseed about where he would get that kind of money in cash-starved Arkansas.

"Judge," Stephens drawled, "I brung it with me." He reached into a pocket of his baggy coat, fished out a wad of bills and tossed it on the table. He renamed the business Arkansas Oklahoma Gas Company.

Eight years later, another government antitrust injunction allowed Stephens to buy what became Arkansas Louisiana Gas Company from Cities Service for $24.5 million, but he had two years to divest lots of the stock to avoid holding-company rules. And he would have to make the poorly performing company highly profitable to sell any stock. He slashed costs and from a friendly state Public Service Commission got a couple of modest rate increases, mostly on large industrial users of gas like Ham Moses's Arkansas Power and Light Company and the big aluminum plants near Benton. Stock prices shot up and investors gobbled up the stock. But Stephens needed more than that, since he had borrowed millions to make the deal, so the company began charging all its customers the prevailing fair-market price of gas for the fuel it was pumping from its own wells in any gas field. One Monday morning in February 1957, the Arkansas Supreme Court ruled that the practice violated the law, because the company was producing the gas at costs well below the regular field prices it had to pay for gas produced independently. Arkla's stock sank.

In the next three days, Stephens demonstrated his political wizardry and the breadths of his friendships and debtors. On Tuesday morning, a friendly legislator introduced a bill in the House of Representatives to permit a utility to pass on to its customers the fair-field price for the gas it produced. The bill was read twice and referred to a committee. The committee recommended the bill to the House the next morning and the bill jumped to the top of the calendar. The House in late afternoon approved it 83 to 7. It was rushed to the north end of the Capitol and introduced in the Senate, which read its title twice and referred it to a committee. The committee the next morning sent the bill to the full Senate, which passed it and sent it to the governor for his signature. Arkla stock soared again. The company became one of the best-performing utilities in the country. Insiders at the Capitol who bought the depressed stock that week made big dividends. Many legislators were rewarded in other ways for their toil that week. A state senator who was superintendent of a poor east Arkansas school district became a public relations consultant for the company, and a representative who performed similar service became the public relations consultant and then vice president of an Arkla subsidiary, Arkansas Cement Corporation, which was formed the next year. A freshman representative from Pine Bluff who operated a service station was hailed by an employee that Saturday morning with the news that someone had dropped by the station to tell him that Arkla trucks in that part of the state would thereafter be filling up at his pumps. Stephens also loaned him the money to buy a farm near his childhood home. A legislator from Union County asked for a case of Falstaff beer, which was delivered to his room at the Capital Hotel. A south Arkansas legislator who was an insurance broker started insuring some Arkla properties.

Six years later, when Stephens himself was in his second term as a representative from Grant County, legislators circulated a petition signed by every member of the House pledging to elect him speaker at the 1965 General Assembly, although in two terms he had never taken the floor to speak on any matter. Stephens didn't want to be speaker, so he quit.

On the morning after McClellan's miserable showing in the 1972 Senate primary, Witt Stephens and one of his political agents, insurance broker Jack Gardner, got on the telephone and reached Stephens's network of rich and influential friends across the state. Meet Stephens the next morning, they said, in the board room of the Union National Bank at Louisiana Street and Capitol Avenue in Little Rock, which was chaired by his friend Herbert H. McAdams Jr. of Jonesboro. It was what was commonly called a "put session." Everyone knew what was expected. More commonly, such sessions were held at Coachman's Inn, a Stephens-owned motel off East Capitol Avenue near Interstate 30, but McAdams's board room would provide more privacy.

Describing the gathering to me a year or two later, Gardner remembered these business nabobs around the large conference table: Stephens; McAdams; John A. Cooper of Bella Vista, a millionaire developer; Dan Portis of Lepanto, a big landowner in Poinsett County; Harry W. Parkin of Little Rock, a printing company executive; Maurice Smith of Birdeye, a big farmer and a member of the state Highway Commission; Dallas P. "Pete" Raney of Little Rock, who ran another bond house; Bennie Ryburn Sr. of

Monticello, a banker and automobile dealer; Truman Baker of Searcy, a car dealer and former member of the state Highway Commission; K. O. Yancey of Searcy, a banker; Vance Thompson Sr. of McCrory, a millionaire inventor and developer; Jack Pickens of Little Rock, a building contractor; H. L. Hembree of Fort Smith, a transportation executive; Haskell Dickinson of Little Rock, a contactor; state Senator W. K. Ingram of West Memphis, a contractor; Joe Mahony of El Dorado, a lawyer and longtime Stephens friend; and a few more whose names slipped Gardner's mind.

McClellan started the meeting with a doleful monologue about having run out his string and thinking that his time was over. He figured that he was probably beaten and that it might be wisest for him to just go through the motions in the two-week runoff rather than waste any more money on a losing cause. Cooper had flown Orval Faubus down from Huntsville on his private plane and the former governor said they should all vow to fight on. Faubus said he would rather go down to defeat with McClellan than to win with David Pryor. Witt Stephens asked what all of them were willing to do.

Portis, the first, promised to pitch in $5,000 and to get McClellan one thousand more votes in Poinsett County in the second primary than he got in the first one. McAdams pledged a much larger sum, and it went around the table. Stephens, the last, said simply, "Boys, I'll take care of the rest." It is probable that he didn't have to spend a dime. Gardner estimated that $250,000 was raised, or at least pledged, that day, but his figure was probably high. For the next ten days, McClellan blitzed the media with advertising. County organizations surveyed the voting rolls and chased down people who had not voted in the first primary and urged them to vote the second time and arranged to haul them to the polls if they needed it. McClellan stood to pick up very few of the Boswell voters, and the overall turnout was sure to be lower because few contested races would be on the ballot. People who went to the polls went just to vote for a senator.

McClellan got 22,000 more votes in the runoff than in the preferential. Pryor gained only 18,000, mostly Boswell voters. McClellan's margin of victory was 16,000.

Vital as all the voter-turnout work was, it was McClellan himself who was the difference. Someone told him that he must not look old and dispirited. He picked up the pace and put on a show of vigor everywhere he went.

The campaign hammered Pryor as a politician who would take away people's guns. The National Rifle Association backed McClellan. As a freshman in the Arkansas legislature in 1961, Pryor had introduced a bill prohibiting people from carrying loaded shotguns in their vehicle inside city limits. A little boy waiting for his mother inside the car on a grocery-store parking lot in Camden had picked up a loaded shotgun, somehow pulled the trigger, and blown his head off. Townspeople were enraged, so Pryor introduced the gun bill. It passed the House of Representatives 98 to 0 but the NRA got involved and stopped it in the Senate. The rest of his career Pryor was accused of wanting to take away people's guns.

And there was the Debate.

As young challengers nearly always do, Pryor immediately challenged McClellan to a debate after the first primary. Against advice, McClellan accepted. That was not the conventional wisdom, but the old man decided it might be his only chance. After forty years of often nasty campaigning and presiding over tumultuous organized-crime and labor-racketeering hearings, he was confident that he could handle anything that came up. Pryor was a neophyte and McClellan figured he would be nervous in front of the lights and cameras in a live hour-long show. McClellan got to the studio early and from a distance watched Pryor wait for the show to start, the biggest event of his career. McClellan thought he detected some fidgeting. He would take the fight to his young hometown neighbor. There would be no quarter, even for Edgar Pryor's boy.

The race had already settled on a single issue: Pryor's support from labor unions. Unions were never popular in Arkansas and the scandals involving the International Brotherhood of Teamsters and its corrupt leaders, Dave Beck and Jimmy Hoffa, were still on people's minds. President Richard Nixon had just pardoned Hoffa, who had been serving prison time for witness tampering, reminding voters again of the corruption in the union— and by inference all labor unions. (The Teamsters were the single union that supported Republican politicians; it had supported Nixon.) Hoffa had not yet disappeared.

McClellan began by belittling Pryor's six years in the state legislature and six years in the U.S. House of Representatives, where he had accomplished little in comparison with all the public works and the rackets investigations that had headlined McClellan's own long career. Mainly, he talked about Pryor's support from organized labor, including the financial support from union political-action committees. McClellan always referred to union leaders as "bosses" and said that, unlike Pryor, he would never do their bidding when the union bosses cracked their whips. Pryor insisted that he was proud that he had the support of the working stiffs rather than the rich folks. The election, he said, was not about the past thirty years but the next thirty, and not about who had power in Washington but how and for whom it was used. He would use it for the common working people.

It was back and forth until, finally, came the exchange that turned the election. Pryor said his union gifts averaged fifty cents a worker.

"My financial help comes from the pockets of worn overalls and from cookie jars and from a lot of people, and all the people right here in Arkansas," he said.

McClellan rattled off contributions to Pryor's campaign from union PACs, from $1,000 to $12,000.

"We talk about fifty cents donated out of overall pockets and out of cookie jars," McClellan rejoined. "I believe he said cookie jars. Listen, this is no overall pocket money."

"This is no cookie-jar nickels and dimes," he said, wagging a finger at Pryor. "Take a look at this. Big out-of-state contributions to Pryor. They total $79,887.16. Yes, that's a cookie jar—quite a cookie jar indeed."

The labor contributions paled alongside the money from the rich and powerful in McClellan's campaign treasury, but Pryor had no such evidence to rebut McClellan's taunts.

The debate had the largest television audience of any political event in the state's history, and McClellan's cookie-jar rejoinder is all that most people took away from it. Pryor would acknowledge that it was probably decisive. Perhaps more than anything, McClellan looked sharp and decisive.

While the debate seemed to blunt Pryor's momentum, he and everyone around him were still confident. He made no preparation for losing, including a concession speech. On election night, as soon as the trend was clear, he went to his election headquarters at the Sheraton Hotel and in front of the TV cameras made the best speech of his life. He praised McClellan for his strength, courage, and fighting spirit, and over cries of disapproval from many of his supporters, declared that the senator deserved to win. He would later tell me it was an approach to politics that he shared with Dale Bumpers: Either in victory or defeat, you never lose by being magnanimous.

Witt Stephens was watching at home that night. He decided that he would do his damnedest to get David Pryor elected to something the next time he ran. It would be in twenty-four months.

Winthrop Rockefeller (front row, center), in hospital scrubs and with his hands still bandaged from injuries suffered in a kamikaze attack on his ship at Guam in April 1945, poses with fellow crewmen. Courtesy of the UA Little Rock Center for Arkansas History and Culture

Winthrop Rockefeller and Barbara "Bobo" Sears Rockefeller cut their wedding cake after "the wedding of the century" on Valentine's Day 1948. They divorced six years later. Courtesy of the UA Little Rock Center for Arkansas History and Culture

Jim Guy Tucker in Vietnam circa 1966.
Courtesy of the UA Little Rock Center for Arkansas History and Culture

Representative Jim Guy Tucker and President Jimmy Carter in 1977.
Courtesy of the UA Little Rock Center for Arkansas History and Culture

Governor Dale Bumpers, 1973.
Courtesy of the UA Little Rock Center for Arkansas History and Culture

Governor Bumpers campaigning, 1974.
Courtesy of the UA Little Rock Center for Arkansas History and Culture

David Pryor campaigns for governor in 1974 in Pocahontas.
He is with state Senator Nick Wilson of Pocahontas and the
Randolph County clerk, Lucille Stolt.
Courtesy of the author

Senator J. William Fulbright.
Courtesy of the CALS Butler Center for Arkansas Studies

Governor Faubus in 1962, after dedicating a state highway at Gu-ion in Izard County.
Courtesy of the *Arkansas Democrat-Gazette*

Jim McDougal outside the U.S. courthouse in Little Rock in 1995, where he was convicted of financial fraud.
Courtesy of the *Arkansas Democrat-Gazette*

Lieutenant Governor Bob Riley shakes hands with Governor Bumpers, who is about to address the state legislature in 1973. The man to the right of Riley is the Senate chaplain of the day.
Courtesy of the *Arkansas Democrat-Gazette*

Governor Rockefeller in 1967 with (behind him) his wife, Jeannette; son, Winthrop Paul; and stepson, Bruce Bartley.
Courtesy of the *Arkansas Democrat-Gazette*

207

Governor Faubus shows off a hole in the sole of his shoe in 1956 with Adlai Stevenson (left), the Democratic nominee for president, who was campaigning in Little Rock. Senator John L. McClellan is on the right. Faubus was reprising the iconic photo of Stevenson with a hole in his shoe, which was taken at a Labor Day rally during the 1952 presidential campaign.
Courtesy of the *Arkansas Democrat-Gazette*

Governor Sid McMath (right) and President Harry S. Truman march in a parade in Little Rock in June 1949, honoring veterans of the 35th Division in World War II. McMath, the Democratic nominee for governor in 1948, broke with many other Southern politicians, including Arkansas governor Ben Laney, and supported Truman against the Dixiecrat candidate, Strom Thurmond, who carried four Deep South states. Laney ran against McMath in 1950, claiming that he had betrayed the cause of segregation.
Courtesy of the CALS Butler Center for Arkansas Studies

Hillary and Bill Clinton, circa 1980.
Courtesy of the CALS Butler Center for Arkansas Studies

David Pryor, with his wife, Barbara, campaigning for governor in Harrison in 1974.
Courtesy of UA Special Collections

Former antagonists Senator McClellan (left) and Governor Pryor after McClellan addressed the legislature in 1977, shortly before his death. Courtesy of UA Special Collections

David Pryor, the sophomore tailback for the Camden Panthers, later the leading passer and rusher for the team. Courtesy of UA Special Collections

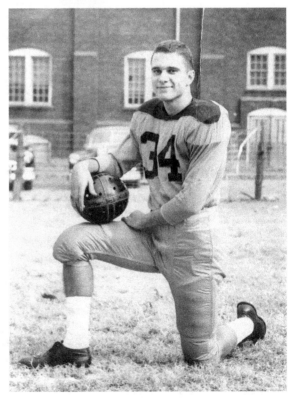

Musical politicians: Bill Clinton and "Cowboy Ray" Thornton, circa 1990.
Courtesy of the *Arkansas Democrat-Gazette*

W. R. "Witt" Stephens, financier, utility magnate, and gray eminence of Arkansas politics.
Courtesy of UA Special Collections

Orval E. Faubus of Huntsville campaigning for governor in October 1954 at the White River Carnival at Batesville. He is talking to his Republican opponent, Mayor Pratt Remmel of Little Rock. Faubus won with 51 percent of the vote, but Remmel made the strongest showing by a Republican in a statewide election since 1872. At the mayor's side is his nine-year-old son, Pratt Remmel Jr., later a social and environmental activist. Faubus handed the boy a buckeye to keep for good luck.
Courtesy of UA Special Collections

Barbara Pryor, campaigning for her husband in 1972.
Courtesy of UA Special Collections

President John F. Kennedy speaks at the dedication of the Greers Ferry Dam on the Little Red River near Heber Springs in October 1963, seven weeks before his assassination in Dallas, Texas. The six members of the Arkansas congressional delegation, Governor Faubus, and Arkansas dignitaries are arrayed behind him. Courtesy of the Arkansas Democrat-Gazette

President Kennedy and Governor Faubus en route to the Greers Ferry dam dedication in October 1963. Courtesy of the Arkansas *Democrat-Gazette*

President Kennedy began his speech by joking that he would have been obliged to come to Arkansas if U.S. Representative Wilbur D. Mills had merely wanted him to sing "Down by the Old Mills Stream." Mills (wearing glasses) is over Kennedy's right shoulder..
Courtesy of the *Arkansas Democrat-Gazette*

Sheffield Nelson campaigning for governor in 1990.
Courtesy of the *Arkansas Democrat-Gazette*

*Frank White takes the oath of office as governor in 1981
from Chief Justice Richard B. Adkisson. Former Governor
Orval Faubus is behind him. Faubus would become his
director of veterans affairs.*
Courtesy of the Museum of American History, Cabot Public Schools

Winthrop Rockefeller and the author, 1964.
Courtesy of the author

X
Past and Prologue

Dale Bumpers had a momentous decision to make in the spring of 1974 and time was running out. The deadline for filing to run in the party primaries was approaching and several men, including David Pryor, were waiting nervously to see whether Bumpers would run for a third term as governor or challenge Senator J. William Fulbright, who had already announced that he was running for a sixth term. It was not a matter of political life or death for Bumpers because, whichever choice he made, he was confident of an easy victory. He had raised taxes and fostered integration in his first term but a year later still defeated Democratic and Republican opponents in landslides. No Democrat was even contemplating running against him if he ran for a third term, but several were hoping he would run for the Senate and open that avenue to them. Republicans, by necessity, would find a sacrificial lamb to run for the office to give the party a claim of legitimacy.

But Bumpers also had a pathological hatred of his job. Years later, after he had been in the U.S. Senate a while, he had some yearnings for his old job, because a governor could actually get things done—in his case, more than any governor in the state's history—while in the Senate progress was measured by tiny steps and many years, especially if you were assigned to minor committees like Small Business and Aeronautics. Bumpers had been ensconced in the governor's office only a few days in 1971 when it dawned on him that he was the chief executive, if only the figurehead in many cases, of a bureaucracy of twenty-five thousand employees and a few thousand citizen members of boards and commissions. On any given day, he began to calculate, a few of them were cheating, profiting off their public duties, or else just making decisions inimical to the public interest. And he was responsible for every one of them. He had had to fire an employee in his office only weeks after taking office for trying to influence a state agency's business-permit decision. He would imagine headlines about corruption in his administration. It would not matter that he would not be involved in the scheming. He needed a job without that overhanging fear.

But if he ran for the Senate, he would be opposing a man with whom he had no disagreements—both had been opposed to the Vietnam War for years—and whom he admired. Moreover, Fulbright had let it be known in 1970 that he favored Bumpers over both Orval Faubus and Winthrop

Rockefeller. Bumpers counted that as a small debt, though it had little to do with his lopsided victories over both men. He shared many ardent supporters with Fulbright, even on his own staff—people who would not be happy if he challenged the old intellectual they thought was Arkansas's single claim to distinction.

As the deadline for filing for political offices approached in 1974, Bumpers announced that he would make his plans known the coming Saturday morning. On Thursday morning, he called Bradley D. Jesson and Douglas Smith at Fort Smith, lawyer friends who had been his legislative assistants every time that the legislature met, and asked them to come to Little Rock Friday morning to talk about the legislative session that would follow the fall election. Jesson, the state Democratic Party chairman, and Smith both had encouraged Bumpers to run for president in 1976 and to run for re-election in 1974 in preparation for it. Bumpers lived with the presumption that his father had always expected one of his boys, Carroll or Dale, to be president one day and lead the nation out of the wilderness, as Franklin Roosevelt had done. Bumpers had been on the short list for vice president at the 1972 Democratic national convention, but Senator George S. Mc-Govern chose Senator Thomas Eagleton of Missouri.

Bumpers was intrigued enough with the idea of running for president that one Saturday early in the year he had quietly flown to Iowa, the first state in the nominating marathon, just to get a sense of the place where all presidential campaigns begin and where every candidate must spend an inordinate and usually fruitless amount of time trying to collect enough votes to give him a sendoff. Bumpers spent all day Saturday fidgeting and shivering in a snowbound Holiday Inn in Des Moines and then caught a plane home the same evening. It dampened his excitement about running. He began to doubt that he was temperamentally suited for a long, grueling, and nasty campaign and perhaps not the brutal political warfare that the presidency itself always entailed. Bumpers would repeat the Hamlet agony in 1984 and 1988, but more openly. He took some early steps toward running—speaking in 1984 at a couple of Democratic cattle shows, to some acclaim—but then each time bowed out, owing to some real or imagined disqualifying excuse: chronic knee pain, his wife's health, the prospect of having to raise lots of money, the likelihood of a Republican victory, and, finally, his friend Bill Clinton's consuming ambition for the same office.

On that Friday morning in the spring of 1974, Jesson and Smith huddled with Bumpers at the Governor's Mansion and prepared for the presidential run. They talked about a legislative program for January 1975 with an eye for what would raise his profile for a national campaign. They adjourned for a working lunch at Hank's Dog House on West Roosevelt Road and then wrapped up in mid-afternoon. Smith and Jesson agreed that they would come to Little Rock for the first quarter to help him pass the legislative program, which Jesson would describe in 2013 as "good window dressing" for the presidential race. None of the three ever mentioned the decision that Bumpers was to reveal the next morning. Jesson and Smith just assumed from his demeanor and his silence about the decision that he was running for re-election. Back at Fort Smith in late afternoon, Jesson's senior law partner, Hugh Hardin, an old friend of Bumpers but also a close friend of Fulbright's chief of staff, Lee Williams, asked Jesson what Bumpers was going to do. He is running for re-election, Jesson assured him.

"Great," Hardin said, and he wrote a two-thousand-dollar check to the Fulbright campaign and rushed it to the post office so that it would be postmarked before Bumpers made his announcement.

Listening to the radio Saturday morning, Jesson heard the news that Bumpers was running for the Senate against Fulbright.

"I was never so surprised at anything in my life," Jesson said. Hardin called and asked him, "What happened?" Jesson said he didn't have a clue.

Pondering with his wife that Friday night about what to do, Bumpers would recall twenty-five years later, he was overwhelmed again by thoughts of the daily fear of corruption and wrongdoing that plagued him every day as governor. He had to get out. Running for the Senate would forestall a presidential race in 1976, because it would look callous to voters that he had asked for a six-year term as their senator and then immediately run for president, but it still looked like a Senate race was the only tolerable option. Also, he had gotten a Gene Newsom poll that showed that Fulbright was almost certain to be beaten by someone, even Jim Johnson, who had come close in 1968 and was waiting for another clear opening when there would be no other serious candidate besides him and Fulbright. The poll showed that Bumpers would beat Fulbright in a landslide. If Fulbright's career was over, Bumpers figured, it would be better for the state if he and not Jim Johnson was the senator.

J. William Fulbright was stunned. It was an act of betrayal that he would brood about for more than a decade after the election, until his wife, Betty, persuaded him to get in touch with Senator Bumpers and have lunch in Washington. They exchanged regrets and confidences and became great friends. Betty made her husband acknowledge that if he had had the choice, he would have picked Bumpers to succeed him. Bumpers would deliver the eulogy at Fulbright's funeral.

Meantime, the campaign and the election were both humiliating for the proud old man. Bumpers never uttered even an indirect criticism of him. He said he respected Fulbright's great contributions to the country and his leadership in trying to turn the country away from war and a confrontational foreign policy. Fulbright did his best to paint Bumpers as an unprepared dilettante who would be useless in Washington. At the suggestion of

a group that, unknown to Bumpers, was opposed to hunting and the killing of wildlife, Bumpers had once naïvely signed a proclamation for "Be Kind to Animals Week." Fulbright's ads suggested that Bumpers was a dangerous liberal who was against hunting and guns. Bumpers found an old Polaroid snapshot of himself shouldering a shotgun and holding a fistful of bloody ducks by their necks, and he ran it in a small ad in the Little Rock newspapers. He admitted embarrassment that he had been talked into running the ad.

In the first campaign event of the season, the Pope County Democratic Women's rally at Russellville, Senator Robert C. Byrd of West Virginia—the Senate whip, Fulbright's friend, and the longest-serving

J. William Fulbright

senator in history—appeared on stage with Bumpers and Fulbright and endorsed his friend, warning that it would be a tragedy for Arkansas if it exchanged the seniority of one of the Senate's giants for a novice. The network of business titans who had teamed up two years earlier to salvage the Senate seat of John McClellan redoubled their efforts for Fulbright. Witt Stephens, who nursed grievances with Bumpers going back to the young lawyer's early efforts to force Stephens's gas companies to increase the piffling royalties they paid to landowners in the big gas fields of western Arkansas, was especially exercised. Fulbright outspent Bumpers ten to one. A Newsom poll for Fulbright a few days before the primary showed Bumpers with a giant lead, slightly bigger even than Bumpers's margin in the spring poll that had fixed his determination to run for the Senate. James D. Blair and Brownie Ledbetter, who were running the Fulbright campaign, took the poll to Betty Fulbright at the Sam Peck Hotel. Don't share it with Bill, she told them. Fulbright sometimes enjoyed campaigning and seemed to find a little encouragement everywhere he went. The poll was too disillusioning. If you show the poll to him, he will quit immediately, she said. They would deal with his disillusionment as best they could after the election.

At the State Capitol and at political events around the state—I was traveling with Orval Faubus most of the time—the evidence of the shellacking that was coming was hard to miss. The Arkansas Education Association's political-action committee interviewed the two candidates at its offices across the street from the Capitol. Fulbright, the founder of the Fulbright international exchange program and once an educator himself, could claim to be a good friend of education. With some reservations, he had voted for President Lyndon Johnson's landmark law that provided substantial federal aid to public education for the first time. In Fulbright's interview in the morning, York Williams, an African American minister and teacher at McGehee in the Arkansas Delta, told him that people were struggling desperately in the Delta. Young families were poor but there were no daycare facilities where they could leave their children while they worked to keep bread on the table. Couldn't the federal government provide money for such things that would widen the educational opportunities for poor people?

Fulbright responded archly. Why, what do you mean poor? he asked. He had been in McGehee only a few days earlier and farmers told him that the crops were unusually bountiful and commodity prices were extraordinarily high for such circumstances. That community and those throughout the Delta seemed to be prospering rather well, he said.

That afternoon, when Bumpers met with the teachers, Williams asked him essentially the same question. Bumpers said Williams was right. In fact, he said, his most distressing failure as governor was the defeat of a $1 million appropriation he had sought in 1973 to match federal Medicaid funds for child-care services for poor parents in communities like McGehee. He said he was distracted at the time and regretted not making the effort that it would have taken to get the extraordinary votes (seventy-five in the House and twenty-seven in the Senate) to pass the bill.

The AEA sent teachers a recommendation that they vote for Bumpers.

Although the race attracted unusual national attention, owing to Fulbright's prominence, it was one of the quietest Senate campaigns on record. Bumpers spent little money and provoked no headlines. Although it was unintentional, his wife might have burnished his credentials a little. Betty Bumpers had organized an effort that spring to get every child in Arkansas immunized against the common childhood diseases, called Every Child in '74. She would expand the effort nationally after the couple went to Washington. One Saturday shortly before the primary, the National Guard, county health offices, the state Health Department, civic groups, and medical organizations collaborated in a massive immunization. It virtually eliminated measles, whooping cough, chicken pox, and the other communicable childhood diseases in Arkansas. Bumpers himself never talked about it.

The next Monday morning I spotted Bumpers entering the Capitol under the Capitol steps. I grabbed my notepad and chased after him to ask him something that was on my mind. As he reached the top of the marble steps to his second-floor office, he veered to the right before I could catch up. When I reached the floor, he had pinned the Capitol reporter for the *Commercial Appeal* at Memphis against the wall between the governor's and the secretary of state's offices. The reporter, who harbored a healthy skepticism of all elected officials of every stripe, had written a column for the Sunday *Commercial Appeal* denigrating the immunization campaign. Betty Bumpers's real purpose in the immunization campaign, he wrote, was not the health of kids but to get her husband elected to the Senate. I had not read his column but Bumpers had. Jabbing his finger into the reporter's chest, Bumpers said the reporter was free to write anything he cared to about him but not about his wife. He uttered a physical threat to the reporter if he ever again questioned Betty Bumpers's honor or motives in print.

Bumpers defeated Fulbright 380,000 to 204,000. A turnout of nearly 600,000 in one party's primary was pretty high for those days, but that was before voter suppression—through such sophisticated devices as photo identifications, purges, caging, and precinct closures—once again became a working political strategy. By comparison, although the number of registered voters had doubled by 2018, forty-four years later, the turnout in the combined Democratic and Republican primaries and a nonpartisan judicial election totaled a mere 312,000.

◻◻◻

David Pryor had waited for Bumpers's announcement of his political plans in the spring of 1974 with more anticipation than anyone, although he had been tethered to a hospital bed in Little Rock for two weeks with a broken right ankle in a cast and a life-threatening blood clot, the results of a skiing accident on an Aspen slope. Before going to the Rockies, Pryor had visited Bumpers and encouraged him to run for a third term as governor and then, upon re-election, promptly announce that he was running for president in 1976. He thought Bumpers would be the Democrats' most exciting candidate, certainly more dynamic than Georgia's former governor, Jimmy Carter, who would win the nomination and the presidency. Bumpers promised to think about it. Pryor had a personal motive, too. The Senate was still his ambition, but his chances in 1978, when McClellan would certainly retire, looked forlorn, because he had been whipped in 1972 and his supporters disillusioned. (His principal supporters also were having their tax returns audited by the IRS every year, thanks to McClellan.) Also, U.S. Representatives William V. Alexander, Ray H. Thornton Jr., and John Paul Hammerschmidt were waiting in the wings for McClellan's job, and Attorney General Jim Guy Tucker, the most charismatic politician in the state next to Bumpers, would obviously seek the job, too. Before the 1978 season, Pryor needed an election victory and a high-profile office, both of which an open governor's race in 1976 might afford him. He was not ready to run in 1974 and, he figured, neither were his supporters. Bumpers's announcement that he was not, after all, running for re-election but for the Senate was a downer. Now, Pryor did not have the luxury of waiting two years to begin his resurrection.

While Bumpers and his Fort Smith pals Jesson and Smith were conferring at the mansion that Friday about the phantasmal 1975 legislative agenda, Pryor was lying in bed at the University of Arkansas Medical Center. A nurse came in and asked if he could take a call from a Mr. Stephens. Pryor picked up the bedside phone. The man on the other end did not identify himself, but Pryor recognized the guttural voice.

"Are you going to run for governor?" Witt Stephens asked, without even identifying himself. Pryor said he was not sure, but at the moment he did not think so.

"Well, if you do, I'm going to help you," Stephens growled. "I helped beat you last time, and I owe you one."

Pryor said he didn't know what Bumpers was going to do the next day. Stephens was sure that Bumpers would run for the Senate. Stephens did not say so but, after eight years in the wilderness under Rockefeller and Bumpers, he wanted to have a friend in the governor's office again. He had long ago come to think of brotherhood with the governor as Nature itself.

It was natural that Pryor should be shocked by the call and a little disbelieving that Witt Stephens would actually support him, and even more that he would, or even could, swing the rest of the formidable organization of rich and conservative shakers behind him for any office—especially if, as seemed likely, Orval Faubus ran again. Pryor shortly came to believe it. When Faubus called, Stephens tried to discourage him from running, but the former governor just did not seriously believe that Stephens would actually support Pryor, and he didn't believe that the other notables—people like Dan Portis, Truman Baker, Bennie Ryburn, and even Sheriff Marlin Hawkins in Conway County—could be siphoned away from the patron who had given them a dependable friend at the Capitol for twelve years. But they all went over to Pryor.

Faubus was deeply hurt and embittered with all of them, but especially Stephens. I traveled with him for a couple of weeks and his despair was palpable. In his speeches he first began to attack Pryor for being the willing puppet of a group of rich and powerful kingmakers, and sometimes he would identify Stephens or John Cooper, the Bella Vista developer, depending upon where he was speaking.

"A certain number of would-be governor-makers met in a small hotel room in Little Rock and conspired to elect the next governor of Arkansas," Faubus said. Many listeners had to wonder, "Weren't those the same guys who were pulling your strings for twelve years?"

A third candidate entered the race: Lieutenant Governor Bob Riley, a college professor and a friend of Pryor. Riley had dropped out of high school after the attack on Pearl Harbor in December 1941 and enlisted in the Marine Corps. He led a rifle-squad assault on a Japanese machine-gun placement on Guam in July 1944 and was hospitalized off and on for a year from multiple injuries that left him crippled. He lost his right eye and thereafter wore a black-leather eyepatch, which became his trademark. Vision in his good eye was limited. Riley was part of Sid McMath's GI Revolt after the war and was elected to two terms in the state House of Representatives from Pulaski County while he was going to school at the University of Arkansas. Eventually, he earned a doctorate in education and taught economics and political science at Little Rock Junior College and then Ouachita Baptist College at Arkadelphia. He was elected lieutenant governor in the

Democratic sweep of state offices in 1970. When Bumpers opted not to run again, Riley saw it as probably his only chance to reach his ambition, the office once held by the sainted McMath, the hero of Guadalcanal. Riley was a witty raconteur but, with no money, no organized support, and the sheer physical hurdles of barnstorming around the state with Claudia—his wife, driver, and guide—he was a small factor in the race. Faubus and Pryor left Riley alone, and he them. I have a photograph of my son, then three years old, tugging on Dr. Bob's black eyepatch at an event at Bryant.

Bob Riley

Perhaps because all the attention was focused on the race for the Senate, little about the campaign was memorable, except Faubus's schizophrenia. He wanted to campaign as a reformer to reach younger voters and promised a fresh team of bright young minds at the Capitol, but he simultaneously had to tear down the youngster Pryor. In only carefully selected venues, mainly east Arkansas, he would mention darkly that Pryor had supported school integration back in 1957–58. He called Pryor a tool of both the union bosses and the corporate bigwigs. One of those elites that Pryor had inherited was Donald J. Tyson of Rogers, who ran the big meat-packing conglomerate, Tyson Foods. Although he pitched in some cash, Tyson's big role in the Pryor campaign was unsolicited. Some churlish foe had painted "Fuck Pryor" in giant letters on the north side of Pryor's Little Rock campaign headquarters just west of downtown on Center Street. Tyson spotted it when he went to the headquarters for a campaign-finance meeting and pointed it out to the campaign staff, which, naturally, had already seen it. He telephoned from the Tyson offices at Springdale a couple of days later to see if the vulgarity had been scrubbed off. No one had gotten around to it. Tyson and a friend bought a crate of spray paint at a hardware store, flew to Little Rock, borrowed a ladder, and covered the offensive letters in a blaze of yellow.

Not even Faubus was surprised at the election results. Pryor escaped a runoff by collecting 298,000 votes to Faubus's 193,000 and Riley's 93,000. Riley, whose great ambition was to be governor, realized it after all. Two weeks before his term as lieutenant governor was to end, Governor Bumpers resigned to take the oath as a senator, making Riley the governor for two weeks. His chief of staff was Jim McDougal, his faculty colleague at Ouachita Baptist College and the mastermind of the palace revolt in the Young Democratic Clubs in 1965. McDougal will reappear in the final chapters of this story.

Pryor was never proud of his euphoric victory speech on election night. He had told a sobbing Francis Cherry exactly twenty years earlier that someday he would personally avenge the poor man's defeat by Orval Faubus. He told the cheering crowd that he was sending a telegram to Cherry's widow at Jonesboro with the message: "Dear Mrs. Cherry: The score is settled." He regretted it almost immediately. It violated his vow to be charitable in either victory or defeat. In his 2008 autobiography, *A Pryor Commitment*, he apologized for the inhumanity. He wished he had found a way to apologize for his arrogance after Faubus, the year before his death in 1994, visited the hospital where Pryor was in recovery from a massive heart attack and left a note hoping they could let bygones be bygones.

It was a summer of calamity and burlesque for anyone trying to make sense of political intrigues and the whims of the electorate.

Cragg Hines, a former United Press International reporter at Little Rock, was in Washington covering Congress for the *Houston Chronicle*. He telephoned me one evening to relate a conversation that he had had at a suburban service station that afternoon with Fred Coleman, an Arkansas-reared railroad lobbyist. Coleman was worried about his friend Wilbur D. Mills, the legendary chairman of the House Ways and Means Committee, author of the Medicare-Medicaid law and briefly a candidate for president in 1972. Wilbur was drinking heavily and Coleman understood that Wilbur and his wife, Polly, were having trouble and might be estranged. He said the congressman was hanging out at a nightclub called the Silver Slipper, where there was a stripper who seemed to have his eye.

Cragg thought it was bizarre and couldn't be true. Wilbur was the most serious man in Washington. Everyone knew that he went home every evening to sup with Polly and fell asleep studying the tax code. I was intrigued by the story owing to my own experience with Mills in the summer of 1972, when he made the quixotic race for president and collected only delegate votes from Arkansas and Massachusetts. On the first day of the convention at Miami Beach, Senator George S. McGovern of South Dakota, who had won most of the primaries, had wrapped up the nomination when California seated a delegation by the unit rule, which meant that McGovern would get all that state's votes. At least, that is what I reported for the next morning's *Gazette*. That evening, Mills threw a party for the Arkansas delegates in the penthouse of the Willard Intercontinental, his headquarters hotel in Miami Beach. I was sampling the caviar—the first I had ever consumed—and talking to a very florid Mills, who was sipping a whiskey sour. He told me that McGovern had been blocked and that he had to meet early the next morning with Senator Henry M. Jackson of Washington and Representative Shirley Chisholm of New York to decide which of the three would take the presidential nomination. I said I thought the California delegate decision had put McGovern over the top.

Judy Petty

"Oh, no," Mills exclaimed. It was over for McGovern. Mills said he had no consuming interest in the nomination but he would take it if "Scoop" (Jackson) demurred. Then one of the other two, he or Shirley Chisholm, would be the vice-presidential nominee. I thought, "Am I that incompetent as a reporter, or has this great man lost his wits?" Two years later, Fred Coleman seemed to offer the answer.

I called Roy Bode, the *Gazette*'s correspondent in Washington, and suggested that he see what he could learn about Coleman's story about Mills and the stripper, especially if the Millses had split up. Bode didn't want to, but he did call Gene Goss, Mills's chief of staff. Goss said that it was all gossip, but every married couple had its ups and downs over the years. We didn't publish anything. For only the fourth time in his eighteen terms in Congress, Mills had an opponent that year, a Republican named Judy Petty of Little Rock, who had been an aide of Governor Winthrop Rockefeller.

In October, a couple of weeks after Fred Coleman expressed his concern

"I just worship the ground I walk on."

about Mills, federal park police in the District of Columbia stopped Mills's car on a bridge over the Tidal Basin for not having its headlights on. Mills, who apparently was not driving, was drunk. Annabel Battistella, who performed at the Silver Slipper under the stage name Fanne Foxe, "the Argentine Firecracker," leaped out of the car and vaulted over the bridge rail into the shallow Tidal Basin near the Jefferson Memorial. A reporter wandered onto the scene and was curious when he saw a man with a bloody face and broken glasses who looked a lot like Wilbur Mills. The next day, he checked the police report, which suggested that Mills was there. Mills first denied it, and then admitted that Mrs. Battistella lived in the apartment building where the Millses lived and that she had too much to drink at a social event that evening. This was his statement:

"After a few refreshments, Mrs. Battistella became ill and I enlisted the help of others in our group to assist me in seeing her safely home. As we proceeded home, she attempted to leave the car and I attempted to prevent it. In the ensuing struggle, her elbow hit my glasses and broke them, resulting in a number of small cuts around my nose."

When it was revealed that she was a stripper at the Silver Slipper, no one was buying his innocence. He came back to Little Rock and held a rare news conference with the tightlipped Polly Mills at his side. It was much ado about nothing, he said. He was concentrating on getting re-elected. That proved to be easy. He won 80,000 to Petty's 56,000. Shortly after the election, Mills showed up at the Pilgrim Theater in Boston, where the suddenly famous Fanne Foxe was performing. Outside her dressing room, an inebriated Mills, wearing a business suit, preened with the buxom stripper for the television cameras.

"All I'm trying to do is launch her career," Mills said. "My wife's in on it."

It was over for the distinguished congressman. By now an embarrassment to the leadership of the House, he surrendered the chairmanship of the Ways and Means Committee and quietly served his last term. He devoted his post-political life to helping people conquer alcoholism. Battistella published a memoir, *The Stripper and the Congressman*, in which she said she had become pregnant during a seventeen-month affair with Mills and aborted his child. No one, as far as I know, tried to check the dubious truth of her claim.

Senator Warren Magnuson of Washington, who went to the House of Representatives in 1938 with Mills and became a lifelong friend and late-afternoon drinking companion, lamented the simultaneous collapse of his old friends from Arkansas, Mills and Fulbright. It had been a terrible political season, he wrote to a Senate colleague.

"First Bill Fulbright was knocked off by Bumpers," Magnuson wrote, "and then Wilbur was bumped off by knockers."

The Tidal Basin incident ended an ancient canon of the Fourth Estate, that alcohol and womanizing were private matters outside the proper concern of the public and of the press, because they did not touch on grave matters of state. The next year, Representative Wayne Hays of Ohio left the House after his secretary revealed that he had hired her on his congressional staff and given her a big raise to be his mistress. Sex was never off limits for political reporters again, as Gary Hart and Bill Clinton would discover. Sex would grow as a reporting priority for the next forty-five years, culminating in the carnal extravaganza of the Donald Trump era.

□□□

The combustible summer of 1974 also fed the brief vaudevillian political career of Joseph Harry Weston, twice an enigmatic candidate for governor. Such were his reckless attacks and disregard for civility and truth that Weston could have been the poor man's Donald Trump, but he lacked the essential accouterment of riches. Bereft of Winthrop Rockefeller and his wealth and prestige, the Republican Party in 1974 was looking for a nominal leader and it had to fend off Joe Weston, the editor of the *Sharp Citizen* at Cave City.

Weston was a native of Little Rock, where he worked as a youngster for a short-lived newspaper called the *Little Rock Daily News* and became a friend of John F. Wells, a newspaperman, printer, publisher, and political activist. Weston wended his way around the country and the publishing business until 1971, when Veterans Administration doctors at Poplar Bluff, Missouri, said that, owing to some illnesses, including diabetes, he needed to get his affairs in order. He bought eighty scrub acres near Cave City with his wife and stepdaughter and began publishing the *Sharp Citizen*, using crude but inexpensive technology taught him by Wells and using Wells's commercial press at Little Rock. Weston typed columns of stories on mimeograph sheets and topped them with hand-lettered headlines that screamed scandals like "Rat Poison Deliberately Fed into Public Drinking Water for More Than a Quarter of a Century." He accused dignitaries in Cave City and rural communities nearby of crookedness and sexual improprieties and ventured into attacks on state officials like Bumpers ("Bumpsy" he called him), McClellan, and highway executives. His favorite targets were an aging banker at Cave City (pop. 807) named Eagle Street ("the bastard tyrant of Sharp County") and the circumspect and pious state representative from Izard County, John Elvis Miller, whom he usually called "the Lizard of Izard."

Weston's paper attracted little attention, though he circulated copies around the State Capitol after picking them up at Wells's printshop and before heading to the hills to plant them on café and service-station counters and on windshields of unattended cars and pickups. He began to get some national attention, notably in the *New York Times*. The American Society of Newspaper Editors printed in its quarterly journal a flaming Weston letter accusing big newspapers of being house organs for corrupt politicians and institutions, which earned him an invitation to appear on a panel at the organization's national convention with Ben Bagdikian, the media critic, and Gloria Steinem, the editor of *Ms.* magazine.

After twice having criminal charges filed against him for inflammatory articles about neighbors and hiding out to avoid legal service, Weston finally won a reprieve from the Arkansas Supreme Court, which declared the state's old criminal-libel law unconstitutional. It was the only law in the country that allowed people to be jailed for writing articles that demeaned someone or a business.

In Trumpian style, Weston decided that he was wasting his notoriety if he did not run for public office, and in the spring of 1974 he filed for governor as a Republican. He claimed to be a disciple of Winthrop Rockefeller. To save the moribund party from having Editor Weston, as he styled himself, as its standard bearer, Republican regulars got Ken Coon—a biology teacher, state president of the Jaycees, and the state Republican chairman—to file for the office and give Republicans an alternative to Joe Weston. Hardly anyone ever voted in the Republican primaries, but the party persuaded 4,500 Arkansawyers to vote in the primary and nominate Coon, who lost badly to Pryor. Two years later, the party had to scrape around at the last minute again to get a retired plumber, Leon Griffith, to take Weston on and save the party the embarrassment of having Weston as its nominal leader.

Weston's legal troubles piled up as he took on judges and eventually the entire state Supreme Court, alleging they were all involved in fraud and conspiracies. One day, he walked into the Capitol pressroom with a stack of papers still warm from Johnny Wells's press.

"Boys," he announced, as he slapped a copy of the paper on my desk, "I've got a blockbuster for you today." The front-page headline proclaimed in giant penciled letters that William Ward Goodman, the state highway director, had just made off with millions of state highway dollars.

"Joe," I said, as he dropped papers on the desks of other Capitol reporters, "you may have a little problem with this one."

"How's that?" he asked.

"Ward Goodman is dead," I said.

"The hell you say," he said, stunned. "Who killed him?"

"No one," I said. More than a year earlier, Goodman—a reticent highway engineer who had been elevated to the director's job—had fallen dead of a heart attack two floors above us while he was testifying at a Senate committee hearing on a bill requiring the Highway Department to withhold union dues for employees who had joined a fledgling union for state workers. Weston had missed the news.

"Well, you can't win 'em all," Joe said cheerily as he finished distributing the paper in the pressroom and headed for other offices around the building.

By his stepdaughter, Joe fathered a son and named him Joseph Freepress Weston. He expected the boy to take up his crusade someday. But his mounting legal troubles, bills, and failing health forced an end to the *Sharp Citizen*. He died in 1983.

XI
A Coon Dog Has Its Day

Unlike Dale Bumpers, for David Pryor the stars did not always line up, no matter what course he chose. Bumpers had raised a raft of taxes when he first took office in 1971 and more in 1973, and he announced that he was not going to "chase smokestacks" to bring polluting industries to the state, but still the economy boomed and new jobs mushroomed. Nature smiled on Arkansas. Crops flourished, commodity prices soared, farm income exploded, and the state treasury overflowed, creating yearly surpluses that Bumpers spent on new buildings and equipment at the state medical institutions, colleges, universities, and new state parks. In the fall before Pryor succeeded him, Bumpers called a special legislative session to spend all the carryover funds from fiscal 1974 on capital projects, leaving the pantry bare for Pryor. To combat inflation, the Federal Reserve chairman, Alan Greenspan, raised interest rates, and as Pryor took office in January 1975 the country was experiencing the beginnings of stagflation—the rare double whammy of inflation and recession. Pryor had to set about reducing state spending almost on his first day. Unemployment soared above 9 percent in the spring. But, as Bumpers would always remind him, in the midst of the gloom Pryor did get to have his picture taken dedicating all the new buildings and parks financed by his predecessor's boom years.

While destiny always seemed to smile upon Dale Bumpers from his first to his last days in political office, for David Pryor storm clouds and political setbacks were never far away.

Like nearly every new governor, Pryor did not arrive at the Capitol on inauguration day with a lot of promises or reform ideas, beyond being a careful steward of the taxpayers' money. Bumpers had adopted and achieved all the prescriptions laid out by progressive groups in the stagnant 1960s. Except one: a new constitution that would abolish the restraints left by constitution writing in Arkansas's depression years of the 1870s and 1930s. That had been the goal of the small band of Young Turks in Pryor's youthful years in the legislature in the early '60s. A constitutional convention in 1969 and 1970 had written a constitution that did just that, but voters did not ratify it at the general election in 1970. Pryor thought a new convention, learning from the 1970 defeat, might draft a constitution that avoided the pitfalls that he suspected produced the defeat. He would give the state a modern constitution, the dream of his old mentor, Virgil Butler. It could be the surest legacy of what he anticipated would be a short spell in the governor's office.

To avoid the expenses of an election on whether to hold a convention, the election for the delegate seats, and a lengthy convention, Pryor proposed to limit the convention to thirty-five delegates: He would appoint twenty-seven of them from around the state; five others would be state representatives and three would be state senators, chosen by those bodies. To avoid too many controversies and the pitfalls of tampering with constitutional provisions that were sacred cows with certain groups, such as industry, the bill spelling out the mechanics of the convention and the timetable for ratifying the new document limited the scope of the delegates' work. Large parts of the existing constitution would automatically be part of the document that would be submitted to the voters at a special election in the fall, so the delegates could not change them.

The legislature enacted the bill, the delegates were appointed, and the convention was set to begin in late spring. Republican lawyers Ed Bethune and Cliff Jackson, who represented Lynn Lowe of Texarkana, a perennial Republican candidate for office, sued to stop it, alleging a number of violations of constitutional law. As soon as the thirty-five delegates assembled at the Capitol, the Supreme Court declared the act unconstitutional and disbanded the convention. The seven justices split four ways, but four of the justices found the act invalid in some way. Since constitution writing was the sole province of the people, the court held, the legislature could not tie the hands of the delegates or of the people to change the constitution in any way that they wanted. Delegates and the voters had to be free to change any part of the constitution they desired. The majority implied, but did not say flatly, that delegates needed to be elected by the people and not chosen by the governor and the legislature. Chief Justice Carleton Harris and two other senior justices, George Rose Smith and Frank Holt, strenuously disagreed. Harris said none of the majority's conclusions had any foundation in the Constitution. Five months into his term, Pryor's plan for a quick and certain revision of the Constitution was dead. He offered another solution two years later—a statewide election of delegates, a full and unfettered convention, and then a ratification vote in 1980—but that process also ended in defeat.

A couple of months into his term, Pryor was relaxing at the mansion one night when the mayor of Pine Bluff telephoned him in a panic. The mayor was at the city fire department, where all but two of the city's sixty-one firemen had walked off the job to protest the fire chief's refusal to resign, the city's refusal to fire him, and the lack of any grievance procedure for firemen or other municipal workers. The city had no fire protection. Pryor called the adjutant general of the National Guard and had him mobilize a National Guard unit at Pine Bluff to take over the six fire stations until the strike ended. So David Pryor, the paladin of the working stiffs, the earnest friend of labor unions, became a strikebreaker. The president of the Arkansas State AFL-CIO, J. Bill Becker, condemned the action. The firemen soon came back to work and the Guardsmen went home, but unions never forgot what they considered to be a betrayal by the man they had backed in every race. Pryor would always maintain that his first obligation was to protect people and that not to have met that emergency would have put politics above duty. Unions abandoned him in his next race for the Senate, in 1978.

Trash was a lifelong obsession of Pryor. He saw it everywhere: plastic and Styrofoam cups and straws along streets and roadsides and in streams, junkyards, rotting tires, and abandoned vehicles. Driving back from Dumas to Little Rock one day with his childhood friend and administrative assistant Don Harrell, he saw youngsters in a car ahead of him throwing McDonald's wrappers and plastic cups out the window. He had Harrell pull up beside them and he shouted at them to stop. He went behind their car, wrote down their license number, and told them he was going to turn them in to the State Police for littering unless they went back and picked up all their trash. He waited while they did it. So he introduced a bill in the legislature, the Litter Control Act, that levied a small tax on manufacturers and distributors of products that required throwaway containers made of plastic, Styrofoam, or other synthetic materials. The bill made it an offense to litter and to leave abandoned vehicles, tires, or other refuse anywhere but on the owner's property. A variety of state and local agencies were to enforce the act. It seemed to be a popular bill. It passed with sizable majorities and was to go into effect on July 1.

It proved to be a major embarrassment for Pryor. Local businesses began to complain to legislators about the new law, particularly after the state Revenue Department sent a postcard to businesses telling them bluntly that they were to start paying the litter tax on July 1 and warning them about the penalties. Legislators began to get telephone calls asking whether they had voted for the new litter law. Some legislators said they couldn't remember or sidestepped the question. The Associated Press circulated an article naming every legislator in both houses who had voted for it and the town where he or she lived, and all the daily newspapers in the state carried the story. Lawmakers besieged the governor, begging him to include a repeal bill in the call for a special session that he planned to fund kindergartens. He tried to offer a restrained, partial repeal that would keep some provisions intact, but legislators wanted the law gone without a trace, and they succeeded. Thirty years later, Pryor was still irked by the garbage despoiling the countryside and by the repeal of his litter law.

But the environmental initiative was neither Pryor's boldest venture nor his bitterest rejection. That was the Arkansas Plan, a novel initiative that Pryor hoped would resolve a recurring conflict over state funding of municipal and county government and also invigorate civic action at the local level. It was Pryor's most serious political miscalculation. He misjudged the ardor for civic engagement by local politicians.

Bumpers had turned aside the big drive by city and county officials and their lobbying associations to carve out 7 percent of the state's general revenues each year, but with Bumpers out of the way they were contemplating another effort. President Richard Nixon's New Federalism, which included an experimental revenue-sharing program with the states in 1973, was an inspiration. Pryor and a young scholar who interned in his office for a while—Steve Nickles, a doctoral student at Columbia University—came up with an elaborate revenue-sharing plan of their own. The state would cut the personal income tax by 25 percent. Cities and counties then would be empowered by law to levy their own income taxes and devise their own plans for dividing it among local governments and for spending it. It would return taxing and spending powers to the people at the lowest level. Voters had just amended the state Constitution to overhaul county government. For the first time, counties would have a real legislative branch and a strengthened chief executive: the quorum courts and county judges. It seemed to be the perfect moment for the Pryor plan to promote the new civic engagement at the grassroots. He promoted the idea in 1976 as he was coasting to re-election. He called in legislators to line up support for the bill in the 1977 legislative session. County and municipal officials were immediately skeptical. It put the burden on them to raise taxes for local services; state legislators and the governor could handle the heat for levying taxes better than they could.

For Pryor, this called for textbook civics. He scheduled regional hearings around the state, where he and a few other state officials could address the

citizenry, explain the plan, and absorb their suggestions and criticism. At one of the first, on the Arkansas State University campus at Jonesboro, Pryor told people that the state tax cut and the enlarged local powers would be like handing their taxes back to them. They could then use their savings by levying the taxes locally for vitally needed services in their communities, or they could just spend it on a new coon dog. It was their choice. George Fisher, the *Arkansas Gazette*'s perspicacious political cartoonist and a dog lover, immediately labeled it "The Coon Dog Plan." In Fisher's daily cartoons, which followed the progress of Pryor's fight for the Arkansas Plan, Pryor always had a coon dog at his side, once holding up cue signs for him as he addressed the legislature on the plan. Pryor, in fact, never appeared in a Fisher cartoon again without the lovable hound at his side. The legislation also permitted counties to divide the money with schools if they so chose. The Arkansas Education Association, the Arkansas School Boards Association, and the association of school administrators let it be known that they would rather the state, not quorum courts, be responsible for school funding.

His friends in the Senate passed the legislation, but the House of Representatives demurred. It died a quiet death. The defeat of his biggest initiative as governor seemed to most of us to forecast trouble for Pryor in the big Senate campaign in 1978 that he and nearly everyone else knew was coming. His health failing, John McClellan had announced that he would not run again and died that fall, clearing the path for Pryor. If anything, his fight for the Coon Dog Plan reinforced his popularity with the rank and file. Only city and county politicians were vexed.

Although it was the legislative branch that he loved and where he would spend thirty of his thirty-four years in public office, most of Pryor's major legislative initiatives as governor by the spring of 1978 had produced bitter fruit. It reinforced his conviction that the U.S. Senate was where he was supposed to be.

Populating the administrative branch, on the other hand, was the executive prerogative that gave him immense satisfaction. Even when they created political problems for him, Pryor found real joy in making unorthodox appointments to major administrative offices and to boards and commissions that regulated scores of government programs. When he had to name a State Police director, he passed over the top-ranking officers of the State Police, who were backed by the state's most powerful senator, Max Howell, and named a young sergeant, Doug Harp, who headed the detail assigned to the governor and who had impressed Pryor with his intelligence and honesty. He appointed the first woman, Elsijane Trimble Roy, and the first African American, George Howard Jr., to the Arkansas Supreme Court. He put the first woman, Patsy Thomasson, on the state Highway Commission. He put a woman and/or an African American on nearly every college and university board, the state Board of Education, and the Board of Higher Education. His first big appointment after his inauguration was to the state Highway Commission. Maurice Smith of Birdeye, who was finishing a ten-year term on the commission and wanted another, enjoyed the support of all of east Arkansas and had joined Witt Stephens's phalanx of rich bankers and businessmen who had supported Pryor over Orval Faubus in the recent election. Instead, Pryor named David Solomon, a bow-tied lawyer from Helena who had shown no interest in the job and who was shocked at the offer. Spurning Smith cost Pryor dearly in the legislature, where Smith's friends overrode the governor's veto of a bill in which Smith had a family interest.

When McClellan died in November 1977, Pryor went to his apartment in

Little Rock and offered to appoint his widow, Norma, to complete his un-expired term, but she was not interested. Every politician in the state and every kingmaker wanted the job, a one-year stint in the nation's capital and the lifetime privilege of being known as a former United States senator. In-stead, Pryor appointed Kaneaster Hodges Jr. of Newport—a farmer, lawyer, and sometime Methodist preacher who was little known outside Jackson County, where he had been a city attorney and deputy prosecutor. Hodges had been a friend and had gone to Little Rock when Pryor took office in 1975 to run his legislative operations at the first session of the General Assembly. Senator Hodges would vote to ratify the Panama Canal Treaty, which was immensely unpopular in the rural South, raising the prospect that Pryor's opponents in the approaching Senate race would charge him with appointing the man who helped give away the Panama Canal to Pan-amanians. Feelings were still so high in 1980 that Senator Bumpers's vote for the treaty nearly defeated him.

With the state plunging into a recession, there was little prospect for in-dustrial gains, so for director of the state's economic development agency Pryor wanted a promoter, someone who could keep business spirits high through the doldrums. He decided that Frank D. White, an ebullient bank-er with a booming voice and a bearish grip, was his man. Since their college days, Pryor had known and liked White, a Democrat who would one day switch parties and become a Republican governor. White was the leader of the Arkansas Jaycees, a network of likeminded cheerleaders. He was an associate at the Commercial National Bank, where his perpetual gregari-ousness sometimes got on the nerves of his boss, William H. Bowen, who happened to be the chairman of the Industrial Development Commission. Bowen told Pryor that White would be perfect for the job. He met Pryor's prescription for the state's development champion. He was buoyant and he had ideas.

One was that Arkansas should open an office in Europe, where indus-trialists were supposed to be looking for opportunities to invest in the booming American economy. It was the hot job-creation idea of the time. Bekaert Corporation, a global steel company headquartered in Belgium, was building a big plant at Van Buren to manufacture steel wire, and there were sure to be other prospects. Mississippi, South Carolina, Virginia, and other states had set up offices in Europe to recruit investors, and White said Arkansas had to keep up. White set up a junket to Europe to explore the prospect. Pryor would lead the delegation to Belgium, Germany, and the

United Kingdom, which included White, Bowen, several legislators, and a couple of newsmen, including me. The trip brought a few embarrassing moments for Pryor. After the Belgian hosts at a dinner next door to the European Parliament in Brussels had lifted toasts to the Arkansawyers, one in French and another in Dutch, Representative Boyce Alford stood with his wine glass and toasted the Europeans in the only foreign words he knew: "Campho-phenique!"

At a reception for the delegation at the elegant Savoy hotel in London hosted by Elliott Richardson, the American ambassador to the Court of St. James, Pryor introduced Senator Virgil T. Fletcher of Benton to the tuxedoed ambassador, who was famous for resigning as attorney general in 1973 after refusing to fire the independent counsel who was investigating Nixon for the Watergate crimes. "Glad to meet ya, Elliott," Fletcher said, while tossing peanuts from the *hors d'oeuvre* table into his mouth. "Where ya from?"

When the group visited other state offices in Brussels and Munich, Germany, the office directors said a key to recruiting investors was a director who was fluent in a European language, either French or German and preferably both. Everyone agreed that a European office would pay dividends, as it seemed to be doing for other states. The legislature back home enacted legislation creating the office and an appropriation. Pryor said he would personally interview the top candidates for the director's job and choose the best one. A committee of the Arkansas Industrial Development Commission interviewed the two finalists, one who spoke Dutch, French, and German, and the other a junior banker at Conway named Bunny Adcock, who said his wife had taught French in high school. Adcock was a leader of the Jaycees with White and later a golf coach at the University of Central Arkansas. White recommended Adcock for the job and the commission hired him. I crossed the Capitol to the governor's office to get Pryor's reaction. He was in Dallas but Don Harrell, his press secretary, said the AIDC couldn't have hired Adcock because the governor intended to interview the finalists and hire the director. Harrell got Pryor on the phone at Dallas and handed the receiver to me. Pryor kept insisting that I misunderstood the AIDC's action, because White knew that the governor intended to make the final selection. I read him my notes. Back in Little Rock later in the day, Pryor summoned White to his office and chewed him out. The Brussels office never landed a single company or a single job. A few years later, Governor Bill Clinton converted the office to a Washington lobbying office and gave the job to Anne Bartley, a daughter of Jeannette Rockefeller by her first marriage. When Frank White defeated Clinton after one term, one of his first acts was to close the Washington lobbying office.

❑❑❑

If life as the state's First Citizen was not a source of enduring contentment for David Pryor, being the First Lady was much worse. Barbara enjoyed the social and analytical aspects of politicking, for which she proved to be a big asset, but the all-consuming nature of the governor's job depleted her indulgence, if not his, and nearly her sanity. Every waking hour he was mentally and emotionally wired to the problems of governing. She felt like a stranger in the household. The social demands on her, in addition to raising three boys, were unexpected. So were the risks of public visibility. When the first lady got a frizzy hairdo, a fad for a while for some of the younger set, it became a matter of statewide conversation, not all of it kind. Well into their first year in the mansion she decided one day that she couldn't do

Barbara Pryor

it another day, and she told David and then the boys. She moved out and resided awhile in their lake cabin in Hot Springs and then in Little Rock. She enrolled in classes at the University of Arkansas at Little Rock, tried to get a job, and developed an interest in filmmaking after meeting a former writer for Pryor's little weekly newspaper who had gotten into the filmmaking business.

In the fall of 1976, shortly before she rejoined the family at the mansion and while her husband was running for re-election, Barbara was the executive producer of the film *Wishbone Cutter*, a sort of low-budget Western horror movie that was filmed in the Ozarks, mostly in Marion County around the Buffalo River. The film, about a Confederate cavalryman who goes into the river country in search of a cache of diamonds revealed to him by a dying Reb but supposedly hidden in a haunted mountain protected by a demon, was written and directed by Earl B. Smith, whose only

"Personally, I think it's disgusting."

previous credits were as a screenwriter for a couple of spooky films. Barbara got twelve investors to put up about a million dollars for the project. The film was released in the early spring of 1977, after she had returned to the mansion.

It was a doomed undertaking. The film called for the demise of a couple of horses, and the American Humane Society protested that the film crew had killed four fine animals in the mountains of Marion County, a matter that would have escaped notice had the film not been associated with the first lady. Barbara said no, that they had obtained the dying animals from a rendering plant and that they were disposed of humanely.

Wishbone Cutter premiered on March 31, 1977, at Little Rock's new round theater at Asher and University Avenues. My wife and I attended. Barbara was introduced and made a few remarks. Bill Lewis, the *Arkansas Gazette*'s film and music critic, began his review the next day this way: "The Academy Awards are just over, but if they gave one for Worst Picture *Wishbone Cutter* probably would be safe against all the competition that may come up by next March."

His review brought up the horse deaths again and called them "a gross violation of all humane sensitivity." Smith, the writer and director, released a statement attacking Lewis and the *Gazette* for a politically motivated diatribe. A few days later, the Pryors threw a reception for some foreigners at one of the historic downtown museums. I was in the mingling crowd when I felt a sharp pain in my left calf. Barbara Pryor had kicked me.

"That's for that terrible review of *Wishbone*, Ernie," she said.

"I didn't write the review," I replied. "That was Willard Lewis's."

"I saw who wrote it," she replied. "But he's not here, and you are!"

I said I would speak to him about it. Bill told me that he might have been a trifle harsh.

XII
"Forget All Feuds"

Familiarity need not breed contempt. If people have had time to gain some intimacy with a politician and like him or her, that is about all that matters. Ideology, profound achievement or lack of it, memorable catch-phrases, founts of money, eloquence or lack of it—none of it will matter. So it was with David Pryor in 1978, when he set about, again, to reach the U.S. Senate, his life's goal. After three statewide campaigns and four years in the most visible job in the state, Pryor had given people no reason to either dislike or distrust him. He had always been the best-liked kid in his class.

Jim Guy Tucker

Everyone with whom he served in the legislative halls at Little Rock and Washington, even those who rarely voted with him, liked him. Nothing historic came of his four years running the state government, but neither had there been a hint of scandal nor reason to harbor any suspicion of self-dealing or of a self-serving pursuit of power. Never had the state seen a politician with an ego so muted, who never boasted or claimed superiority in any sphere or over any foe. Pryor's frustrated Republican opponent that fall, Tom Kelly of Little Rock, ridiculed Pryor's likability by calling him "Arkansas's Pet Rock," a reference to a brief merchandising phenomenon of the time.

Pryor was going to win the Senate seat in 1978 unless another candidate could establish his own likeability with an equal or greater number of voters or else raise a burning economic or social issue with the voters. None presented itself that summer, and so likeminded were his opponents that they found no latent issue that might separate them from David Pryor or minimize the likeability quotient.

No U.S. Senate seat since 1944 had been open to all comers, with no daunting incumbent on the ballot, and every aspiring politician yearned to run. The 31-year-old attorney general, Bill Clinton, whose ambitions exceeded everyone's, thought seriously about it, but rather than take the risk of running against a field of strong candidates, all holding bigger offices than his, he took the bird in hand. He would hardly be challenged in a race for governor. The Senate race was the chance of a lifetime for all four congressmen—Bill Alexander in the First District, Jim Guy Tucker in the Second, John Paul Hammerschmidt in the Third, and Ray H. Thornton Jr. in the Fourth—but Alexander, a Democrat, and Hammerschmidt, the only Republican in the delegation since Reconstruction, concluded that their chances were too remote, especially with the popular Pryor on the ballot. Thornton and Tucker, however, thought the stakes were too high to pass up and that their chances against Pryor were close to even.

A Harvard graduate with the deepest dimples in Christendom and a penchant for bravado, Tucker enjoyed a powerful base in Pulaski County, where he had been a popular prosecutor who went on raids with the police, kicking down doors and once firing shots into a ceiling to scare a hiding thug out of the attic. After Harvard, Tucker entered the Marine Corps to fight in Vietnam, but when he was discharged after three months for an auto-immune disease, he went twice to Vietnam as a freelance war correspondent and wrote a book about it, *Arkansas Men at War*. Fresh out of law school, he volunteered to a partner at his law firm, John Haley, the chairman of the state Board of Corrections, to be committed to the state penitentiary as a convicted felon so that he could expose criminality in the corrupt system, but he was removed when Governor Rockefeller found out and ordered officials to get him out before his throat was cut. After his term as prosecuting attorney, Tucker was elected attorney general twice. In his first term, he tried to get the state Public Service Commission to require Arkansas Power and Light Company to install expensive scrubbers on the two units of a coal-burning power plant that the utility was about to build near Redfield to remove sulfur and nitric oxides from the smokestack emissions. Forty-five years later, in 2018, the utility agreed to shutter both its coal plants rather than install scrubbers or continue the dirty emissions. Tucker had easily won the congressional seat of the retiring Wilbur D. Mills in 1976 and, as a freshman, played a role in Social Security reform.

Sending Guardsmen to replace striking firemen at Pine Bluff cost Pryor dearly in the Senate primary. When he appeared at the Arkansas State AFL-CIO convention in the summer of 1978 he got a cold reception. The convention endorsed Tucker for the Senate, and individual union groups followed suit. So did the Arkansas Education Association, based on the governor's intervention in the firemen's strike and his failure to deliver substantial salary increases for teachers.

Thornton believed he could neutralize Pryor's base in south Arkansas since he had held Pryor's congressional seat there for six years. As a member of the House Judiciary Committee in the summer of 1974, Thornton had cast three decisive but perilous votes for impeachment articles against President Nixon. It raised his profile but also embittered the silent Republicans in Arkansas, who still voted in the Democratic primaries. A fourth candidate, A. C. Grigson of Texarkana, an accountant, entered the race to raise some burning issue that he could never quite articulate on the stump. Thornton would always believe that, had it not been for Grigson's eight thousand votes, mostly from southwest Arkansas, he rather than Tucker would have made the runoff against Pryor, and the demographics might then have favored him.

By the spring of 1978, Witt Stephens regretted having had a soft spot for David Pryor in 1974 and throwing his network of power brokers from around the state behind him in the governor's race against Faubus. Now Pryor was running against his nephew, Congressman Ray Thornton, who had been counsel for his utility, Arkansas Louisiana Gas Company. Everyone who had attended the big "put" session to raise money in 1972 for Senator McClellan's runoff against Pryor and who then switched to Pryor in 1974 returned to the fold in 1978. They all gave the maximum contributions to Thornton's primary campaign. It would not be enough. Pryor received 198,000 votes, Tucker 187,500, Thornton 184,100, and Grigson 8,100. Short of a majority, Pryor was forced into a runoff with Tucker but won it handily, 265,800 to Tucker's 218,400.

Two sagas in that election that on the whole played inconsequential roles in Pryor's victory had freakish but lasting effects on political fortunes both in Arkansas and across the country. It is not a stretch to say that they have followed Jim Guy Tucker and Bill Clinton the rest of their lives and contributed to the future misfortunes of both men, including Clinton's becoming the second American president to be impeached and Tucker's becoming the first Arkansas governor to resign from office over a criminal conviction. The reader will need to follow the threads as we navigate the years.

While Pryor had to fight his way into a runoff with Tucker, Clinton easily won the nomination for governor over four opponents without a runoff. Clinton had heard about a young political consultant and pollster in New York named Dick Morris who had helped relatively unknown candidates win, and he hired him. Morris was a partner of another New Yorker, Richard Dresner. Originally they were Democrats but had begun to handle both Republican and Democratic candidates. I never knew what Morris contributed to Clinton's campaign for governor, but Clinton thought he was a political genius. Clinton saw Tucker, another cerebral but swashbuckling Ivy Leaguer, as his chief future rival in the Arkansas political firmament. The day after his own victory, Clinton sent Morris across town and told Pryor that Morris could devise a strategy for defeating Tucker, who had real momentum after coming so close to the governor in the preferential primary. Morris would become internationally famous sixteen years later, in 1994, by moving into the White House and resurrecting President Clinton's fortunes after the disastrous midterm elections cost Democrats the U.S. Senate, House of Representatives,

Ray Thornton

and most governor's offices. He devised a strategy he called triangulation, which was to co-opt Republican issues and talking points like welfare, banking reform, and shrinking government. Morris became even better known in 1996 when, while managing Clinton's re-election campaign, he had to resign during the Democratic national nominating convention after a tabloid revealed his relationship with a prostitute, with whom he was photographed consorting on a hotel balcony. Morris had let the call girl listen on another telephone while he and President Clinton talked about political strategy.

Back in 1978, Morris's strategy was to find something in an opponent's past or his voting record that ran against the grain of conservative voters. With Tucker, it was his largely liberal record in his single term in Congress. Tucker voted with Democrats and, more narrowly, with liberal Democrats in the few roll calls that reflected ideological bents, like the Nuclear Non-Proliferation Act, the Clean Water Act, the Humphrey-Hawkins Full

Employment Act, the Pregnancy Act, and the National Energy Conservation Policy Act. Tucker also was supported by the union movement in Arkansas. On the evening that Morris's first television commercial against Tucker ran on Little Rock stations (it said Tucker took orders from the union bosses and that he voted nearly all the time with eastern liberals), Pryor was campaigning in northeast Arkansas and would not be returning to the Governor's Mansion until late evening. Morris was in the living room of the mansion with Billy Roy Wilson, Pryor's old friend and campaign manager, waiting for Pryor's return. Barbara Pryor, the governor's wife, happened to be watching television in another room and saw the commercial. It reminded her of the commercials McClellan had run against her husband in the Senate race in 1972, which accused him of being a servant of labor bosses and eastern liberals. McClellan had turned Pryor's defense that his union contributions came from the overall pockets and cookie jars of working men and women against him. She stormed into the living room and demanded to know who was responsible for the terrible commercial for her husband. Morris meekly raised his hand and said he guessed that it was he. She ordered him out of her house and told him not to come back. Morris went back to his hotel room and prepared to return to New York. It was agreed that he would not go back to the mansion and that the commercials against Tucker would be softened.

Whether the union and liberal baiting cost Tucker the election, as it presumably had Pryor in 1972, it is impossible to know, but Tucker was madder at Clinton than at Pryor. Clinton had no reason to meddle in the Senate race except for personal ambition—a need to stymie the man he saw as his rival some day. Relations between them were never warm again. Tucker ran for governor four years later, when Clinton was making a comeback against Frank White, and was beaten after a rancorous campaign. They were about to clash again in 1990 in Clinton's final race for governor, but Clinton dried up his financing and Tucker backed down and instead ran for and was elected lieutenant governor. Their two years sharing the executive branch were tense and often confrontational, particularly when Clinton was outside the state borders campaigning for president and Tucker was the acting governor. While Kenneth Starr, the special prosecutor in the Whitewater snipe hunt, was pursuing Clinton for seven years, 1994–2001, the only big quarry he bagged was Clinton's longtime adversary, who had to resign the governor's office after he was convicted of misapplying the proceeds of a loan in a private business transaction ten years earlier. When, in his final days in office, Clinton pardoned a number of people—including his brother Roger, Susan McDougal, and Marc Rich, the millionaire who had fled the country to avoid trial for avoiding payment of $48 million in taxes—he offered no grace to his old rival, though he later apologized for not doing so.

Another imbroglio in the Senate campaign caused only a ripple in that rather calm election but crested in succeeding waves over the next twenty years. It involved a feud among three Little Rock businessmen, with the collaboration of two investigative reporters for the *New York Times*. The five men engaged in a long-running tag-team match that eventually produced the investigation that led, in 1998, to the second impeachment of an American president.

It all began in the late spring of 1978 when an investigative reporter who worked in the financial section of the *New York Times* got a tip about some arcane regulatory dealings in Arkansas involving the energy moguls and financiers Witt Stephens and Jackson T. "Jack" Stephens, whose nephew Ray Thornton happened to be running for the Senate. The reporter came to Little Rock to do the story and eventually got it published, a few days before the preferential primary in which Thornton was knocked out of the runoff. The Stephenses, Thornton, and his campaign staff would always believe that the *Times* story and the follow-ups in the Arkansas media cost Thornton the Senate seat, at least in tandem with A. C. Grigson's handful of votes. The *Times* reporter, Jeff Gerth, would return to Little Rock fourteen years later and, with the help of the same Little Rock contact, write the Whitewater story that produced the seven-year criminal investigation that led to Clinton's impeachment.

It was presumed at the time, in March 1992, that Gerth's Whitewater story—a long, baffling, often misleading, and occasionally inaccurate piece published on the great paper's front page—was the reporter's and the *Times*'s first incursion into the "incestuous" (to use the journalistic currency of the time) worlds of Arkansas business and politics. Actually, it was the latest installment in a series of tit-for-tat articles in the *Times* that furthered a war of Shakespearean intrigue between an ambitious young businessman, Sheffield Nelson, and the Stephens brothers, who had accumulated one of the South's great fortunes. Readers will remember Nelson from Chapter V, which recited the successful campaign by liberal insurgents led by Sam Boyce and Jim McDougal to overthrow the old regime in the Young Democrats of Arkansas. Nelson, who had just gone to work for Arkansas Louisiana Gas Company as executive assistant to the CEO, Witt Stephens, was supposed to assume the presidency of the political organization in 1965, backed by the controlling supporters of Governor Faubus, but Nelson was defeated in a Byzantine scheme cooked up by McDougal to keep Nelson and his supporters out of the convention hall until the voting had finished. The setback delayed the onset of Nelson's political career for two decades. He would run for governor twice and head the state Republican Party at the beginning of its renaissance in the 1990s.

In 1978, I was a stringer—an occasional reporter of Arkansas doings—for the *New York Times*. I had a tiny and clandestine role in all those stories, from 1978 through 1992, sufficient only to give me some inside knowledge of the intrigues on both sides.

This is how it all happened.

☐☐☐

When he acquired Arkansas Louisiana Gas Company, a big but floundering natural-gas distributor, from Cities Service in 1954, Witt Stephens left the investment house that he had started during the Great Depression largely in the hands of younger brother Jack, although he continued to dabble in bond trading at the firm. Together, Witt and Jack acquired large energy interests outside Arkla, particularly in the gas-rich Arkoma Basin of western Arkansas and eastern Oklahoma. Some of it they held individually and some through Witt's small distribution company in the Fort Smith region, Arkansas Oklahoma Gas Company, but mostly they were held through Stephens Production Company, a subsidiary of the brothers' investment company. In 1973, at the age of sixty-six, Witt retired as president and CEO of Arkla and handpicked his successor, his loquacious executive assistant Sheffield Nelson, whom he considered almost a member of the family. Nelson, who had picked up a law degree while he was in Stephens's office, was only thirty-two. There may have been method to Stephens's choice beyond his admiration for the young man's business acumen—a successor who would be yoked by loyalty to the Stephenses' good fortunes. Witt would soon regret the promotion.

The family's large gas holdings were valuable on the open market, but there were a few intractable problems, at least as long as Witt was running Arkla. Other than Arkla's pipeline network, there was no way to transport the Stephenses' gas from western Arkansas and Oklahoma across Arkansas to the Mississippi River, where interstate pipelines could deliver it to meet the growing demand in markets in Missouri and the industrialized Ohio River Valley. The brothers' gas that was sold to Arkla, moreover, was tied up in long-term contracts negotiated in the 1950s and '60s at pennies per thousand cubic feet, far below the prices that were paid for gas on the open market. The brothers naturally thought their gas was as good as gas from new wells and that they deserved payment for the true current value of gas. They wanted to renegotiate the old contracts with Arkla and also to transport their gas through Arkla's pipelines to the interstate pipelines along the Mississippi River, where it could be marketed to meet the high demand in the industrial regions. Stephens offered to pay a fee to Arkla to use its pipelines. While Stephens was running Arkla, those transactions would have appeared to be self-dealing.

Nelson refused to go along. He said his obligation was to the company, its shareholders, and customers, not to his mentor and patron. The Stephenses and other producers, leaseholders, and royalty owners in the Arkoma gas basin were Arkla's captives. Nelson considered it poor economics for Arkla to liberate the captives so that they could sell their gas beyond the state or to renegotiate old gas-purchase contracts and pass those higher costs on to Arkla ratepayers. It was an argument that would prevail when the legislature defeated a bill requiring Arkla to transport the gas to other markets. It was a shock that the whippersnapper Nelson won in the legislature, a jurisdiction where Stephens had prevailed against any comer for twenty-five years. It was little comfort that what they sought, the unimpeded transportation of energy across artificial barriers, eventually was seen as a matter of national interest and national policy.

That dispute was still raw in the spring of 1978 when Jeff Gerth boarded a plane for Little Rock to do the article about the Stephenses. Gerth had been a freelance reporter in San Francisco, where he caught the eye of Seymour "Sy" Hersh, the famous investigative reporter for *The New Yorker*, the *New York Times*, *The Nation*, and other publications. Gerth had helped Hersh on a couple of stories on a contract basis and then joined the *Times* as an investigative reporter for the financial section.

The preferential primary for the U.S. Senate was a few weeks away. The Stephenses, obviously, supported their nephew Thornton, and Nelson supported Jim Guy Tucker. Either Thornton or Tucker was likely to reach a runoff with Governor Pryor. It always seemed obvious that Nelson had tipped Gerth on a potential story involving the Stephenses and Thornton, but Nelson told me that Gerth seemed to have gotten information from someone else when he called Nelson. He said Gerth telephoned him "out of the blue" and asked Nelson to tell him what he knew about Witt and Jack Stephens. He said he told the reporter about the brothers and how they had made their wealth, but he suggested nothing derogatory. Nelson called Gerth "a bulldog of a reporter" who got the story that appeared in the *Times* on his own. I never asked Gerth about his original source. A rate analyst at the state Public Service Commission, the regulatory agency where Gerth got the information for his article, had recently left the commission and gone to work for Nelson, but he swore to me years later that he had not provided the tip to Gerth, Nelson, or anyone else.

Before flying to Little Rock, Gerth had telephoned me from New York and said he was going to do an article on the Stephens brothers, who were the subjects of big stories in *Fortune* magazine and other business periodicals for owning the largest investment banking house in the nation off Wall Street. Gerth asked for some help in doing his story about the brothers. I told him that I could provide him with a long series of articles that I had written the year before for the *Gazette* about how the brothers had accumulated their wealth and political power over the previous forty-five years. He said he had those articles already and asked if, for a start, I could get the annual reports of the Union Life Insurance Company, which Jack Stephens had bought in 1959, and deliver them to the hotel in Little Rock where he would be staying. He arrived that day and went to the state Public Service Commission offices in the Justice Building on the Capitol grounds. That evening he called and asked if I could meet him for a beer. Gerth told me that he had a bombshell of a story that would "blow Ray Thornton out of the Senate race." He would, of course, not tell me what the story was, because, naturally, I would be compelled to get the story for my paper, the *Gazette*. That is the competitive nature of the business. Before he could write the story, Gerth had to get the Stephenses to try to explain things.

I wondered what there could be at the Public Service Commission that would scandalize Thornton, who had many years earlier represented his uncles' utility in some proceedings, but never before the regulatory agency. Thornton's biggest contribution to the utility had been to design a service vehicle for the company. I went to the commission the next day to look for any recent filings that might affect the Stephenses and found nothing suspicious other than a year-old rate filing by Arkansas Oklahoma Gas Company, the tiny Stephens gas utility on the state's western border.

For days, Gerth stayed around trying to talk to the Stephenses and complained to me almost daily about the runaround he got from the Stephens offices. He especially needed to talk to Jack Stephens, but he could not get him on the telephone or find anyone who would set up an appointment. All he needed was to give one or both of the Stephenses a chance to talk. If one of them said simply "no comment," that would suffice, because the newspaper's policy was that no critical article could be published without the subjects having a chance to explain or justify their actions. Gerth asked if I could get one or both of the men to talk to him; after all, Witt Stephens was quoted extensively in my series the year before. I suggested that he show up at the Stephens building at East Capitol Avenue and Scott Street at daylight and wait for the men in the parking lot or else hang out around their homes and catch them as they were leaving for work or coming home. Finally, he said it was obvious that they were avoiding any conversation with him, so he was flying back to New York and would continue trying from there to get them on the phone. He called periodically to express his continued frustration in trying to talk to the Stephenses, especially Jack. He wanted my help but he could not share what his story was all about.

Finally, he called and told me excitedly that he had set up a golf date with Jack Stephens and they would talk about the matter on the golf course. At Little Rock, he was frustrated again. It turned out that Stephens was not expecting Gerth at a Little Rock Country Club golf course but at the Augusta National Golf Club on the Georgia–South Carolina border, the site of the annual Masters tournament. Stephens, a lifelong golf aficionado, was chairman of the club and had a home there. Feeling that he had been tricked again, Gerth returned home.

Emon Mahony Jr., an El Dorado acquaintance of mine from our youth and later the legislative assistant to Senator McClellan, was the CEO of Witt's west Arkansas company, which turned out to be the subject of Gerth's article. Two weeks before the election, Mahony received a call from someone at the *Times*. It could have been Gerth but Mahony didn't remember the name. The person wanted to ask him a few questions about the Stephenses and the gas company. Mahony, who had heard about the brouhaha at Little Rock, said he would be happy to talk to the man in a few weeks—i.e., after the primary. The person told him it had to be right then, because the story would be running the following Monday. Mahony refused. The article would actually be published the next Wednesday. Gerth finally persuaded his editors that Stephens was avoiding him simply to prevent publication of the story. Gerth called to alert me that the story would appear in the financial section of the *Times* the next day, although altered from his original account. I alerted the *Gazette*'s managing editor that the *Times* would be carrying a blockbuster story that would impact the Senate race, but I didn't know what it was. The *Gazette* subscribed to the *Times* news service.

It was anything but a blockbuster. Under the headline "The Stephens Empire Faces a Challenge," Gerth's 1,800-word article devoted its first dozen paragraphs to an account of the Stephenses' great wealth and political power and Jack Stephens's friendship with Naval Academy classmate Jimmy Carter and his acquaintance with Bert Lance. It then reported the nut of the story: Witt's little gas company in Sebastian County had in recent years quadrupled the price it paid for gas that it bought from the Stephenses, including Stephens Production, which was more than it was paying other royalty owners for gas. It was paying Stephens producers 97 cents per thousand cubic feet of gas while paying independent producers only

68 cents. Witt's gas company maintained in the filing that it could pay the higher price under a 1957 law, the Fair Field Price Act, which allowed a gas company to pay the current market price for gas that it produced itself and pass along that cost to its ratepayers. The Public Service Commission staff maintained that it could not charge the "fair field price" because the producer, though part of the family, was not part of an integrated utility. The company had applied to the Public Service Commission for a rate increase the year before and the disparate payments were reflected among the documents the company had filed with the agency. Someone had tipped Gerth on the documents—*not me*, Nelson insisted—and that was the summary that Gerth had come to Little Rock to find.

The dispute, which was common in energy regulatory cases, and Gerth's account of it were so esoteric that no Arkansas reader was likely to comprehend the scandal. After nearly a year, the commission still had not ruled on the rate increase, owing probably to the ambiguity over pricing gas from Stephens wells and independent producers. Much of Gerth's article unflatteringly recapitulated the Stephenses' accumulation of power and money over the decades and repeated an unattributed quote from my interminable series of articles on the Stephenses the year before: "Witt rounds up the chickens and Jack carries them to the slaughter."

Gerth's story never mentioned Ray Thornton, although the candidate's name must have appeared in Gerth's original copy.

I wrote an article for the *Gazette* about the little controversy, and the Associated Press did a revised and shorter piece for the other media. Stories appeared in papers in western Arkansas but triggered no controversy. Still, Thornton and the Stephenses thought it had just enough impact in the communities served by the gas company to sink Thornton there—he finished third in those counties—and tilt the election to Tucker and Pryor. Thornton's kinship with Witt Stephens was expected to be a source of strength for him in the region, not a detriment.

What Gerth didn't know, presumably, was that Jack Stephens was getting advice from a colleague of Gerth at the *Times* about avoiding Gerth's inquiries. Wendell Rawls Jr., commonly known as "Sonny," was a Tennessee boy who had graduated from Vanderbilt University and won a Pulitzer Prize at the *Philadelphia Inquirer* for exposing atrocities at a Pennsylvania mental hospital. He moved to the Washington bureau of the *New York Times* as an investigative reporter when Jimmy Carter became president. Rawls did some of the reporting on Bert Lance, the Georgia banker and Carter friend who ran the Office of Management and Budget until investigations turned up evidence of mismanagement and corruption at the Calhoun First National Bank of Georgia when Lance was chairman of the board. Lance resigned as director of the OMB, probably at President Carter's urging, but later was acquitted on nine charges of corruption. Jack Stephens had had financial dealings with Lance in the Georgian's banking days. The federal Securities and Exchange Commission once filed a civil complaint against Lance, Stephens, and others accusing them of violating securities laws in a furtive effort to take over a Washington, D.C., bank-holding company, but the matter was settled without a decision about any wrongdoing.

Rawls told me that Stephens had been a valuable confidential source for some of his reporting on Lance. The reporter and the financier struck up a friendship, surely the only journalistic friendship Stephens ever enjoyed other than with Orville Henry, the sports editor of the *Gazette*. He valued privacy and distrusted reporters, not least among them me.

Rawls, who had spent some time in Little Rock and in my home in 1974 when he was covering politics for the *Philadelphia Inquirer* and writing about the Fulbright-Bumpers race, told me that Stephens had called him in 1978 and said that some reporter for the *Times* named Gerth was in Little Rock working on a story about the brothers and Thornton. Gerth was calling the office trying to talk to him. Word had circulated in the executive offices at Arkla, where Witt Stephens still had friends, that the *Times* reporter was going to expose the Stephenses for something and damage the Thornton senatorial campaign. Jack Stephens wondered if Rawls knew what Gerth's story was about. Rawls didn't, and he also thought Gerth was a poor reporter. Like Rawls, Gerth apparently had worked some on the Bert Lance stories. Rawls told Stephens to just avoid at all costs having any conversation with Gerth, because the *Times* would not run a story without some comment, even a "no comment," that could be attributed to one of the Stephenses. Stall him, Rawls advised. Gerth's story was obviously intended to influence the Senate election. Stephens assumed that Sheffield Nelson was behind it.

When Gerth's article appeared in the *Times*, Jack Stephens called Rawls and demanded to know what had happened, since Rawls had assured him that no story would appear until the paper had a response from the Stephenses. Rawls apologized. He said he was surprised that the *Times* ran the story.

That was not the end of the gas fight. About three o'clock in the morning, six days after the primary that ended Thornton's run for the Senate and eight days before the runoff between Pryor and Tucker, I received a call from a lawyer friend of Tucker asking me to meet him right then in a wooded thicket off Highway 10 in western Little Rock. I spotted him in the darkness smoking a cigarette and leaning against a pine tree, reminiscent of Deep Throat in the Washington parking garage. He told me that Jack Williams of Texarkana, David Pryor's campaign treasurer, had approached his old college buddy John Pickett, who was a Pryor appointee to the state Public Service Commission, and urged him to go along with the rate increase sought by Witt Stephens's little west Arkansas gas company. Pickett, who became disturbed about the *ex parte* communication after talking to his colleagues on the commission, was going down to the Pulaski County prosecutor's office the next morning to report the conversation. The implication was that Pryor's campaign was angling to get the support of the Stephenses and Thornton supporters in the runoff the next Tuesday by assuring them that Witt would get his rate increase. Pryor had appointed two of the three commissioners—Pickett and Scott Stafford.

At the courthouse a few hours later, Pickett said Williams had talked to him twice about the Arkansas Oklahoma rate case that Jeff Gerth had exploited and had expressed the hope that Pickett and the other two commissioners could see Stephens's side of it. Pryor and Williams held a news conference at the campaign headquarters, where Williams insisted that Pickett had misinterpreted their conversations. All that he meant, Williams said, was that he was sure that Pickett would keep an open mind about the matter and do what was right. Pryor said that while he was not sure that Williams should have had any conversation at all with his old friend, Williams had no criminal intent.

The dispute dominated the news for the rest of the election cycle. Pryor said Tucker was going to wind up with egg on his face and accused Scott Stafford, a longtime Tucker friend and colleague while Tucker was prosecuting attorney and attorney general, of masterminding the red herring. Pryor had appointed Stafford to the regulatory board. Tucker said no, that it was he who exposed the nefarious plot to get Stephens a rate increase. Dick Morris counseled Pryor not to get caught up in the gas rhubarb but to keep the public's attention focused on Tucker's liberal congressional voting record, for spending and taxes. He did. I thought Pryor was in deep trouble on election day. He wasn't. Most people were not going to believe that David Pryor would do anything even slightly corrupt. Lee Munson, the prosecuting attorney, issued a short statement after the election saying he found nothing to prosecute in Pickett's complaint.

Readers will pardon me for leaping forward in this narrative to the next phase of the collaborative feud of businessmen and journalists, rather than following a tight chronology.

❑❑❑

Five years later, the Stephenses had a chance to get even with Nelson, through the same medium, the *New York Times*.

In December 1981, Nelson concluded a deal with an old Little Rock friend, Jerral W. "Jerry" Jones, later the owner of the Dallas Cowboys football franchise, to sell Arkla's half-interest in leases on fifteen thousand acres of prime gas-producing land in the Aetna and Cecil fields of western Arkansas to a company in which Jones was a partner, Arkoma Production Company. Jones, a former Razorback football player and insurance man, had gotten into the gas- and oil-drilling business in the late 1970s. Meeting at a hunting cabin in east Arkansas, Nelson and Jones worked out a deal in which Jones's production company would buy Arkla's half-interest in the leases, Arkla would lend Jones money to drill, and Arkla would contract to buy at current market prices all the gas that Jones found. They signed so-called "take-or-pay" contracts, which had been common in periods of gas scarcity. The utility would pay for all the gas that Jones's company produced in its successful wells, whether it could actually take the gas or not. Arkla would lend him three million dollars, interest free, to undertake the drilling. The Arkla board of directors approved the deal on New Year's Eve.

An Arkla news release announced the arrangement and presented it as an especially good deal for the gas company, because Arkla would be avoiding the risk of drilling dry wells and it would get a firm supply of gas. Brief stories about the deal appeared in the *Arkansas Gazette* and *Arkansas Democrat*.

Nelson soon retired as president of Arkla, at the age of forty-three, but remained a while as chairman of the board. Jones landed on the board of Arkla a few weeks after the deal was consummated and proceeded in a few years to reap a nice fortune, with which he purchased the Dallas Cowboys franchise from H. R. "Bum" Bright in 1989 for $140 million. In 2018, *Forbes* magazine would value Jones's franchise at $4.8 billion.

Before the announcement, Witt Stephens heard about the deal from

Arkla geologists at the Shreveport, La., headquarters who thought it was a sellout. Arkla's leases were in a part of the Arkoma Basin where there was almost no risk of failure. It was a very rare exploration that did not hit gas. As long as it held the leases, Arkla could just drill whenever it needed more gas.

Sometime after the little story appeared in the business pages of the *Arkansas Gazette* and *Arkansas Democrat,* Witt invited me to lunch in the executive dining room of the Stephens building across Capitol Avenue from the *Arkansas Democrat* headquarters. I was an occasional guest at the legendary cornbread lunches, where Witt and old political friends and adversaries, like U.S. District Judge Henry Woods and former Attorney General Ike Murry, swapped yarns. There always seemed to be a particular purpose for my invitations, uttered usually at a private audience in Witt's office before lunch. Witt asked if I had read the Arkla story about the gas deal Nelson struck with Jerry Jones. Well, he said, it was a rotten deal for the company and for the ratepayers but a bird's nest on the ground for Jerry Jones and his young partner. Arkla would bankroll their exploration so they would experience no risk whatever. They would reap an immense fortune at the expense ultimately of the ratepayers and, though Witt left it unsaid, shareholders of Arkla like himself. (He did not mention that the Stephenses, since they owned the other half-interest in the disputed leases, would reap some financial benefit from the Arkoma deal.) Somebody ought to expose the deal, Witt said.

By then, I was no longer a reporter but an editorial writer, but when I got back to the office, I dutifully mentioned Witt's tip to my old friend from El Dorado, Leroy Donald, the chief writer in the *Gazette*'s business section. Beyond the original stories based on the company news release, no story appeared in either Little Rock newspaper. Whether Witt also passed the tip to someone at the *Democrat,* I do not know.

Eighteen months later, someone at Stephens—Jack Stephens himself, no doubt—called Sonny Rawls at Atlanta and told him about the Arkoma deal, which by then was already gathering wealth for Jones and causing financial tremors at Arkla. By that time, Rawls had left the *Times* Washington Bureau and was the roving Southern correspondent for the paper. Rawls flew to Little Rock and wrote a 2,000-word article about the Arkoma contracts for the *Times,* which appeared in the paper on July 23, 1983. The article suggested that the deal was enriching Jones and that there were multiple conflicts of interest for Jones and Nelson. It mentioned Nelson's recent announcement that he probably would run for governor in the next election.

The gist of Rawls's article was that Arkla's gas leases in the Aetna and Cecil fields were worth far more than the $15 million Jones was paying Arkla. Quoting the state geologist, Norman F. "Bill" Williams, Rawls suggested that the real value of the gas reserves was around $250 million. Arkla itself was financing $11.5 million of Jones's $15 million purchase price at 10 percent annually, which was 2 percent below the prime rate at the time and 3.5 percent below what Arkansas banks were then charging their best corporate customers. Rawls quoted Nathan M. "Mac" Norton, the chairman of the Public Service Commission, as being skeptical that the arrangement was a good deal for Arkla, the utility that he regulated. The article left the impression that the deal for Jones was the biggest bargain since Spindletop but a bad one for the utility, and, vaguely, maybe someday a payoff for Nelson.

Although he had been quoted extensively in Rawls's article, Nelson said it was wrong or misleading in many particulars and had libeled him. He flew to New York, met with *Times* editors, told them the article was politically motivated—the Stephenses, he said, had sicced the reporter on him to damage his political career—and demanded a retraction. He threatened to sue the newspaper for libel. He obtained letters from a couple of people quoted by Rawls who said they had been misquoted or their remarks taken out of context. He told me later that he had expected the *Times* to make some kind of retraction, but it never did. He decided not to file the libel suit, because the suit would have dragged on for years and damaged Arkla on Wall Street.

A libel suit, of course, would have been pointless. The U.S. Supreme Court had settled such matters forever in 1964, in the landmark *New York Times Co. v. Sullivan* decision. A public figure, which Nelson obviously was, cannot be libeled unless he can prove that the publication printed material that it knew to be false and defamatory, had actual malice for the person, and had set out purposely to harm him by printing an untruth. Rawls always defended every word of his story. By the time his article appeared in the *Times*, he had already resigned over some assignment dispute with his editor that had nothing to do with Arkansas. He became assistant managing editor of the *Atlanta Journal-Constitution* and later an independent film producer and journalism professor.

The *Times* article, and Nelson's reaction to it, revived interest in the Arkla-Arkoma deal and in the old Stephens-Nelson dispute. The controversy triggered a few articles about the case in the Arkansas media. A group of Arkla shareholders filed a lawsuit against Nelson and the Arkla board, but the suit was settled out of court and dismissed. Governor Clinton asked the Public Service Commission to investigate the deal to see whether it was harmful to the utility and its customers, but the agency seemed to make only a cursory examination. The Arkoma controversy soon subsided and lay doggo for another four years.

Nelson, meantime, laid the groundwork for the political career that had always been his ambition. Despite the alliance with Faubus disciples in his 1965 race for president of the Young Democrats, he was at heart a progressive. He worked for the liberal Senator Edward M. Kennedy in his run for the Democratic nomination in 1980 against President Carter, who was backed by his Naval Academy classmate Jack Stephens. In the fall of 1983, when Governor Clinton proposed a sharp increase in the severance tax on natural gas to support his education reforms, a tax vigorously opposed by the Stephenses, Nelson went to the Capitol to testify for the tax. He said it was pitiable that the commonweal had received so little compensation for all the finite resources that had been taken forever from the earth because Arkansas had collected minuscule taxes on their harvesting. Natural gas was a particularly flagrant example. The tax was only three-tenths of a penny on each thousand cubic feet of gas taken by the producers. Texas, by contrast, taxed producers hundreds of times that rate—7 percent of the current market value of the gas. But observers might be forgiven for suspecting that Nelson's animus for the Stephenses lay behind his ardor for the severance tax.

Clinton's tax bill needed three-fourths of both houses to pass—the governor himself fell mute and did little to corral votes for the bill—and it failed. Nelson would try repeatedly over the years to raise the gas severance tax, the lowest in the United States, twice pushing for initiated acts to levy a tax close to what nearby energy-producing states like Texas, Oklahoma, and Kansas levied. His final effort forced Governor Mike Beebe and the legislature in 2008 to enact a small production tax. Fearing that voters would approve the sizable tax that Nelson was proposing in an initiated act, gas producers urged the governor to call a special legislative session to approve a bill they had written that imposed a much lower tax than Nelson's.

Also, when Clinton's economic-expansion program in 1985 included legislation to expand competition for state bond financing, over the objection of the Stephenses, the state's biggest municipal-bond underwriters, Nelson endorsed it. Clinton had appointed Nelson chairman of the Arkansas Industrial Development Commission in 1984.

While Nelson had been counting on Clinton leaving the governor's office in 1986 to run for the U.S. Senate or else to prepare for a race for president in 1988, clearing a path for Nelson to run for governor, Clinton was not ready to give up a job that allowed him to control his own destiny. He ran again, with marginal opposition. Nelson decided that his political fortunes could never hinge on Clinton's foibles, so he planned to switch parties and run in 1990 as a Republican, against Clinton if it were necessary. His timing proved to be terrible. The bubbling dispute over the Arkoma contracts exploded in 1988 as Nelson began preparing for the 1990 campaign, dooming his political ambitions again and again.

Hold on to the thread. A few chapters hence, we will return to the Stephens-Nelson feud and the men's surrogates at the *New York Times* and see how they dramatically changed the course of American history, including the republic's second impeachment of a president.

Let's return to the political chronology. Where were we? Oh yes, 1979.

XIII
Caesar and Cleopatra

First impressions of politicians, which may betray no more than super-
ficial physical skills, usually prove unreliable, but not always. A rangy
Yale law student with big hair had hung around the Arkansas delegation
to the Democratic National Convention in the delegates' little boutique
Miami Beach hotel in July 1972, hoping vainly to pry more than a single
delegate, his pal Stephen A. "Steve" Smith of Huntsville, away from their
allegiance to favorite son Wilbur Mills and get them to vote instead for
Senator George S. McGovern of South Dakota. I carried away no impres-
sion of the law student. He and his Yale girlfriend had spent the summer in
Texas organizing for McGovern, but if she showed up with him at Miami
Beach I have no recollection of it. Soon after joining the law faculty at the
University of Arkansas at Fayetteville, he went to the State Capitol in the
spring of 1974 to file as a Democratic candidate for Congress from the
Third District. He hailed me from across the room in the secretary of state's
office and came over to tell me how much he admired my reporting for the
Gazette, a common gesture that is expected to yield a favorable cast to the
reporter's mentions of the politician.

Bill Clinton's first real outing was a week later at a big rally on the Arkansas Tech college campus sponsored by the Pope County Democratic Women's Club. The Russellville rally kicked off every political season.
Democratic candidates for statewide, regional, and local offices always appeared and were given a few moments to introduce themselves. I went up
mainly to catch the first joint appearance of Governor Dale Bumpers and
Senator J. William Fulbright after Bumpers entered the race for the Senate. Fulbright's powerful friend Senator Robert Byrd of West Virginia, the
Democratic whip, was the keynote speaker and did not disappoint. With a
stoic Bumpers sitting a few feet away, Byrd endorsed Fulbright and warned
that it would be foolhardy for Arkansas voters to swap a man of Fulbright's
seniority and power for a neophyte, whose name he did not utter.

Candidates for lower offices were asked to line up at the edge of the stage
ranked by the office they were seeking, and each was brought forward to
speak for up to two minutes—only one minute for candidates for local
offices. As the program reached the four congressional candidates in the
Third District, the crowd was milling around the arena noisily drinking,
eating, and chatting with each other. All the speakers went largely unheed-

ed. When it was Clinton's turn to speak, within twenty seconds the din had subsided and the throng listened raptly and applauded at the end. It was a remarkable phenomenon, which didn't happen to any other candidate. Looking over my notes, I found nothing that Clinton had said that was notable or even worth mentioning in an article about the event. People who probably had never heard of him obviously were inspired by something, but what?—his bearing, his physical magnetism, the quiet huskiness and sincerity of his voice?

At the Old South Restaurant later that night I had a sandwich with David Pryor, who was running for governor. He had lined up behind Clinton for the speaking and watched the nervous young man (he was twenty-seven) pull a piece of paper from his jacket pocket and start scribbling. Pryor said he had an impulse to tug on Clinton's arm and give him some sage advice: Young man, don't talk from notes but just get up and tell them who you are, why you are running, and that you hope they'll consider voting for you. Keep it simple.

"Boy," Pryor said, "I'm sure glad I didn't." Like me, Pryor wondered what magic the fellow possessed. A quarter century later, people were still trying to figure it out.

A couple of weeks after the Russellville speech, Clinton and the other three Democratic candidates for Congress—who included a veteran state senator from Fort Smith, the largest city in the district—addressed the Arkansas State AFL-CIO convention at Hot Springs, and the excited delegates from around the state spontaneously stuffed buckets with small campaign contributions, even before they voted to endorse him. He missed a majority in the Democratic preferential primary that May but won the runoff in a breeze.

U.S. Representative John Paul Hammerschmidt, who had defeated the veteran James W. Trimble in 1966 to become the first Republican congressman from Arkansas since Reconstruction, was wildly popular in his fourth term, having defeated each of his Democratic foes in 1968, 1970, and 1972 by better than two to one. The fallout from President Nixon's near impeachment for Watergate crimes, his resignation, and his pardon by President Gerald Ford helped Clinton in his first general election against a Republican that fall, but Hammerschmidt eked out a victory with 51.8 percent, the only close race of his career.

Whatever he ran for in 1976, Bill Clinton clearly was going to be the man to beat.

It was attorney general, the only statewide office that had no incumbent in that election. Clinton won the charm contest easily against the secretary of state and Attorney General Jim Guy Tucker's deputy. Tucker ran for and was elected to Congress.

Attorney general is a perfect steppingstone to higher office, because the state's chief counsel does not have to cast risky votes or take an unpopular stand on anything, but instead prosecutes dastardly convicted criminals on appeal and undertakes popular litigation of his own choosing to protect consumers. As attorney general, Clinton fought, on environmental grounds, Arkansas Power and Light Company's application to build a second coal-fired generating plant, this one in Independence County, without also installing scrubbers to reduce greenhouse gases from the plant's smokestacks. (The utility in 2018 finally agreed to close the plant rather than install scrubbers, which were then required by federal rules or instead convert to cleaner and cheaper energy sources.) Clinton lost the coal fight, but it confirmed him as the people's champion.

By this time, he had married his Yale sweetheart, Hillary Rodham of suburban Chicago, who had joined him on the UA law faculty. When they moved to Little Rock after the 1976 general election for him to assume the duties of attorney general, Hillary joined Rose, Meek, House, Barron, Nash & Williamson, Arkansas's oldest law firm and second-oldest business, after the *Arkansas Gazette*, for which the Rose firm had been counsel during much of the newspaper's existence. I barely knew her then, but she would soon send my boss a legal opinion recommending that the paper not publish a lengthy article that I had written about the evidence behind federal indictments of a prominent Little Rock businessman, which the U.S. District Court for the Eastern District of Arkansas had quashed at the request of the Justice Department. The publisher took her side and didn't publish my story. It was not a personal clash, but there would be others.

That legal dispute deserves some elaboration, not because it has any direct relevance for political history but because, at least in my retrospection, it sheds some light on the personal specter that chased Hillary Clinton all her career, through her calamitous presidential campaign in 2016.

◻◻◻

Harry Hastings Sr. owned the largest liquor distributorship in the area, Moon Distributors. Rumors circulated for years, fed by the Organized

Crime and Intelligence Unit of the Little Rock Police Department, that Hastings was cozy with the "Dixie Mafia," a crime syndicate in New Orleans reputed to be run by Carlos Marcello out of the family's restaurant, Mosca's. (A nearly windowless shack across the Mississippi River from New Orleans, Mosca's earned a national reputation owing to the writings of A. J. Liebling and Calvin Trillin in *The New Yorker*. By my personal affirmation forty years ago, it does prepare one of the South's great indulgences, Oysters Mosca.)

The Little Rock Police Department's organized-crime team, headed by Forrest Parkman, itself had developed a reputation as a smalltime crime syndicate. See, for example, Roger Glasgow's 2016 memoir, *Down and Dirty Down South*, the lawyer's account of how the Organized Crime squad helped set him up for a bogus smuggling rap at the Mexican border in 1972. The *Union Station Times* carried an article in 1975 alleging that Parkman's men also had tried to stash marijuana in the car of Jim Guy Tucker, who had been the prosecuting attorney and was sometimes at odds with the police leadership.

The Hastings-Parkman rivalry got personal. Parkman sued Hastings and another businessman for defamation and for holding him up to public ridicule, claiming that the businessmen had maliciously told one of Parkman's deputies, Kenneth Pearson, that Parkman had raped two women. The Pulaski County circuit judge who heard the case dismissed Parkman's suit, and in the spring of 1975 the Arkansas Supreme Court upheld the dismissal, wondering how Hastings and his friend could have held the cop up to ridicule if their accusation was recorded by Pearson but was never rendered to print and never heard by another soul until Parkman filed his suit and the public prints wrote about it.

Six months later, Parkman got even with Hastings for winning the lawsuit. He sprang a petty thief named Rayburn Hamilton out of the city jail and commissioned him to set up Hastings for a federal rap. They wired a microphone to Hamilton's chest and sent him on several visits to Hastings, whom the crook knew from some past association. In a series of visits and telephone calls, all secretly recorded, Hamilton talked to Hastings about stealing diamonds and other paraphernalia, and he piqued the liquor dealer's interest in finding some free truck tires and an industrial air compressor, expensive paraphernalia that Hastings's distributorship always needed.

Lieutenant Parkman wanted Hastings to be charged in federal court, where he would be prosecuted by U.S. Attorney W. H. "Sonny" Dillahunty, so Hastings's and Hamilton's crime needed to be an interstate job. Hamilton and two cronies arranged with Parkman's help to "steal" an air compressor from an obliging dealer and sell it to Hastings's two sons for $1,000. Hamilton maintained that he had told the Hastings brothers that the compressor was stolen, although that conversation was not taped and there was no evidence to support his claim. Lieutenant Parkman, working with the Mississippi Highway Patrol, the Mississippi attorney general, and Armstrong Tire & Rubber Company, arranged for the driver of an eighteen-wheeler loaded with Armstrong truck tires to leave the key in the ignition when he stopped for coffee at a truck stop in Senatobia, Mississippi. Hamilton and his confederates jumped in and drove the big truck to downtown Little Rock. They parked it on East Third Street beside Dailey's Office Furniture store, four blocks east of the *Gazette* building.

According to the tapes, which I later laboriously transcribed over four days, Hamilton told Hastings excitedly that he had stolen a full load of truck tires for him. Where the hell are they? Hastings asked.

When Hamilton told him that the stolen cargo was parked on one of the city's busiest streets, Hastings cursed and told the thug to get in the truck and meet him at his duck-hunting lodge near Stuttgart. At that point, Parkman got the FBI involved for the first time so that it would obtain a federal search warrant to enter Hastings's hunting premises. Dillahunty secured grand-jury indictments of Hastings and the two accomplices in the "theft" of the truck tires and of his two sons for taking an air compressor that they knew to have been stolen.

Before the case was to go to trial before U.S. District Judge Terry Shell in the summer of 1977, the U.S. Department of Justice asked the court to dismiss the charges, because the Little Rock police's rogue manner in setting up the crimes made prosecution of the men fundamentally unfair. It said Parkman and his men had overstepped the bounds of constitutionally permissible police behavior in setting up the arrests and that prosecuting the five men would be repugnant to the sense of fairness that was a fundamental doctrine of the Fifth Amendment. Judge Shell emphatically agreed and dismissed the charges.

Bill Williams, a member of the vice squad and a former *Gazette* photographer, had wired Hamilton and rigged up the recording system. The tape recordings were offered to the *Gazette,* and Bob Douglas, the managing editor, took them. He thought both the content of the tapes and the manner of the arrests constituted news and asked me to transcribe the scratchy and sometimes nearly indecipherable tapes. I did and wrote a lengthy article, consisting almost entirely of quotes from the tapes. It could easily be deduced from the tapes that Harry Hastings Sr. did not recoil at the concept of a little larceny, whether of diamonds or tires, but also that Forrest Parkman and his men would go to any lengths to trap their prey. The dialogue between the con and the businessman provided amusing reading, owing to Hastings's salty language and his sometimes derogatory references to his wife and other family members.

Hugh B. Patterson Jr., the *Gazette*'s publisher, sent the article to the Rose law firm, and I went over to its conference room on West Markham Street while Webster "Webb" Hubbell and Vincent Foster, two lawyers whose names will be recognized from the Whitewater era twenty years later, perused it and asked if I could back up certain sentences.

"It's in the tapes," I said each time. Foster and Hubbell said they saw no risk of libel, because the recordings substantiated everything I had written.

The next day, a lengthy opinion arrived. It was from the firm's newest partner, Hillary Rodham, who had not been present at our meeting. She advised the paper not to publish the story. While there seemed to be no risk of libel, she said the story violated the privacy rights of Mrs. Hastings and perhaps other members of the family on matters that had nothing to do with the crimes. Her opinion was studded with citations from case law on the privacy rights of individuals and the right to protection from self-incrimination.

Although I had had private misgivings about the efficacy of a story that added little to the relevant public knowledge of a famous case except titillating dialogue and the implication that Hastings had a predisposition for venality, to no avail I argued for only editing out the most offending passages and publishing the story. The *Arkansas Times*, then a magazine, obtained the tapes months later and devoted much of a monthly issue to them.

Hillary's brief suggested something more broadly about the article than the violation of the privacy of Mrs. Hastings and the sons by printing the old man's unflattering references to them. Publication of Harry Hastings's maunderings to the con, mostly disconnected from any expectation that he was engaged in a crime or that the jabberings would see publication, raised questions for Hillary Rodham about the sanctity of personal information that had no relevance to an alleged crime or to the public's right to knowledge about a public activity. To her, the Fifth Amendment's promises of due process and protection from self-incrimination were a constitutional guarantee of privacy for the individual, even for a man with disreputable impulses like Hastings. While she acknowledged that the newspaper probably risked no monetary damages from publishing the story, she said the paper might consider its duty to respect the privacy rights of even a man for whom the paper had no brief.

It was many years later, and repeatedly, that I was reminded of her legal essay on my Hastings story, which I had wanted to be published mainly because I had spent more than a week transcribing the trashy tapes and composing the article. The opinion exposed an unfortunate aspect of her character—not an undesirable one, but one that would serve her badly in a life devoted to politics. It was a literal obsession with personal privacy, a refusal to yield the private matters of her family, her business dealings, or how she went about her work, because they were nobody's business. Just as they were not entitled to paw through the disreputable musings of an old man, people were not entitled to pry into what she considered the personal space of her life.

In politics, a privacy obsession is not sustainable. If you don't want reporters, congressmen, Republican investigators like Brett Kavanaugh and Rod Rosenstein, or just nosy voters rummaging through the billings of your law clients, your personal business transactions, or your private conversations with family, friends, or coworkers, which mutate into emails that become subject to freedom-of-information laws, you are going to experience a sea of troubles. It would lead circuitously to her husband's impeachment and to the end of her dream to be president of the United States. In ensuing chapters, we'll have reasons to delve into that passion again and again.

Bill Clinton would be attorney general of Arkansas for two years, governor for almost twelve years, and president of the United States for eight years—in all, eight electoral victories, with a single intervening defeat in 1980 followed quickly by redemption and resurrection. It was a remarkable political run, for controversy and political enemies always chased him and yet he ended each stretch implausibly popular, even after becoming the second president to be impeached. His policy achievements in all the political offices over twenty-two years were not historic but creditable, a judgment I think history will ratify.

History should also reflect that all of it—the politics and the policy—was a dual achievement of husband and wife, and sometimes a dual failure. When he was running for president in 1992, Clinton said that, if he were elected, Americans would be getting two for the price of one. It did not enhance either of them, particularly Hillary, in the minds of many voters. They were electing a president, not a team, and they thought she would be taking on airs by claiming such a role. First ladies from Eleanor Roosevelt to Nancy Reagan had often created highly public roles for themselves, but outside the instruments of government.

In truth, from the race for attorney general forward the Clintons were always a team, although not always a perfectly harmonious one. Bill Clinton was always an ambivalent decision-maker, never quite sure which instinct and which advice to follow. He often seemed to go with the last person who talked to him about an issue. He listened to people—often to too many people—but none was rarely as persuasive as his wife. Big changes in political strategy and abrupt policy shifts usually could be traced to an overnight discussion with the governor's (or president's) wife.

The origin of Hillary's remarkable leverage with her husband would be a subject of disagreement among Clinton's advisers—critical psychoanalysts concluded that it was guilt over his philandering—but I always thought he had a genuine admiration for her intellect, her scholarly exceptionalism, and perhaps for her early work in the Watergate investigation of President Nixon. He translated her intellect, sometimes woefully, into smart political judgment, which isn't the same thing. He would collar me sometimes to complain about unflattering editorials or columns. His ultimate riposte was that his wife had expressed the correct judgment about my editorials or columns: "Hillary says my own newspaper is the only one in the country that doesn't give me credit for welfare reform."

She saved his political career and his presidency, in very public ways and in quieter, unreported ways. She also imperiled his political career, most notably in refusing to turn over her law firm's private billing records related to her trifling legal work in the 1980s for Jim McDougal and his little thrift institution in Little Rock. Her rigidity led to the Whitewater prosecutor's relentless pursuit of the couple and to the president's impeachment for causes that had nothing to do with any transaction that she or her husband had ever made.

So the decades-long Clinton saga—the rise and fall of "Clintonism," as a few writers called it—may be said to chronicle the meshing and clashing of their profoundly different personalities and emotional needs, and how those very personal dramas played out in the great national crucible of politics and governance. Books would be written about Bill's and Hillary's upbringings in stressful households of rural Arkansas and suburban Chicago, how those experiences formed the character and personalities of the couple, and how those in turn shaped the great national dramas and crises of their reign, from Gennifer Flowers to Monica Lewinsky and impeachment. This was the whole object of William H. Chafe's psychological narrative *Bill and Hillary: The Politics of the Personal* and a thesis also of *In Search of Bill Clinton: A Psychological Biography* by John D. Gartner. The authors of *A Woman in Charge* by Carl Bernstein (of Woodward and Bernstein fame) and of the massive *Bill Clinton, an American Journey* by Nigel Hamilton tried their hands at Freudian analysis, and so did others on smaller tablets. The Clintons' own autobiographical efforts carry more than a little introspection about how they came to be who they were—Bill's *My Life* obviously far more than Hillary's *Living History*, which strove to give the Rodham household a wholesome all-American caste.

Far be it from me to engage in any such personality analysis of the Clintons. Neither I nor any reporter in Arkansas spent any time investigating the personal lives, especially the childhoods, of the Clintons or any other politician. We learned more during the first presidential campaign and its aftermath than we already knew about his private life and ancestry. Clinton himself was still learning. Six months into his presidency, in 1993, he discovered, along with the rest of the country, that his father, William Jefferson Blythe Jr., who drowned after a car wreck in Missouri three months before he was born, was a bigamist who had conceived two other children out of wedlock and left a trail of wives and ex-wives across the Southwest. An investigation by the *Washington Post,* starting with birth registries, turned up that bit of ancestry. Clinton, as best we could discern, was more intrigued than mortified by the discovery. For Hillary, it is safe to say, the only thing more abashing would have been such a discovery in her own family and the publication of it.

Without engaging in the scrupulous psychoanalysis that the professors Chafe, Gartner, and others undertook, we do have to recognize the part that the child's turbulent home played in both his marriage and how he reacted later to the vicissitudes of politics and governance. We do not have to speculate much about that home life. Clinton wrote and talked about it, although he didn't draw many conclusions. Without a father, Bill was left off and on for a few years to be reared by his maternal grandparents, a loving and paternal grandfather who would pass on to the boy his tolerant and even brotherly affection for the black underclass of the community, and a grandmother who was not so charitable to even her kin, including Bill's mom. His mother, Virginia Dell Cassidy, a strong-willed woman who went off to educate herself as a nurse anesthetist soon after he was born, was a powerful force influencing both the strong and weak character traits of the boy. Virginia, by all accounts, liked to flirt and have a good time, and her appearance—heavily made-up, coquettishly attired—tended to amplify that behavior. She was not a beauty, but she stood out in every crowd, and Bill adored her. Growing up, he was witness to her various liaisons. And it was she who encouraged her handsome and graceful son to always pursue the prettiest girls. (At the beginning, she didn't care much for Hillary, who wasn't the sex queen that Virginia thought her son deserved.)

Virginia had married Roger Clinton Sr., a blustering, twice-divorced Buick salesman in Hope, when Bill was four years old. Roger's heavy drinking and suspicious nature led to frequent rages and occasional violence against his wife and sometimes his small son, Roger Jr. Bill, who had adopted the Clinton name, stood up to his stepfather at the age of fifteen and threatened physical retribution after one violent episode. It made him a hero to the family, including, strangely, his stepfather. More than anyone, it was the stepson who kept some uneasy peace in the family and, at the end of the stepfather's life, visited him in North Carolina repeatedly to pacify the old man's sorrow and regrets when the wife and son wouldn't.

Hillary's father, Hugh Rodham, was not haunted by Roger Clinton's demons, but neither was he a model husband, although in her memoir she talked about how much she adored him and he her. Other family members, neighbors, and friends said he was moody and mentally abusive to his wife, who had herself experienced a sorrowful childhood—abandoned by her parents and then disrespected and virtually enslaved by the grandparents who took her in. Dorothy Rodham was determined that her daughter get everything she had been denied: admiration, encouragement, a great education, and most of all a stable family. No abuse, no disrespect, no embarrassment was ever worth severing the family. It was a lesson that Hillary obviously absorbed.

Like Clinton, Hillary was the family champion—to her mother, to her brothers, and also to her father, who was proud never to have voted for a Democrat or a liberal but who expected his daughter, his Goldwater Girl, to break all the barriers. Like her mother, Hugh wanted Hillary to go to the best college, get the highest degree, reach for the loftiest goals.

Those were the closeted underpinnings of the marriage and partnership that Bill and Hillary Clinton brought in January 1979 to the Arkansas Governor's Mansion and to the drama of leading a rustic and insular state out of the uncivilized wilderness.

XIV
Two for the Price of One

For a Rhodes Scholar and Yale law graduate with universally admired political skills, a tumultuous mandate from the voters, and the uncanny Hillary Rodham for a silent partner, running the state of Arkansas was going to be a skate around the park for Bill Clinton. No one ever addressed his first gathering of the General Assembly with more ease or greater confidence. He and Hillary had been at Yale when Dale Bumpers, with no governing or political experience, no statewide network of supporters, and only one friend and a few acquaintances in the legislature, walked into the State Capitol for the first time in 1971 wondering what in the world he was doing there—but Clinton knew what Bumpers had accomplished in four years without seeming to have lost a skirmish or ruffled a feather. Clinton had run with the support of the key financial and business interests, labor, farm leaders, and every African American organization and community leader in the state. He brought with him to the governor's office a couple of young brains from the legislature who had helped Bumpers and Pryor fashion and pass progressive programs, and added one of Hillary's nimble feminist friends from Wellesley, Nancy "Peach" Pietrafesa, and her talented husband John Danner to his executive brain trust. He recruited young stars from out of state to run health, human services, education, and energy agencies. What could go wrong?

Just about everything. Two years later, Clinton would be swimming in self-pity, blaming one group or another, one strategic error or another by his team, and perhaps even himself, for the destruction of his career. The most gifted politician in the state's history would be only the third governor in 145 years to be defeated after one term. Nearly everything, including his successes, went wrong.

His inaugural address was an eloquent manifesto of what he stood for and what he expected to do as governor. He was going to work for greater equality and against the abuse of power; seek to ease the burdens of the poor, the aged, and the disabled; raise economic opportunities for people through better education and business development; and use the levers of government to recover and protect clean waters, land, and air, which were

273

being harmed by energy exploration and unhealthy development practices (like forest clear-cutting and tree farming, which went unmentioned at the moment).

As he would at every legislative session in his nearly twelve years, he had a raft of bills that he asked legislators to sponsor, many of them consequential but others more window dressing than substance. The legislature passed nearly all of them, but sometimes after altering them in ways that made them unpopular. In one way or another, he or his aides and agency heads managed in little more than a year to antagonize the forestry and poultry industries, bankers, physicians, the state's largest utility, the big trucking companies, and, with the help of the president of the United States, a sizable part of the voting population of west Arkansas. Sorting through the detritus of his electoral defeat in two-thirds of the counties in 1980, he gleaned a profound political lesson: Don't squander all your political capital at once. But there were many lessons to be learned.

His admiring lawmakers altered his bill to raise highway-building funds by raising fees for registering cars and trucks—"car tags" as they came to be called. That, more than anything, cost him the election the next

Bill Clinton

year, because it unsettled hundreds of thousands of car and pickup owners.

He could, and would, blame the car-tag misadventure on the legislature, although in the end he reluctantly went along with a sellout to the trucking and shipping industries. Nothing that any governor ever tried to do was more popular than improving highways, streets, and roads. Clinton wanted a big highway program, and he proposed increasing motor fuel taxes by a penny a gallon and raising revenues from vehicle license fees by 50 percent, mostly from big trucks. The fuel tax, as always, sailed through both houses with three-fourths majorities, but not the registration fees.

Henry C. Gray, the state highway director, persuaded Clinton that the state's major highways were being torn up by the big interstate shippers and eighteen-wheeler loads, and that car owners were subsidizing the big shippers and haulers through fuel taxes and registration fees. Studies by the federal Bureau of Public Roads showed that one 73,000-pound load did more road damage than hundreds of thousands of cars. Gray actually wanted to make the big interstate trucks pay a tax for each ton and for each mile traveled on Arkansas highways—the "ton-mile" tax, they called it. Like the big trucks, cars and pickups had been paying a license fee every year based on the weight of the vehicles, which meant that people who owned old cars paid more for their car tags than did owners of sleek and lighter new models. The governor was tormented by the hostility between the forces of the trucking industry and their shipping allies, on the one hand, and the Highway Department's director on the other. Gray wanted the truckers to pay their share of taxes for road maintenance, and the industry wanted the gross weight limit on the highways raised from 73,280 pounds to 80,000 pounds, which Gray—called by his critics King Henry—opposed. Clinton vacillated, first pleasing the industry, then the Highway Department, then the industry again.

Clinton's vehicle-registration bill, drawn up by Gray, changed the fee system for pleasure vehicles and pickups so that they were based not on their weight but on the model year and the invoice price on the model. Cars were so light that they had little to do with road damage. Car tag fees would be based on the vehicle's value, not its weight.

The Senate narrowly passed the bill—it needed the votes of three-fourths of the members of both houses—but the poultry industry, Riceland Foods, other shippers, and the big transportation companies stymied the bill in the House of Representatives. The industry prepared amendments to the bill that restored the weight system for cars and pickups, raised the weight fees for trucks only slightly, and raised it sharply for cars and pickups. The road program would get about the same amount of revenues Clinton sought, but it would come primarily from car owners, not the big transportation companies and their shippers. Lobbyists, primarily for the poultry industry, had enough legislators from the mountain region locked down to keep anything opposed by the industry from passing. Clinton relented, the House passed the industry bill, and he signed it.

Every month, one-twelfth of the people went to the courthouse to renew their car tags, stood in line for the usual confusion about bringing all the requisite documents reflecting assessment and payment of property taxes, safety inspections, and liability insurance—only to discover that the cost of tags for their old cars had nearly doubled. Wherever Clinton went in the election year of 1980, people confronted him about their car tags. Don Tyson, the head of the poultry giant Tyson Foods, wrote a letter to the *Gazette* urging people to vote against Clinton because he threatened to wreck the shipping and transportation industries by trying to make them pay high taxes and not allowing them to haul 80,000 pounds. People followed his advice, but for the opposite reason.

By early fall 1980, Clinton knew the extent of the damage and talked with aides (and, one evening, his campaign manager Harry Herget and me) about calling a special session a couple of weeks before the election and repealing the car-tag law, but everyone concluded that it wouldn't undo the damage and would only make him look weak as well. A few days after the election he telephoned me, asking what I thought about the idea of calling a special session before leaving office in January and repealing the law, thus denying Frank White, the new governor, credit for the good deed. I tried, in the few instances in which he asked for it, to avoid giving him advice, but I wondered if it would do anything more than remind people again of what he had done. Eventually, he chose just to apologize to people, publicly, profusely, and repeatedly.

The Grand Gulf Affair was a subtler problem, because it cost him financial and organizational support, but it would roil politics for Frank White's single term and Clinton's subsequent ten-year sojourn. Arkansas electricity customers eventually would pay $4.5 billion—roughly $6,500 each—to a utility holding company to generate power that they didn't need at a nuclear plant in Mississippi. Clinton had actually sought to protect them from the costs, but he managed never to reap any credit for it and, instead, antagonized a powerful industry that operated in nearly every county in the state. When he was attorney general, Clinton had questioned whether Arkansas customers would have to pay for two proposed nuclear power plants in Mississippi, and was assured that Arkansas already had all the power generation that it would need for many years.

Clinton's energy department—notably four young conservationists—discovered that Arkansas Power and Light Company actually had joined three sister subsidiaries in Mississippi and Louisiana in what was called a "system agreement" to pay for two big nuclear-powered generating plants at a port on the Mississippi River south of Vicksburg called Grand Gulf. Arkansas would bear thirty-six percent of the costs of the power stations and probably another one called Waterford that was planned near New Orleans. The cost of the first station had already soared from $1.5 billion to $3.5 billion and it was still rising. Construction had not begun on the second station; it would ultimately be abandoned. A separate subsidiary of the parent Middle South Utilities would build and own the Grand Gulf stations. Arkansas Power and Light had built its own nuclear stations at Russellville and big new coal-powered stations in Jefferson and Independence counties that were producing more power than Arkansas was projected to need for many years, but under the system agreement it was on the hook to bear more than a third of the costs of Grand Gulf.

Clinton's reformers—Walter W. "Wally" Nixon III, who had been a lawyer on Clinton's attorney-general staff, along with Scott C. Trotter, Basil Copeland Jr., and James Strangways—put together a detailed article exposing the state's giant obligation. Clinton and Hillary worked on the article, too. It carried an editorial slant that the agreement cast an unfair burden on the people of Arkansas and would also impair its economic development through excessive rates. I was on the editorial staff of the *Gazette* and arranged to publish the 7,700-word article on the front page and an inside page of the *Gazette*'s Sunday opinion section on August 31, 1980. It would carry the byline of Bill Clinton, probably the first byline of a governor ever to appear in an Arkansas newspaper. The article was already in type and the pages already designed when Clinton decided to call Jerry Maulden, the young president of Arkansas Power and Light, and alert him that an article was appearing Sunday in the *Gazette* under Clinton's byline about the agreement to share the cost of the Grand Gulf stations. Maulden, who was something of a champion of the little man owing to his own upbringing (and also a national board member of the NAACP), begged him not to do it. Maulden said he was trying to alter the system agreement and fashion a better deal for Arkansas. Clinton's article would imperil any chance he could get it done. Clinton agreed.

The next morning, he wanted to pull the article. I insisted that it was too late, that the article was in type and the pages already designed. Nixon and Trotter, jeopardizing their jobs, said to run the story and credit it to them and to Copeland and Strangways rather than to the governor. That is the way the article appeared, under the headline "Grand Gulf: A Corporate Haze That Spells Trouble for Arkansas." The four authors were identified as officials in Clinton's Department of Energy.

The article seemed to have little public impact that fall, perhaps because the subject was so arcane, although the message did get out that people were going to see a hike in their monthly electricity bills at some point, several years away. But Clinton would get no credit for trying to hold down people's energy bills—at least in that election. Had his byline appeared on the article, it would have caused a sensation and might have burnished his image as a protector of the little people. As it happened, Hillary Clinton would blame Nixon and Trotter for Clinton's defeat by insisting on publishing the story and turning the powerful electric industry against him. Clinton would come back in 1982 as a roaring paladin of the biscuit cookers.

The article hurt him subtly in the 1980 election. Two months before the election, Frank White, the Republican candidate, inherited the financial and organizational backing of the big utility, its executives, and probably its employees and far-flung contractors. White's first action as governor, minutes after delivering his inaugural address in January 1981, was to scribble an executive order to the Department of Energy firing Wally Nixon, Scott Trotter, Basil Copeland, and Jim Strangways. Ironically, White would come around to their way of thinking. Late in his ill-starred term, White mused publicly about the value of a little socialism: a state takeover of the state's largest power industry.

The dispute would drag on for a decade. Lawsuits and regulatory cases went up and down through federal and state courts. The state Public Service Commission, led by Clinton appointees, did not want to pass the Grand Gulf costs on to Arkansas Power and Light's (today Entergy's) residential and industrial customers, which put it at odds with the holding company and its subsidiaries, the regulatory agencies in Mississippi and Louisiana and, ultimately, the Federal Energy Regulatory Commission and the United States Supreme Court. The dispute went to the Supreme Court three times. A pivotal issue was whether a federal agency could require a state to impose rate increases on utility customers, since conservatives always argued that the Constitution's Commerce Clause left such matters to the states.

Justice Antonin Scalia—who would in other matters, such as health care, rule that the federal government was barred from imposing such rules on commerce—held for the Supreme Court that Arkansas regulatory agencies and courts, and those in other states, could not interfere with power-pooling arrangements approved by a utility holding company and the federal power agency. A dissenting opinion wryly observed that it was a strange opinion for a bunch of conservatives, because Congress in the Federal

Power Act of 1935 had specifically directed that retail energy rates were the sole jurisdiction of the states. In a federal appellate court ruling at one point, a District of Columbia appellate judge named Robert Bork held (in, mercifully, a dissenting opinion) that Arkansas should bear nearly all the cost of Grand Gulf, not just thirty-six percent. It was noted at the time that Mississippi and Louisiana were governed by Republicans and Arkansas by the lone Democrat. Although Bork had been one of his law professors at Yale, Clinton would cite that opinion in opposing Bork's nomination to the Supreme Court. The U.S. Senate subsequently denied Bork a seat on the court.

In 1985, Clinton's Public Service Commission yielded and approved a rate increase on Arkansas residential and industrial customers that would pay for 32 percent of Grand Gulf's costs, adding the unusual legal language, "We hate to approve this settlement." Fortunately, Mississippi canceled plans for the second unit when demand for electricity fell far below the old projections from the 1970s. The Arkansas subsidiary finally was able to exit the system agreement and end the subsidies in 2013, after ratepayers in the state had already coughed up $4.5 billion to pay for the plants in Mississippi and Louisiana.

☐☐☐

Style became an unexpected handicap for the stylish new governor. He hired three whiz kids to run his office: his best friend, Stephen A. Smith of Huntsville, who had been elected to the Arkansas House of Representatives in 1970 just as he turned twenty-one; Rudy Moore Jr., a Fayetteville lawyer who was elected to the House with Smith; and Danner, a Californian and Harvard business graduate who had married Hillary's best friend, "Peach" Pietrafesa. Pietrafesa joined the staff, too, as the governor's education liaison. The problem mainly was that Smith, Moore, and Danner all sported well-trimmed but luxuriant beards before the mountain-man look became modish outside the Ozarks. People tended to associate beards with hippies and radicals. Legislators and others who went to see the governor would complain that they had to deal with the hippie guys. The conservative *Arkansas Democrat*, whose editorial writers, managing editor, columnists, and editorial cartoonist savaged the Clinton administration almost every day, took particular delight in razzing "the bearded troika," whose heavily camouflaged features appeared regularly in caricatures and cartoons. One

Saturday morning in the summer of 1980, Clinton summoned all three to the Governor's Mansion. He and Hillary asked if they would mind shaving their beards. Monday morning and for the rest of the year, all three showed up with shining chins.

By the end of the year, John Danner and Steve Smith were gone, under circumstances that reflected badly upon some weakness of character in the governor.

Danner and Pietrafesa did not mesh well with the governor's staff, maybe because they had a little Yankee brashness and pushiness. Everyone was expected to do things their way. Moore and Smith finally went to the mansion on a Saturday morning to report to the first couple that the staff was near insurrection. A few were saying John and Peach had to go or change, or else the staff members would quit. It was especially tough for Hillary, because the couple had picked up and come to the benighted state at her beckoning. But neither she nor Bill could tell them that they were no longer needed or even talk to them before they packed up and left for California. Moore was given the unpleasant task of telling the couple that they were fired. Their desks were clean Monday morning when the staff arrived.

In his memoir twenty-four years later, Clinton recorded his sorrow at the way he and Hillary had handled it, not even saying "goodbye, we're sorry, and thank you for severing your careers and coming here to try to help us." He also expressed his regret many years later to Rudy Moore, the old friend whom he had tasked that day to do the dirty work for him and who was embittered by the experience.

Steve Smith left under only slightly more ennobling circumstances. He was an environmentalist with connections to the Ozark Society and the large conservation movement. They were concerned particularly about the clear-cutting policies of the timber and paper-products industries. Vast swaths of hardwood forests through the Ouachita Mountains and the Southern Plain of south Arkansas were cleared of hardwoods, and pine seedlings were planted in their stead. The pine monoculture altered the natural environment of the state and stripped the natural habitat of food for the creatures of the woods. Clinton put Smith in charge of a timber task force that would study the issue. After a number of hearings, the task force submitted its work and its recommendations to Clinton, who liked them and passed the preliminary report on to leaders of the timber and paper-products industries. They told the governor how much they despised it. Smith had already enraged the industry by referring to them nonchalantly as "corporate criminals." Clinton seemed to be shocked by the response and decided to just shelve the whole project. Smith quit and went home.

"I decided I had better things to do with my life," he said years later. It would be the evening before Clinton's inauguration as president, twelve years later, before the two old friends talked again.

When he was elected attorney general, Clinton brought along one of his law students at the university, Peggy O'Neal, by then a fresh member of the bar. He designated her as the state purchasing agent after getting the legislature to repeal a statute that said the purchasing director had to be at least thirty years old. O'Neal was painstaking and overzealous, irritating state agency heads and legislators with nitpicking rules on bidding and purchasing. O'Neal also became a regular quarry of the *Democrat*'s editor and daily columnist, John Robert Starr, who said she was emblematic of the incompetent and inexperienced youngsters Clinton had brought into government. Clinton became consumed by Starr's diatribes. He read every word and would ask people, "Why does he write such trash?" With the rest of us who opined rather than reported, he would call up and rage for a few minutes, pointing out how you had misjudged things, and then spend thirty minutes glossing things over so that you would not hang up mad at him. Clinton couldn't figure out why Starr hated him. After the election, he would figure it out and fix it.

Before Clinton became governor, hardly anyone in the state had noticed that his wife did not use his name. The references in the newspapers to "Hillary Rodham" seemed to readers to be some baffling media formality. But, before long, there was talk everywhere that the governor's wife wouldn't take his name. People had just never heard of such a thing. Was it just airs, or some Yankee feminine phenomenon? Frank White was razzing Clinton about his wife not taking his name. What kind of man wouldn't make his wife take his name? Hillary felt obliged to explain that she kept her name for professional reasons having something to do with her law practice. No one was buying it. Clinton sensed that it had become a political problem, but he wasn't convinced it was a decisive one. They fixed the problem when he ran again.

Another collateral problem was the couple's business partner in a tiny mountain real estate development, James D. McDougal. McDougal, a former aide to Senator J. William Fulbright and a political science professor at Ouachita Baptist College, was Clinton's liaison with the Highway Department and the state agencies that regulated financial institutions.

McDougal believed that one reason the state lagged in economic development was that banks tended to be overly conservative, preferring not to lend money for local development but to keep their money safely invested in government securities. He proposed that the state induce banks to be more progressive in their lending practices by requiring them to maintain a certain loan-to-investment ratio to be eligible to hold idle state treasury funds. Community bankers across the state were alarmed by the proposal. Though the governor never tried to implement McDougal's plan, many bankers began to see Frank White's appeal. McDougal left the governor's office with Steve Smith before the election and together they acquired a tiny bank in the mountain village of Kingston.

A few years later, McDougal would buy a small savings and loan company and put his philosophy into practice, handing out loans to anybody and eventually dying penniless in a federal prison for his nonchalant banking practices and for his inability to tell a special prosecutor some crime that could be pinned on Bill Clinton or his wife.

Two big initiatives that Clinton announced in his inaugural address were to raise the pay of school teachers, who had fallen back to the lowest paid in the land in the last recession, and to do something about the paucity of health care in rural Arkansas, particularly in the desperately poor Mississippi Delta. Both initiatives ran into trouble. He was going to raise teacher pay $1,200 each year of the biennium, and he squeezed other budgets to set aside the funds for the pay increases. But a national recession in 1979 forced a reduction in general-revenue allocations and the $1,200 increases didn't materialize. Clinton fretted that lots of teachers, who had endorsed his election in 1978, might have abandoned him, but that probably was not the case. He achieved a few other school reforms—the first programs for gifted and talented children, the creation of the Governor's School at Hendrix College for gifted students, and better equity in the distribution of state school funds.

Doctors were another matter. Clinton shared Dale Bumpers's concern about the lack of doctors and medical facilities in rural areas. He appointed Dr. Robert Young, who ran a rural health clinic in West Virginia, as the director of the state Health Department. Young developed a plan to establish a network of rural clinics that would be staffed mainly by nurses and nurse practitioners. Physicians would attend each clinic at least once every two weeks. The Arkansas Medical Society and the Board of Health, made up of physicians, opposed the plan. The Carter administration in Washington approved an experimental grant to fund the clinics. Four were established and work was begun on three others. Clinton started a loan fund to help doctors set up offices in small towns, passed an appropriation to set up a radiation therapy institute at the state medical center, and passed another to provide income supplements to family doctors in rural communities. But the medical profession still resented the young West Virginian's notion of providing care by people without a medical degree. The Arkansas Medical Society called for Dr. Young's resignation. When Clinton left office, state support for the rural clinics was slashed. Clinton figured many doctors voted for Frank White.

The last culprit in Clinton's quick political descent was President Jimmy Carter, whose high popularity in Arkansas was also in descent, owing to his inability to free fifty-two American hostages held in Tehran by student revolutionaries who remembered America's role in overthrowing the country's democratic government in 1953 and installing the brutal Shah.

But Carter had another problem, which he shared with his 1976 Arkansas campaign chairman, Bill Clinton. Fidel Castro, the Cuban dictator, loosed a flotilla of thousands of rebellious Cubans to the Florida shores in the six months before the 1980 election. Throngs of despairing Cubans who were victims of an economic collapse tried to gain asylum in the Peruvian embassy, and Castro agreed to send them all, along with criminals in Havana jails, to the United States. They were ferried to the port of Mariel, where they were loaded onto an armada of boats headed to the Florida shores. Carter decided to load them onto planes and distribute them among vacant military installations around the country, including the Army training post at Fort Chaffee.

Packed into the unairconditioned barracks, the Cubans soon became rebellious, broke out of the compound, and roamed down the road to the nearby town of Barling, terrifying the residents. Some fifty people were injured slightly in the melee. Clinton visited the post and vented his rage at the commander for letting the Cubans break out of the compound and terrify the community. He got President Carter to promise publicly that he would send no more Cubans to Fort Chaffee. But when more Cubans arrived in the late summer Carter had to break his promise and flood Fort Chaffee again. Clinton battled with the military commanders over how tough they should be in controlling the Cubans. They cited the Posse Comitatus Act, enacted during Reconstruction, which prohibited federal military forces from enforcing domestic laws. After midnight, Clinton took a commander around Barling and showed him women sitting in the doorways of their homes with shotguns in their laps. The commander said, all right, we'll keep them locked up and stifle any disobedience.

It is doubtful that the Cuban affair had much to do with Clinton's defeat, but he thought it did. White ran TV commercials with pictures of marauding Cubans outside the Chaffee gates and speculated that all the Cubans would be settling in Arkansas and taking people's jobs. He said the problem arose from Clinton's cozy relationship with the unpopular Carter and the state needed to get rid of both of them.

The election returns did not support the notion that Carter dragged Clinton down. Ronald Reagan beat Carter in Arkansas by only five thousand votes, and Carter probably would have won without the thirty-six thousand votes cast for moderate-to-liberal splinter-party candidates. White beat Clinton by thirty-two thousand.

XV
To Elba and Back

B ill Clinton's exile was longer by a year than Napoleon's, but while Napoleon went back to his old imperial ways Clinton spent his exile in the more fruitful pursuit of the reasons for his defeat and the ways that he could regain and hold power. If he had another chance, Clinton would pick his fights more carefully and infrequently, look for his own compromises before he had to accept dangerous ones, avoid (insofar as he could) antagonizing really powerful groups like the poultry and wood-products industries, and leave no slight unpunished, even for a day. And have his wife use his surname.

Frank White proved to be the perfect foil, too. White was a big, ebullient man who loved meeting and gabbing with people even more than Clinton did. He was frank, literally, to excess. He said the first thing that came into his head, often made rash decisions, and uttered clumsy remarks that he soon regretted—and admitted it. His impulsive remarks made him look bumbling, even when most people liked the positions he took, such as signing a bill directing science teachers to instruct kids in Genesis's account of the creation of the universe in six days. After his own defeat in 1982, White found his calling as a stand-up comedian. He was in demand as a toastmaster, where his self-deprecating humor and gibes at his critics and opponents, like Clinton, brought down the house.

The two men were not dissimilar in their childhood traumas, although, unlike Clinton, White never mused publicly about the experiences. White was born Durward Frank Kyle Jr. in Texarkana, Texas. His father died when he was seven, his mother married Loftin White of Dallas, and Frank changed his name to Frank Durward White. His stepfather died when he was seventeen, and he and his mother moved back to Texarkana. He landed an appointment to the United States Naval Academy, graduated, and was commissioned in the Air Force as a pilot. He was jolly and effusive, a natural salesman and promoter. He was an instant success as a broker at Merrill Lynch & Co. at Little Rock and came to the attention of William H. Bowen, a lawyer who became president of Commercial National Bank and a friend and adviser of three governors. Bowen hired White at his bank, and unintentionally sponsored his political career by suggesting to David Pryor that the gregarious fellow who knew no strangers would be the perfect director of the state's industrial-development program. They would later fall out over

White's attacks on Clinton, of whom Bowen was a lifelong ally.

Bowen was alternately captivated and flummoxed by White. He told me that White would burst in unannounced at a bank board meeting, hail everyone in the room, and then pester Bowen over some trivial office problem like where to order paper clips. He decided that White would be better running the state's industrial development program, where being totally unabashed would be an unalloyed asset.

Being Pryor's industrial promoter gave White the bug to get into politics, where he realized that his natural camaraderie would be an asset that few could match. No one ever failed to like him. In the spring of 1980, he decided it was time to go for it. I ran into him in the Capitol rotunda as the filing deadline for running for office was approaching. He wanted to run for Congress, but Ed Bethune, the former prosecuting attorney at Searcy, had upset the Democrats in 1978 and become the first Republican since Reconstruction to be elected to Congress from Central Arkansas. White thought Bethune would be hard to beat for a second term, and it was only two months between filing and the Democratic primary, which was not enough time for him to raise a war chest or to organize for a campaign. Besides, he thought he needed a little campaign seasoning. Clinton might even be vulnerable to a primary challenger, owing to the car tags, but if White switched parties and ran as a Republican he would have seven months to build a political network, make himself known across the state, raise some money, and run a creditable race. He would have to get several thousand votes in the little Republican primary, but it would be easy to do that against the soft-spoken Marshall Chrisman, who ran a gravel company at Coal Hill and who had served one unobtrusive term in the House a dozen years earlier. Then, even with a loss to Clinton, White would be primed to run a winnable statewide race in 1982. So he announced that the Republican Party was a more suitable home for him and put down his filing fee for governor.

When Monroe A. Schwarzlose, a wheezing old turkey farmer who drove himself around the state and slept in a rusting pickup truck, got more than thirty percent of the vote against Clinton in the May primary while never running a campaign ad of any kind or making even a slightly sensible speech, White realized that he might, after all, really have a chance of winning. Whoever he met was likely to vent his anger at Clinton over the big hike in his car or truck license fees. Everything began to fall into place: Arkansas Power and Light executives pouting over Clinton's Grand Gulf

exposé, the marauding Cubans at Fort Chaffee and Carter's welching on his promise not to send Clinton any more Cubans, the brouhaha over Clinton's bearded and suddenly clean-shaven aides, concern about the deepening recession. Nothing was going well for Clinton, and the polls showed White inching up. Still, on election night Frank White probably was more surprised than Clinton.

When he was sworn in, White had no ideas about what he wanted to get done at the first legislative session, beyond repealing the Clinton law raising registration fees on cars and trucks, but lots of men had taken office without having much of a program in mind. Dealing with an overwhelmingly Democratic legislature was not going to be a problem for him as it had been for Winthrop Rockefeller. Veteran Democrats were his floor leaders, although the floor jobs were not demanding since White had no program that he wanted to advance. He was going to be frugal with the taxpayers' money and eliminate waste in government, and he was not going to raise taxes. (He did sign a bill giving cities and counties authority for the first time to levy their own sales taxes.) He shortly found himself in the same straits that had handicapped his boss David Pryor. Five months into his and Ronald Reagan's administrations, the country fell into the deepest and longest recession since the Great Depression. Unemployment ran into double digits for much of 1981 and 1982, White's re-election year. Recessions are never good times for chief executives to stand for re-election, although nothing White did or did not do had anything to do with the economic conditions. He had to repeatedly order reductions in spending in nearly all state agencies.

Impulsive, offhand remarks, never ill-intentioned, began to create an image of a guy who was not sure of what he was doing. He ascended to the office by proclaiming that his election had been "a victory for the Lord," which brought some jeering. When the legislature several weeks into his administration passed a law requiring public schools to give "balanced treatment" to the biblical account of creation if they ever mentioned evolution, White signed it into law. Although most Arkansawyers thought the Bible should be taught instead of the Darwinian theory of evolution, the law caused a storm of controversy. A lawsuit ultimately led to a federal court order invalidating the act as a violation of the

U.S. Constitution. Attorney General Steve Clark, embarrassed at having to defend the law in a trial that invited national attention, did not appeal the decision, which brought him condemnations from the television preachers Pat Robertson and Jerry Falwell, who doubted that Clark was a real Christian. White had never given much thought to the proposition before its sponsor, Senator Jim Holsted of North Little Rock, told him about his bill. White said he told Holsted that, sure, if Holsted could pass the bill in both houses he would sign it. He volunteered later that he had signed the bill without reading it. Governors sign hundreds of bills every session without reading them, although you presume that they all read truly consequential bills. White came off looking careless and unserious. In all of George Fisher's cartoons caricaturing the governor afterward, White always carried a half-peeled banana, emblematic of the ape's place in the evolution of man.

A trustee at Hendrix College passed along to me a letter that Governor White had written to the school, reporting that he understood that the faculty of the Governor's School for gifted kids, which took place on the campus every summer, taught Bill Clinton's values. Henceforth, White wrote, he expected the school to start teaching his, not Clinton's, values. The *Gazette* published excerpts from the letter, which caused a small furor. On his last day in office, White said dashing off the impulsive letter was one

of the things he most regretted about his short tenure.

It reflected a basic characteristic of White: a sincere if sometimes reckless honesty.

Early one Saturday morning a few weeks into White's term, my telephone rang about daylight. My wife answered the phone and woke me up saying that Governor White was on the phone. She told him that I was still asleep.

"Well," White said, "roll him out!"

When I picked up the receiver, his voice was a roar.

"Ernie, you lied about me this morning! You made me look like a liar."

"How's that, governor?" I asked.

I had written an editorial criticizing the governor for signing a bill exempting equipment used in agriculture, nurseries, and sod farming from the sales tax, which would cost the state treasury about $25 million a year. I wrote that he had vowed a few weeks earlier, before taking office, to veto the bill if it reached his desk, with the sound reasoning that such exemptions made the sales tax increasingly unfair and that it would reduce state revenues for schools and other needs. At every legislative session since 1963 that I had covered, one or more industry or retail interests would approach the legislature about exempting their products from the sales tax. Typically, you got the legislature in one state to adopt the exemption, and then nearby states had to grant the same exemption to be competitive. White said my statement about his promise was wrong, that he had never said he would veto the bill.

"I always supported that exemption," he said. In fact, he said, he had committed to farm groups before his election that he would back the tax exemption.

I said that I was certain that he was quoted in the newspaper in December as saying that he would veto it.

"No sir! No sir! No sir!" he kept exclaiming.

I said I would go down to the office and check the papers, and if I was wrong I would write an editorial for the Sunday or Monday morning paper correcting the error and apologizing.

"Will you do that? That'll be great," he said.

I drove down to the office, rummaged through the December *Gazette* and *Democrat* files, and found articles in both papers reporting the governor-elect's opposition to the exemption and his promise to veto the bill if both houses passed it. I made copies of the stories from both papers and enclosed them with a brief letter to the governor wondering if he and I had miscommunicated in some way, because it was clear that he had made the remarks.

Several days later the governor returned my letter by mail. Across the top, he had scribbled:

"Ernie, you were right. I was wrong. Frank."

Bill Clinton would never have made such a blunder, but if he had, he wouldn't have admitted it.

White got everything he wanted out of the session. The legislature abolished the Energy Department—although on his first day in office he had fired the four chief offenders, the men who had written the Grand Gulf story for the *Gazette*—and also the Department of Local Services, although state Senator Nick Wilson of Pocahontas had instigated that action because Clinton's director of the department had refused to hire Smokehouse Jackson for a vacant job as a regional emergency coordinator in Izard County. White considered it a victory to sign any bill abolishing an agency or a job.

Early on, White made an appointment that irked both Republicans, who were already unhappy that he was filling his cabinet mostly with Democrats, and also African Americans. Apparently at the urging of Witt Stephens, White appointed Orval E. Faubus as director of the little state veterans' affairs office. Faubus badly needed a job, because he couldn't keep up mortgage payments on his Fay Jones–designed home on a ridge overlooking the town of Huntsville. Stephens felt a little guilt for having abandoned Faubus for David Pryor in the 1974 Democratic race for governor. After the voters bounced White out of office in the next election, Stephens Inc. hired him.

But White would continually demonstrate that he had a tin ear for political realities. Utility regulation was a big issue for voters, which was easy to grasp. They didn't like for their utility bills—gas, electric, or telephone—to go up. Both Jim Guy Tucker and Clinton, as attorneys general, had earned plaudits for fighting utility rate increases. People didn't grasp the intricacies of the system agreement that committed Arkansas to pay more than a third of the cost of nuclear power plants being built in Mississippi, but they did understand that it was somehow going to increase their electric bills. The chief executive merely needs to take care that his fingerprints aren't on any rate-increase order.

When a vacancy on the three-member Public Service Commission opened on his second day on the job, White picked his candidate, Sandra Cherry, a capable lawyer in the U.S. attorney's office, and sent her a few blocks south to Arkansas Power and Light Company's offices to interview for the position. She talked to Jerry D. Jackson, the company's general counsel and a former Public Service Commission member. Both Jackson and Cherry seemed to be embarrassed about the interview. White insisted that he was not trying to please the utility but merely thought that Cherry might benefit from Jackson's firsthand knowledge of what the PSC job entailed. But it cast suspicion that the governor might be friendly toward a rate increase for the company.

White soon landed a second appointment to the commission, former state revenue commissioner Walter Skelton, when one of Clinton's appointees, Frank B. Newell, resigned under pressure from state senators who had utility investments and thought they detected a bias by Newell against utilities. AP&L applied for a rate increase, and White's two commissioners granted a hike that raised the utility's revenues by $104 million a year, the largest utility rate increase in the state's history. Shortly afterward, the governor took a free ride on AP&L's jet to Richmond, Virginia, so that he could talk to executives of a manufacturing company and discourage them from closing a plant in Arkansas.

The rate increase probably sealed White's doom.

Whatever the cause—perhaps criticism by Clinton that the governor was selling out to the utilities—White became a champion of utility reform late in his first year. He began to talk half seriously about the state's buying AP&L and operating the utility as a public service, as several Arkansas cities—among them Jonesboro, North Little Rock, and Hope—already did. That could forestall the rate increases that seemed likely to come down when the Grand Gulf power plants in Mississippi were completed. He called a special legislative session and urged the lawmakers to pass a law outlawing a practice known as "pancaking." Utilities had been able to file for a rate increase and charge the higher rates while they awaited the Public Service Commission's approval. They would put the payments in escrow for repayment to customers if the rate increase or any part of it was denied. White didn't get the full law that he proposed, so he said he would use friendly persuasion in the future to get utilities not to implement rate increases while their cases were pending before the Public Service Commission.

From the day he left the Capitol in January, Clinton seemed determined to run again in 1982. Nearly everyone counseled him to wait and let people forget the car tags. He reached out to almost everyone he knew for their views about what went wrong and what he needed to do to win again. He went to lunch one day at the Little Rock Country Club with Hugh Patterson, the *Gazette* publisher, and me. The discussion was all about the *Arkansas Democrat*'s savage opposition. He said the paper's unrelenting attacks cost him the election. I pointed out that nearly all the *Democrat*'s circulation was in central Arkansas—Pulaski, Saline, and Faulkner counties—but he won there decisively in spite of the newspaper's ritual criticism. Where he was beaten decisively was rural Arkansas, across the southern half of the state and in the rural mountain regions, where the *Democrat* scarcely circulated. He thought about that a moment and said that business leaders in those towns probably took the *Democrat* rather than the *Gazette* and that they spread the word in their communities about how bad his

administration was. He said he did not think he could run again as long
as the *Democrat* was likely to keep savaging him and his administration.
It would be hard to get people to join his administration if they knew they
were going to be ridiculed in the paper the way his aides and department
heads had been in his first term. Hugh told him that he paid far too much
attention to the *Democrat*'s columnists and editorials. Criticism came with
the job, Hugh said.

Our advice was pointless anyway. Clinton's wife soon figured out the
solution to the newspaper problem: John Robert Starr, the newspaper's
crusading managing editor, was egocentric, maybe a narcissist. Starr could
be cultivated and, if not made a fan, he might be neutralized. Clinton had
summoned an associate from the McGovern presidential campaign who
lived in the Rio Grande valley, Betsey Wright, to Little Rock to help him
organize his papers and, it turned out, help him chart a path back to the
office. She agreed with Hillary's strategy.

By the summer of 1981, Starr's daily column began to mention running
into Bill or Hillary at lunch, as others of us downtown cafe habitués often
did. Clinton seemed to Starr to be a changed man—mature, thoughtful,
more conservative. You would read in Starr's column that Clinton had
complimented him on something that he had written. At lunch at an Asian
restaurant across Second Street from the *Gazette* building, I would spot
Starr and Hillary deep in conversation at a corner table. I always made it
a point to drop by the table and speak, since Bob Starr and I back in the
1960s had been friendly competitors at the Capitol, he for the Associated
Press and I for the *Gazette*.

Starr actually began to write glowingly of his old quarry. You read that
Hillary's father, Hugh Rodham, who had moved down with his wife from
Chicago, was a big fan of the editor and loved everything he wrote. When
Starr went to the hospital for some surgery, he wrote that Hugh Rodham
had come to visit him. Starr never missed an edition of the paper; he wrote
columns from his hospital bed.

For the next nine years, the *Arkansas Democrat* rarely had an unkind
word for Clinton, his wife, or anyone in his administration. Clinton and his
staff went out of their way to alert Starr to Capitol stories. Joan Roberts, his
press secretary, said her first assignment every day was to find some way to
accommodate the *Democrat* editor. She told me that she talked to him by
phone most days. If Starr wanted to talk to Clinton, she had orders to find
the governor and put him on the phone.

Hillary thus saved her husband's career for the first time. The capstone was that she let it be known at the start of the comeback campaign that henceforth she was Hillary Clinton, not Hillary Rodham. She had used her maiden name mainly for professional convenience, although she said she was proud of her family name; she had always been Hillary Clinton at heart, but she realized that it offended many voters that she didn't use her husband's surname. She was often at his side when he spoke, gazing admiringly at him as all political wives are supposed to do. For the next ten years, she would be his best political asset.

By the spring of 1982, beating Frank White looked increasingly likely. But Clinton had to win the Democratic primary first, and that was problematic. Jim Guy Tucker, who had lost the runoff race for the U.S. Senate to Pryor two years earlier, was running, along with Joe Purcell, the former attorney general, lieutenant governor, and state party chairman, who was an uninspiring campaigner but the rare politician who had never made an enemy. Monroe Schwarzlose signed up again, as did state Senator Kim Hendren of Bentonville, whose family would later dominate Republican politics in northwest Arkansas.

Tucker looked especially formidable. His only loss and only close race was his defeat four years earlier in the runoff for the U.S. Senate seat. But Clinton never seemed worried much about him. Well before Clinton announced and after Tucker had indicated that he would run for governor, my wife and I dined one night at the home of our friends and neighbors, Gloria and Robert Cabe. Gloria, our state representative, had been defeated like Clinton in the last election. She would later be Clinton's aide and chief of staff. Clinton, who lived a few blocks away during his exile, knocked on the door after dinner and came in. He had not yet said he was running, but we fell to discussing the race. How do you run against your twin, I asked, pointing out that both he and Tucker were polished Ivy League liberals?

Clinton went into a comedy routine. He was on the stump warning people about the dangerous fellow traveler, a secret socialist.

"Why," he said, "he got educated up yonder at Harvard, in Massachooosetts! And, Lord, I've even heard it said that *James* Guy Tucker is a card-carrying member of the A C L of U. Is that who you want running your state government?"

Indeed, Tucker had filed the first lawsuit for the Arkansas chapter of the American Civil Liberties Union in 1969. He represented a couple from Fayetteville, members of the Southern Student Organizing Committee, who were talking about civil rights to youngsters in the student union at Henderson State University at Arkadelphia. They were arrested and jailed for violating a state law prohibiting "offensive talk" at schools after they refused an order by the dean of students to leave the campus. Tucker won the case. The Arkansas Supreme Court, in *Neal v. Still*, reversed their convictions and invalidated the speech statute.

Clinton never made that talk on the stump, or anything like it. Tucker went after Clinton early for commuting the sentences of a number of convicted criminals to time served. Clinton had commuted the sentences to reduce crowding in the packed penitentiary. Tucker's ads featured a 72-year-old man whom Clinton had freed and who shortly afterward killed an old friend in a fight and then rode a dirt bike through the front door of the Pottsville Citizens Bank to rob it. Clinton apologized for freeing the man and the others and said he would never do it again. He criticized Tucker for having been opposed to the death penalty and ran slick ads criticizing Tucker for missing many votes in the U.S. House of Representatives in 1978, when Tucker was in Arkansas campaigning for the Senate. The commercials showed a forlorn couple at the breakfast table ruminating about how terrible it was that taxpayers had paid Tucker his fat salary while he wasn't at work in Washington, while their meager wages would be stopped if they didn't show up at their jobs.

The barrage of ads, on television and radio and in newspapers, sank Tucker. Both men ignored Joe Purcell—cartoons called him Honest Joe and put Abe Lincoln's stovepipe hat on his head—because there was nothing even slightly defamatory they could resurrect about him. Clinton got forty-two percent of the vote and faced a runoff against Purcell two weeks later. Joe was a political enigma. He had been municipal judge at Benton in 1966 when he filed for attorney general, and voters elected him over the colorful Bruce Bennett although they knew nothing about him. His neighbors at Benton had bought a big ad in the *Gazette* listing their names and telephone numbers and urging people to call them and ask them about Joe.

In June 1982 utility rates, thanks to White, the PSC, and AP&L—and, of course, Clinton—had become the big issue. Electric rates had just jumped and the specter of Grand Gulf was on the horizon. Although Hillary had privately excoriated Scott Trotter and Wally Nixon for costing Bill the election in 1980 by launching the overblown Grand Gulf story and infuriating AP&L and its friends, the pair were back in good graces. Together, and with the Clintons' secret assistance, they wrote an 8,500-word amendment to the state Constitution rewriting the utility regulatory code to tightly limit the profits that the energy monopolies could earn from the ratepayers. It created a seven-member Ratepayers Utility Board to represent the interests of various classes of customers in rate proceedings and provided for the three members of the Public Service Commission to be popularly elected. Nixon and Trotter headed an organization called Ratepayers Fight Back. They began circulating petitions to get the approximately 75,000 signatures of registered voters that were required to get it on the ballot.

Owing to our old relationship, I was kept apprised, confidentially, of the progress of work on the amendment. I knew that the Clintons were behind it and that it would be part of the gubernatorial campaign. But I thought it was a bad amendment, because it put matters into the Constitution that shouldn't be in a basic charter. While the provisions, except the election of commissioners, might have merit, they should be in statutory law, not the Constitution. But Trotter and Nixon thought it had to be in the Constitution or else the legislature could repeal or amend it anytime by a two-thirds vote. I wrote editorials in the *Gazette* saying the amendment should not be put on the ballot and should not be ratified.

Joe Purcell

Immediately after the preferential primary, Trotter and Nixon went to Purcell, who refused to sign the petition to put the issue on the ballot while making essentially the arguments I had raised. Clinton ceremoniously signed the petition. I wrote an editorial excoriating Clinton and praising Purcell. The morning the editorial appeared, a week before the runoff election, Clinton called Hugh Patterson and asked to have lunch with the publisher and the editorial board, which included James O. Powell, the editorial page editor, and me. Both strongly agreed with my editorials. We were to lunch with Clinton at the Capitol Club at the top of one of the bank towers.

When the three of us arrived, Bill and Hillary both greeted us. My intrepidity quotient dropped. From my off-the-record conversations I knew what Hugh and Jim Powell didn't know (and what Bill and Hillary didn't know that I knew), which was that the ratepayers amendment was essentially the Clintons'. I couldn't expose Wally and Scott for talking out of school and sharing that knowledge with me.

The table discussion got around to the matter at hand. Clinton said that perhaps we didn't understand his position on the ratepayers amendment. When he signed the petition, he said, he was not endorsing the amendment but simply saying that it was an important issue for voters and that they should have the right to vote on it. Voters might either ratify it or defeat it, but it was their decision, not his. I asked him what he actually thought, as a lawyer, about the amendment. Was this something that should be in the Constitution? After all, the whole constitutional reform movement that all of us supported aimed to remove provisions that were put into the charter long ago and that now were outmoded. He wouldn't answer, but repeated his purpose in signing the petition. He didn't want to declare a position on the amendment, but preferred to leave it up to the voters to decide if the law would be workable. I asked how they could decide that, since the amendment was 10,000 words—longer than the declaration of rights, executive, legislative, and judicial articles of the Arkansas Constitution combined—and a voter would not have time in the voting booth to read even the long ballot title. Hugh Patterson joined in to support me. Clinton was flustered, but he did not become argumentative. I asked him how he would address the matter when he was teaching constitutional law at the University of Arkansas. I said we were not going to quote him but that we'd like to know what he or perhaps both of them thought of it as constitutional theory.

Hillary had said nothing. Finally, she leaned forward and jabbed a forefinger at me.

"Look," she said, "do you want to beat this amendment? Because they will get the signatures and it will be on the ballot."

Sure, I said.

"Well, you've got one chance to beat it, and that's Bill," she said. If Joe Purcell wins the nomination next week and he comes out this fall and says he's studied the amendment and thinks it's bad and that people should vote against it, she asked, do you think that would make any difference to voters? After all, Purcell didn't even want to let people vote on it. On the other hand, if Bill Clinton, who had helped put the issue on the ballot, were to say that he had decided the state would be better off without the amendment, wouldn't that be likely to make a difference to people?

"Well, I guess so," I said. But I turned back to Clinton and asked if he was telling us privately that he knew the proposal should not be in the Constitution and that he would oppose it before the election. He repeated his mantra that all he had wanted to do was give voters a chance to make up their own minds about whether the ratepayers proposal was the right way to deal with the utility problem. Clinton was clearly flustered.

Hugh, my boss, finally cut me off.

"Goddamn it, Ernie," he said. "That's enough. Hillary's absolutely right. With Bill's help this fall, we'll beat that damned amendment."

I wanted to say that I knew it was their amendment and that they had had a hand in drafting it, but I couldn't betray the confidence of Trotter and Nixon.

We departed in good humor. Walking back along Louisiana Street to the office, Hugh was buoyant. He was glad that we had had the discussion. He felt confident that, with Clinton's leadership, the amendment would be beaten. I interjected that, regardless of Hillary's implication, neither of them had ever flatly said that it was a bad amendment or that Bill would oppose it. Hugh said I was too skeptical and that he had no doubt about their intentions.

They got the necessary signatures and the amendment was placed on the November ballot. Clinton ran hard against White's knuckling under to the utilities and then, in late summer, announced his support for the amendment and urged people to vote for it. Hugh Patterson was furious. He raged that the Clintons had lied to us at lunch. I insisted that they hadn't, that Hillary had deftly left that impression but she hadn't lied. Clinton had never answered the direct question of whether he did or would oppose the amendment. Clinton told me later that Hugh had called him and given him the worst cussing he had ever gotten.

The next Monday, the Arkansas Supreme Court handed down its decision in a lawsuit (*Dust v. Riviere*) challenging the validity of the amendment. It ruled five to two that the ballot title itself—707 words long—was so long and complicated that an Arkansas voter "cannot intelligently make a choice based on that title." Justice Darrell Hickman, a fishing buddy of mine who wrote the majority opinion, included the full ballot title in his opinion and invited "any disinterested person to read it in the time one would ordinarily use in a voting booth and understand the changes that the amendment proposes." (Voters were allowed three minutes in a voting booth if they were voting on machines and five minutes if they were voting on paper ballots.)

Justices Steele Hays and John Purtle, who dissented, said that while both the amendment and its ballot title were terribly long and complicated it was not the court's place to say that a voter could not comprehend them sufficiently to cast a confident vote.

Clinton feinted at trying to pass portions of the amendment in a statute at the 1983 legislative session, but it went nowhere.

The Supreme Court ended the ratepayers movement, but it did no damage to the Clinton campaign. He received 55 percent of the votes in a record turnout for an off-presidential-year election. A measure of Clinton's political education in exile was that he coasted to victory in all his elections in Arkansas thereafter, including a thrashing of White again by nearly two to one, four years after the pivotal comeback campaign.

❑❑❑

Between the election and Clinton's inauguration in January, Witt Stephens invited me to join his group for one of the famous cornbread lunches in the Stephens Building and to a private tête-à-tête in his office beforehand.

"What's Bill going to do about Orval?" Witt asked. Was Clinton going to keep Orval Faubus on as the director of the Office of Veterans Affairs?

I said I didn't know, but I presumed that he would replace Faubus.

"Why would he do that?" Witt asked, looking incredulous. He said Faubus was doing a good job and that he badly needed the little salary.

Clinton got 98 percent or more of the African American vote, which was largely responsible for his victory, I said. He could not afford to defy those voters instantly by keeping their old nemesis on the public payroll.

Witt said he understood but that, by and large, Faubus had been a good governor. He was an especially good administrator and Witt expected that people would understand that and accept Clinton's keeping him on in one of the most minuscule and inconsequential state agencies, where he would never do anyone any harm. I said Faubus might have been a good administrator, but that sending troops to block nine black children from going to school at Central High School would be viewed by many as unforgiveable.

Witt said he was honeymooning out of the country with his new bride when Faubus did that. He said he didn't exactly agree with what Faubus did but that, being overseas, he was not where he could have given Faubus advice as the schools were opening in Little Rock in 1957, even if the governor had asked for it. Witt's brother, Jack, who was appointed to the University of Arkansas Board of Trustees by Governor Sid McMath, was instrumental in admitting the first African Americans to the university's professional schools in 1949.

Witt told me that, if the *Gazette* published an editorial giving the new governor grace to keep Faubus on the job, he figured that Clinton would do it. I had no proof of it, but Witt obviously had talked to Clinton about keeping Faubus. Clinton probably told him that the *Gazette* would rip him to shreds if he did that.

Although I felt some charity toward Faubus by then, I went back to the paper and wrote an editorial saying that Clinton was morally obligated to replace Faubus, which appeared in the next morning's paper. Clinton fired him.

After that I expected never to get another invitation for peas and corn-bread at the Stephens building, but if anything, the invitations picked up. Only once did Witt ever express the slightest disappointment at my failure to heed his advice or suggestions at these visits. That was over my serial editorials and columns urging Governor Clinton and the legislature to raise the severance tax on the production of natural gas. Witt took the severance tax personally.

The Stephenses were one of the few powers that Clinton would cross in the next ten years. He would pass a bill in 1985 giving Wall Street and local bond houses an even chance to compete with Stephens Inc. for underwriting Arkansas's municipal bond business. Clinton also appointed the Stephenses' nemesis, Sheffield Nelson, to chair the Arkansas Industrial Development Commission. Although Witt continued to give lip service to supporting the Democrat, brother Jack did not forgive the slight.

XVI
One at a Time

George Fisher's cartoons in the *Arkansas Gazette* throughout 1982 caricatured Bill Clinton garbed in sackcloth like a penitent monk and throwing ashes on his head, or else lashing himself with a whip—abasing himself for jacking up car-registration fees and for other sins. By inaugural day in 1983, he had discarded the hair shirt and brimmed again with confidence, but he didn't discard the lessons. There would still be the profusion of administration bills at the beginning of every General Assembly, but they were focused at each session mostly on a single issue—education, roads, or economic development, with an occasional feint at environmental protection or government ethics.

Although his Public Service Commission resisted paying for Grand Gulf until the Reagan administration and the U.S. Supreme Court said Arkansawyers had to come up with the money, he didn't antagonize the utilities again, or the paper and wood-products industry, or the banks, or the transportation, poultry, and other shipping industries. He had achieved a decade of peace with the *Arkansas Democrat*, so that about the only printed criticism of him and his administration thereafter came in the form of an occasional editorial or column in the *Gazette* lamenting some shortcoming or needless compromise or an editorial in the Republican-leaning *Pine Bluff Commercial*. It was as close to political nirvana as one could achieve in a democratic society.

Education was the ticket to stardom and ultimately the presidency. It was not merely a political calculation. Both the Clintons, I am convinced, were passionately committed to raising the educational achievement of Arkansas children, the same way that Rockefeller, Bumpers, and Pryor had been. It was *a* solution, if not *the* solution, to everything. Aside from her role in myriad governmental school reforms, Hillary brought the HIPPY (Home Instruction Program for Parents of Preschool Youngsters) early childhood program to central Arkansas and helped start Arkansas Advocates for Children and Families, which became a powerful advocate for better schools and family services the next thirty-five years. Whatever the results on the ground from the legislated school reforms, including taxes and tougher standards, the Clintons' around-the-clock advocacy for school improvements perceptibly raised awareness with the population. Arkansas's high school-dropout rate fell and the college-going rate of high school graduates, previously the lowest in the country, improved over the decade.

As I uncharitably pointed out from time to time, to Clinton's irritation, he owed us one. Early in his first term, in the summer of 1979, the Arkansas Supreme Court ruled in *Public Service Commission v. Pulaski County Board of Education* that Arkansas was wildly violating the Constitution by assessing property for tax purposes at grossly unequal rates, from below three percent of market value in some counties to as high as twenty-one percent in Pulaski and Washington counties. Since the state subsidized schools in adverse proportion to their local ability to tax themselves, it meant that counties that assessed their property at higher rates were subsidizing schools in counties that assessed and taxed themselves at very low rates. The Supreme Court ordered every county to reassess all property and to do it uniformly according to its actual market value. The order incited a panic, at least among politicians. Reassessments would double, triple, quadruple people's property taxes, or worse, which would make Clinton's car-tag increases look like rounding change.

Clinton summoned the legislature to Little Rock and submitted a rough constitutional amendment requiring millage rates to be rolled back after every county's property reappraisals. Lobbyists for the railroads, utilities, timber companies, the Arkansas Farm Bureau, hobby farmers, and other real-estate interests descended on the Capitol. Land interests and corporate owners of large personal property wanted to alter the law to allow certain properties to be reclassified and assessed at something besides their market value. One complicated proviso after another was added to the already bewildering proposal, seemingly but not publicly with the governor's blessing. Marcus Halbrook, the venerable director of the Legislative Council, who drafted some of the language, finally went to key sponsors in the Senate and House of Representatives, urging them to pull the amendment down while he could rewrite it. He said he frankly could not make sense of the amendment and that no one could be sure what it would do. It was too late, he was told, because legislators were weary and wanted to get out of town that week. They would fix it by another constitutional amendment after the voters approved it.

While Clinton said people needed to approve it to avoid big increases in the property taxes, only the *Arkansas Gazette* and the Arkansas Education Association opposed the amendment. Voters ratified it by a ratio of three to one. I wrote editorials and columns, which were characteristically too arcane for anyone to grasp, explaining that the big tax increases after re-

TO LEAD OR NOT TO LEAD—THAT IS THE QUESTION—
WHETHER 'TIS NOBLER IN MIND TO SUFFER
THE SLINGS AND ARROWS
OF OUTRAGED SPECIAL INTERESTS
OR TO TAKE ARMS AGAINST
A SEA OF TROUBLED CONSTITUENTS...
FOR WHO WOULD BEAR THE WHIPS
AND SCORNS OF CLARENCE BELL
AND LLOYD GEORGE?
THUS THE LEGISLATURE
DOTH MAKE COWARDS
OF US ALL!

appraisals could be negated without the radical constitutional changes and that the amendment would virtually freeze local school revenues for many years and perhaps actually reduce them in some areas. That indeed was the effect, and the legislature discovered in 1981 that there was no way to fix the law after the reappraisals had begun. A justice of the Arkansas Supreme Court would call it "the Godzilla of constitutional amendments."

"Nobody knows what it means," Justice Darrell Hickman wrote in a dissent to a decision erroneously interpreting the amendment (the court subsequently corrected its mistake). "It was the child of fear and greed."

Amendment 59 was not one of the missteps for which Clinton apologized in his penitent rounds in 1982, but he, indeed, tried in 1983 and subsequently to make up for the harm that Amendment 59 did to school funding.

In the wake of the property-tax decision, the courts took up the attendant issue of funding public education, which had roiled the legislature at nearly every session for the previous thirty years and would vex all three branches of government for the next forty-five years. That case, *DuPree v. Alma School District*, would give Clinton the chance to launch his and Hillary's big school offensive. Since the Great Depression, schools were funded primarily from state revenues, with the corollary goal of overcoming the vast differential in the educational offerings between children in communities with fat property-tax bases and those in districts with little local property wealth to tax.

When the legislature assembled in 1983, Clinton said the goal was to make a great leap forward. Five years earlier, a state-funded study of Arkansas education led by Dr. Kern Alexander of the University of Illinois concluded that schools in Arkansas were about the worst in the land. A child in Arkansas would be better off, he wrote, in a school anywhere else in America. As the long regular legislative session of 1983 was ending, a national commission making the same assessment of the country's schools issued its dramatic report, *A Nation at Risk,* saying that the United States was losing its economic edge over the rest of the world by failing to keep pace with other advanced countries in educating its children. Governors in other Southern states—Virginia, South Carolina, North Carolina, Tennessee—were getting national attention for their progressive school reforms, including higher taxes, salaries, and accreditation standards. It was, again, a perfect culmination of events for the Clintons.

At the regular session of 1983, while the *DuPree-Alma* case was making its way to the Supreme Court, Clinton sent the legislature a bill creating a study commission to recommend an overhaul of the state standards for accrediting schools across the state. The legislature passed it, and Clinton appointed the commission members and made Hillary the chairman. With Hillary nearly always presiding, the commission held hearings in towns all over the state listening to educators, parents, and business leaders about how the schools were failing or succeeding and getting ideas about what schools should be doing that they were not doing. She reported back a couple of times to the Arkansas Legislative Council, which met monthly, and legislators were impressed. "Gentlemen," said Representative Lloyd George of Danville, the unofficial chair of the country-boys caucus, "I think we've elected the wrong Clinton."

Many schools, particularly in small towns and rural areas, were not offering students the range of courses in science, mathematics, and the arts that would equip them to compete in the technological world, she said. Children in every school should have access to counselors and to instruction in at least one foreign language. She said communities put too much emphasis on athletics and not enough on academics, and that Arkansas was never going to get ahead until schools gave them at least equal attention, both in prominence and funding.

Heretical as it sounded, and absurd as was the notion that it would actually happen, academic and athletic equality proved to be a popular suggestion. Hillary Clinton meant it, even if almost no one else did.

Meantime, at the end of May, the Supreme Court handed down its landmark ruling in *DuPree v. Alma*, a six-to-one decision that sought to end a century of injustice for Arkansas children. Since 1874, the Arkansas Constitution had required the state to provide a "suitable" education to every child in the state, and both the state and U.S. constitutions required that it do so equitably. The court avoided any effort to spell out what a suitable education was—it would address that twenty years later in the *Lake View* school case—but it said the inequalities from one school to the next had to be ended then. Arkansas consistently had funded its schools, Justice Steele Hays wrote, in a way that never came close to any measurement of equality. Counting both local property taxes and state aid, the yearly expenditure per child among some four hundred districts ranged from $873 to $2,378. He said the system promoted greater advantages for children in richer communities and diminished opportunities for those in the poorer ones, a transparent violation of the state and federal constitutions' promise of equal protection of the laws.

It was the springboard and also the political cover that Clinton needed to raise taxes to support the schools. Without new taxes, the only ways to close the huge gap in funding among districts cited by the Supreme Court would be to drastically reduce spending in many districts (cutting salaries and/or laying off teachers) and give the money to other districts, or else to sharply reduce spending on law enforcement, corrections, and health care and transfer it to schools. While his wife continued her community school hearings, Clinton spent the summer talking about the need to invest in the future of Arkansas children. By the time he called a special legislative session in the fall, a poll showed that a substantial majority of Arkansawyers thought a sales tax increase would be all right if it benefited the schools. Clinton expected the session to pass taxes for education, devise a new formula for distributing the money equitably among the schools, and deal with a raft of other ideas the Clintons had hatched, some of them arising from Hillary's community hearings. One would cost him, at least for a few years, his strongest constituency but build his overall popularity: a basic-skills test that teachers and administrators would have to pass to keep their teaching licenses.

Before the session, Clinton invited the *Gazette* editorial board—James O.

Powell, Jerry Dhonau, and me—to the mansion for coffee and to discuss the plans he was still formulating for the session, mainly the taxes. But it was there that he first broached the idea of a test for teachers—perhaps the standardized national teacher-licensing test. Hillary had talked about such a test after receiving complaints from parents at the hearings that some teachers sent notes home that were ungrammatical or that misspelled words. He said the test, if they went that route, probably would not be a condition for teachers keeping their jobs but would be used for evaluations and remediation. It would turn out to be much different.

I suggested that a sales tax would make the already regressive tax system more punitive for the poor, whose children already were the most disadvantaged by the school-finance system. Could he not seek a balancing ability-to-pay tax, like raising the corporate income tax rate or imposing a real severance tax on natural gas? Every other gas-producing state in the country collected production taxes many times higher than Arkansas's, which was three-tenths of a penny per thousand cubic feet of gas. He said he might do something like that, although such a tax would be hard to pass since it required the votes of three-fourths of each house. I said a gas severance tax would not raise a lot of money unless there was a lot of new exploration, but I thought legislators might be hard-pressed to vote for a substantial tax on nearly everyone but vote against one that would cost no one but gas producers and cause the owners of mineral rights a trifling reduction in royalties.

The governor did suggest a few days later that he might introduce a gas severance tax to balance the regressivity of the sales tax, but he was not sure. Witt Stephens invited me to lunch the next day. After he got into the gas business in the 1940s, Witt always took talk about raising the severance tax personally. When Governor Ben Laney and the legislature raised severance taxes on most minerals to raise a little money for the starved treasury in 1947, they actually slashed the tax on natural gas, perhaps upon Witt's lobbying—I never asked him about it. In 1957, when Governor Faubus got the legislature to raise the production taxes on nearly all minerals, he and Witt struck a deal. They would double the tax on natural gas—from three-twentieths of a penny per thousand cubic feet to three-tenths of a penny, which had an invisible impact on the treasury. But Faubus could say that he raised the severance tax.

In his office before lunch, Witt asked if I thought Clinton would try to pass a severance tax. I said I didn't know anything more about it than the governor's own speculation that he might do it.

"Ernie," he said, "if Bill raises the severance tax he'll never get elected to any office in this state again." He went on to say that I was wrong when I wrote that all the other gas-producing states had higher severance taxes than Arkansas. Louisiana has no severance tax, he said, explaining that he knew that for a fact because Arkansas Louisiana Gas Company was head-quartered at Shreveport, Louisiana. He said the company had never paid a dime of tax on the gas that the company's exploration subsidiary produced in that state. I called the Louisiana tax division in the afternoon to confirm that they were collecting severance taxes on gas, but I didn't try to quarrel with Stephens about it.

Representative Joseph K. "Jodie" Mahony II, my old El Dorado friend, introduced the governor's very modest severance tax bill, but it died a quiet death. It never passed even the House. Mahony told me later that he saw no evidence that the governor lobbied legislators to vote for the bill.

Years later, Mahony's younger brother Emon, who had been president of Witt's west Arkansas gas distribution company in 1981, told me that Witt had telephoned him asking what in the world his big brother was doing introducing Clinton's severance tax. Emon was unaware of it. Witt clearly expected him to do something about it. Emon wrestled with the quandary for days. He didn't want to call Jodie and pressure him to withdraw the bill or to discourage him from trying to pass it. He didn't call Witt back and dreaded hearing from him again. He read the papers closely to see what happened to the bill. Finally, Witt called him about another matter and finished by saying that Emon should not worry about that gas-tax matter because he thought it was taken care of. My hunch always was that Witt called the governor, who told him that he did not need to fret about the tax because there was no chance the bill could get the three-fourths vote and there was no point in his trying hard to get it passed.

The sales-tax bill, which raised the tax from three to four percent, barely got the simple majority it needed to pass, perhaps because of the teacher test. Representative Bobby Glover of Carlisle told me that he agreed to vote for the sales tax only on the condition that there was a mandatory teacher test. He said several other House members were with him.

When the final version of the teacher-test bill stipulated that it would be a basic-skills test that would be required for relicensing, the Arkansas Education Association opposed the bill. Teachers at Little Rock's Central High School circulated a petition, signed by most of the faculty, saying bring it on because they were happy to take any test. But it was immensely unpopular with the profession statewide. Teachers considered it an affront to the whole profession and personally demeaning. Many teachers refused to take the test and had to leave the classroom, others failed it, and many who were no longer teaching but had maintained their certification did not take the test and their certifications were voided.

The teacher-test battle and Clinton's school-reform campaign won him national attention. Clinton and Peggy Nabors, the president of the Arkansas Education Association, engaged in debates on the teacher test, including one on CBS's *Phil Donahue Show*. Although there was no evidence that the test raised the quality of classroom instruction, it gave Clinton a big political boost. Fighting with the teachers' association and also the Arkansas State AFL-CIO won him the admiration of conservatives, particularly a certain contingent that hoped that the test would rid their schools of the black teachers inherited through desegregation. (That didn't happen.) The AFL-CIO fell out with the governor and, like the AEA, did not endorse him in the next two elections, owing both to the teacher test and to Clinton's reneging on a commitment to amend his sales tax bill to give low-income people an income-tax rebate for the sales taxes they paid for groceries. Labor and the AEA would return comfortably to the fold only when he ran for president in 1992.

Twice more, in 1987 and 1991, Clinton would return to education at the regular sessions of the General Assembly, each time either raising the sales and use tax rate (by half a percent in 1991) or expanding the collection base to more commercial items, like cigarettes, cable television, interstate telephone calls, and used vehicles of all kinds. The money was not earmarked for the schools and the legislature diverted some of it to other causes, but teacher salaries and scholarships were the rationale for the new taxes.

Re-election in 1984 was a breeze. In the Democratic primary, Clinton faced his old friend Lonnie Turner of Ozark, a lawyer who was sore over the new school standards devised by Hillary because he thought they would kill rural schools; Monroe Schwarzlose, who ran for the third and final time but hardly left his house in Kingsland; and Kermit Moss of Monticello, a college business professor and humorist whose letters and satirical essays in the state papers about politics and Clinton usually began or ended with the same exclamation that would lead his obituary twenty-six years later: "Mercy me, sakes alive, and carrot coffee!" Moss's occasional whimsies offered the only antidotes to a somnolent election season other than, of course, the wacky vaudeville of Sheriff Tommy Robinson, a Clinton protégé who got himself elected to Congress and then set out six years later, with the help of Republican plotters, to end his patron's career before he could run for president.

True to his plan to stick to one big issue at a time, in his third term Clinton concentrated on economic development. Arkansas's old economic model of agriculture and factory and processing businesses, which depended on unskilled and low-paid workers, had landed the state near the bottom of nearly every index of economic well-being, Clinton said as the General Assembly convened in January 1985. Rather than adversaries, he said, government and business should be partners in development. He had a basket of ideas culled from innovations in a number of other states and a stack of bills ready for lawmakers to sponsor. The legislature would pass nearly every one.

The state would create enterprise zones in depressed urban areas where tax breaks and other incentives would encourage investors to locate businesses. Many of the innovations involved tax breaks of one sort or another for businesses as an incentive to build or expand in the state. Ten bills, most of them from the governor's basket but others from lobbyists for commercial interests, exempted commercial and industrial products and equipment from the sales and use taxes. All of them were signed into law. Another five were enacted in the 1987 legislative session. One act created the Arkansas Science and Technology Authority, which was supposed to develop new technology businesses. Another expanded the Arkansas Housing Development Authority's ability to issue bonds for low-income housing and also industrial and agricultural development. Another gave income tax credits for businesses that created new jobs. The state's public employees pension funds were encouraged to invest five percent of their funds in Arkansas business projects. The handful of state-chartered banks were given authority not only to lend money but also to take equity positions in commercial and agricultural industries.

I was dubious that all the business tax breaks, particularly the sales- and use-tax exemptions, would produce an economic boom, and I wrote columns and editorials to that effect. The long and deep national recession that set in early in the administration of Ronald Reagan—ten consecutive months of double-digit unemployment—finally ended about the time that Clinton regained office. After the big federal tax cut of 1981, Congress and the president increased federal spending and raised taxes five of the next six years, and the economy surged about the time Clinton took office again. Arkansas's did, too, but in special ways. In a reversal of recent trends, Arkansas had a better record of creating manufacturing jobs than most other states. Did Clinton's tax incentives and the other innovations to encourage investment help? It was hard to prove one way or the other.

One strategy that did work was globetrotting. Every succeeding governor would embrace the idea. Whatever its success, traveling around the country and the world in pursuit of industry and jobs was good politics. Whether it was Clinton's magnetism and charm or good luck, his trips seemed to produce new industries and to save others. He flew to New York to persuade the president of International Paper Company not to close its big Camden mill and move the jobs to New England. The company president wanted some tax and union-bargaining concessions, and Clinton got them for him. He arranged for Arkansas shoe man Don Munro to buy a shoe plant at Clarksville to keep it from closing. He flew to Japan to talk the president of Sanyo out of closing its television plant at Forrest City. Clinton called Sam Walton and persuaded him that Walmart and Sam's stores should stock Sanyo TVs, which kept the plant going. A similar intercession with Walmart kept a shirt factory open at Brinkley. He was instrumental in getting NUCOR Steel to build its big steel plant at Blytheville.

Until Republicans took control of the government after 2010, highway funding in Arkansas was never a political struggle, as long as highways were to be built by gasoline and diesel taxes. People everywhere want better roads and streets. Conservative and liberal lawmakers from both parties always were willing to vote for fuel taxes, and no legislator was beaten in the next election after having voted for them. Clinton was wary of proposing another highway program after his defeat for having raised car registration fees in 1979. He was thinking about referring a highway tax program to the voters at a special election in 1985 or at the 1986 general election. I reminded him that Dale Bumpers had the same notion in 1973 until a legislator from Stuttgart rebuked him. Representative Wayne Hampton, a former highway commissioner, told Bumpers that people had elected the two of them and the rest of the lawmakers to make those decisions, not just punt the tough decisions back to the people who had elected them.

I went to the digests for each legislative session back to 1957, plotted all the tax increases for highways and general revenues going back to Faubus's 1957 tax program, examined the roll calls on each of the bills, and compared them with results from the next elections. Not one legislator who had voted for one of the income, sales, motor fuel, or severance taxes in those twenty-seven years had been defeated in the next election. I wrote a column for the *Gazette* summarizing those results and speculating that if the legislature raised fuel taxes, voters would hold the legislators and the governor harmless for raising their taxes.

Clinton proposed a four-cent-a-gallon increase and the legislature passed it easily. In 1991, the last session before he ran for president, he asked for another four cents a gallon. The legislature amended the bill to five cents a gallon and passed it. In a painful show of either timidity or hypocrisy—I leaned toward the latter explanation—Clinton vetoed the bill. Both houses promptly called the roll and more than three-fourths of the members over-rode his veto, giving him a bigger highway program than he asked for and at no political risk whatever. He had his cake and ate it, too.

The 1986 election, the first after the state Constitution was amended to give constitutional officers four-year terms, was nearly as breezy as the 1984 one. Clinton had a chance in the same season to beat up two old nemeses, Orval Faubus and Frank White—Faubus in the Democratic primary and White in the general election. Faubus, who was never able to get a job after leaving the governor's office in 1967, except briefly as a teller at a little branch bank at Huntsville and as Frank White's veterans-affairs director for two years, was hurting for cash. Clinton had fired him from the veterans office and then stopped the state Parks and Tourism Department from buying Faubus's mountaintop home to use as a tourist retreat. Faubus was having trouble keeping up the mortgage payments. Faubus always collected cash along the campaign trail, and perhaps he thought that, although he probably wouldn't win the election, he could earn a little tribute from sympathizers along the way. The campaign cost him very little.

Clinton piled up more than sixty percent of the vote against Faubus and then White.

Both men hoped that family problems and drugs—a dangerous fusion—might make Clinton vulnerable. Tommy Goodwin, the State Police director, had told Clinton that agents had evidence that his brother Roger was dealing cocaine and asked how the governor wanted him to handle it. Clinton told him to handle it like he would any other suspect. Clinton told Hillary and his chief of staff, Betsey Wright, but not Roger or their moth-

er. The police trapped Roger selling more cocaine and arrested him. He served fourteen months in prison. When it was revealed that Clinton had been told about the investigation and didn't alert his brother or his mother, a few people considered it family disloyalty, but it probably enhanced his popularity.

His brother's problems were not a suitable issue for an opponent to bring up, but Roger and Bill shared a friend, Dan Lasater, a racehorse owner, investment banker, owner of a ski resort at Angel Fire, New Mexico, and general *bon vivant*. Roger apparently helped Lasater and his friends in some way to get cocaine for their parties and was named as an unindicted co-conspirator when Lasater and the two partners of his Little Rock bond house, former state senator George E. "Butch" Locke and David Collins, were indicted shortly before the 1986 election on charges that they provided cocaine for social gatherings. Being named as an unindicted co-conspirator meant that Roger probably gave investigators evidence.

White couldn't accuse the governor of being a druggie, but he had to find a way to keep the Lasater scandal in front of the voters along with the insinuation that the governor could have been involved in some way with the drug activity. The Lasater, Locke, and Collins investment house on Loui-

Front Runner

siana Street got some of the state's bond business after Clinton's 1985 Development Finance Authority reforms that expanded its bonding authority and opened the underwriting business to in-state and Wall Street competitors of Stephens Inc. White accused Clinton of favoring his drug-abusing friend with lucrative state bond business. Clinton pointed out that White worked for the big Stephens investment firm, which got nearly all the underwriting before his 1985 reform and most of it afterward.

Clinton got a tip that in a scheduled televised debate White might make a dramatic demand that the governor undergo a drug test to prove that he wasn't partying with the drug-snorting playboys. That, indeed, is what White did, and thanks to his nervy political adviser Dick Morris, Clinton was prepared. He responded that he and Betsey Wright, his executive secretary and campaign manager, had already submitted their urine to drug tests and were free of psychotropic substances. Clinton then insisted that White and his own colorful campaign manager, Darrell Glasscock, also have their urine tested. He included the two campaign managers—Betsey and Darrell—because he figured Glasscock might refuse to take the test. Glasscock, who grew up in the burlesque of Louisiana politics, managed several Arkansas political campaigns and ran for office several times, alternately as a Democrat and a Republican. Glasscock avoided indictment ten years later when his business companion, Secretary of State W. J. "Bill" McCuen, went to prison for several fraudulent schemes, one of which was to split with Glasscock the profits from a scam sale of flags to the State Capitol. Glasscock sniffed trouble, didn't cash his $53,000 check, and escaped charges. He died in Bogota, Colombia, in 2017.

It was an entertaining campaign, as any race would be with Dick Morris and Darrell Glasscock calling the shots, but there was never any tension about how it would come out.

Longevity in office and now being the first governor with a four-year term did not strengthen Clinton's ties with the legislature, as Orval Faubus's lengthening reign had done twenty years earlier. He ran into resistance trying to raise more taxes and close tax loopholes, primarily to fund education, as special interests like the poultry industry kept enough legislators in line to prevent the extraordinary majorities that often were needed to pass fiscal legislation. He called a special legislative session in 1988 and asked the lawmakers to pass an ethics bill drawn up by Scott Trotter and others who by then were associated with Common Cause, the national political reform organization. It required extraordinary disclosures by legislators, other government officials, and lobbyists, and outlawed certain conflicts of interest. The measure ran into the stiffest resistance in the state Senate, where in earlier years he had nearly always prevailed. The session disbanded without passing the legislation. Clinton announced that he would put it on the ballot through an initiative campaign and submit it to the voters. His friend Webster Hubbell, whom he had appointed chief justice of the Supreme Court for a brief term and would later install as deputy attorney general of the United States, redrafted the ethics bill and the voters approved it in the 1990 general election, although Trotter would later discover that it had been amended to exempt the executive branch from a few of the ethics restraints.

More and more, as his national visibility rose and he was in demand as a speaker, the governor traveled out of the state. When he did, the lieutenant governor became the acting governor. On one occasion, both Clinton and Lieutenant Governor Winston Bryant were both outside the state's boundaries, and Senator Nick Wilson of Pocahontas became the acting governor for a couple of days. Wilson had been a strong ally of the governor in their earlier years, but he felt betrayed once or twice by Clinton's changing

commitments. He went to the governor's office and appointed a bunch of people to state boards and commissions to fill vacancies that Clinton had failed to fill. He also demoted Clinton's chief of staff, Betsey Wright, and made her liaison to the state Transportation Commission, an agency that had been abolished by an act written by Wilson and signed by the governor. Her demotion lasted only until Clinton returned.

Governor of Arkansas was becoming a tedious job.

XVII
The Southern Mind Redux

Lee Atwater would have better served his race—meaning either the human one or the white one—if he had devoted his energy to only one of his two limitless talents, focusing on rock music rather than the political knavery that he pursued with such audacity and success for the pivotal decade of the 1980s. He gave the country Ronald Reagan and George H. W. Bush at their worst, and, had Atwater not died from brain cancer at the age of forty, Bill Clinton undoubtedly would never have been president of the United States. Nevertheless, Atwater did treat Arkansawyers to one of the most audacious elections of the century, in 1990.

Atwater grew up in South Carolina, downstate from where Wilbur J. Cash wrote *The Mind of the South*, the classical treatise on Southern culture and mentality that became an intellectual rite of passage for generations of young Southerners. *The Mind* had begun as a series of essays for H. L. Mencken's *American Mercury*, which were then enlarged into the book. It was a celebrated achievement that put Cash, a journeyman newspaperman, in popular demand. Atwater never knew Cash, because ten years before Atwater was born, the celebrated author got married, delivered a famous commencement address at the University of Texas, and hanged himself by his necktie in his hotel room. Atwater surely read *The Mind of the South*, because his short career as a political consultant and manager reflected a thorough grasp of Cash's notions about the common mental groundings of men of the Old South, as well as a sizable part of the rest of the national populace. If he didn't read Cash, Atwater would have figured it all out intuitively anyway. Cash summarized his whole book about Dixie dwellers in one of its paragraphs:

> Proud, brave, honorable by its lights, courteous, personally generous, loyal, swift to act, often too swift, but signally effective, sometimes terrible, in its action—such was the South at its best. And such at its best it remains today, despite the great falling away in some of its virtues. Violence, intolerance, aversion and suspicion toward new ideas, an incapacity for analysis, an inclination to act from feeling rather than from thought, an exaggerated individualism and too narrow concept of social responsibility, attach-

ment to fictions and false values, above all too great at-
tachment to racial values and a tendency to justify cruelty
and injustice in the name of those values, sentimentality
and a lack of realism—these have been its characteristic
vices…

Atwater calculated early that catering to those vices would win elections,
certainly in the South and with only slightly less probability in the nation
at large. He specialized in finding ways to exploit those prejudices and direct them against aspiring politicians, usually Democrats. The first was
Tom Turnipseed, a populist former George Wallace acolyte who ran for
Congress in South Carolina in 1980. Running the Republican's campaign,
Atwater ran a fake push poll that told people Turnipseed was suspected of
being an NAACP member, and he mass-mailed letters from Strom Thurmond, the twentieth-century South's most famous bigot, warning South
Carolinians that Turnipseed planned to turn America over to communists
and liberals. But his cleverest gambit was to plant a fake reporter at a news
conference to ask Atwater whether it was true that Turnipseed had jumper
cables affixed to his brain because he was crazy. Turnipseed's mental illness
as a boy—he had talked often about his suicidal impulses as a teenager and
electroshock treatments—became the big issue that beat him. Turnipseed
and I both served in the 1990s on the board of an organization called The
American Forum that produced progressive op-eds. He told me that he
had received a sorrowful letter from the dying Atwater in 1990 apologizing
for making fun of his juvenile illness and exploiting it for political gain.
Atwater said learning that he had a fatal brain cancer had taught him hu-
mility, humanity, and love.

Beating Turnipseed, and soundly, merited a job in the new Reagan White
House as the deputy to Ed Rollins, the president's political director. Rollins
would later marvel at how Machiavellian Atwater was—"utterly ruthless"—
as the chief strategist for Reagan's 1984 re-election campaign. He said Atwater directed a dirty-tricks campaign against Representative Geraldine
Ferraro, the Democratic vice-presidential candidate, insinuating that she
had mob ties. He would run George H. W. Bush's successful campaign for
president in 1988 and was responsible for the nasty Willie Horton campaign that turned Michael Dukakis's seventeen-point lead into a lopsided
defeat. (Governor Dukakis gave the convicted murderer, a black man, a
weekend furlough and he raped a woman and beat up her boyfriend.) At-

water had declared that he would "strip the bark off the little bastard [Du-kakis]" and "make Willie Horton his running mate." (After converting to Catholicism and repenting his sinful life in his dying days in 1991, Atwater sent an apology to Dukakis for the "naked cruelty" of his attacks on the governor and his wife, who had her own emotional problems.)

Atwater became a partner in the Washington political consulting firm of Paul Manafort and Richard Nixon's dirty trickster, Roger Stone, both of whom would surface ingloriously thirty years later in the investigation of corruption in the Donald Trump campaign and White House.

In a recorded interview with a historian when he was in the Reagan White House, Atwater explained "off the record" how political strategies based on race had to change over the decades from outright racism to coded terms that raised the same hackles with whites in the South and elsewhere. In 1954, a politician could yell "Nigger, nigger, nigger," he said, but by the end of the 1960s that had become taboo. Politicians had to develop issues that would trigger the same responses in people, such as espousing cuts in gov-ernment programs like food stamps and welfare that many white people tended to associate with African Americans.

"You follow me?" Atwater asked. "Because, obviously, sitting around saying, 'We want to cut this,' is much more abstract than even the busing thing, and a hell of a lot more abstract than 'Nigger, nigger.' So, any way you look at it, race is coming on the backbone."

But we were talking about Arkansas. After George H. W. Bush was elect-ed president, he fulfilled Atwater's dream to be chairman of the Republican National Committee, in charge of the party's whole agenda of controlling all three branches of government. Still, Atwater considered his primary job to be the re-election of his friend and benefactor in 1992, which he private-ly doubted could be done, because Bush was such an anemic politician. At-water's job was to create the most favorable circumstances possible for him. The first task was to eliminate or else weaken the strongest Democratic contenders. Atwater had already concluded that Bill Clinton was the Dem-ocrats' best shot, even though few Democrats and no other Republican at the time thought so. The South had become the GOP's base, and it would remain so well into the twenty-first century. Bush's re-election depended first upon holding the now solid Republican South, from Texas to Virginia. Clinton was a Southerner, with higher political gifts than anyone in either party, and his chairmanship of the National Governors Association and his founding of the moderate Democratic Leadership Council had raised the profile of a figure from a state that historically was inconsequential in any national drama.

Clinton had pondered running for president in 1988 but, to Atwater's relief, he backed out in the summer of 1987. He had invited supporters to Little Rock for the likely announcement at the Excelsior Hotel, but he maintained in his memoir that a remark from Chelsea on the fateful morning changed his mind. She asked where they were going for vacation and he said that if he ran for president he wouldn't take a vacation. She said that she and Hillary then would go somewhere without him. He said he realized then that if he announced for president he would have little to do with her for the next year and a half and maybe the next five and a half. It persuaded him that he needed to devote the next four years to her and to finishing the job as governor. Jim Powell, editor of the editorial page of the *Gazette*, wrote an editorial saying Clinton must not run because he needed to finish the job in Arkansas. Clinton would cite the editorial in his memoir, though it probably had little to do with his decision. He went to the press conference at the Excelsior and announced that he was not running. Atwater knew that 1992 would be different and that Clinton would be hard for Bush to beat. The task was to beat him in the governor's race in 1990, if Clinton chose to run again rather than devote himself entirely to the 1992 presidential race, or else to cripple him so badly in the state race that he would be damaged goods in 1992.

Atwater knew the perfect agent for the hatchet job: Congressman Tommy F. Robinson of Little Rock. Robinson shared Atwater's Machiavellian impulses and was ambitious for a bigger job than congressman, which he hated, but he had to be persuaded to become a Republican and also to run against the man who had launched his career in 1979 by elevating him from the lowly job of suburban police chief to a member of the governor's cabinet.

It was too easy.

In May 1989 Atwater held a news conference at Little Rock to talk about national politics, with rumors rampant that Congressman Robinson, then in his third term, at Atwater's bidding was going to switch parties and run for governor in 1990. Robinson was good material for the Republicans and Atwater said he hoped Robinson would take that step. He predicted that the Democrats would nominate a Southerner for president in 1992, which would be their only chance of winning, but he said it would have to be a real Southerner, not a fake one like Clinton. Two months later, Robinson appeared with President Bush in the Rose Garden to announce the switch. He would explain his decision later by saying that the Democrats had become the party of "homosexuals and weirdos."

Soon afterward, Atwater summoned two Republican operatives from Arkansas, J. J. Vigneault and Rex Nelson, to the Republican National Committee offices to strategize about Robinson's race. Both men were already working for Robinson in official or unofficial capacities. Vigneault had been chairman of the Reagan-Bush campaign in Arkansas in 1984 and Atwater had brought him into the Republican National Committee offices as a regional political director. Now he was assigned to run the Robinson campaign in Arkansas. Nelson, a Republican whose career alternated between journalism and politics, had been an adviser to Judy Petty, the congressional candidate who had challenged Wilbur Mills in 1974, and was recruited that summer to help Robinson.

Atwater was blunt about Clinton. He was the single Democrat that Atwater believed would be almost certain to defeat Bush in an ordinary campaign. Presuming that he would run for re-election in 1990, Clinton had to be defeated or else his reputation so besmirched that he would not be a viable candidate for president two years later.

"You boys have to remember, I don't give a fuck who the governor of Arkansas is," Atwater explained. "My only job as chairman of the Republican National Committee is to get George Bush reelected."

"We're going to take Tommy Robinson and use him to throw everything we can think of at Clinton—drugs, women, whatever works. We may or may not win, but we'll bust him up so bad he won't be able to run again for years."

He said the RNC would provide them whatever was needed to nominate and elect Robinson as governor: money, research, staffing, and media expertise, anything.

Atwater neither offered nor asked for any knowledge or rumors of Clinton's extramarital amours. It was not a moral issue with Atwater, who was a legendary adulterer himself, having used the RNC credit card to pay for hotel trysts with a girlfriend in Virginia. He talked a *Washington Post* reporter out of publishing anything about his affair with a White House staffer, because it would hurt innocent people.

Tales of Clinton's womanizing, or at least rumors, were already circulating in Washington. Atwater's team—his executive assistant at the RNC was Mary Matalin, later a partner in the extrapartisan marital team of Matalin and James Carville, the latter Bill Clinton's own acerbic political adviser—was spreading the rumors far and wide, especially with the Washington press corps.

A week before the *Arkansas Gazette* closed in October 1991, I received a call at the paper from a *Washington Post* reporter, who was in Little Rock in anticipation of Clinton's formal announcement that he was running for president. The reporter was assigned to chase down the womanizing rumors before Clinton's announcement, perhaps so that Clinton could be asked about them at his announcement. He wanted to talk to me about them, offering to do so off the record. It was clearly an unwelcome assignment. He had the names of a number of women, largely the same list that Larry Nichols circulated after Clinton fired him from the state development-finance office for running up big telephone bills consorting with the Contra rebels in Nicaragua. I said I had heard the same rumors but that I had no personal knowledge about any of them and would not discuss them with him. He persisted over the phone and finally asked about one woman in particular.

"Well," I said, "she's in the cubicle next to mine. Let me let you ask her." He begged me not to put her on the line, but I did. It was Deborah Mathis, who wrote a column and an occasional editorial for us and had a previous career as a television reporter at all three Little Rock stations.

Deborah told the reporter that she was delighted to be asked but she had never had sex with the governor nor had he ever been indiscreet other than his naturally flirtatious mien. She and a film crew had gone to the mansion once to talk to him, and a cameraman had joked with her about it afterward. She said the rumor had circulated for years.

Atwater was convinced that in Tommy Robinson they had recruited the right man to take Clinton out, but they had to be sure first that he got the Republican nomination. Another Republican might not be willing to go to the depths needed to beat Clinton. He would be proved right.

Robinson had grown up on the south side of the Union Pacific tracks in the blue-collar suburb of Rose City. He was a buddy of Jerry Jones, who bought the Dallas Cowboys a few months before Robinson went to the White House Rose Garden in July 1989 to be introduced by President Bush as the GOP's newest congressman. Jones's daughter, Charlotte, was the congressman's chief of staff. Within a year, Robinson would be calling his old pal a crook and his own career would be over. But in the summer of 1989, Robinson was at the pinnacle: feted at the White House, his exploits recounted in articles and videos across the nation, a glamorous future assured by the masterminds of the Grand Old Party.

Handsome and photogenic, Robinson had bounced around in minor law-enforcement jobs before becoming chief of Jacksonville's small police force. He was a publicity machine who sought out reporters and regularly got his name in the papers for crime work in the town. He talked tough but also seemed to have a progressive streak, such as bemoaning the gun culture celebrated by the National Rifle Association. To Clinton, he seemed like a natural to be director of the Department of Public Safety, which in the past had been a figurehead overlord of the State Police, the National Guard, and smaller public-safety units. But within months he was feuding with the people who ran the agencies.

Within a year, all the constant publicity had given Robinson a leg up in the race for county sheriff in 1980. He visited the *Gazette* and *Democrat* seeking their endorsements. He told everyone what they wanted to hear. The editorial page editor of the *Gazette* penned a glowing editorial endorsing the young progressive, but before it was to be published I persuaded him that, while Robinson was smart and brassy, there often was little truth behind his boasts. We held off endorsing him. For a candidate for county sheriff, TR, as he became known, had a remarkable band of rich and powerful backers, much of it owing to Rose City friendships with young men who navigated to power, including Jerry Jones and the heads of the state's two largest utilities, Arkansas Power and Light Company and Arkansas Louisiana Gas Company. He won by a landslide over the gentlemanly Ken Best while his patron, Clinton, was going down to defeat by Frank White.

Normally a languorous part of government that makes the back pages of the paper once a month or so, the work of the county sheriff under Robinson became an unceasing carnival, a spectacle that fed not only the Little Rock media but the rest of the state and sometimes the nation. Within months, Robinson had already spent nearly his entire budget for the year on flashy new uniforms, equipment, and cars, as well as higher pay, and he was demanding more appropriations from the county administration and the Quorum Court and threatening recalcitrant officials.

Recounting Robinson's escapades in the four years at the courthouse would fill a captivating book; as it happens, Gene Lyons wrote two of them, both good reads, *Widow's Web* (1993) and *The Hunting of the President* (2001), the latter in tandem with Joe Conason. I will try to briefly encapsulate the highlights.

Angered by publicity about overcrowding and serial escapes from his jail, Robinson blamed the state penitentiary, because it was overcrowded and was not accepting more prisoners from the counties. Robinson loaded a bus with prisoners, hauled them to Cummins Prison, and chained them outside the gates in the summer sun. Then he surrounded his jail with armed deputies and instructed them to shoot state troopers or correction officials if they tried to return the prisoners. He told newsmen that he would arm and deputize them if the state police proved too much for his own men. To stop a rash of liquor-store robberies, he posted signs in the windows of participating liquor stores showing the barrel-end of a shotgun and warning robbers that deputies were in the back of the store ready to kill them. The robberies stopped in rural areas, but a clerk was shot to death in a Little Rock store. After a federal judge appointed a special master to oversee the county jail, Robinson ignored him. When the county judge and the female clerk who dispensed money for county agencies refused Robinson's request to give him money for some jail expenses without the OK of the court-appointed master, Robinson alerted cameramen and photographers and then had his deputies handcuff the county judge and his sobbing clerk and throw them in jail. U.S. District Judge George E. Howard Jr. then ordered Robinson jailed at Memphis for contempt of court for refusing to allow the court-appointed jail master to enter it, which elicited from Robinson a racial taunt about the "token judge."

Finally, there were his serial blunders after the murder of Alice McArthur, who was found shot to death in a closet of her home; she was clutching a bouquet of flowers. Robinson alerted photographers and, in the mid-watches of the night, dragged her husband, defense attorney Bill McArthur, out of his bed, handcuffed him, and tossed him in jail for murdering his wife. Little Rock police then arrested the real killers: two men who had posed as floral deliverymen, and Mary Lee Orsini, who they said had hired them to kill McArthur's wife. All three would be convicted and Orsini, who had earlier beaten charges that she had murdered her own husband or had him killed in their bedroom, would die in prison. Robinson had arrested McArthur after talking to Mrs. Orsini. Robinson feuded with the prosecuting attorney, Dub Bentley, over the case and then dragged McArthur from his home in the middle of the night a second time and jailed him, claiming that he had evidence that the attorney was plotting the sheriff's murder. Robinson said McArthur had met with two hired guns in the woods near Malvern on a certain day. It would turn out that McArthur was in the Pulaski County Courthouse that day and was spotted there by numerous witnesses, including a judge, the prosecuting attorney, and several journalists who covered the courthouse. The two young men whom Robinson arrested after they told him about the meeting in the woods with Bill McArthur admitted that they were merely playing a stupid practical joke on the sheriff that got out of hand when Robinson took them seriously and arrested McArthur.

To every sensible observer of all this, Robinson was either a buffoon, a dangerous megalomaniac, or an unhinged exhibitionist. But, like Donald Trump thirty-five years later, his electrifying showmanship was what mattered. The electorate in the rural precincts from border to border loved it. Someone was finally taking on a black federal judge and all the other smug bastards in Little Rock.

When the congressional seat in central Arkansas became open in 1984, Robinson filed for the seat and all eight counties voted him in, over a fairly stellar field comprising Secretary of State Paul Riviere, a lanky, dimpled twin of actor Warren Beatty; Dr. Dale Alford, who had once represented the congressional district after championing the segregationist cause in Little Rock's school crisis; Thedford Collins, a smart African American consultant; the reformist state Senator Stanley Russ of Conway; and the durable Republican, Judy Petty.

In January 1985, Robinson joined a Congress already spellbound by another barreling former sheriff, James Traficant Jr. of Ohio. On the job, Robinson was considerably more sedate than the colorful Traficant, who wore crazy outfits, sported wild hairdos (later revealed after his arrest to be a toupee), and raved against federal agencies on the House floor. Traficant eventually was convicted of bribery, racketeering, and tax evasion and was expelled by the House of Representatives by a vote of 420 to 1.

After his defeat in the governor's race in 1990, Robinson himself was somewhat disgraced by revelations that he was the chief abuser of the House of Representatives bank, on which he had written 998 hot checks in his short span in Washington.

At the Rose Garden ceremony where Robinson was inducted into the Republican Party, the gallery included Mary Anne Stephens, the youngish wife of Jackson T. Stephens, the head of the big family investment house. Clad in a brilliant red dress, she beamed and clapped at the announcement and at Robinson's short remarks. It raised the question of whether the Stephenses had helped Atwater persuade the congressman to switch parties.

Jack Stephens had given heavily to the campaigns of Reagan and Bush. After all, it was already known that Sheffield Nelson, the family enemy, was also switching parties and running for governor as a Republican. Stephens now had two thankless foes running for governor, Nelson and Clinton, and one potential savior in Tommy Robinson.

Mary Anne Stephens, a political neophyte, ran Robinson's campaign for governor, at least figuratively; Atwater was calling the shots from Washington until the first of March, when he collapsed at a fundraiser in Washington and was diagnosed with brain cancer. After Robinson was beaten in 1990, Mary Anne romanced the legendary old coach of the Super Bowl champion Miami Dolphins, Don Shula, a neighbor to the Stephens vacation compound on Indian Creek Island in Miami. She promptly divorced Jack, married Shula, and began to cut TV commercials with him. She got Jack's Indian Creek estate in the divorce and also a million dollars a year for life. She would continue to make news for years, Tommy Robinson–style, by suing Jack's younger son for diminishing his late father's estate and potentially risking the end of her million-a-year alimony, and also by complaining to a Florida board that it had no right to impoverish the Shulas by raising ad-valorem taxes on their four-million-dollar compound.

No one had anticipated that Robinson would have to face Sheffield Nelson before he could take on Clinton, or perhaps they assumed that Nelson would do something else rather than face the popular Robinson. Nelson had been a big supporter of Robinson, owing to their mutual friend, Jerry Jones. But Nelson's ambitions had always been as consuming as either Clinton's or Robinson's. The reader will remember that, as a youngster fresh out of college and working as Witt Stephens's office assistant at the gas company, Nelson had tried to take over the Young Democratic Clubs of Arkansas but was foiled by renegades led by Jim McDougal, who would later become a friend and business partner of Clinton and then Nelson.

Nelson would have been characterized as a liberal in the 1980s. He helped run Senator Edward M. Kennedy's presidential campaign in Arkansas in 1980 and championed much higher severance taxes on the industry that he led. He supported Bill Clinton and was appointed by Clinton to chair the Arkansas Industrial Development Commission. He waited for Clinton to move on so that he could run for governor, and waited…and waited. Clinton always decided to do one more term. When it became clear that Clinton was going to run one more time in 1990, Nelson saw his political future dimming as long as he was a Democrat, especially with two other dimpled young stars—Jim Guy Tucker and Steve Clark—waiting in the same wings. He had to strike then, and his best chance was the Republican Party, which had prevailed in the last two presidential races in Arkansas, and it was a Republican of lesser stature who had defeated Clinton in 1980.

Now he would be taking on both the flamboyant Robinson and his own nemesis for fifteen years, the Stephens family and political organization. Nelson had no close connections in the GOP; Robinson had Jack Stephens, Stephens's wife, and rural Republicans who loved his combative style and theatrics.

It was both a delicate and a volatile situation: two old chums now in a death struggle for their political careers. It was not apt to turn out very well for either one.

Nelson and Jones, partners in the Arkla Gas hierarchy and also the architects of the gas-lease deal that had made Jones a quick mega-millionaire, jointly owned a duck-hunting club, and they hired Robinson to "manage" it. The three men hunted, drank, and partied together.

Robinson apparently had only a little trouble embracing Atwater's take-no-prisoners strategy. If you got in a race to win, lifelong friendships could not stand in the way. Gingerly at first—Jerry Jones's daughter, after all, was his chief of staff—Robinson attacked the gas-leasing deal between Nelson and Jones that had made his pal a multimillionaire in a couple of years, but without personally disparaging his old friend. Nelson had put Jones on the Arkla board of directors and assigned him rights to the richest gas field in the region for $15 million, partly financed by Arkla, and after Jones made a fortune from the leases Arkla had to buy it all back from Jones for more than ten times the $15 million. It was a bad deal for the gas company's customers, and Sheffield Nelson, the president, was to blame for making such a lousy deal, Robinson said. Gas customers across the state were paying dearly and they should blame Nelson, he said.

The exchanges got nastier and nastier, and Robinson threw aside his earlier restraint. He implied that his old Rose City friend was a crook. Jones raged to an emissary that he had bought life insurance for the ungrateful bastard and paid his family's medical bills, and his thanks was to be called a crook. Jones's daughter promptly quit the congressman's staff.

The trio had another connection. Nelson and Jones had formed a company, bought a farm in Monroe County, and leased it to Robinson for $25,000 a year. When he had not remitted his payment by year's end, Nelson announced the farm arrangement in January 1990 and said Robinson had reneged on his lease payment. If he couldn't even manage a little farm, Nelson wondered, how could he manage the state's affairs? Nelson and Jones were going to expel Robinson from the farm, although he was having it managed for him while he was in Congress. That caused another exchange of insults among the three.

Nelson landed the last blow. Shortly before the primary, his campaign—someone at least—arranged for Robinson's confidential medical records from the House of Representatives to be leaked to the Little Rock media. Congressman Robinson had told the House's attending physician in 1985 soon after arriving in Washington that he drank more than a pint of bourbon every day and used a strong sedative that was supposed to cause paranoia. In a state where three-fourths of the counties were dry, Robinson knew that his rural admirers would not find his drinking exploits and drug use amusing. He cried foul and accused Nelson of somehow stealing the records of his confidential conference with the physician, which were supposed to be inviolate.

The public melodrama had a secret aspect. Although Bill Clinton himself always said he never feared the Robinson candidacy, his big support-

ers and some of his campaign team were not so confident. A few of them organized an effort to persuade thousands of Clinton partisans who were not registered as Democrats to vote in the Republican primary for Nelson, figuring that he would be easier to beat than Robinson, owing to the growing scandal over the Arkoma gas deal. Crossover voting had always been common but rarely effective. Until the 1990s, few Republicans voted in their own primaries because there were few races on the ballot and nearly every county officeholder was decided in the Democratic primary. There were suspicions that Republicans sometimes voted for the weaker of the Democratic candidates. When Winthrop Rockefeller was governor, the Democratic machine would get people to run against him in the little Republican primary hoping to sidetrack Rockefeller there. It never was close.

James L. "Skip" Rutherford, a public relations director for Arkla after Nelson left the company and a close adviser to Clinton, called numerous people to organize crossover votes for Nelson, although he said Clinton had mildly discouraged it. A total of 86,977 voted in the Republican primary, and Nelson won by 7,515 votes.

Until he died in late winter, Atwater kept up with the campaign. Had he remained active, you have to believe that he would have counteracted the crossover and medical deceits with a last-minute bombshell or charge. Instead, he was praying with a Jesuit priest in Washington and penning mortifications to the men he had savaged.

Everything, starting with Atwater's freak of fate, proved to be fortuitous for Bill Clinton. He had no particular reason to fear his re-election chances in 1990, other than a public weariness with him after a dozen years of currency and the pent-up frustrations of ambitious young men who were awaiting their turn at stardom, like Sheffield Nelson. For Nelson, the remedy was the Republican Party, where there were still traces of the progressivism of Winthrop Rockefeller. For three others—Jim Guy Tucker, Steve Clark, and Thomas C. McRae—switching parties was not an escape but a surrender.

Since his defeat at Clinton's hands in 1982, Tucker had practiced law and accumulated some wealth by developing real estate and cable television franchises across the country and in Great Britain. But politics had always ruled his ambition. He announced his plans to run for governor in 1990 early, obviously hoping that it would encourage Clinton to forego another race and organize his 1992 presidential race. He and Clinton exchanged a few barbs but, knowing that Clinton would corral nearly all the available money, Tucker surrendered when Clinton formally announced he was running and filed as a candidate for lieutenant governor instead. The decision proved to be both fortuitous and unfortunate. Clinton's election to the presidency elevated Tucker to the governorship in 1992 but made him the misdirected target of Republican wrath, which led to his conviction on a variety of trumped-up charges and his resignation from office in 1996.

Steve Clark was not going to be deterred. With a deeply dimpled chin, a linebacker's physique, and a perfect coiffure, Clark was a troublesome rival. He was the longest-serving attorney general in Arkansas history, he had been a faculty colleague of Bill and Hillary Clinton at the U of A law school, and he had been Governor Pryor's chief of staff for two years. He had been a model attorney general, too. He told the legislature that the separation-of-powers doctrine prohibited the lawmakers from vetoing the rules of executive agencies. When the legislature passed the creation-science bill in 1981, he warned legislators that the courts were apt to rule that it violated the U.S. Constitution's establishment clause, and when a lawsuit was filed in federal court challenging the act he insisted upon defending it himself, rejecting the pleas of the law's rabid defenders that he claim the

Bible's account of the creation in six days as the law's defense. He argued instead that describing the school curriculum, whether wisely or not, fell within the scope of legislative power. When U.S. District Judge William Overton ruled that the law violated the First Amendment's free-speech and religious-establishment clauses, Clark didn't appeal the decision, angering evangelicals like Rev. Jerry Falwell, who doubted that the attorney general was a real Christian. The popular televangelist Pat Robertson denounced Clark on his *700 Club* show, suggesting that he was an agent of Satan.

Thanks to an *Arkansas Gazette* reporter who was pursuing an entirely different quarry, Bill Clinton never had to contend with Clark. The attorney general, who had argued eight cases before the U.S. Supreme Court, was convicted of misusing state funds and resigned before the election. He already had pulled out of the governor's race, soon after the *Gazette* published articles about his abuse of his expense account. Clark was sure that Clinton or his supporters had planted the story of his accidental misdeeds with the *Gazette*. Actually, Clinton had nothing to do with it.

In January 1990, a few days after Clark announced his plans to run for governor, Max Brantley, the city editor of the *Gazette*, made an assignment to Anne Farris, a reporter. Brantley suspected that Secretary of State William J. McCuen, an amiable scalawag, was cheating the state on his expense account and perhaps in other ways. Bill McCuen had taken trips, one of them to Hollywood, with two lovely staffers accompanying him. (A few years later, McCuen was convicted and sentenced to seventeen years in prison for bribery, tax evasion, and accepting a kickback, but it had nothing to do with his companions or his travels.) Brantley told Farris to search the records in the state auditor's office and compile a record of the expenses for which the taxpayers had reimbursed McCuen. While she was at it, for comparison, she should look at the same records in the same time span for the other six constitutional officers. Brantley was sure that it would show McCuen to be the reckless scamp that the press corps was sure he was.

Farris came back with a different story. McCuen's expenses were not out of line with the others. The only one that stood out was Mr. Clean, the suspicionless attorney general, who had put scores of expensive dinners and lunches on the attorney general's Visa card. Farris wrote a lengthy story about the seven officers' spending, including Clinton's, and leading with Clark's exorbitant spending. The seven constitutional officers had spent $365,616 the prior year, $115,729 of it by the attorney general. The article mentioned several expensive meals and recorded Clark's guests.

The next morning, John Brummett was at his desk in the *Gazette* newsroom when a woman who was listed as one of the guests at a lunch at the Capital Hotel restaurant called and said the article was in error—she had not been Clark's guest at lunch. Another lunch voucher listed Judge Richard S. Arnold of the U.S. Eighth Circuit Court of Appeals and Carl S. Whillock, president and chief executive officer of the Arkansas Electric Cooperatives, Inc., as guests at a $243.78 lunch at Alouette's, Little Rock's fanciest restaurant at the time. Both wanted a retraction because they had not been at such a lunch. It looked especially bad for Judge Arnold, because the attorney general sometimes practiced before him.

Farris went back to the auditor's office and, along with other reporters, got a list of all of Clark's credit-card expenses for the previous couple of years along with the guests at each. Clark often had recorded the business discussed at the business lunches. Farris also went to the attorney general's office and got all his long-distance telephone bills, which identified the people whom he had called. Some apparently were to girlfriends or friends with whom the attorney general had no business. Then she and other reporters telephoned the lunch and dinner guests and phone-call recipients around the country. Many said they had, indeed, dined with Clark and that he had picked up the tab. Just as many said they had not. Clark's family had a history of alcohol problems. He had a habit of picking up the tab at parties, some at which he was an invited guest. Cocktails frequently were part of the tab. One group of state employees threw a party at a west Little Rock diner and invited Clark. He went back to the kitchen and paid the bill and a generous tip, over the protest of a couple of members of the party. Unbeknownst to them, Clark charged the expenses on his state Visa card and put their names on his voucher, which got them subpoenas when the prosecutor began to look into the *Gazette*'s reporting.

Arkansas's constitutional officers collected the lowest salaries of their breed in the country, and for recompense the legislature gave them expense accounts with fewer requirements than for other state employees. Constitutional officers did not have to record the guests at business lunches or mention any business that was discussed. Had he not recorded all the false guests, he would not have gotten into trouble—at least nothing more than an article about his spending more than the other six elected officials. But Clark had hired a former classmate at Arkansas State University as his office accountant. She was a stickler for strict accounting. She insisted that he was obliged to list the guests on each expense voucher, whether the law

required it or not. She refused to submit the vouchers without them. So at the end of the month, Clark would scribble names aimlessly on the back of the vouchers and send them to the auditor for payment. In so doing, he incriminated himself. He was buying meals and cocktails for girlfriends and friends who were not there on official business, and his scribblings exposed it. Prosecuting Attorney Chris Piazza charged him with fraud.

After his conviction in Pulaski Circuit Court, Clark resigned, forfeited his license to practice law, and left the state. His careers in law and politics were suddenly over. He wandered in the wilderness for years but finally conquered his alcoholism, recovered his equanimity, returned to Arkansas, and built a new career in economic development.

Clinton was left with a single credible opponent. Tom McRae was a gangling, self-effacing, introverted man who devoted his life to causes, perhaps because he was driven by his heritage. His great-grandfather, Thomas C. McRae, was a banker, lawyer, and congressman who led the virtuous wing of the populist movement early in the twentieth century. He tried to rewrite the state Constitution in 1919 to make it a more progressive document and argued for higher taxes on business, an income tax, land and forest preservation, and prison reform. He was elected governor in 1920 at the

age of sixty-eight, but the conservative legislature spurned his reforms. The younger Tom McRae, who went to school with me at El Dorado, thought his mission was to finally instill his grandfather's ideals in the public life of the state. He joined President John F. Kennedy's Peace Corps and worked with the poor in Nepal. He met his Scottish wife in Cairo, Egypt, after their public-service stints (she had been a volunteer in Malaysia). He was running the Model Cities program at Texarkana when Governor Bumpers asked him to join his administrative staff. For more than a decade, he ran the Winthrop Rockefeller Foundation, where he sought to use Rockefeller's money to foster rural development, sustainable farming, and equal rights. When he died of Lou Gehrig's disease a few years after his race for governor, Bumpers said McRae would have been a great governor.

Predictably, he raised virtually no money for the race. With Nelson, Tucker, and Clark sidetracked, he became Clinton's only viable opponent, owing mostly to his visibility running the Rockefeller charity.

He was a terrible campaigner. Serious, soft spoken, a preternatural policy wonk, McRae induced sleep every time he made a political talk or even a statement. No slogans, no catchphrases—only lectures on proper planning, balanced development, environmental degradation, tax policy.

The culmination came under the dome in the rotunda of the State Capitol, where McRae planned to present a part of his program to assembled reporters. He didn't have the money for televised commercials. He suggested in the rotunda that Clinton was out campaigning for president—he was in Washington that day—while the affairs of the state went unaddressed. In the midst of his lecture, a woman nudged her way through the reporters and cameramen to confront McRae, who had a life-size poster of Bill Clinton at his side. It was Hillary. She said McRae's own Rockefeller Foundation reports had recognized Clinton's good work in education and development and suggested that he should be ashamed of himself. When McRae would start a tentative reply, she bearded him some more. Brought up as a chivalrous Southern gentleman, McRae could only stammer and blush. He didn't dare admonish a woman, especially the First Lady. Clinton wrote in his memoir that Hillary had plotted the confrontation when they spoke on the phone the previous evening.

All the media recorded his confusion and embarrassment. McRae was not going to win anyway, but the humiliating episode cost him any momentum. Clinton received 54.7 of the votes in the primary, McRae 38.7 percent, and four also-rans the rest.

Disposing of Sheffield Nelson in the general election was chancier. Clinton picked up on Tommy Robinson's charges about Nelson's and Jones's gas-leasing deal. He asked the Public Service Commission—he had appointed all three commissioners—to look into the old deal again to see to what extent it had impacted ratepayers. When it finished its investigation after the election, the commission ordered Arkla to refund $17 million to the ratepayers. The commission had no authority under the law to require Jones to reimburse either ratepayers or the gas company. Nelson sought to make it appear that Clinton had advocated higher taxes and spending with a last-minute commercial that carried a one-second clip from Clinton using the phrase "tax and spend." Clinton rushed a radio commercial responding to it and attacking Nelson to stations overnight the day before the election. He had vowed in 1980 never again to let an attack go unaddressed.

While the matter of Dan Lasater and his alleged cocaine distribution seemed to have short legs, more credible character issues were percolating. Larry Nichols, an angry and slightly paranoid man whom Clinton had directed his Development Finance Authority to fire, called a press conference on the steps of the State Capitol and released a list of five women who he said had had affairs with Clinton. Nichols, who said he was a Clinton supporter, had pestered the governor's office for months to find a job for him in state government, and he finally landed one at the development office. Soon he was sitting in his state office and making long-distance calls to support the Contra rebels in Nicaragua, who were trying to overthrow the leftist government of Nicaragua. Bill Simmons, a reporter for the Associated Press, wrote a story about his having made some 120 calls at the taxpayers' expense, which got him fired. Simmons asked Clinton about the five women whom Nichols had named. He denied the affairs and suggested that the reporter call the women. All denied it, although much later a couple of them would say that they had had sex with Clinton and one, the famous Gennifer Flowers, would claim to have had a twelve-year affair with him. No newspaper and only one radio station carried anything about Nichols's accusation then. Nichols would carry on his crusade against the Clintons for another twenty-six years. A Nichols video claiming that he had helped Hillary Clinton murder people would figure in her defeat for president in 2016. A *New York Times* columnist would recite a conversation he had overheard at an adjoining restaurant table in a Midwestern city among women who had seen the video and were voting for Donald Trump rather than the killer.

Nelson, in the final crucial days, could not bring himself to release a racy television commercial that implied that Clinton, whose images but not his name appeared in the ad, was involved in illicit sex with women and perhaps other shady doings. Jerry Jones and Nelson's own people had assembled what they thought was evidence, or at least credible accounts, of his womanizing. Nelson thought his own reputation might have been ruined by what he thought was scandal mongering over the Arkoma deal, but he quailed at releasing the ad.

Lee Atwater—or Tommy Robinson—would have had no hesitation.

Having disposed of two big challengers, beating Robinson cleanly without dirtying his hands and Nelson with the renewed largesse of the Stephens family, Clinton found his standing strengthened for his last bouts with the legislature and his political courage reinforced. Robinson and Nelson had complained that Clinton's tax increases had not achieved the goals he sought and they had promised not to raise taxes, for anything. Clinton had hinted that he wanted to do more for education, health services, and the highways.

The 1991 legislative session would prove to be his most productive. His tendency to be wishy-washy—as Fisher's cartoons often portrayed him—and to please the last person who talked to him seemed to vanish. In 1989, he had vetoed a bill written for the National Rifle Association that prohibited cities and counties from adopting ordinances that regulated firearms in any way, and narrowly made his veto stick. In 1991, an NRA lobbyist came to town to see to it that the gun bill votes stuck this time. He met Clinton in a hallway outside the Senate and told him that, if he vetoed the NRA bill this time and ran for president in 1992, the NRA would see to it that he was crushed in Texas and other nearby states. Although Clinton was telling people, at least in Arkansas, that he doubted he would run for president, he told the NRA man that he looked forward to the battle in Texas. He got friends in the Senate to hold up the NRA bill until the session's last days. It passed by huge margins in both houses and was delivered to his desk. He waited until the legislature had adjourned *sine die* and vetoed it. The NRA would be the one big interest group that Bill Clinton would stand up to. In his first term as president, he signed into law the Brady Handgun Violence Prevention Act, also known as the "Brady Bill," which required federal background checks on firearms purchases and imposed a five-day waiting period on purchases, and also a ten-year ban on the purchase of assault weapons.

Beyond that display of fortitude, Clinton got the legislature to pass the biggest highway program in history (except for Sid McMath's big bond program in 1949) and a nickel-a-gallon tax on motor fuels, to raise the sales tax for schools by half of one percent and collect taxes on the sale of used vehicles, to toughen the penalties on polluters, and to expand medical services for the indigent under Medicaid. Reminiscent of 1979, his youthful confidence was restored enough to embolden him to tackle the country next. What could go wrong?

XVIII
War and Peace

B y the last decade of the twentieth century, newspapers were already playing a diminishing role in political discourse in Arkansas and everywhere else, although the Clintons would discover as soon as they began their quest for the presidency that one reporter writing about one insignificant event in their distant past could still profoundly change their destiny as well as the country's. Newspapers and printed journals of all kinds would be supplanted more and more each year by electronic forms of communication and a constantly expanding profusion of social-media platforms where real news and informed opinion became indistinguishable from propaganda, rumors, and the manipulations of any individual, group, or foreign power with designs upon American elections and the formation of government policy.

In Arkansas, muting the voice of newspapers first followed the old-fashioned route: hardening competition and a shrinking market. At noon on October 18, 1991, two weeks after Clinton had announced his presidential candidacy, the media company that owned the *Arkansas Democrat* bought the assets of the *Arkansas Gazette,* and the oldest paper west of the Mississippi River closed, ending a struggle in which the proprietors of both papers had been hemorrhaging tens of millions of dollars a year. The next morning, the *Democrat* arrived on people's doorsteps with a new nameplate, the *Arkansas Democrat-Gazette*, with the former title of each appearing in its old font—𝕲𝖆𝖟𝖊𝖙𝖙𝖊 in the Old English Blackletter that the paper had used since 1819—but the paper's contents representing the work only of the *Democrat* staff. The only *Gazette* staff members who were retained were two columnists whom the surviving paper was obliged to pay, even if it didn't publish their columns, because they had ten-year employment contracts. After a nine-year respite, the *Democrat* and its managing editor returned to their unrelenting enmity toward Bill Clinton and now to his candidacy for president. The hostility of his state's leading newspaper had only a marginal impact on Clinton's campaign in 1992; Arkansas was the only state in which he received a majority of the votes against George H. W. Bush and Ross Perot in what was essentially a three-man race. But the end of "the newspaper war" and of the independent *Gazette* would produce a notable, though incalculable, effect on Arkansas's politics and the scope of government. The state was gradually following the trend of other Southern states after the passage of the civil-rights laws of the 1960s, away from the old Democratic Party of both Jim Crow and Franklin Roosevelt and toward the increasingly rightward-leaning Republican Party. The transformation would be nearly complete in twenty years, but it might have been no different—and the quality of the paper perhaps much worse—if the *Gazette,* not the *Democrat,* had survived under its last owner, the Gannett Company, Incorporated.

Thus, readers may excuse a slight diversion from our story, for the "newspaper war" and its armistice, or surrender, were both a cause and a reflection of the shifting political and social currents.

J. N. Smithee, a former Confederate soldier who had once edited and owned the *Gazette,* acquired a newspaper at Little Rock in 1878 to battle the *Gazette.* He named it the *Arkansas Democrat.* The *Gazette* accused Smithee of making his newspaper sound like the house organ for the Democratic Party to hide the fact that he actually was allied secretly with the liberal carpetbaggers of the Republican Party. Smithee never seemed to be a Republican but rather a leader of the populist faction of Democrats, who favored free silver and repudiating the state's debt. He would soon sell the *Democrat* to satisfy some legal and financial problems and acquire the *Gazette* again, before selling it again, this time to the Heiskell family, and then committing suicide in 1902. The papers would compete head to head for most of the twentieth century, but not so much philosophically. Both were editorially conservative and affiliated themselves, like nearly every journal and nearly all the white people in the state, with Jim Crow and the Democratic Party. The *Gazette* raged against the personal income tax when the legislature and Governor Harvey Parnell enacted the tax in 1929. J. N. Heiskell, the editor, wrote that taxing income and wealth would stymie economic growth and bring doom. Sure enough, as soon as Arkansas— which had the lowest taxes, lowest per-capita income, and highest per-capita government debt in the country—imposed a personal and a corporate income tax, all of America fell into the deepest and longest depression in history. Forty years later, when Governors Rockefeller and then Bumpers sought to increase the tax, the newspaper reversed its stance and endorsed raising income-tax rates. The rates were raised under Bumpers, and the state prospered. Thus, if it had dared, the newspaper could have claimed to have been proved, by divine guidance, right both times.

The *Gazette* was the leading paper—in readers, revenues, and every other way—until the school crisis at Little Rock in 1957, when its unpopular stand against the governor's efforts to forestall integration set it back a few years. By the mid-1960s it had regained a bare lead in circulation and advertising, but the changing habits of newspaper readers left afternoon papers nearly everywhere struggling to compete. The *Democrat*, owned and run by K. A. Engel and then his nephews from 1926 until 1974, declined steadily. Its daily circulation was only half the *Gazette*'s when Engel's heirs sold it to the Palmer Media Group for $3.7 million. Walter E. Hussman Sr., the son-in-law of Clyde E. Palmer, who had started the chain of daily papers at Texarkana, Hot Springs, El Dorado, Magnolia, and Camden, named his son publisher of the *Democrat*. Walter E. Hussman Jr., then only twenty-seven, struggled to turn the afternoon paper around and couldn't. After three years, he approached Hugh Patterson at the *Gazette* about a ten-year joint-operating contract, under which the *Gazette* would print Hussman's afternoon paper on its presses, they would share some operating expenses while maintaining separate staffs, and the Palmer group would get a small percentage of the overall profits.

Patterson made a business decision, an unpardonable one by hindsight. Little Rock was about the smallest and poorest of the thirty-four American cities that still had competing newspapers, and the arrangement seemed to him likely to only impoverish both, because the Little Rock market was not growing and the afternoon paper was almost certainly going to continue losing subscribers and advertisers. The *Gazette*'s owners were not getting rich, but it beat subsidizing the losing *Democrat* operations for a decade.

It seemed like the final blow for Hussman, but in desperation to keep a place in Little Rock he came up with a few bold plans. He had one advantage, a very big one, if he chose to risk it. The parent company had lucrative newspaper operations in the five south Arkansas cities plus other money-making media assets that could subsidize a losing business in the capital. The *Gazette* had little more than its newspaper plant. How could Hussman make the *Gazette* unprofitable, unsustainable?

He decided to abandon the afternoon market and publish the *Democrat* in the morning, head-to-head with the *Gazette*, an act that at the time looked suicidal. He made personal classified advertisements free, for as long as a person wanted to run one, and reduced display advertising rates to a small fraction of the *Gazette*'s. Although the *Gazette* had a huge advantage in display advertising from big merchants like Dillard's department stores, because advertising in the *Gazette* reached people with more spendable income, classified advertising was the paper's principal source of revenue. Hussman learned of a "total market coverage" strategy in another city: throw the new morning paper free in the yards of nearly every home. You might subscribe to the *Gazette,* but you also got the *Democrat* free. Its classified advertising section grew larger by the week; the *Gazette's* shrank.

To Hugh Patterson and his business manager, J. R. Williamson, at least, it seemed suicidal. The rest of the Palmer Media Group could subsidize all this for a while, but what sane businessman, even one with all those assets, would do that for long?

Hussman added staff to beef up the reporting to try to compete with the *Gazette's* news coverage. He added pages to the daily paper and opened the news hole, again to show that it could match the *Gazette's* daily offerings of national and international as well as state and local news. The *Democrat's* operating losses were mounting, but the rest of the media company's assets were still making money.

The *Democrat* expanded its sports coverage, where it had lagged behind the *Gazette* and its renowned sports editor, Orville Henry. Hussman would eventually lure away Henry himself, along with thousands of his devotees, when the new corporate owners of the *Gazette* slashed Henry's lengthy columns on the Arkansas Razorbacks or just didn't run them at all. Orville called me one Friday night from Fayetteville and said Jack Stephens—the financier, former University of Arkansas trustee, and Razorback financial supporter—had brokered a deal for him to work for Hussman. He didn't want to do it, but he was going to do it the following Monday unless the Gannett bosses at the *Gazette* agreed to match the deal and reprimand the new sports copy editor who was tearing up his stories. I called Max Brantley, the *Gazette's* metro editor. Saturday morning, Brantley talked to Walker Lundy, the editor who was sent to Little Rock by Gannett, and told him that Orville was going to go to the *Democrat* if he didn't match Hussman's deal.

"And we care?" Lundy asked wryly. He was glad to be rid of an old guy who was paid too much and was too wordy. Lundy liked very short sentences and snappy articles about lighthearted topics, such as food and movies. He cared nothing about the Razorbacks. Max persuaded him that Henry was an important asset and it would be a blow if he went to the *Democrat.* Lundy finally agreed. He called Henry several times on his business phone at Fayetteville, not his home line, and got no answer. Orville's wife, Ann, let the phone ring. Monday, Henry went to see Hussman and they announced that his Razorback reports would appear in the *Democrat* in the future.

The *Gazette* had always refused to compete with all the small daily papers in the Arkansas newspaper contests, for the best sports story, editorial, photography, general excellence, etc., believing that it was unfair to small papers with limited staffs and resources. The *Democrat* entered every contest, and when it won most of the awards it publicized the triumph in news stories, full-page ads, and in the radio and television media. Arkansas's Award-winning Newspaper, the ads proclaimed. That would change after Gannett bought the *Gazette* in 1986 and the new publisher ordered all of us to enter every Arkansas contest. The *Gazette* started winning most of the awards. Having been a judge in several such contests, I thought they were all silly. Uninformed judges choose the flashiest stories, editorials they agree with, columns that match their own sense of humor, and page designs and typography that match their own publication's.

Four years after the *Gazette* closed, the *Democrat-Gazette* printed a big story and an ad proclaiming that it had won first place for deadline news reporting in a regional newspaper contest. It was for a massive article on the death of Orval Faubus that had appeared in the paper the morning after his death in December 1994. The contest judge obviously did not know that newspapers maintain obituaries on prominent people, which they can drop into the paper when needed. It must have appeared to the judge that it was a whale of a feat for someone to quickly compile eight thousand words on the former governor when he died just before the newspaper's deadline. I had written that article for the *Gazette*—the last news article I wrote the weekend before I was kicked upstairs to write opinion in January 1979. Over the next twelve years I had updated it occasionally, such as when Faubus ran for governor the ninth time, when his wife Elizabeth divorced him, and when she was murdered. My article was still in the *Gazette* computer archive when Hussman's people took over the newspaper in 1991. A *Democrat-Gazette* editor altered it slightly to insert comments about Faubus's death and to transpose some of Faubus's own accounts of his feats in the 1957 school crisis for mine. I actually was happy to see the product of my labors, that long weekend in 1979, finally in print.

By 1984, Hugh Patterson had realized his misjudgment in turning down the joint operating agreement. The *Gazette* was still barely profitable, but only by shrinking the paper's news hole every day, reducing the daily pages, leaving staff vacancies unfilled, and skimping on other operating costs. Regular staff raises came to a halt. It was clear by then that Palmer Media and Hussman could and might continue the strategy forever. The *Demo-*

crat was still far from profitable, but it was improving.

Patterson filed a lawsuit in U.S. District Court, alleging that the *Democrat* owners were violating federal antitrust laws by giving away or selling their product at far below cost in order to drive the competition out of business. It might have been an open-and-shut case on its merits, but there was a trial before a jury. The optics were not particularly good for the *Gazette*. It was still profitable and the *Democrat* wasn't. The *Gazette* trustees had given Patterson a nice bonus the previous year. The *Gazette's* chief litigator was a fancy Houston barrister, an antitrust specialist, who came to court with an expensive three-piece suit, fancy shoes, and a gold watch chain across his vest. I went to the trial one day and thought the *Democrat's* bow-tied attorney, Philip S. Anderson, was wearing an old suit worn shiny at the elbows, but I might have been mistaken. The plebeian jury might have been forgiven for wondering, what's wrong with giving your product away or cutting prices?

The jury delivered a verdict for the *Democrat* in March 1986, and Patterson went shopping for a buyer for his paper. A Florida entrepreneur in Patterson's tow toured the *Gazette* building one day that summer, but Patterson snuffed him as a buyer after learning that he owned a dog-racing franchise. A dog racer was not going to own the *Arkansas Gazette*. By 1986, newspaper organizations like Knight-Ridder, the New York Times Company, the McClatchy Company, Scripps Howard, and Landmark Media were not acquiring papers in the few remaining competitive markets, because the cost and risks were too high. Gannett, the largest media company in the world, was.

Gannett, which owned more than a hundred newspapers, television and radio stations, and other media, acquired the *Gazette* on October 31, 1986, for $51 million. Allen H. "Al" Neuharth, Gannett's cocky chairman, rode a stretch limousine for two hundred yards down Louisiana Street from his hotel to the *Gazette* building to announce the purchase to its employees. The message was, we have deep pockets. They did. Gannett expanded the staff, enlarged the paper, set up more bureaus around the state, gave many employees nice salary increases and better health insurance and pensions, and hired more African Americans and women. It was soon losing more money than the *Democrat*. It also sought to introduce a different perspective of what a newspaper should be: more colorful, less tedium and detail in reporting on government and public affairs, more emphasis on cultural and social affairs, and much shorter and snappier articles. Gannett soon

sidelined the *Gazette*'s editor, Carrick Patterson, son of the former publisher, and hired Walker Lundy, who had recently been fired from the same
job at the *Fort Worth Star Telegram*. Lundy seemed to fit the Gannett mold,
but he liked off-beat stories that would make readers scratch their heads
and wanted columnists to write about themselves, using the first-person
pronoun as much as possible so that readers would identify with the writer.

Unstated was Gannett's wish for a more conservative and congenial
slant for the daily and Sunday opinion pages. Liberalism did not sell in
the South. It would turn out that Hugh Patterson had received an unwrit-
ten commitment from Neuharth to preserve the *Gazette*'s liberal editorial doctrine, which Neuharth apparently was happy to do, since he liked
owning the oldest newspaper west of the Mississippi River, a paper that
had won two Pulitzer prizes and other tributes for its stands in 1957 and
other racial conflicts. Neuharth retired as the chairman shortly after the
purchase. The new publisher of the *Gazette*, William T. Malone, was a Republican who had helped manage Neuharth's pride and joy, the national
newspaper *USA Today*, and whose wife worked for Vice President George
H. W. Bush. Malone was persuaded by businessmen whom he met that the
Gazette's stagnant or waning circulation and advertising were the product
of a liberal editorial page that offended a deeply conservative populace and
particularly business interests.

Malone would try subtly for three years to change it, finally firing Lundy,
the man he had hired as editor, after Lundy fled to Florida to visit relatives
on the Friday before the 1988 presidential election. (The *Gazette* opinion
staff, ignoring Lundy's persuasion, had prepared an editorial endorsing
Michael Dukakis against Bush that would run in the Sunday paper. Malone
had assigned Lundy, who was not so conservative himself, to sit in on ed-
itorial-page conferences and to use his leverage to prevent such miscar-
riages as endorsing a Democrat.) Malone himself then left soon afterward
for a job at another Gannett paper. The next publisher, Craig Moon, set
out to be more direct in altering the paper's liberal vestiges by ordering
the editorial staff in January 1991 to start holding weekly conferences
in his office, where all editorial decisions would be made subject to his
approval and that of his editor, J. Keith Moyer. It became my presumption long afterward that Gannett had intervened at that point and told
Moon that negotiations were under way to sell the paper to Hussman. The
editorial conferences never occurred—Moon and Moyer stood us up for
three weeks—and we went about spouting deviant apostasies for the dura-

tion of the newspaper, another nine months.

What became known historically as "the newspaper war" should be ascribed to John Robert Starr, a longtime Associated Press writer and bureau chief, whom Hussman had hired to be the managing editor of the *Democrat*. If Starr, who was the AP's Capitol reporter when the *Gazette* assigned me to the Capitol full time in 1964, held any special enmity toward the newspaper we were not aware of it. But that enmity became apparent quickly after he became the *Democrat*'s managing editor. The *Arkansas Times*, then a monthly magazine, ran a lengthy article about his campaign against the *Gazette* and the unfolding "newspaper war." For the magazine's cover, Starr, wearing a battle helmet, posed for a picture squatting on top of a *Gazette* paper rack, clenching a knife in his teeth. Hussman said he nearly fired Starr over the stunt.

Starr wrote a daily column for the op-ed page, 365 days a year, passing on his opinions about everything but mostly about two subjects, the perfidies of Bill Clinton and the *Arkansas Gazette*. His job was to run the paper's news operation, not its opinion pages, which should have called for the paper's editor and management to avoid judgments about politicians and public issues for fear that it would influence the objectivity of his reporting staff or color the readers' perception of that objectivity. But Starr unlimbered on Clinton and his staff on everything they did during his first two-year term, which seemed to invigorate the paper's reporters and affect the play that the administration's miscues received in the paper. Meantime, he wrote often about how the *Gazette*'s news coverage over the years was dictated by its liberal editorial page, especially when Orval Faubus was governor. Starr was an admirer of Faubus.

After the Clintons opened their successful charm offensive in 1981 to proselytize the *Democrat* editor, his daily columns turned their focus more keenly to the real enemy, the *Gazette*—its reporting, its history, its editorial dishonesty, its poor business ethics. Sometimes it was personal, but usually not. In his columns, I eventually lost my name and became simply "the wet-noodle liberal." He wrote on a number of occasions that the *Gazette* refused to publish letters to the editor that took exception to its editorials or its news coverage. Being the one responsible for culling the dozens of letters that the paper received each day to fit the small space set aside for them, I knew it was not true, but Hugh Patterson instructed us not get into an exchange with Starr.

One day the *Democrat* op-ed page published a lengthy letter criticizing

344 The Education of Ernie Dumas

the *Gazette's* stance on some matters and also for refusing to publish critical letters, including the one he passed on to the *Democrat*. Our policy actually was to give first priority to letters taking issue with the *Gazette*, unless the letter attacked the paper for something that it had never said or a position that it never took. Starr's column, which ran alongside the man's letter, said the accompanying letter had been sent to the *Gazette* but that the paper had refused to publish it. He chastised the *Gazette* again for not printing letters that criticized it. Our policy was to keep every letter we received for a year, whether we published it or not. I did not remember receiving his letter and could not find it in my file of unprinted letters. I called the man at his home. He first insisted that he had sent the letter. I said I had never received it and asked how he had addressed it. I told him our policy was to print all such letters and that if he actually had read the paper's editorial page he would know that. He finally said he had not mailed it to us because he didn't read the *Gazette* but had read in the *Democrat* that the *Gazette* did not publish such letters. I offered to clip a few critical letters from recent issues and mail them to him. He apologized and asked if I wanted him to tell the *Democrat* of his mistake. I said it was his call.

After Gannett and Walker Lundy were running the *Gazette*, Starr repeated the accusation. Lundy sent me a one-sentence memo asking how we justified not printing letters that criticized us. I reviewed all the letters that were printed in both newspapers for the previous three months and sent him a summary. The *Gazette* had printed a number of critical letters during that period and the *Democrat* had not printed a single one, perhaps because it had not received any.

Starr's relentless attacks on the paper, and attacks by other sources connected to the *Democrat*, had little to do with the *Gazette's* demise five years after Gannett's purchase. Starr only reinforced the low esteem in which a significant part of the community had long held the paper and its editorial policies. Hussman's shrewd business strategy and his determination did the job. He was willing to risk the family fortune and the liquidity of its business empire to stay in Little Rock and prevail in a place he knew would never again support two newspapers. After four years, Gannett's executives and board concluded what Hugh Patterson had come to realize, that Hussman had the resources and the will to stay in the battle indefinitely. Unlike Gannett, he didn't have shareholders wondering what the corporation owed Arkansas that made it willing to sacrifice corporate profits in a tiny market that held little hope for the kind of profits that investors had come to expect. It sued for peace, proposing that they buy out Hussman, or he them. Hussman chose the latter option.

When the publisher and editor suddenly abandoned interest in reshaping the *Gazette*'s editorial policies, we figured that something was up. In late summer 1991, rumors were suddenly rampant that Hussman's company was buying the *Gazette*. Bob Douglas, the *Gazette*'s former managing editor and by then chairman of the Journalism Department at the University of Arkansas at Fayetteville—and sometimes a consultant and litigation witness for the Palmer media chain—telephoned me that weekend and said it was true. The sale had to be approved by the U.S. Department of Justice. The surviving paper would be called the *Arkansas Democrat-Gazette*. U.S. Representative William V. Alexander of the First District talked to the Justice Department and confirmed for us that the sale was awaiting a determination that, to satisfy antitrust rules, there was no buyer willing to continue competition in Little Rock. There was idle talk in the newsroom about employees buying and operating the paper. It was an absurd notion because most of the employees struggled to meet their rent or mortgage payments.

In the Dallas airport, a *Gazette* reporter ran into Harry Z. Thomason, a native of Hampton, a town across the Ouachita River from my birthplace. Thomason was concerned about the published rumor that the *Gazette* would be sold and closed. Thomason and his wife, Linda Bloodworth-Thomason, were successful film producers and also close friends with the Clintons. If there might be an employee buyout, he was willing to get involved and to put up a little cash. A half dozen or so employees hired Walter Davidson, a lawyer who was head of Common Cause in Arkansas, to look into the matter for us. He told the Justice Department that employees were trying to arrange a deal with other investors to buy the paper. It was ludicrous and all of us knew it. On Thursday, October 17, Davidson told us that he had been warned that the employees might be sued jointly by both parties for a frivolous effort that was costing both Gannett and Palmer Media millions of dollars a month. He let the Justice Department know that afternoon that we had folded. The sale and the *Gazette*'s closure occurred at noon the next day. At that moment, all our computers went offline.

The absence of the *Gazette*, which had served from time to time as a beacon for newspapers for Arkansas's first 172 years as a colony and state, would affect politics and social change in many ways, some not to my personal liking. In another way, however, it was fortunate for the Arkansas citizenry. It is depressing to contemplate what a Gannett *Gazette* would be like today. If the rest of the Gannett empire is any measure, in a world of crumbling newspaper journalism it would be a mere shadow of today's *Democrat-Gazette*.

XIX
To the Co-Presidency

I f Arkansas's first couple found it hard to co-exist with John Robert Starr, an occasional pesky reporter, or pedantic editorial writers, they would discover that a bigger stage brought only aggravation on a titanic scale. In the summer of 1991, when Clinton was traipsing around the country and encouraging speculation that he was running for president, he got a call from a White House aide whom he had begun to think of as a friend, as he tended to do with nearly everyone he met. Roger Porter was an off-and-on Harvard professor, when he wasn't in the service of Republican presidents—Nixon, Ford, Reagan, or Bush I—and he had worked with Clinton when the governor was collaborating with the Bush administration on school and welfare reform. He was Bush's assistant for economic and domestic policy. Porter chatted amiably with the governor and then got down to business. Was Clinton intending to run for president in 1992? Clinton was noncommittal and rambled on about how he thought Bush was missing some opportunities.

"Cut the crap, Governor," Porter finally interjected. The news media always needs someone to crucify, to destroy personally, he said, and if Clinton ran "we're going to give them you." That, anyway, was Clinton's memory of the conversation. They had heard the rumors about personal peccadilloes and, whether they were true or not, Porter said that was what the campaign would become. Clinton's character would be impugned beyond redemption. Lee Atwater, who was supposed to run the gentlemanly Bush's re-election campaign, had just died, but his wraith still hovered over the capital.

Bill Clinton—Hillary, too, probably—had concluded after his 1980 defeat and regeneration in two years that he could give even better than he could take and that he was adroit enough to handle anything that the Republicans threw at him. Porter's threat only exhilarated him.

Atwater had figured correctly that Clinton was the most skillful, likable, and adaptable candidate in the Democratic Party's stable. President Bush's short war in the Persian Gulf, in which the United States and its allies drove Saddam Hussein's Iraqi army out of Kuwait in forty-two days, made him immensely popular when the campaign got underway in the fall of 1991. New York governor Mario Cuomo, a Periclean orator, was the Democrats' strongest candidate, but he calculated that Bush was unbeatable and didn't run. When Rev. Jesse Jackson and Senator Al Gore of neighboring Tennessee decided not to run—Gore's son had been badly injured in a car accident—it left the South clear for Clinton. The post–Gulf War swoon was short lived. The country was battling through a mild but intractable recession. Bush's retreat from his 1988 vow—"Read my lips: no new taxes"—damaged him even more than he had feared. Ronald Reagan had gotten away with a no-tax promise, but not Bush. Reagan had promised at a rally at the Little Rock Convention Center a few days before the 1984 election that taxes would be raised "over my dead body," but he raised taxes over and over, including the big tax-reform act of 1986 that made Donald Trump and other big real-estate developers pay federal taxes, at least until they could get Congress in 1991 to restore their benefit. When the primaries arrived in 1992, too late for new Democrats to enter, Bush was in trouble.

Porter's promised character assassinations were not long in coming, although it would be hard to prove that many, if any, of them had their genesis in the White House or the Republican National Committee's dirty-tricks brigade. Their origins were local and sometimes years old.

The single national Republican plot to embarrass Clinton never materialized, at least during the campaign. Bush's Justice Department tried to get the U.S. attorney for the Eastern District, Charles A. "Chuck" Banks, a Mississippi County boy, to find a way to file charges again against the Clintons' former friend and associate James D. McDougal. Banks had prosecuted McDougal in 1989 for allegedly defrauding his little state-regulated thrift, Madison Guaranty Savings and Loan Association, but a jury acquitted him in 1990. Fresh charges against McDougal in 1992, even if they again went nowhere, could indirectly ensnare the Clintons and raise questions in the public mind about their character. Banks took seriously the principle that justice should be independent of politics and he refused to undertake an obviously politically motivated prosecution during a campaign.

But Larry Nichols's old list of five Clinton paramours still circulated. Reporters who came to Little Rock to write profiles of the young presidential candidate had the women's names and pestered them and others to get a sense of the truth. No one wrote an article then, but in January the cover of the monthly supermarket tabloid Star blared "MY 12-YEAR AFFAIR WITH BILL CLINTON" above a photograph of Gennifer Flowers. It quoted Flowers, a cabaret singer who had worked briefly for KARK-TV and a couple of radio stations in Little Rock, as saying that she and Clinton had been lovers for twelve years, starting when he was attorney general and ending in 1989. The *Star* editor confirmed that the paper had paid Flowers for the story. Clinton publicly denied that it was anything more than a friendly relationship, but then on January 28 Flowers had a press conference with the editor of the *Star* and her Little Rock attorney, Blake Hendrix, at the Waldorf Astoria hotel in New York City, where she circulated snippets of taped telephone conversations with Clinton that she said showed Clinton expected her to lie about their affair.

The claim of a twelve-year affair would be proven ridiculous, owing partly to her own subsequent account of her life during that period, but it also became clear, by Bill Clinton's own admissions years later, that theirs was something more than a friendship, whether it lasted one day or months. Flowers had talked openly with women co-workers at KARK-TV about her amours. She mentioned Clinton but mostly she talked breathlessly about weekends with her lover Evel Knievel, the daredevil stuntman who hurtled over canyons, barricades, and strings of cars and trucks on his motorcycle. The women eventually began to be dubious about her Knievel affair. The owners of a Little Rock radio station told me when Flowers surfaced in 1992 that they had hired her for a brief time to spin records from a studio near Little Rock. They said she volunteered that she was having an affair with a preacher in North Little Rock who was madly in love with her and had given her jewelry, but she never mentioned either Clinton or Knievel.

The Flowers bombshell, or even a hint that it was coming, would have driven any other candidate from the race. And it would have driven Clinton from the race had not Hillary said they were going to fight it and move on. They sat together for a grilling on the ABC show *60 Minutes*, which followed the Super Bowl. She insisted again upon their mutual love and respect, using a memorable invocation of a country music star.

"You know, I'm not sitting here, some little woman standing by her man like Tammy Wynette," she said. "I'm sitting here because I love him, and I respect him, and I honor what he's been through and what we've been through together. And, you know, if that's not enough for people, then, heck, don't vote for him."

There can be no doubt that her gritty performance on the show saved his career. At the time, it won her wide admiration for standing by her flawed husband, but it also played a role in the long-developing public perception of who she was and what motivated her—ultimately the narrative that the marriage was a mere arrangement for their mutual political ambitions.

Despite her insistence that she loved him and he her, her handling of the
revelations and allegations of affairs over the next seven years, combined
with her obsession with the sanctity of private lives—everyone's, but theirs
in particular—confirmed the notion by people who perhaps wanted to believe it anyway that the marriage was an arrangement for political convenience. But for the daughter of Dorothy Rodham, it was what every woman
must try to do.

Most people were eager to forgive a man in those days, if he showed a
little penitence, but for wives, reactions were more complicated and lasting. People, even women, tended to be more skeptical of wives' motives.
Shouldn't she have cast him aside or else let him handle the matter the best
that he could? That's what wives generally did. Or else, she must just be
coldly calculating their future careers. The images from that night, shown
repeatedly on television for years, would haunt her as she tried to refashion
herself without giving away too much about herself. At every turn in her
career, I would always remember my occasional encounters with her and
those of other reporters and editors at the paper, all reflecting her deep
suspicions about reporters and the media generally and her insistence on
keeping her life and the lives of her family as private as possible: her legal
opinion to the publisher of the *Gazette* that killed a long article of mine,
because it invaded a domain of privacy of the family of a man accused of
a heinous crime; her fury at reporters who tracked her and her husband
down while they were on vacation; her suspicion of newspaper people who
showed up at the Governor's Mansion for social events; her orders—yes,
that's the word—that the media let her daughter have a normal childhood
and not try to report on her school doings or photograph her. Bill Clinton
wouldn't have minded any of those things, but she did.

Hillary Clinton represented something new in presidential politics: a
wife who was a career woman with credentials at least as impressive as her
husband's, a wife who was going to have, by her husband's own account,
an important role in governing the country. Those things may have been
responsible for some of the efforts by newspaper reporters to turn insignificant events in the lives of the couple into serious-seeming scandals. After
all, if she's going to be a co-president of the United States, no matter is too
trivial to put on the front page.

Gennifer Flowers would not be the last one to test the resilience of Hillary's resolve to keep her private life and, insofar as she could, that of her
husband sacrosanct. The challenges would come almost weekly that spring

and summer. Her handling of all the inevitable issues, starting with Gennifer Flowers, became a sort of Rorschach test, forcing voters of both sexes to wrestle with questions about how a woman should handle the sometimes-conflicting roles of home, marriage, public life, and governance.

Bill Clinton was dogged by one stigma after another. His casual remark that he had once tried marijuana but didn't inhale brought widespread ridicule. His old friend Steve Smith, who had enjoyed a few joints in their days at Fayetteville, told me that it was true: Clinton would never touch the weed. Clinton's draft problems—which were similar to those of hundreds of thousands of American men of the era, including George W. Bush, Dick Cheney, and Donald Trump—caused him weeks of grief, partly owing to his being caught not only rationalizing his efforts to avoid the draft but also fudging the truth at one point, which he acknowledged in his memoir.

The couple would weather all the revelations and their occasional miscalculations, and that fact itself became his principal strength. Voters were impressed that the guy just wouldn't give up. Four years earlier, in the 1988 Democratic campaign, Senators Gary Hart and Joe Biden, both leading contenders, had dropped out of the race owing to allegations of sexual impropriety (Hart) and plagiarism (Biden). Not being a quitter became Clinton's most admirable trait. When he rose from near the bottom of the pack to second place in the New Hampshire primary, he became the Comeback Kid. After Clinton swept a string of Southern primaries, only California governor Jerry Brown among the big field of candidates staggered on toward the national convention and Clinton's inevitable victory. With all the splinter-party candidates, especially Ross Perot, who captured millions of Republican voters that fall with his anti-deficit rhetoric, Clinton coasted to an easy victory over President Bush.

□□□

While the Clintons survived all the character diversions that Lee Atwater had envisioned and then were promised by Roger Porter, one series of attacks that had nothing to do with sex, hallucinogens, or draft dodging—but, rather, an old Arkansas business rivalry—would follow the Clintons the rest of their days and would lead, arguably, to the second impeachment of a president of the United States. It would forever be referred to only as "Whitewater."

The groundwork for Whitewater has been laid in earlier chapters, but let's recapitulate its salient elements. Witt Stephens, the legendary investment broker and gas mogul, hired young Sheffield Nelson out of college in 1964 to be his executive assistant at Arkansas Louisiana Gas Company (now CenterPoint Energy). When Stephens retired as president nine years later, he handed the reins to his protégé. Call it ingratitude or independence, but the new CEO soon rejected overtures from his old boss and the Stephens family's gas production business, first refusing to renegotiate Arkla's old long-term gas-supply contracts with the Stephens interests and then refusing to transmit the Stephenses' gas in the Arkoma basin through Arkla's pipelines to interstate transmission pipelines along the Mississippi River so the Stephenses could market their gas for good prices in the industrial regions of the Ohio River Valley and beyond. The feud escalated for the next twenty years and spilled repeatedly into state election campaigns and finally the presidential election of 1992. Nelson, who shared some of Clinton's charismatic qualities, also coveted high political office.

The intrigues were carried on through surrogates: two national reporters for the *New York Times*. Nelson collaborated with Jeff Gerth, an investigative financial reporter who came to Little Rock in 1978 and again in 1992 and each time filed unfavorable articles on Witt and his brother Jack. First, it involved an arcane royalty dispute involving a tiny gas distribution company at Fort Smith owned by Witt Stephens, whose nephew was running for the U.S. Senate in 1978. Another *New York Times* reporter, Wendell "Sonny" Rawls Jr., who had had dealings with Jack Stephens in the so-called Bert Lance scandal during the Jimmy Carter administration, privately advised the Stephenses on how to steer Gerth away from the little gas story, which the *Times* eventually published anyway in bewildering detail shortly before the Senate election. The Stephenses' nephew, of course, lost the election to David Pryor.

Then, in 1983, owing almost certainly to a tip from Jack Stephens, Rawls came to Arkansas and wrote an article for the *New York Times* about how Nelson had arranged the sale of Arkla's mineral leases on 15,000 acres in the gas-rich Arkoma Basin to a small production company owned by his friend, Jerral W. "Jerry" Jones, for the absurdly low price of $15 million, mostly financed by Arkla itself. Jones would use his huge early earnings from the Arkoma deal to buy the Dallas Cowboys professional football franchise. The sale and the lucrative arrangements with Jones by 1983 was costing Arkla a fortune and beginning to imperil its financial health. The story suggested a conflict of interest by the two friends. They were hunting buddies and shared other business arrangements, and Nelson had put Jones on the Arkla board. Nelson, who had just announced plans to run for governor in 1984, flew to New York to meet with editors of the *Times* and threatened to sue the paper for libel if it did not retract the scandalous implications in Rawls's story.

The Arkoma gas deal would embroil Nelson in controversy for the next ten years. He did not run for governor in 1984, but he finally did in 1990. The Arkoma deal still proved to be such a blight that Clinton beat him in the general election. The Stephens family had been virulent foes of Clinton after he changed state finance laws to permit Wall Street brokerages and Clinton's friend Dan Lasater to carve away a considerable part of Stephens Inc.'s bond-underwriting business. But they joined Clinton's camp in the fall of 1990 after their candidate for governor, Tommy Robinson, lost to Nelson in the Republican primary and they faced the prospect of a governor who was unusually inimical to their interests. They wanted anybody but Nelson in the governor's office. Although after Witt's death in December 1991 the Stephenses were uniformly Republican and were major contributors to the party and its candidates for state and national offices, they decided that state pride obliged them to also back the local boy for president. At least he would be out of their hair.

In January 1992, three months after Clinton announced his candidacy for president, Gerth arrived in Little Rock to look into the candidate's economic circumstances, as he told me in our first telephone conversation about his investigations. I had ceased being the *Times*'s Arkansas stringer a decade earlier, but we had talked numerous times when he was working on the first Stephens article in 1978, and he knew that I was familiar with the sources of the Stephenses' economic and political clout and with Clinton. I figured he had talked extensively to Sheffield Nelson, who would be quoted critically about the Stephenses and their tightness with the new presidential candidate in the article that the *Times* published on February 5. Gerth wondered if I was familiar with any legal work that Hillary Clinton might have done for Stephens Inc. or the family. If she did, I said, it was not of sufficient magnitude that it had made the newspapers.

"Wealthy Investment Family a Big Help to Clinton," the headline on Gerth's story in the *Times* proclaimed. It was the first of a string of major stories by Gerth in the *Times* that suggested, often spuriously and sometimes inaccurately, that the governor and his wife enjoyed close and unethical relationships with powerful financial interests in Arkansas that rewarded the businesses with government assistance and tepid regulation. The articles in the world's leading journal would form a narrative that would follow the Clintons, especially Hillary, the rest of their careers. The February 5 article on the Clintons and Stephenses began by recounting Bill Clinton's appeal to the Stephenses in the final days of his 1990 race against Nelson to help him borrow money to answer Nelson's last-minute onslaught suggesting that Clinton planned more big tax increases. The drift of Gerth's article was that the Stephens family had enjoyed immense power both in business and the government, which Clinton and his wife had facilitated. Witt Stephens had, indeed, enjoyed a reputation as a kingmaker in Arkansas politics from the late 1940s through the '60s, but while Witt's and his family's business interests were no less successful financially after that, their political influence had been in steady decline since 1971. Even the young Sheffield Nelson had overpowered them in the legislature after their standoff over renegotiating supply contracts and piping Stephens gas to Midwestern clients through Arkla's pipes. Clinton in 1985 had ended Stephens's total dominance of municipal bond underwriting, but he earned their grace again in the 1990 governor's race by taking down their nemesis Nelson, who had beaten their man Tommy Robinson in the Republican primary.

"Mrs. Clinton has had connections, too," Gerth reported. "According to a Stephens official who asked not to be identified, Mrs. Clinton once represented them in litigation. Public records also show that her firm has represented a number of Stephens entities." He didn't mention which public records showed that.

On the record, top Stephens officials, including chairman Warren Stephens, have always said they knew of no legal work Hillary had ever done for them. Lawyers at the Rose firm who worked closely with Clinton could recall no work that she had done for Stephens Inc. or any kind of legal work for the big financial house that she could have been called upon to do. The Rose law firm, like several other big law firms, had done bond and other work for Stephens. Even if she had handled some legal matter for the company, it would have been neither illegal nor unethical, unless it involved some clear conflict with the governor's regulatory prerogatives, and there was no suggestion that it was. Gerth wrote that her annual income for lawyering had been below $100,000 before 1991, the previous tax year.

After Gerth's article, the Clinton-Stephens nexus would become a frequent topic of national news and commentary. The common implication was that her work had to raise ethical questions since her husband was in charge of the whole state government and nearly every business, even if only by paying taxes to the state, was under some kind of regulatory jurisdiction. The article pointed to no advantage that the government under Clinton had given to any Stephens enterprise.

A band of reporters surrounded Hillary at a campaign event in Chicago on March 5 and asked her about her representation of Arkansas businesses and local agencies, such as a municipal airport commission. She snapped, "I suppose I could have stayed home and baked cookies and had teas, but what I decided to do was to fulfill my profession, which I entered before my husband was in public life."

A torrent of criticism followed. Critics said she was denigrating women who did not follow a career outside the home.

Three days after her cookie riposte, Jeff Gerth landed a story on the front page of the *Times*—Whitewater—that would bedevil the Clintons for the next ten years and arguably lead to the president's impeachment. The furor set off by Gerth's story would last until the fall of 2000, when the third special federal prosecutor to examine the matter admitted that Whitewater had all been much ado about nothing. The Clintons had done nothing illegal. The prosecutors by then had spent upwards of sixty million dollars investigating the little land project and its offshoots.

Gerth telephoned me one day in February 1992 asking if anybody had ever written anything about the Clintons' investment in a remote vacation development called Whitewater in 1978, before he became governor. Yes, I said, it was fairly common knowledge and it had caused a minor dustup in the governor's race in 1986. The Clintons and Jim and Susan McDougal had borrowed some money and bought 230 acres of remote wilderness land on a ridge overlooking the White River and Crooked Creek in Marion County and tried to develop it for vacation homes and fishing cabins. Clinton had been elected attorney general, and Hillary had left the law faculty at Fayetteville with him and joined the Rose law firm at Little Rock. Interest rates at the time had soared high into the double digits, the worst inflation spiral of the century, and no one was borrowing money for such pleasure ventures, which the Clintons realized too late. The stupidity of the venture became apparent to them before long. McDougal, who had sold them on the project, couldn't sell a single lot because no one was borrowing money anywhere, but the couples were paying high interest on their loans. Clinton's political career would rise and fall and rise again in the next fourteen years, while McDougal would work briefly for Clinton in the governor's office and then try his hand at running a couple of small financial institutions—in the worst climate for such enterprises since the 1930s—before losing everything and sinking into despair.

In 1992, when Gerth arrived in Little Rock, a federal jury had vindicated McDougal on charges that he had defrauded his little savings and loan company, but he was jobless and living in penury in a trailer at his friend Bob Riley's home in Arkadelphia. McDougal's mother had moved in with him after Jim's father's death. She told him that Bill Clinton had telephoned there one night and that she had beseeched him to find a state-government job for her desperate son, who suffered from clinical depression. McDougal said his mother told him that Bill had promised her that he would try to find a job for Jim in the government. Clinton never did get him a job. McDougal said he never expected Clinton to come through, but he resented that Bill had broken his old mother's heart.

McDougal was nursing that slight when his friend and former business partner Sheffield Nelson introduced him to Gerth, who was investigating the Clintons' background for the *Times*. McDougal had gone to Nelson, a lawyer, asking him to sue his old friend Lieutenant Governor Jim Guy Tucker over $59,000 that he thought Tucker owed him. McDougal was happy to oblige Gerth and tell him all the troubles he had had with Tucker, and also the troubles with the Clintons over the old Whitewater development and Hillary's lucky investment in stock futures. He would quickly regret it. For his trouble that day, McDougal would die eight years later to the day after Gerth's Whitewater story appeared in the *Times*. He died on a cot in "the hole"—solitary confinement—in a federal prison near Fort Worth, Texas, because, although willing, he could not give the special prosecutor any evidence that either Clinton had committed a crime. He had only his claim that Clinton had once asked David Hale, at a chance meeting of the three, if he had approved a small-business loan to Susan McDougal's media company—a fraudulent loan application that Jim McDougal had prepared.

McDougal, who had once been on the staffs of Senator McClellan and Senator Fulbright and was a bill clerk of the U.S. Senate when he was twenty years old, was teaching political science at Ouachita Baptist College at Arkadelphia in 1978 when he hit upon the idea of a vacation development on an Ozark trout stream. A real-estate agent at Flippin told him about the riverside land that was for sale. It was not accessible by road, but McDougal flew over it and it looked like it could be a good site for vacation cabins. Years earlier, McDougal had made Fulbright and other Senate staffers some money by having them invest with him in a couple of subdivision developments in Saline and Faulkner Counties. Fulbright was amazed that McDougal had cleared more than $100,000 for him in the Saline County project and told people that the scamp was a wizard.

Since he had masterminded the Young Democrats' revolt in 1964, McDougal was widely known as an eccentric rascal with unusual political ingenuity. As a boy in the White County community of Bradford, the son of a feedstore owner, he was consumed with politics. He had a volume of the great orations in history, and he memorized many gaudy flourishes, such as William Jennings Bryan's Cross of Gold speech at the 1896 Democratic National Convention, Frank Clements's "How long, O America, how long?" peroration at the 1956 Democratic convention, and the bombastic diatribes of John L. Lewis, the scowling industrial unionist who brought high wages and pensions to America's mineworkers. He loved political scraps and to make speeches. At the age of twenty, he was sometimes a campaign stand-in for Faubus, whom he admired for his occasional populist impulses before he was co-opted by fatcats like the Stephenses. To McDougal, Faubus's blocking integration at Central High School had been only an aberration. McDougal would always work in soaring flourishes borrowed from Winston Churchill, Franklin Roosevelt, Lewis, or Bryan.

Like his father and grandfather, he suffered from a severe bipolar disorder. Twice, in manic phases—1982 in northwest Arkansas and 1994 in southeast Arkansas—he ran for Congress, losing to John Paul Hammerschmidt in 1982 and to a Democrat in the 1994 primary in the Fourth District. He would blame his 1982 race for his two prosecutions and the legal troubles growing out of the Whitewater quagmire. He believed that Congressman Hammerschmidt had sicced national Republicans and Reagan's bank regulators on his little bank at Kingston to sidetrack him, and claimed in his memoir that the conniving government regulators disillusioned him. He said he developed "an outlaw mentality" that he carried for the rest of his life.

"I prefer to think of myself as a good pirate in the tradition of southern populists, quick to bend the law to defy the establishment," he wrote.

It is doubtful that Hammerschmidt had ever given McDougal a second thought.

McDougal made his last quixotic race in 1994 as the first Whitewater independent counsel's investigation of Whitewater got underway and he was being summoned to Washington to testify before congressional committees about the old land deal and his dealings with the Clintons, Tucker, and Hale.

Hillary liked McDougal's idea of developing wilderness estates when he described it to her and her husband over lunch in January 1978 at the Black-Eyed Pea restaurant on Rebsamen Park Road in Little Rock. McDougal said Bill showed no particular interest—he never evinced any interest in making money—but he agreed to go along if Hillary wanted to. The Clintons, McDougal, and his wife, Susan—a student he met while he was teaching at the little Baptist college—obtained $203,000 in bank loans to buy the land, form the Whitewater Development Corporation, and begin the rudimentary development on a heavily forested ridge on the White River. Hillary eventually contracted to build a speculative cabin in the woods to entice people to build there, but there were no takers and the whole project foundered. The two couples had trouble paying down their bank debts. When congressional investigators and sleuths for the Resolution Trust Corporation got into the old files of the Whitewater Development Corporation many years later, they found numerous notes back and forth and baffling side transactions trying to salvage the project in some way, all of which found their way into national news stories in the 1990s.

"Clintons Joined S. & L. Operator In an Ozark Real-Estate Venture" was the headline on Gerth's blockbuster article on the front page of the *Times* on March 8, 1992. The front page of the *New York Times*, then as now, proclaims to the news world each day what big issues the press should be following.

The headline sounded scandalous, because savings and loans had recently collapsed all across the country, costing the taxpayers billions of dollars in bailouts. Numerous scandals reaching into politics—Lincoln S&L and the Keating Five (Senator John McCain and four other senators), Silverado S&L (President George H. W. Bush's son Neil), and Vernon S&L (House Speaker Jim Wright)—had turned "S. & L. Operator" into an ominous phrase. Here was a governor, who was supposed to be regulating a few of the thriftless thrifts, actually going into business with one of the miscreants.

The headline was blatantly wrong. McDougal was not an "S. & L. Operator" in 1978, and Clinton was not the governor. The Clintons had entered a real-estate venture not with an S&L operator but with a teacher at a small Baptist college and his wife. McDougal would not set up a small state-chartered savings and loan in Little Rock until four years later, after he had worked for a while in the governor's office in 1979 and after quitting the governor's office and running a tiny bank for a while in the unincorporated community of Kingston in Madison County. In 1982, while Clinton was out of office and McDougal was running for Congress, McDougal acquired a small thrift in Woodruff County, renamed it Madison Guaranty Savings and Loan, and then moved it to South Main Street in Little Rock, where he began handing out loans to virtually anyone who asked for one. He had gotten into trouble as the governor's economic-development adviser for criticizing Arkansas banks for being too conservative in lending money for start-up businesses. With his little thrift, McDougal put his philosophy into practice, right after the Reagan administration had deregulated the institutions and encouraged them to go out and throw money at entrepreneurs, not just homebuyers. Like about a third of the nation's thrifts, McDougal went at it with abandon and lost everything. In his case, he lost his businesses, his reputation, and eventually his life. Scores of "S. & L. operators" across the country were prosecuted or subjected to civil lawsuits for recoveries from their freewheeling and sometimes self-serving ways.

One of McDougal's development investments at Madison Guaranty was Campobello Island in New Brunswick, Canada, once a vacation escape for his hero Franklin Roosevelt. McDougal got Sheffield Nelson and Jerry Jones—remember them from the Arkoma gas imbroglio?—to invest as limited partners. Desolate, dreary Campobello was a financial disaster, too, but the receiver for the federal Resolution Trust Corporation was a former Razorback teammate of Jerry Jones, and he handed the pair a profit on their investments in Campobello before bailing out McDougal's thrift—but not McDougal himself—with tax funds and turning it over to a Little Rock bank.

Like hundreds of S&Ls across the country, McDougal's thrift had begun to get in trouble in 1985, when federal examiners said inflated profits from speculative investments might have jeopardized the company's solvency, but it would be a couple of years before state and federal regulators put it into receivership and the U.S. attorney brought charges against him.

Gerth's story about Whitewater and the Clintons gave an ominous cast to all the intricate arrangements the two couples made while trying to salvage the little investment, all the while promoting the idea that the governor and his wife had an ethical conflict in having done business with a man who in the future would operate a savings and loan association. That story and those that followed suggested that McDougal, not the Clintons, bore the brunt of the losses, which seemed to be part of McDougal's pique. Gerth's story made Madison Guaranty sound like a financial behemoth. He called it "one of the largest" state-chartered S&Ls in the state, when it was actually one of the tiniest S&Ls in the state and the country. State-chartered banks and thrifts were few and tended to be very small operators. Most large thrifts were federally chartered.

The March 8 story was not the last on Whitewater, even in the campaign. That article and subsequent ones suggested that Hillary Clinton, whose law firm did legal work such as title opinions for Madison Guaranty, might have exercised undue influence on the state securities commissioner, Beverly Bassett, a Fayetteville lawyer whom Clinton had appointed to the post. Bassett had approved a plan suggested by McDougal and drafted at the Rose law firm for rescuing the company, but McDougal ignored it. Bassett later moved to put McDougal's firm into federal receivership.

Gerth would write more long investigative articles on the Clintons for the *New York Times*, all with the same dark hints that something was cunning and sinister about what the Arkansas couple had done—not stupid, but wrong. What the lead on the original Whitewater exposé should have said, if it were worthy of reporting at all, was that this ambitious Yale-educated couple now wanting to run the country had fourteen years earlier gone into debt for a real-estate project in a poor and rugged area that had little chance of success, even in a normal business climate, much less in the raging inflation of 1978. But Gerth was not alone. There was pressure on reporters for other major journals to catch up with the *Times* on the Clinton scandals. One was Susan Schmidt of the *Washington Post*, who regularly got confidential "leaks" from the independent counsel—notably from the young zealot Brett Kavanaugh—about what the prosecutors and FBI agents were finding in the Clintons' machinations in the Arkansas government and with the Arkansas power establishment.

One of Gerth's bombshells was that in 1978, when Clinton was attorney

general and running for governor, Hillary invested $1,000 in the cattle fu-
tures market and closed her account the next year after reaping a profit
of $99,000. The scandal was that she had been guided in the trading by a
young lawyer named James B. "Jim" Blair, who would in the future become
general counsel for Tyson Foods. In Gerth's telling, the powerful Tyson
Foods helped the future first lady make a small killing in the market in
order to gain leverage with the man who would one day be governor and
then perhaps senator or president. Gerth proceeded to recount how the
food giant, after helping her make $99,000, ran roughshod over pollution
laws and reaped millions in aid from the state government under Clinton.
He wrote that Tyson had obtained $9 million in loans from the state gov-
ernment under Clinton. I was intrigued when I read the story, because
the state had no such loan program. I tried to call Gerth, who had told
me about his story before he wrote it, but couldn't reach him, so I told the
Times's national editor that the sentence was an error and probably ought
to be corrected. A few weeks later, a correction appeared on page two of
the paper. It did not say what the error was, only that Tyson received no
loans from the state. The *Times* has since become more transparent about
its mistakes.

Hillary opened the account in October 1978 and cashed out the next
year—right before the bull market crashed. What Gerth failed to mention
was that Blair and others in his orbit stayed in when Hillary got out, and
they lost a fortune. A broker named Robert "Red" Bone, who founded Ref-
co, Inc., a brokerage at Springdale, was the wizard who advised all of them.
After the crash, he became a villain. Gerth failed to mention that the connection with Blair was not business with Tyson Foods but personal. Blair's
wife, Diane, the eminent political scientist, was Hillary's best friend and
confidante for life. Jim and Diane were in the Clintons' wedding, and Bill
performed the Blairs' wedding. The couples vacationed together. When
Diane Blair was dying of cancer in 2000, Hillary telephoned her daily from
the White House and visited her at Fayetteville just before she died. Tyson
Foods had nothing to do with her relationship with the Blairs and her stock
trading. Don Tyson, the CEO, had written a letter to the *Gazette* in 1980
urging Clinton's defeat. While Tyson and the poultry industry were invet-
erate polluters in a state whose population was never bothered much by
industrial and agricultural pollution, Clinton had twice, in 1979 and 1991,
passed laws that stiffened regulations and fines for Tyson's pollution.

But there might have been an ethical slip that Gerth missed in his reporting on the ancient cattle trades. One of the lawsuits filed against Bone and his brokerage after the crash was by Hayden McIlroy, a prominent banker at Fayetteville, who stayed in the cattle trades when Clinton withdrew and lost $800,000 as a result. McIlroy blamed Refco and Bone. One of his lawyers was Hillary Rodham of the Rose firm. Looking through the case file when the cattle story broke in 1994, I noticed that she had withdrawn as counsel for McIlroy. My assumption was that a senior partner at Rose, upon hearing from Hillary that she had once traded with Refco, said that she ought to withdraw from the case because it presented the appearance of a conflict of interest. The case was fifteen years old then and I did not follow up to learn if that was the cause. McIlroy lost his case before U.S. District Judge Henry Woods, who had alerted me to the suit, and also before the Eighth U.S. Circuit Court of Appeals.

Her Tyson-aided cattle-futures profit, as Gerth and others ruthlessly characterized it, would resurface whenever Hillary ran for office, a dark reflection on her character.

It could be said in defense of Gerth, who was adept at digging into financial transactions, that he always acted on the fundamental impulse of reporters and the whole news business, which is to expose fraud, deceit, and incompetence by people who do the public's business, or the same faults plus excessive greed by those whose commerce affects the public health and welfare. That is the mission of reporting and of every good newspaper. But too often the impulse is not regulated by good judgment—a determination not to be unfair and not to create a false narrative just to get a big headline. It is a special danger for the breed called investigative reporters, whose job is not to report daily occurrences but to go beneath the surface to expose wrongdoing. There is an instinct to overlook exculpatory details if they detract from your narrative or to ignore common human failings that explain why something went wrong. If you have spent days or weeks working on a story, you must have at least a small bombshell to show for your wages. Everything must sound sinister, even if the details seem ordinary. Good editors should spot evidence of overreaching, but everyone wants to beat the others to a good story.

Gerth late in the decade would share a Pulitzer Prize, as did Sue Schmidt at the *Washington Post*; he lost credibility soon afterward when he was exposed as having unfairly destroyed the reputation and career of Wen Ho Lee, a nuclear scientist at Los Alamos National Laboratory who was accused of stealing secrets for Communist China, although Gerth's stories had not identified him by name. Eventually, the judge apologized to Lee for putting him in solitary confinement and denounced the government for misconduct. The federal government and five news organizations paid Lee $1.6 million to settle a civil suit. As for Hillary, Gerth and another *Times* reporter in 2007 wrote the most vindictive of all the Clinton books—*Her Way: The Hopes and Ambitions of Hillary Rodham Clinton*—with the obvious purpose of undermining her campaign for president in 2008.

Early in Bill Clinton's presidency, committees of the Senate and House of Representatives began to hold hearings to get to the bottom of the *Times*'s bewildering Whitewater revelations, along with a cascade of other dust-ups—Clinton's firing of President Bush's travel-office staff, the handling of some FBI files in their first weeks in the White House, and, finally, the suicide of the deputy White House counsel, Vince Foster, Clinton's kindergarten classmate and next-door playmate at Hope, whose body was found in Fort Marcy military park with his father's antique pistol at his side. A shredded note in his wastebasket back at the White House complained about newspapers destroying people's reputations and lives for fun. Foster apparently was not alluding then to the *Times* but to the *Wall Street Journal*, which had carried several editorials doubting the character of Foster, a paragon of lawyerly virtue who happened to possess his former law firm's billing records on Madison Guaranty.

When Whitewater wouldn't go away and Republicans chanted for the appointment of an independent counsel to investigate the fifteen-year-old Whitewater transaction and Foster's death, Clinton, his wife, and his top aides conferred by transatlantic phone in January 1994 while the president was in Moscow. David Gergen, a Republican counselor whom Clinton had hired, had been arguing for Hillary to turn over the law firm's billing records on Madison Guaranty to the *Washington Post*, which was clamoring to see them and was now competing with the *Times* for who could publish the most details about Whitewater. Gergen said that would end any questions about whether there was some misconduct in Hillary's representation of McDougal's little company. She refused. Those were confidential private records and none of the public's business, none of Congress's business, and none of the newspapers' business, she said. Clinton and others pleaded also, according to Gergen, but she would not relent. She and Clinton agreed by telephone that night that he should have the attorney general appoint an independent counsel and put the whole mess behind them.

George Stephanopoulos offered the worst advice any aide ever gave to a president. He argued that an independent counsel appointed by the attorney general would soon settle the whole crazy matter and it would go away. Meantime, the White House could get back to doing the people's business. Clinton's chief counsel, Bernard Nussbaum, who had experience with the Watergate prosecution twenty years earlier, pleaded with the president not to do it, because an independent counsel, especially one who might be appointed by a partisan judicial panel, would be a partisan himself who would never quit until he unearthed something, however flimsy, that could be used to impeach the president. Clinton would write in his memoir that accepting Stephanopoulos's advice and ignoring Nussbaum's was the worst mistake of his life.

The first independent counsel, a former Republican federal judge named Robert B. Fiske Jr., investigated the most urgent matter, the wild charge by right-wing radio commentator Rush Limbaugh that the Clintons probably had their friend Foster murdered for some unknown reason that might be connected with the acreage near Flippin. Federal and local investigators had already concluded that it was a suicide. When Fiske concluded the same thing and suggested that he wasn't finding any wrongdoing by the principals in the Whitewater and Madison Guaranty matter, a federal judicial panel fired him and appointed Kenneth B. Starr, whom Clinton had previously removed as the solicitor general. Starr hired a young Republican lawyer, Brett Kavanaugh, to direct a fresh investigation of Foster's death to see if it could be pinned on the Clintons. After spending three years and a few million dollars in the pursuit, Kavanaugh's sleuths could find nothing to support anything but suicide, the same conclusion that local and federal investigating agencies and two bipartisan congressional committees had reached. Kavanaugh went back to private practice, only to rejoin Starr's team when they stumbled upon evidence that Clinton had had sexual liaisons with Monica Lewinsky. Kavanaugh and Starr widened the investigation of the old Marion County land deal to include a former Arkansas state employee's claims that Clinton had once exposed himself to her, as well as the allegations that he had had an office affair with Lewinsky and lied publicly and under oath when he said he hadn't. They pursued that until the Republican House of Representatives impeached the president for not being truthful about his trysts with Lewinsky. Decades later, Kavanaugh parlayed it into a seat on the U.S. Supreme Court.

The leitmotif of all the newspaper stories in the New York and Washington papers and their spinoffs, and the interminable congressional investigations, was that the cunning and dishonest Clintons had gotten away with something crooked in the bewildering web of transactions among Mc-Dougal, David Hale, and their Arkansas associates, although no one could figure out just what it was. The story should have been that the Clintons did not get away with a dumb business deal in 1978 but rather paid dearly for it—and also for not being completely candid and forthcoming in the aftermath of the reporting. The Whitewater investigations did persuade the Clintons that they might have improperly claimed a tax deduction for Whitewater losses, and they sent the IRS a check for the delinquency and penalties.

Nussbaum was right about a special prosecutor, at least the second one, Kenneth Starr, and the highly partisan staff of attorneys he put together. Starr would later claim that one unnamed person on his investigative staff had actually voted for a Democrat in the last election, so it couldn't have been partisan.

Robert H. Jackson, the only person ever to hold the offices of solicitor general, attorney general, and justice of the U.S. Supreme Court—he was also the chief American prosecutor at the Nuremberg trials of Nazi war criminals after World War II—once warned against overreaching law enforcement and judiciaries and against skirting due process in an unrelenting search for grounds to take down an individual rather than to correct an injustice. Everyone, even the most sainted individual, has broken the law, often with harmless intentions, he said. What he had in mind was exactly the independent-counsel process as it was carried out in the 1990s.

Neither Jim McDougal's escapades nor the exposés of Gerth and his competitors kept the Clintons out of the White House, but they altered the trajectory of Arkansas politics. The independent counsels—first Fiske and then Kenneth Starr—followed the traditional prosecutorial path to get their quarry: first find people who fudged in a business transaction by misapplying loan proceeds or lying on an application, flip them into a plea agreement to divulge something unsavory about a higher-up, and keep going up the ladder until you reach the quarry, in this case the Clintons. FBI agents and assistant prosecutors interviewed women who were rumored to have had affairs with Clinton, captured computers used in the governor's re-election campaign, and hauled former aides and campaign workers be-

fore a grand jury to explain memos and justify expense checks to campaign workers. None of it had anything to do with the special prosecutor's
mandate, which was to determine if there was criminal conduct involved
in the business transactions flowing from the Whitewater Development
Corporation. The prosecutor charged Clinton's friend and longtime supporter Herby Branscum Jr., the president of the little Bank of Perryville and
former Democratic state chairman and national committeeman, of using
bank funds to reimburse himself for contributions to Clinton's 1990 gubernatorial campaign and of causing a bank employee not to report to the U.S.
Treasury Department a loan the bank had made to Clinton's campaign. The
reporting requirement was intended to tip federal agents on money-laun-
dering drug smugglers. Branscum refused to capitulate and was tried in
the federal district court, along with his bank partner. Branscum testified
about all the transactions for two days and was acquitted.

Jim Guy Tucker was not so fortunate. Tucker, who was lieutenant governor until he became governor upon Clinton's election in 1992, was characterized in many national articles as a close ally of Clinton. They had been
rivals almost from the beginnings of their careers and had fought bitterly in 1982 when both men were recovering from political rejections. But
Clinton and Tucker shared two relationships: their fragile friendship with
Jim McDougal and the mutual enmity of Sheffield Nelson. McDougal and
Tucker had been bachelor roommates when McDougal worked for Fulbright and Tucker was starting his law practice. McDougal and Clinton got
acquainted when McDougal was working for Fulbright and Clinton was
an intern for the Foreign Relations Committee. Clinton occasionally drove
Fulbright around the state during his 1968 Senate race with Jim Johnson.
In the memoir that was published soon after McDougal's death, he delighted in recounting Fulbright's aggravation that young Clinton talked too
much and argued with him on national issues while they were cruising
between towns.

As for Clinton's and Tucker's relationships with Nelson, all three men
shared a mutual distrust, based on their ambitions and their almost certain
future rivalries for high office. Clinton eventually defeated both Tucker and
Nelson for governor, and Tucker defeated Nelson in 1994, the last political
race for both men. Nelson sicced Jeff Gerth on both Clinton and Tucker
in January 1992, but Gerth's editors told him they were not interested in
dirt on a mere lieutenant governor and to concentrate on the presidential
candidate. It was still another old political acquaintance, David Hale, who

brought them all together in the clash that brought about Governor Tucker's conviction and resignation and heightened Clinton's risk of impeachment.

On July 20, 1993, the same day that Vince Foster shot himself in Fort Marcy Park, Paula Casey, the new Clinton-appointed U.S. attorney in Little Rock, obtained a federal search warrant for the offices of Hale's small-business lending company. The next day, FBI agents raided the offices of Capital Management Services and carted away Hale's files, which carried evidence of widespread fraud. Clinton's director of the Small Business Administration had referred the results of the agency's investigation of Hale's lending operations to Casey. Hale had advanced more than two million federal dollars to thirteen dummy corporations that he controlled. Although the dummy corporations were not associated with either Tucker or McDougal, both men were friends of Hale and had business dealings with him. Hale also was a Little Rock municipal judge. Readers may remember the Young Democrats' brouhaha in 1965, when McDougal engineered a revolt that stopped Hale, his brother Milas, and other supporters of Governor Faubus from electing Sheffield Nelson as the organization's president. McDougal would later become a friend and business partner of his old rivals.

When Hale, acting on the suggestion of Jim Johnson, claimed the next year that Governor Clinton had encouraged him to make a loan of questionable legality to the McDougals, Casey decided that, since Clinton had appointed her, she should recuse from the prosecution of Hale to avoid the appearance of favoritism. She handed all the evidence to the new independent counsel investigating Whitewater, Robert Fiske, who, after an appellate judicial panel fired him, then handed it off to Kenneth Starr. The appearance of favoritism under Starr, had anyone in the media noticed, was formidable. He prosecuted Hale's partners who were suspected of being Democrats, like Tucker and McDougal, but left alone three delinquent state Republican officials who got loans from Hale. Starr hoped to indict Clinton or at least implicate him in Hale's unlawful loan to McDougal, but no record of Clinton having any transaction or influence with Hale ever surfaced. Hale had supported Tucker against Clinton in 1982 and Frank White against Clinton in 1986, so the governor was unlikely to expect any favors from him, or Hale from the governor. Transactions that McDougal and Tucker had with Hale's lending company formed the grounds upon which Tucker, along with Jim and Susan McDougal, were convicted in 1996. Tucker resigned and Lieutenant Governor Mike Huckabee became governor.

The trial of the McDougals and Tucker received heavy play in the *New York Times* and the *Washington Post,* but, for the jury, the days of bewildering testimony and quibbling about the intricate financial transactions involving Hale's and McDougal's lending institutions and development projects were frustrating. Attorneys for the three defendants and Tucker, too, sensed that the jurors were having trouble figuring out what was wrong and who was responsible. One juror later confirmed it. The lawyers advised the defendants not to take the stand but to leave the prosecutors, including Rod Rosenstein (later Donald Trump's deputy attorney general), floundering. But McDougal, remembering the bravura performance that got him acquitted in 1989, insisted on testifying in his own defense. It was a disaster. This time, he was confused and nonsensical. The prosecutors caught him repeatedly in mistakes, lies, and exaggerations. They kept him on the stand until the defense seemed demolished. McDougal would admit in his memoir that he had convicted the three of them, but he seemed to be regretful only that he had sent his ex-wife to prison.

Tucker also pled guilty to another charge by Starr, that he had cheated the Internal Revenue Service on a cable-television bankruptcy filing. Facing death or a life-saving liver transplant, he pled guilty after an offer of a suspended sentence. Starr had refused during the early phases of the bankruptcy case to identify the part of the revenue code that Tucker had violated. Tucker's lawyer demanded to know the part of the bankruptcy code that he had violated, but Starr refused to say and U.S. District Judge Stephen M. Reasoner ruled that the prosecution was not obliged to give him that information. Starr said that Tucker had cheated the government out of $3.7 million in taxes through a sham bankruptcy of a cable-television business. Privately, the prosecutors would discover from the IRS that the law they were relying on had been repealed two years before Tucker's bankruptcy and that he had not violated the law at all. But they continued with the prosecution anyway, although Starr offered Tucker a deal that he would not seek a prison sentence if Tucker pled guilty. Facing a ruined career and approaching death if he could not find a liver donor soon (he did), Tucker accepted it. But he still had to pay his debt to the IRS. Judge Reasoner finally ordered the special prosecutor and the Justice Department to identify the statute that Tucker had violated so that his tax debt could be computed. In 2001, after Starr had relinquished the job of special prosecutor, the Justice Department conceded that the law did not exist and that Starr had wrongly prosecuted him. The IRS could not determine if it owed Tucker

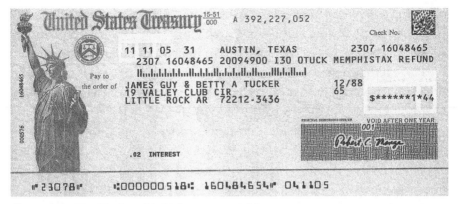

Government to Tucker: $1.44 for your troubles.

a tax refund or if he owed the government. Rather than endure more lit-igation, Tucker and the IRS agreed to drop the matter. The Treasury De-partment sent him a pro-forma settlement check for $1.44. He didn't cash it but framed it and hung it in the hall of his home. For such purposeful malpractice, another lawyer in Starr's shoes in another jurisdiction might have lost his license to practice. Tucker tried to withdraw his guilty plea and have his conviction set aside, but the appellate court, which erroneous-ly said that the U.S. attorney at Little Rock had brought the charges against Tucker, ruled that once a man pled guilty and was sentenced, he couldn't withdraw the plea, no matter how badly the government had screwed up.

Jim Guy Tucker's three, four, or five years as governor—it depends on how many of his acting-governor days you count—were as tumultuous as the rest of his life, so their frenzied ending in July 1996 with his conviction and resignation seemed almost ordinary. He was the rare swashbuckling Harvard graduate. After college, he wanted to go to Vietnam and joined the Marine Corps, but he was booted out twice owing to the rare health problem that dogged him all his life. He went to Vietnam twice anyway as a freelance war correspondent and wrote a book about the Arkansas warriors he met during the conflict. I have related his attempt to expose corruption and brutality in the prisons by getting fake commitment pa-pers and reporting to the Cummins prison as a crook, and that Governor Rockefeller ordered the corrections chairman to get him out before some-one cut his throat. He got elected prosecuting attorney, battled with police higher-ups, led raids and kicked doors down, fired into a ceiling to rout a hiding thug, and made the police reports once by chasing away ruffians outside his apartment building late one night by running into the street and firing shots over their heads. As the attorney general, he battled utilities over rate increases and power-plant emissions. He spent a relatively sedate two years in the U.S. House of Representatives and then gave Governor Pryor a rough time in their race for the Senate in 1978. He made some money in law and private business before making his comeback in 1990.

Clinton knew that Tucker, who would be the acting governor every day that the governor was outside the state's borders, would not be a quiescent seat holder, so he brought in William H. Bowen, the super lawyer and banker, to be a sort of super chief of staff while he was campaigning for president. Tucker fired the governor's real chief of staff while Clinton was out of town. Tucker had no intention of letting Bowen run the shop or of merely doing what Clinton wanted done while Clinton was in Iowa or New Hampshire. The two had a few cross long-distance conversations, but Tucker was unbending. When state matching funds for Medicaid were running low, Tucker called the legislature into special session without consulting Clinton and forced through a tax on soft drinks, which raised about $45 million a year to meet the state's federal match and to avoid a reduction in health services to the disabled and poor. Since sugary drinks were partly to blame for the high incidence of diabetes in the state, he said the makers and the patrons should bear some of the cost of subsidized medical services. While he was attending Clinton's inauguration in Washington in January 1993, his own acting governor, the president of the Senate, Jerry Jewell, pardoned two convicts and eased the terms of three others. Tucker came home and got the legislature to curtail the power of acting governors. He urged the legislature to pass laws that toughened sentences and reduced convicts' ability to get early release from prison. He defeated Sheffield Nelson in a landslide in 1994 to win his own term as governor.

In several ways, Tucker was a mirror opposite of his predecessor. Clinton sought advice, dithered over whose to take, changed his mind perpetually, and then wondered if he had made a mistake. Tucker acted quickly and boldly. He never seemed to have doubts. He cut the budgets of state agencies that could generate their own revenue and channeled the money to the schools. Where Rockefeller, Bumpers, and Pryor had failed—drafting a new constitution—he intended to prevail. He proposed a plan for a swift revision of major parts of the Constitution that would be submitted to the voters. He proposed the biggest highway program in the state's history—a sales tax and bond issue that would build a $3.5 billion four-lane highway system all over the state. By the time those issues reached the voters, Tucker was under siege by the Whitewater independent counsel, and the voters rejected both plans by lopsided votes. He did get the legislature and the voters to amend the Constitution to assure a more equitable distribution of state and local tax revenues among the state's public schools.

His last act was to draft an income-tax reform bill that reduced nearly everyone's tax liability, especially the elderly and people with low incomes, while maintaining the brackets and rates. He resigned before the legislature assembled, but all the Democrats in the legislature sponsored his bill in 1997 and it passed. Governor Huckabee signed it into law and then, when he was running for president a decade later, bragged that he was the first governor in Arkansas history to reduce taxes and claimed that he had forced the reluctant Democratic legislature to pass the bill.

By the midterm in 1994, the co-presidency was not working out to the satisfaction of either the president or his wife. He had had some early success with the Democratic Congress. Within weeks of his inauguration, he had passed a bill creating the AmeriCorps program and his family-leave bill, which guaranteed people up to twelve weeks of unpaid leave to recover from childbirth or medical emergencies. Congress passed his bill to ban the sale of military-style weapons for ten years, over the bitter opposition of the National Rifle Association. Without a vote to spare, he passed an omnibus budget bill that raised gasoline taxes and trimmed domestic programs, setting the stage for the first multiyear balanced budgets—four in a row—in the twentieth century. Clinton needed the vote of his own congressman, but Ray Thornton spurned the intercession of Senator Bumpers and said he had made a campaign promise in 1992 not to vote to raise the federal motor-fuel tax. Chelsea Clinton's future mother-in-law, Marjorie Margolies, a new congresswoman, had to cast the decisive 218th vote and lost her seat in the next election. Clinton brought together Yitzhak Rabin and Yasser Arafat, the prime minister of Israel and the chairman of the Palestinian Liberation Organization, on the White House lawn to sign a historic peace agreement, performing some gymnastics to keep Arafat from hugging Yitzhak and staining the wary prime minister's honor back home. He fulfilled his campaign promise to get enough Democrats on board to ratify the North American Free Trade Agreement (NAFTA), President Bush's prized legacy, although it privately infuriated Hillary, who told her confidante Diane Blair that the NAFTA fight used up too much of the new president's political capital and left little for the important business of health-care reform. He completed his big trade program by getting Congress at a lame-duck session to ratify the General Agreement on Tariffs and Trade. He got North Korea to agree to shelve its development of nuclear bombs and intercontinental missiles.

All of that seemed to be overshadowed by the Whitewater-spawned investigations and media revelations, and by the media's infatuation with silly dustups like the erroneous story that he had held up airline flights at the Los Angeles International Airport while he got a $200 trim by a hair stylist on Air Force One.

By the summer of 1994, as the Whitewater investigations in Congress and by the independent counsel were heating up, the first couple had lost their most vaunted goal, an overhaul of the country's health-care system to give every American access to medical care at a reasonable cost. All the Democratic candidates for president in 1992 had promised it, and Clinton had insisted that it was not even an issue because universal health care would be enacted no matter which of them was elected. Polls showed that an overwhelming majority of Americans wanted universal health care. Just as he had put Hillary in charge of the big education-reform drive in Arkansas in 1983, he put her in charge of a task force that would produce a comprehensive overhaul that he vowed Congress would pass in the first one hundred days. It was an unrealistic goal. The task was far more difficult than either of them imagined, accustomed as they were to a state legislative body that produced nearly a thousand laws in a hundred days.

Hillary threw herself into the work with messianic zeal, leading closed working sessions, making speeches across the country, testifying before congressional committees, and buttonholing senators and congressmen in their offices for long private discussions about the intricacies of the health-care system and how various schemes to cover everyone and finance the system might work. To her, it was the most important domestic undertaking in sixty years. Health care was the Hillary Project. When it failed, it was her failure.

Hillarycare, as critics started calling it, was not totally dissimilar to Obamacare—the Affordable Care and Patient Protection Act of 2010—in that it expanded the private insurance system as well as Medicaid and Medicare to insure everyone. Rather than mandating that individuals had to buy private insurance plans with government subsidies, Hillarycare mandated that employers with seventy-five employees or more provide coverage and pay up to 80 percent of their premiums. The country would be divided into regional alliances, where consumers could choose among at least three comprehensive health plans offered by the insurance industry. It had some of the same coverage guarantees as the later Affordable Care Act.

She apparently never anticipated that others would have different solutions that were perhaps not as comprehensive or costly as hers. She insisted that every single American had to be insured and she was certain that the complicated plan that she and the rest of her team had devised was the only one that would work. Universal coverage was a principle that she insisted could not be compromised. Health care was a community problem; every family went through the physical and emotional traumas of illness and death. Likewise, she said, the whole community had to be invested in taking care of the least and poorest among them.

"Until all people are secure, no one is," she kept insisting.

A congressman from Tennessee produced his own plan for near-universal coverage and so did a congressman from Oregon. The conservative think tank Heritage Foundation had proposed a system similar to what would become Obamacare, based on individual coverage rather than mandated employer coverage, and many Republican senators introduced the bill. The employer mandate became increasingly unpopular. Parts of the insurance industry began running TV commercials ridiculing Hillarycare and suggesting, erroneously, that it would not allow people to choose their doctors and hospitals—the same false claim made by critics of the Affordable Care Act fifteen years later. She became more and more brittle, attacking the plans offered by members of Congress as a surrender to the status quo and to the commercial interests that wanted to keep the system unchanged. She repelled intercessions by friendly Democratic senators that they compromise and live with something that, at least for the moment, would not cover everyone. The president, though he hinted to others that a compromise might be workable, would not tell her that they were going to take something less than the whole pie. As with seemingly everything, he would not override her.

By the summer of 1994, with the mid-term congressional elections approaching, health care was dead and the post-mortems began. Republicans swept the mid-term elections in November and the Clintons faced a hostile Republican Congress led by Representative Newt Gingrich for the next six years. The future of his presidency and their mutual political careers looked grim. Both had suffered personal losses, Bill's mother and Hillary's father. Clinton, normally ebullient even in the worst of times, fell into depression. In December, Webb Hubbell, his old friend and golfing partner who had gone to Washington with him as deputy attorney general, pled guilty to defrauding the Rose law firm on his expense billings and headed to prison.

Bill and Hillary were in Little Rock for a spell during the holidays. I had undergone heart bypass surgery and was lying on a hospital bed in my living room when Clinton telephoned to express his sympathy. Gene Lyons had told the couple about my surgery and Hillary had suggested that he call me. After a perfunctory inquiry about how I was doing, Clinton launched into a monologue about the perfidy of the press—the White House press corps and even the editorial writers at the *New York Times* and the *Washington Post*, who seemed to look for the flimsiest excuse to write negative things about both of them. I interjected that he had surely learned long ago from his experiences at Little Rock that editorial writers carried absolutely no powers of influence. He was not deterred. He offered a couple of theories about why the White House press corps in particular seemed to be united in finding fault with everything he did, but I do not remember what they were. He finally caught himself and apologized for his ramblings. I felt obliged to say something hopeful. I said I was sure he would find a way to make the best of the situation, even with a hostile Congress.

The post-mortems on health-care reform were all about Hillary, starting with her decision at the outset to keep the formative deliberations more or less secret. The teams that were formed to work on different aspects of the health-care problem would work in private until preliminary plans were worked out. It obviously did not sit well with the media and undoubtedly affected the tenor of the reporting. It raised suspicions about what interests were being taken care of behind closed doors, although the big interests like the pharmaceutical companies, physician organizations, and the insurance industry were shut out of the deliberations themselves.

She made no secret of her distrust of the media. Subjecting every suggestion raised in the task-force deliberations to public criticism made it hard to arrive at a considered and rational solution, she believed. In a speech in Nebraska, she referred to "the bane of all people in political life—the unfair, unjust, inaccurate reporting that goes on from coast to coast, north to south, east to west."

Others involved in the project, like the technocrat Ira Magaziner, would conclude that the effort to control the reporting on the work from the outset was a decisive mistake because it affected the developing attitudes in Congress and beyond about the whole project. Her unyielding insistence that hers was the only plan with a moral foundation—taking care of everybody—doomed it in the end, although the profound disagreements, not all of them philosophical, about how medical care should be regulated and paid for, and who was entitled to get government help, have always made it seemingly impossible to achieve the universal system that every other advanced democratic country reached long ago.

On May 30, 1994, *The New Yorker*, the weekly magazine of the American cognoscenti, produced a cover story about the first lady that put a permanent cast on her persona—a brilliant and idealistic woman who was also virulently ambitious, calculating, hardheaded, steely, and, well, unlikable to lots of people who knew her. Likeability would be the big issue in her two losing presidential races.

The 32,000-word *magnum opus*, titled "Hillary the Pol," was written by Connie Bruck, who had interviewed the president and scores of Hillary's friends and colleagues from her college days, her Arkansas sojourn, and her year and a half in the capital. The story covered all her battles—education reform in Arkansas, Whitewater, her cattle-futures trades, health-care reform—in excruciating detail, often with Jeff Gerth's pejorative slants. Hillary came across on the whole as brilliant and hard-working but also deeply political, intensely private, hard to get close to, and not a woman who shared much of herself and her inner musings with anyone but her closest family. It would be a persona upon which crafty opponents could easily install more sinister lineaments. She referred to the first lady's "steeliness." Bruck's piece could be viewed in another light—it remarked upon her high intellect, idealism, dedication, ingenuity, and analytical powers—but readers and listeners always tend to carry away the more inimical impressions.

Bruck began the piece in a way that must have thrilled Clinton and her ardent admirers. It had a long quotation from Lawrence O'Donnell Jr., who was the chief of staff of the Senate Finance Committee. O'Donnell would later be a talk-show star for MSNBC. O'Donnell described Hillary's first appearance before the Finance Committee, which would be handling health-care legislation, in the early spring of 1993:

> Mrs. Clinton came into that room, and she opened the discussion at about four-twenty-five in the afternoon. We

were about eighteen minutes into it when she stopped—I remember, I looked at the clock. And what I had just heard were the most perfectly composed, perfectly punctuated sentences, growing into paragraphs, in the most perfect, fluid presentation about what our problems in this field were and what we could do about them. And then she held her position in the face of questioning by these senators around the table, many of whom know a great deal about the subject. And she was more impressive than any Cabinet member who has sat in that chair.

Everyone Bruck quoted—most of them identified by name, a few anonymous—spoke reverentially of her ability and intelligence, her single-minded dedication to whatever the cause, but a few drifted off into descriptions that would contribute to the popular negative views of her: her reserve, her lack of demonstrative warmth, her shrewdness, her political calculation. They were descriptions that male politicians would not mind, but women were better admired for warmth and congeniality. Hillary would strive mightily over the years to overcome all the stereotypes, but they stuck.

Although the president granted Bruck two interviews and was effusive in his praise of Hillary, the first lady, as usual, had not talked to the reporter. She apparently was furious over the piece. A few days after it appeared, I received a call from her press secretary, Lisa Caputo. I was quoted in the article talking about how Hillary had co-opted the managing editor of the *Arkansas Democrat* and giving her credit for turning the editor and the paper from scourges of Governor Clinton into cheerleaders for most of his last ten years in office. Caputo said she had been talking to others who were quoted in the article and who said they had been misquoted or their remarks taken out of context. She said Hillary figured that was true of mine, too. Bruck had this direct quotation from me: "Hillary and Betsey Wright decided they had to neutralize the *Democrat*. They knew that John Robert Starr had a tremendous ego, that he was weak, that they could pander to him. Before long, you'd see Hillary and Starr at lunch over in a corner. We found it nauseating. And for eight years he wrote very little bad about Bill."

I said that, while I couldn't say whether the quotation was exactly what I had said to Bruck, she accurately described the point I had been making. Caputo thanked me archly and hung up.

It reminded me of my last interaction with Hillary Clinton, in late December 1992, after Clinton's election and before his inauguration. The president-elect's office was on Capitol Avenue in downtown Little Rock, where he was meeting daily with prospective cabinet members and doing interregnum spadework to take office. The closing of the *Gazette* and the dismissal of its staff a year earlier had left me unemployed for a while, but I had started teaching at the University of Central Arkansas at Conway. Every Saturday morning I played table tennis for a couple of hours with a former Nazi soldier at the old YMCA building at Broadway and Sixth Street, where Hillary sometimes came to jog around a little oval track. We met that morning in a narrow hallway as we were both heading to the dressing rooms. She did her best, as always, not to betray her suspicion of a newspaperman who was always finding fault with what public servants were doing. We chatted a moment about the pressures of getting set up to take office. I always tried to break the ice with a weak attempt at humor. I asked her to tell Bill that all I expected of the president for all my editorials endorsing him and praising his good works over the years was to be appointed commissioner of the Internal Revenue Service. Every year, I said, I would order a tax audit of the editor and the owner of the *Arkansas Democrat* (by then the *Democrat-Gazette*), who had given both of us so much grief in past years. It was obviously a joke. She didn't even smile. I interpreted her stern look as saying, "Do you think we would appoint you to *anything*?" She said nothing but walked on to the dressing room.

She just has no sense of humor, I thought. Much later, I would realize my error. She knew newspapermen. She had had enough experience with us. Whatever she said, whether following my comedic line or not, was apt to show up in print (by this time I was writing a political column for the *Arkansas Times*) and there was no telling how her response would be portrayed. Bruck's article only proved again that she couldn't trust any of us. We were all junior-level Jeff Gerths.

Her deep misgivings about the news media—the entire tribe of reporters and their opinionated counterparts—were a natural consequence of Hillary Clinton's abiding obsession with privacy. It was not merely a constitutional value, guaranteed by the Bill of Rights, but a personal one. It was not a character flaw but simply who she was, a product probably of her childhood experience, a legacy perhaps of her mother. It did not suit her for a political career, which rewards extroversion and amiability—qualities that her husband had in spades, in spite of his flaws. Still, she was elected twice, overwhelmingly, to the U.S. Senate from the third most populous state in the union, served a term as secretary of state, and left both jobs with high public approval ratings. But the obsession cost her the presidency.

Her hostility to the press—yes, and her paranoia, too—invited more investigative reporting on everything in which she was involved. The reporting by the *Wall Street Journal*, the *New York Times*, and others that interpreted global philanthropies to the family foundation as malignant efforts to win favors from the senator and secretary of state was an example.

The great email scandal, one of the most preposterous supposed scandals in modern history, cost her the election in 2016. Donald Trump told cheering crowds that she should be thrown in prison for using a private email server rather than the government server when she was secretary of state, or else for having someone destroy many of the old emails after she left office in 2013. She had a substantial lead in the polls until the FBI director announced dramatically a few days before the election that the FBI was reopening its investigation because a new cache of emails had been discovered. It turned out to be a false alarm. There never was any evidence that she had violated the law, even innocently.

Emails were a digital innovation that replaced telephone calls, handwritten notes, or visits to colleagues down the hall. But when President George W. Bush took office, it had begun to occur to government officials everywhere, including in the office of Governor Mike Huckabee of Arkansas, that unlike phone conversations, office conversations, and notes, emails could be considered public records and were subject to freedom-of-information laws. Newspaper reporters could demand the emails. In Washington, the Bush White House and scores of agencies quietly turned to the private server operated by the Republican National Committee.

The first revelation of high public officials using a private server was not Hillary Clinton's, but it did involve an Arkansawyer, the U.S. attorney for the Eastern District of Arkansas, Bud Cummins. Hillary Clinton might have raised the episode in her defense, but she never did.

Karl Rove, the White House political director, wanted eight Republican U.S. attorneys removed because they would not go after Democratic officials before the 2006 elections. The Justice Department fired eight prosecutors, including Cummins, who was replaced by a former political aide of Rove, Tim Griffin, who is now the lieutenant governor. Congressional investigators looking into the political firing of independent prosecutors discovered that Rove's chief deputy was using a gwb43.com email account to discuss firing Cummins and appointing Griffin in his place. Gwb43 stood for George W. Bush, the 43rd president, and the Republican National Committee owned the domain. Investigators considered the private emails a violation of the Presidential Records Act, although no one was ever charged.

Eventually, it was discovered that many agencies and officials were using the private server and protecting their emails from public scrutiny. In 2009, 22 million emails were alleged to have been destroyed, although subsequently they were found on backup tapes. The Obama administration settled a lawsuit filed by two groups seeking access to the 22 million emails but took no action against anyone who might have violated the Presidential Records Act or the freedom-of-information laws. Nobody in the White House screamed or tweeted, "Lock them up! Lock them up!"

Clinton was at first defiant about using her private email server, saying it was for convenience since many of her emails were private family communications that had nothing to do government business. Moreover, former secretary of state Colin Powell had advised her to do it. The State Department server was constantly under attack by hackers. WikiLeaks dumped thousands of State Department emails onto the Internet but none of Clinton's.

She might have explained with perfect candor that she wanted to keep her private and public business away from prying, unfair newspaper reporters. Some of her detractors, maybe even Donald Trump, might have found it plausible and even forgivable.

Afterword

Conventional wisdom has it that American politics, and Arkansas's own strain of it, underwent a sea change sometime around the advent of the twenty-first century, or a decade or so on either side of it—in any case, after the end of my more or less active engagement with politics and the men and women who practiced its arts. The centers of the major parties moved farther toward the extremities, both ideologically and rhetorically. The Republican Party shed the progressive wing that had defined it for most of the party's first century while also subsuming the white-primacy majority in Arkansas and the other states of the old Confederacy—the Democratic Party's once "Solid South." Arkansas was much later than the other Southern states in making the transition to Republican-hood, which in the other states happened after the passage of three federal civil-rights laws in the 1960s by a Democratic president and Congress. Arkansas was later than the others chiefly because, at the time, the liberal Winthrop Rockefeller was the doyen of the Grand Old Party in Arkansas, and a string of transfiguring liberal Democrats starting with Dale Bumpers followed him and kept diehard Democrats in the traces for thirty years. The election in 2008 of Barack Obama as a Democratic president with an interracial lineage completed the transformation. The South and border states like Missouri and Oklahoma were also particularly vulnerable in the culture wars, in which Republicans tried to lay claim to the moral high ground on abortion, guns, homosexual marriage, immigrants, and religious zealotry. By 2014, running as a Democrat for state office in Arkansas was as promising as a Republican chasing such an office in 1954, or anytime since Reconstruction.

After Clinton's departure and Tucker's political garroting, the Arkansas Republican Party stumbled into its embrace of far-right ideologies and into majority status. Mike Huckabee, who became the third Republican governor of the century after Tucker's forced resignation in 1996, actually must count as one of the three or four most liberal governors in Arkansas history. While preaching conservatism, he expanded government-paid medical care for the poor, embraced civil rights, championed citizenship and public services for undocumented immigrants, fought for wholesale school consolidation, and raised taxes for public education, highways, conservation, and long-term care for the indigent elderly and disabled. He expanded the public payroll by 20 percent. If you counted taxation as the first reference

point for liberalism, Huckabee would be Number One. He raised more taxes than any governor in history. Running for the Republican nomination
for president in 2008, he was compelled to deny all of it after a right-wing
organization, the Club for Growth, called him out on his big-government
liberalism. Later, perhaps to escape Arkansas's 7 percent income tax on his
class, he moved to Florida's coastal panhandle, where he complained about
the exorbitant property taxes that Florida made him pay for his three-story
beach mansion on the Redneck Riviera.

The traditional party and ideological rivalry also turned far more lethal.
The other side did not just have poor ideas, but they were also sinister
people dedicated to harming America. Who started it? Ronald Reagan and
Lee Atwater with their attacks on government as an institution? Atwater
for turning political campaigning into armed aggression? Newt Gingrich
for declaring war on a wounded president and his party? Let the historians
settle it.

After the election of President Barack Obama, no Republican in Congress was permitted to vote for anything favored by the president or any
significant bill sponsored by a Democrat. For the first time in history, solely because he was a Democrat (and, although they denied it haughtily, because he was brown skinned), the Republican Senate prevented a president
from filling a vacancy on the Supreme Court, his prerogative under the
Constitution for 225 years.

A greater measure of chivalry still prevailed in the Republican-dominat-
ed Arkansas legislature, but Republicans running for almost every office,
from justice of the peace upward, found ways to express their disdain for
the black president and the local Democrats who were his catspaws. "Liberal" and "liberalism" became terms of opprobrium, and the great liberal
democratic tradition—the thread of American history that gradually had
given meaning to the country's founding premises of equality and human
rights—became a treasonous plot against American values.

The press, once the primary source of knowledge about current events
but in decline owing to technological change, was condemned en masse as
organs of liberalism, out to destroy what was good about America. Adopting a catchphrase from Lenin, Stalin, Hitler, and Mao Tse-tung, President
Trump called the press "the enemy of the people" and threatened to pass
laws to silence critical media.

But you could take some solace in the knowledge that the country has
experienced even more partisan and divisive times, most notably in form-

ing political parties after the adoption of the federal constitution—to the great distress of President Washington—and again in the conflagration over slavery that led to the formation of the Republican Party and to the Civil War. Both times, the nation recovered its equilibrium and moved on toward the high aspirations promised by the Declaration of Independence and the Bill of Rights.

Newspapers have experienced more rancorous times and harsher attacks from more eminent quarters than Donald Trump. In the republic's formative days, newspapers were blatantly partisan. Competing journals espoused the causes of leading politicians and factions. Their harshest critic among all American presidents was Thomas Jefferson, who also penned the great paeans to a free press. "And were it left to me to decide whether we should have a government without newspapers, or newspapers without a government," he wrote, "I should not hesitate a moment to prefer the latter."

But when Jefferson became president and the press supporting Alexander Hamilton, John Adams, and their Federalist accessories began to criticize his deeds, even the Louisiana Purchase, and suggested that he was a Francophile, an atheist, perhaps a traitor, and the owner of a slave mistress, Jefferson changed his tune. In his second term, he asked the attorneys general in New England to prosecute editors and writers for sedition, in the way that President Adams and Congress had attacked his favorite papers through the Alien and Sedition Act, which resulted in the jailing of newspapermen who had written critically about Adams and Congress. The sedition act made it illegal to criticize the president and Congress but allowed them to libel the vice president, which happened to be Tom Jefferson. He pardoned the editors when he became president. After reaping the scorn of newspapers himself, he wrote: "I deplore with you the putrid state into which our newspapers have passed, and the malignity, the vulgarity, and mendacious spirit of those who write for them."

If the press weathered John Adams and Thomas Jefferson, two of the most brilliant men ever to hold national office, it can survive a buffoon, although perhaps not the broader economic and social developments that have left print and newsgathering obsolete and at the mercy of propaganda, in ways Joseph Goebbels never dreamed of.

Money has always and everywhere been the fuel of politics—the most powerful men in Arkansas after the Civil War were lobbyists for the railroads—but it seems to me that it has reached a new dimension with the arrival of the new century. In occasional spasms of progressivism over the past century, the state has tried to limit the power of money or to make its uses transparent to voters through campaign-finance and ethics rules, but every reform falls short. The U.S. Supreme Court has kept the spigots flowing (and in secret), first by defining spending money to elect or defeat politicians as protected free speech (*Buckley v. Valeo*, 1976) and then by a series of decisions striking down statutory limitations on political spending and ending with the landmark decision (*Citizens United v. FEC*, 2010) defining corporations as the owners of individual rights and barring government from limiting what corporations, either commercial or nonprofits, could spend independently to elect or defeat candidates and issues. Arkansas's Asa Hutchinson, then a congressman from northwest Arkansas, introduced a bill in 1999 to ban the use of "soft money," cash that was described as party-building money that influenced elections indirectly. It didn't pass. Hutchinson's own party then spent $245 million of soft money from rich donors and corporations to elect candidates the next year.

The *Citizens United* case raised the issue of whether a right-wing group should be allowed to spend huge amounts of money promoting a nasty film about Hillary Clinton, *Hillary the Movie,* which gave a villainous account of her investment in the old land deal near Flippin, her trading in cattle futures, and other little dustups in the White House in 1993. The Citizens United organization wanted to buy time for the film on cable networks during the 2008 primaries to defeat Clinton, whom the group thought would be the strongest Democratic candidate for president, but lower federal courts held that it was an electioneering expense and was not allowable under campaign-finance laws. The Supreme Court reversed the decision and said the dark-money expenditures should have been allowed.

Justice John Paul Stevens, in one of his last opinions, warned that the precedent would have a devastating effect on elections and on the electorate, by exposing them to the forces of secret wealth. "A democracy cannot function effectively when its constituent members believe laws are being bought and sold," he wrote.

Since *Citizens United*, the tide of soft and dark money has washed into elections in poor Arkansas in escalating waves, even into rural legislative elections. It has exacerbated the polarization of political parties, candidates, and the electorate. *Citizens United* might allow states some leeway in stopping the corruption, but whichever party is in power and benefiting the most from secret wealth will always be reluctant to initiate reform. Right now, but perhaps not forever, it is Republicans.

Arkansas has not been absent from the trend toward greater wealth for fewer people. However the rich come down on the political scales, they exercise steadily rising influence over the policies that officeholders contemplate, biasing the agenda always toward the concerns of the affluent. One way that it has manifested itself is the composite attitudes of those seeking major offices. For a half century, candidates for governor and those who were elected—Republican as well as Democratic—generally embraced the idea that the state's future depended upon a better-educated and healthier citizenry, which meant that raising the state's resources and concentrating them on those deficiencies was the main agenda. Into the second decade of the century, the political agenda became making money for oneself and protecting the assets of the successful (and the holders of the purse strings).

Men began to run for public office to make a better or easier living. Salaries for executive officials and legislators in Arkansas had been the most penurious in the country until voters in the 1970s began raising the floors imposed by the state constitution. In 1974, Governor Bumpers drew a salary of $10,000 a year and a legislator $1,200, although the taxpayers furnished the governor a house and a car. Under the old Jeffersonian system of citizen legislatures, men laid down their plows for a few weeks every year to go to the capital and make the laws for the state and prescribe how the state's paltry revenues were spent. A constitutional amendment ratified in 2014 allows a nervy legislator in the hinterlands to draw down nearly $100,000 a year in salary, expenses, and per diem for actually showing up at the Capitol on the pretense of doing the public's business. Legislators sign a register at meetings of committees of which they are not members and draw per diem and expenses for the day. The state treasury is a well from which you can offer sustenance to benefactors and the like-minded.

The General Improvement Fund (GIF) and judicial-bribery scandals over the past three years gave people a clue about the breadth of the problem. The GIF scandal arose from a single audit of a northwest Arkansas planning district, one of eight in the state that distribute governmental and philanthropic grants for economic development projects. The legislature used the planning districts to launder state money to the 135 legislators' favorite local projects, which the Constitution prohibited them from funding directly. When the audit was turned over to prosecutors, they tracked down bribery, kickbacks, and backscratching by legislators and collaborating lobbyists and consultants. Although only two of them were convicted of taking kickbacks, eleven Republican lawmakers from the area kicked in some $700,000 of state tax receipts to a tiny religious school called Ecclesia College that most people, even in the county in which it is located, had never heard of. The Constitution prohibited the state from singling out a religious school for state aid. The school's director asked for financial help from the legislators on the ground that the school turned out reliable Republican voters.

Ecclesia led the investigators to other criminal enterprises involving legislators, lobbyists, and consultants who conspired to divert millions of dollars of state mental health funds into a private "nonprofit" organization.

Simultaneously, a federal prosecutor in central Arkansas exposed another criminal syndicate in which hundreds of thousands of dollars were funneled to judges and judicial candidates in an effort to turn the judiciary into a protectorate for lax and abusive nursing homes and others that harm individuals through neglect or abuse. One Republican judge went to prison for taking a bribe in the form of multiple campaign contributions, arranged by the former Republican state chairman, in exchange for trimming $4.2 million from a jury verdict against a chain of nursing homes.

Most of the people heading to prison were Republicans, but only because it reflected the relative composition of the legislature and the lobbying ranks.

In the second decade of the century, in Washington and Little Rock, the legislative agenda called for improving the circumstances of the successful through corporate welfare and tax reductions while giving the poor and the feeble tough love, in the form of freedom from government-aided assistance for medical care and nutrition.

No one ever argued that the wealthy needed help and the poor rebukes, but rather that tax cuts for the wealthy and businesses would expand the economy and produce new jobs and higher pay—and, in turn, more tax receipts in the treasury. It never turned out that way, at either the state or national level. The legislature in 2019 lowered income taxes for people earning more than $80,000 a year, with most of the savings going to very richest. If all the history of high-income tax cuts, from 1981 through 2017, is any gauge, it will produce no new jobs, no refugees from high-tax states, and no help to the middle class or the poor.

Republicans opposed a public initiative to raise the state minimum wage, which passed by a healthy margin in the 2018 general election, and they introduced a bill in 2019 to undo the wage increase. The irony was lost that the state minimum-wage was a legacy of Winthrop Rockefeller, the first

Republican governor in the twentieth century. The sponsors repeated the old shibboleth, often recited by editorial writers and the chamber of commerce, that minimum-wage increases drove thousands of workers into the unemployed ranks. On the contrary, every minimum wage increase in the state's history was followed by job growth and lower unemployment.

If he were still around, Dave Cox, the Weiner farmer and gubernatorial candidate, might again offer his guidance to youngsters ascending from school into one of the poorest labor forces in America:

"She's a low-wage state. Git out and git out fast!"

You would have to ask him, "But where would I go?"

INDEX

About the Author

Ernest Dumas started reporting for the *El Dorado Daily News* and *Evening Times* in 1954. For thirty-two years, he was a political and state government reporter and an associate editor, editorial writer, and columnist for the *Arkansas Gazette*, until it closed in 1991. He continues to write for a number of state and national outlets, including the *Arkansas Times*. He has been an author or collaborator on several books, including *The Clintons of Arkansas*, *Waiting for the Cemetery Vote*, and *Dearest Letty*.

Publication Note

Publication of this book was made possible in part by an endowment created by Samuel Isaac Bratton (1945–2014), who figured prominently in Arkansas politics and education for more than thirty-five years.

Bratton graduated from Earle High School in Crittenden County, Arkansas, and earned degrees from Hendrix College in Conway and the University of Arkansas School of Law in Fayetteville.

He was a key figure during former president Bill Clinton's time as governor of Arkansas, serving in many posts, including assistant attorney general, liaison for education, and chief counsel for legal and financial policy. He also chaired the Arkansas Public Service Commission. He was known in Arkansas state government for his deft coordination of fiscal and budgetary matters and was instrumental in shepherding many of Governor Clinton's policy initiatives through the state legislature.

Bobby Roberts, former director of the Central Arkansas Library System, said of Bratton: "Sam loved Arkansas and served our citizens for the better part of three decades. His work on education policy and utility regulation issues helped improve all our lives. He was intelligent, hard-working, and fair with everyone. What more could you want or ask from a public servant?"